AF479192

The Recovery of the Soul: An Aristotelian Essay on Self-fulfilment

In *The Recovery of the Soul*, Kenneth Rankin suggests that the current impasse over solutions to many philosophical problems is the result, in part, of a failure to consider how each of these problems bears on the rest. Rankin shows that a libertarian theory of free will, an A-theory of time, a corporealist theory of personal identity, and a non-relativist interpretation of the foundation of ethics all contribute to or are derived from a psychocentric form of physicalism.

The proposed Modal Identity thesis identifies the mind, or that which ensouls the body, with a strictly physical power, the power to act intentionally from occasion to occasion in any one of several mutually exclusive ways. Rankin argues further that the non-arbitrary individuation of particular physical things derives from the causal powers they possess. The distinctive power that ensouls our bodies is identified as the primary causal power: all other powers derive their status as powers from it in so far as they are constitutive, or instruments, of it.

Rankin demonstrates that many of our ontological preconceptions are Aristotelian in origin. The psychocentric physicalism of the central thesis is a response to Aristotle's question "What is being?" and in the earlier chapters of the book Aristotle's contributions to a theory of being are used as a preliminary study to suggest which parts of these preconceptions should be kept and which revised. Later chapters suggest that failure to resolve many philosophical problems results in part from the failure of Aristotle's philosophy to fulfil its promise.

KENNETH RANKIN is Professor Emeritus at the University of Victoria.

The Recovery of the Soul

An Aristotelian Essay on Self-fulfilment

KENNETH RANKIN

McGill-Queen's University Press
Montreal and Kingston • London • Buffalo

© McGill-Queen's University Press 1991
ISBN 0-7735-0796-5

Legal deposit second quarter 1991
Bibliothèque nationale du Québec

Printed in Canada on acid-free paper

This book has been published with the help of a grant from the Canadian Federation for the Humanities, using funds provided by the Social Sciences and Humanities Research Council of Canada.

Canadian Cataloguing in Publication Data

Rankin, Kenneth, 1920–
    The recovery of the soul
    Includes bibliographical references and index.
    ISBN 0-7735-0796-5
    1. Aristotle – Contributions in psychology. 2. Aristotle – Contributions in theory of perception.
    3. Self-realization. I. Title.
    BF637.S4R36 1991   150'.92   C91-090100-7

This book was typeset by Typo Litho composition inc. in 10/12 Baskerville.

To John MacMurray
1891–1976

Contents

Acknowledgments

I have had generous help from a number of sources at various stages while at work on this book. Nearest in time comes the grant towards publication from the Canadian Federation for the Humanities. Not quite so near are two sets of leave fellowship, travel and research grants from the Canada Council (under its earlier terms of reference) and its later offshoot, the Social Sciences and Humanities Research Council of Canada. Tenure of the fellowships was made practicable by grants of assisted study leave in 1974–75 and 1981–82 from the University of Victoria. It was further eased in the latter year by my appointment as a Visiting Research Fellow in the Department of Philosophy at the University of Melbourne. The University of Victoria has, furthermore, been munificent with other forms of research assistance over the period of my employment within its walls, and likewise the University of Melbourne during our association. To Monash University, in the more remote past, I owe thanks for a fully assisted study leave for 1968. It was then, through a more integrated analysis of intention and time, that I found my way out of difficulties that I had left unresolved in *Choice and Chance* (1962) . My thanks to the granting agencies, the three universities, and their philosophy departments for these various forms of assistance. The respite for intensive rumination was of particular value. The stimulus of the philosophical contacts I made or renewed at campuses in Britain, Australia, and New Zealand was hardly less so. My thanks, also, to the Fellows of the Queen's College and of St Catherine's College, Oxford, for interludes of a more social and relaxing nature enjoyed at their tables during one of my overseas visits.

In certain chapters I reproduce, more or less extensively and with little alteration, passages from articles I have previously published. The articles are "The Non-Causal Self-Fulfilment of Intention,"

American Philosophical Quarterly 9, no. 4 (October 1972), "McTaggart's Paradox: Two Parodies," *Philosophy* 56, no. 217 (July 1981), "The Complete Reality of Substance," *Mind* 91, no. 363 (July 1982), and "Responsibility as an Ontological Basis for Ethics," in Douglas Odegard, ed., *Ethics and Justification* (Edmonton: Academic Printing and Publishing 1988). I am grateful to all the editors and publishers concerned for permission to use these materials.

Various people at various times have become involved in the book's development in other ways. Gary Miller and John Leslie have advised me on matters relativistic and cosmological. Howard Horsburgh and Rodger Beehler commented on a previous draft of chapter 9. A relay of anonymous and astringent readers uncovered infelicities in earlier versions of the work as a whole. Danny Daniels and Charles Morgan domesticated my home computer. Dick Simpson, Jennifer Hilditch, and (over the longest period) Robert Fahrnkopf, as research assistants, kept me scrambling to keep pace with their output. Four sorely tried but remarkably patient typists, Sandra Chellew, Donna Denike, José Winther, and Caitlin Simpson, helped to bring my material into more manageable form. I am grateful to each one of these. Where this final product fails to commend their respective efforts, the fault is mine.

Finally, I wish to thank my major resource – my wife, Jean, who as ever has been the very central pillar of support, and our three children, Oliver, Patricia, and Neil, for the fortitude with which they underwent dislocations or partings imposed by periodic changes of scene.

Introduction

It is more than in time or even in doctrine that Aristotle may now seem remote. That we dwell in the aftermath of the Copernican, Daltonian, Darwinian, and Fregean revolutions has no doubt much to do with the more apparent decline in his influence. As well, however, the institutionalized diversification of interest – to say nothing of loss of nerve – within the community of philosophers has rendered the more profound aspects of his legacy to us, at least temporarily, sterile. Ancient Greek philosophy is commonly seen as primarily the concern of scholarly interpretation and critical exegesis of sundry texts. In that sort of light we are licensed to wrestle with our current concerns with no more than a casual nod, just for the sake of ori-entation, at earlier systems. Some may engage the ancients with more tenacity. But that tends to count as merely a sign of the sort of versatility or excess energy possessed by a cellist who also plays the harp.

This book moves with more circumspection. I believe that atten-tion both to the detail and the overall sweep of Aristotelian doctrine has a constructive role to play in current philosophical enquiry. Two socio-historical sorts of phenomena come to my support. Though not quite distinct, one pertains the more to detail, the other to over-all sweep.

First, the continuing appropriation in current inquiry of the more durable Aristotelian concepts often betrays the imprint of one-sided or equivocal, semi-acknowledged, and half-forgotten interpretations of their original application. Like the other concepts of Ancient Greek origin, e.g. nemesis itself, to be sorely Websterized has been their doom. Second, many of the philosophically most consequential errors are the work of the relatively few thinkers who, on either a grander or a minor scale, almost got their act together. For subsequent generations of philosophers either the error is sanctioned by the achievement or the achievement debased by the error, or more often than not (with impartial unfairness) both at once. On the grandest scale Aristotle is the archetypal approximator. He comes more closely to the truth and yet leads further astray than any other.

Consider first some major results of interpretative imprint. Take for a start the category distinctions between substance quality, quantity, relation, et al. Aristotle placed those on so flimsy a basis that on close scrutiny they give little evidence of being more than well intentioned (see chapter 1). Yet, whether in a spirit of consent or rejection, we commonly proceed as if something solid were there to build upon or demolish.

Likewise the notion we term substance has just on its own been persistently distorted. The Greek word "οὐσία," with its rudimentary equivalence to the English term "being," would seem to have carried a greater specificity than the latter conveys, a specificity appropriate to the primary existential status of just *one* among the various categories, all of which are categories of *being*. No doubt "substance" confers a specificity peculiar to itself. What it underlines is the function of substance as the *subject* of predicates. But first, in that specific function a substance is conceived more narrowly or less ambivalently than Aristotle himself eventually required (see chapter 4). Second, the etymology both of "substance" and of "subject" alike suggests a conception of the function that, not without Aristotle's connivance, has rendered it opaque. To conceive substance as something that underlies leads directly to one or other of two kinds of construction. Thus for some the distinguishability of a substance from its predicates is that of a bare particularity, which lies patent to a purely referential non-judgmental act of acquaintance. For others, as for Locke, it is something even less accessible, i.e. that of an I-know-not-what support of the qualities predicated (chapter 2).

That, incidentally, is my cue in what follows for sometimes replacing "substance" as a category heading by the homespun "thinghood." Though this substitution may stick in the unpractised craw for a while, it is triply apt. It is less prejudicial. It reflects in English the informality of word construction to which the original Greek for the various categories owes its impromptu vigour. And not least, it achieves some of the ambivalence or neutrality between generality and specificity in which "being," though morphemically more neat, is inconveniently lacking.

My final example of this first phenomenon is the superficially trite distinction between matter and form. Examined more closely it turns out to be two main distinctions rather than one (chapter 3). In some of its applications it is an *inter*categorial distinction between a substance and the various properties, etc., that through time it may gain or lose. In this capacity it is a diachronic distinction. In other applications it is an *intra*categorial distinction between correlative aspects within the same broad category, whether it be that of substance or of the properties a substance may instantiate. In this capacity it is a synchronic distinction. But as well as failing to make this absolutely plain – indeed in part as a result of the failure – Aristotle obscures the application in a further way. Ultimately he turns the abstraction of form from its correlative matter in the synchronic application into an existential separation or separability (chapter 4). On this shaky foundation rest some of the foibles of more modern times, e.g. the invention of materialism, whether by clerics as a sin or by laymen as an ontology, our current use of the words "material" and "physical" as virtual synonyms, a confusion of the categorial distinction between mind and matter with a distinction between classes of being, and the willingness, even among those who now call themselves materialists, to suppose that conceivably there *could* be something non-physical even if as a matter of fact there is not.

Consider next the second and more pervasive phenomenon, i.e. consequential error. Take as an example Aristotle's two main principles of metaphysical inquiry and the four more substantive or doctrinal principles in which the heuristic pair have come to fruition (chapter 4). To summon a suitable level of generality I label and formulate at times somewhat freely as follows. The two principles of inquiry head the list.

1 The Path to Enlightenment: that inquiry must proceed from what is more knowable for us to what is more knowable by nature. Thus quite typically he favours what he cites as the opinions of the many and the wise as his point of departure. The final terminus lies, however, in an intrinsic knowability consisting in a form of cognition that is essentially reflexive. His paradigm for this is strictly esoteric. At its utmost extremity, or maybe just beyond, it is an eternal activity of intellectual contemplation that takes itself exclusively as its object, i.e. the Prime Mover.
2 The Integrative Program: that various theoretical sciences are to be subordinated in some way as special to first philosophy, i.e. to a science of being qua being or of first causes.

Next come the four more substantive or doctrinal principles. In each of these each of the heuristic pair finds an application.

3 The Reificatory Principle: that particular sensible substances owe their being as such (in my terminology their "non-arbitrary particular or individual thinghood") to their proximate or mediated instantiation of form. Thus the soul as the form of the body is that to which the latter owes its non-arbitrary thinghood.

4 The Modal Identity Principle: that the soul is a certain kind of power, potency, or potentiality to do certain things.

5 The Psychocentric Principle: that the soul, and more specifically the mind, is the form of forms somewhat as (to use his pregnant analogy) the hand is the tool of tools. It confers being (non-arbitrary thinghood) upon other natural substances somewhat as the skill of the hand confers, to some extent, the utility of the tools it can handle, and conversely as the utility of the tools that the hand has the skill to handle is constitutive of the utility of the hand.

6 The Axiological Principle: that the ultimate reifying factor, or source of non-arbitrary thinghood, is the highest good.

In sponsoring these six archetypal generalities I believe Aristotle to have been, if not much ahead of his own time, at least far ahead of ours. Thanks, however, to the more specific form he gave them, each one is currently in jeopardy, disregard, or total eclipse (see chapter 5). Thus his seamlessly teleological conception of the natural word is at fault for one such decrepitude. For him inanimate and animate substances form a hierarchically structured chain of being, each member of which is motivated, both in behaviour and in exemplification of its species, by teleological potencies, i.e. desires, or perhaps by something more primitive than desires, for ends or perfections. This seamless teleology led him to an interpretation of the manner in which the soul might be said to be the form of forms, which renders both the Reificatory and the Psychocentric principle as in these modern times scientifically obsolete. A further source of consequential error lies in Aristotle's inadequate conception of soul-diversity, i.e. the manner in which the diverse faculties of the soul or their respective activites integrate so as to form faculties or activities of a unitary being. His interpretation of soul-unity in terms of a functional dependence or interdependence within the diversity of faculties has compromised his Modal Identity Principle. A third, though connected, source lies in the unique sort of status Aristotle accords our intellectual activity. In his account of the faculty of intellect he introduces a dualistic conception of the relation between mind and body that squanders the theoretical economy of the Modal Identity Principle's representation of the soul as a power pertaining to the body. It also misplaces the value of being to which the Axiological Principle points. Furthermore, as seen through the miasma of these three sources, both the Path to Enlightenment and the Integrative Program may seem at worst pretentious and at best quixotic in what they respectively enjoin.

Altogether, then, in relation to Aristotle and strictly as philosophers, we are like the human relics of an empire now defunct, who survive on hand-outs, cast-offs, and blood transfusions from regions long since seceded. We huddle in the ruins of an ancient and once thriving city, initial flaws in the design of which are the source of the present debility not least of ourselves. A few, no doubt, may still reflect some of the old glory more faithfully, but only as curators of on-site museums or as tourist guides.

Can we reverse this pathetic decline? For a start I turn back to Aristotle in a spirit not of passive nostalgia but rather of reformatory zeal. I shall apply the first of his two heuristic principles directly to him. He may or may not qualify as many. He does as sufficiently wise. His efforts to traverse the Path to Enlightenment will, therefore, be *our* point of departure on that very same path. In other words, his footprints, though far from distinct, are about to feature – in part at least – as the more knowable to us. My initial aim is to determine precisely how in the application of his two principles of inquiry Aristotle went wrong. Without an explicit rejection of the error, their strength will never emerge. Correspondingly, I react to his specific rendering of the four more substantive principles as to pilot engagements in a conjoint venture. In short, though Aristotle is unavailable to co-opt us (were he otherwise to deign to take that risk), we can and I will co-opt him.

That he still can beguile is due, I believe, to a sense of suspense that continues to tease the imagination. Beneath the surface of unresolved themes that sustain his grand design there stirs, it seems, a better tune ready to erupt in triumphant splendour like the jubilant climax to Beethoven's Ninth. Some may strain their ears for a *sotto voce* revelation in what he actually, or not quite but almost, did say. Others may listen for reverberations and resonances beyond or contrary to anything that can fairly be attributed to him. They may co-opt him in the cause of the Christian or some other faith, or (as in my own case) some ostensibly more secular theme. While I remain susceptible to either type of murmur, it is to one of the latter that I now tune in (chapter 6 to the end).

As in the original version of the Psychocentric Principle, in mine the ultimate reifying factor is essentially psychological. The principal difference is that in mine the psychological and the non-psychological are without any exception distinct categories of *physical* being. In short, as specified by me the principle becomes a physicalist form of psychocentrism. There are differences of a more specific sort as well. These derive, however, from adjustments elsewhere.

Thus, as in the original version, in my version of the Modal Identity Principle the mind or soul (these two no longer to be kept distinct) is a potency of the body. The difference is that I identify this potency not only as *of* a physical thing but also as exclusively *for* that thing's physical behaviour. More specifically, I interpret it in terms of our ability to act (i.e. behave physically) otherwise on certain occasions than, as it turns out, we actually do. In short, the physical category to which the psychological belongs, at least that part that consists of the mind or soul as distinct from its activities, is one of causal modality.

Then again, as in the original version, in my version of the Reificatory Principle mutable particulars owe their non-arbitrary reidentifiability through time, if any, to their possession of causal potency. Thus, like Aristotle, I recognize the mind or soul, by virtue of its being a potency, as the first actuality of the body. The difference lies in how I distinguish this first from the corresponding second actuality. Both belong to the category of causal modality. Each, indeed, is but a different aspect of the same modality. However, the first actuality, i.e. the mind or soul, is a core component of the ability to act otherwise, i.e. what remains general or occasion-loose from one occasion to another in that ability's shift from one particularized form to another. Yet the second actuality does not consist in some behavioural manifestation of a potency whether physical or non-physical. Instead, it consists — at least in its complete fulfilment — in the various particular or occasion-bound forms that the ability to act otherwise takes as an ability according to how an agent's opportunities and other capacities change with the passage of time. Thus both the first and the second actuality of the body, i.e. the occasion-loose and the occasion-bound power, are distinct from the body they inform as one physical category from another.

I then go on to interpret the occasion-bound power as indeterministic, and on that basis — for reasons later provided (6.9) — as the primary sort of causal power. All other kinds of causal power in relation to it are non-primary or secondary. Other causal powers owe their status as powers to being constitutive of this indeterministic power somewhat as the utility of tools owes utility-status to being constitutive of that specific kind of utility that is manual skill. Accordingly, this primary sort of power takes over the function with which Aristotle endows his Prime Mover. It is the source of non-arbitrary thinghood, not only for the agents who possess it but less directly for the other sorts of mutable substance that owe that thinghood more directly to powers that are non-primary. Furthermore, a more radical argument (chapter 8) will show that without the existence of beings who have the primary sort of power, the structure of reality itself would fail to be intrinsically temporal.

The end of the path is almost in sight. First, however, my credentials as a physicalist may need some scrutiny. My form of physicalism is less deprived than what normally goes by that name. It does not delimit the list of physical categories that are to play host to the mind and the mental in the standard way. Thus the mind is not identified contingently or otherwise with a kind of substance, e.g. a pulpy mass of neurons, nor are its activities identified with the various changes within the structure of a substance, e.g. with the electro-chemical processes in certain neurons, nor are its states identified either with structural or functional states of a substance. Instead the mind, its activities, and states are identified analytically with various aspects of the causal modalities that persons have by virtue of having organs of certain kinds, in ways that will be more fully specified later (chapters 6 and 7). Nor is causal modality, including the type here at stake, conceived reductively in the Humean sort of way in favour with, at least, certain physicalists.

In consequence, my form of physicalism does not deny to our introspective reports their declarative status. Nor does it charge them with some kind of epistemic delinquency on the grounds that they fail to make the physical nature of what they report perspicuous. Quite to the contrary – and now once more we forge ahead. It is centred on the fact that the primary causal power is as unique epistemically as it is ontologically. For the possibility of any course of action that it leaves open to an agent to be unconditionally a possibility, the agent must to some degree entertain that course, however tentatively, as a possibility. The intimating of the possibility as a possibility is, indeed, a logically necessary condition of the possibility intimated, and as such belongs to the same modal category as the latter. In short, the ability that is the primary power is self-intimating as well – or, in Aristotle's words, knowable by nature.

This completes the path as newly realigned. As well, however, the other principle of inquiry, the Integrative Program, can now be refurbished. The type of inquiry in which Aristotle has encouraged us to engage turns out to be an articulation of the sort of knowledge that is tacit in what is knowable by nature. As Aristotle in his own way saw, this must constitute a quite separate science, and one to which the others are subordinate. Not only is it different in method and basic data from the rest, but the sort of tacit knowledge it articulates is implicit in, and essential to the realization of, the primary source of the non-arbitrary thinghood of the things that other sciences investigate. In this sense, contrary to a contemporary view, ontology or metaphysics is more than the cleaning lady or odd-job man whose ministrations these other sciences sometimes tolerate. It is the queen of the sciences or, if you prefer, the master science. More succinctly, it is first philosophy.

Finally, we must not omit that for Aristotle his doctrine of being entails a doctrine of value. The Path to Enlightenment and a Path to Fulfilment intertwine. The one departs from the more knowable for us to terminate in the more knowable by nature. The other departs from the good for us to terminate in the good by nature. But the point of departure of the latter falls within that of the former. Likewise, the latter's terminus coincides with the former's. For him in both cases the terminus is the ultimate source of being, i.e. the Prime Mover.

In my version of the Axiological Principle there is a similar coincidence. I maintain (chapter 9) that as bearers of the primary power we not only have a non-arbitrary thinghood that is primary. We also instantiate a good that is unqualified. What links the thinghood and the good in this way is the fact that our possession of the primary power is not only self-intimating. It is self-desiderative as well. More specifically, the primary power is essentially a desiderative power that includes among more special desires a desire for its own continued instantiation. Accordingly, since our non-arbitrary thinghood depends on our possession of a power to which this desire is central, this desire unlike others is non-contingent. It is not a desire that we could conceivably be without.

Two consequences now follow. First, what fulfils this desire must be essentially attractive and an unqualified good. Second, the knowledge that articulates our tacit knowledge of what fulfils this desire, i.e. of our primary sort of power, must contribute to the desire's fulfilment, at least to the extent to which it protects the knowledge from corruption. Since by necessity the primary power intimates itself in this tacit knowledge, the latter is essential to the power's realization, i.e. the realization of the unqualified good (chapter 10).

At first sight, perhaps, this doctrine of value may seem to be egoistic in character. In fact it is quite otherwise. The primary power is a universal, and it is as a universal that we have the non-contingent desire for its continued instantiation. As bearers of this power we are members of a republic of means, i.e. means to its further realization. Part of the evidence, both for this and for the existence of such a thing as a non-contingent desire, lies in the altruistic and categorical nature of our ethical intuitions.

The reader's priorities may be out of step with the sequence of the chapters that follow. Those who distrust the antiquarian trend in the first five, and who fear that the promise of an eventual novelty will lead to fiasco, may want to advance without delay to chapter 6. There they can test my pretensions. Then, if they wish, they can move backwards or further ahead according to how the questions they thus put to themselves unfold. That procedure could be closer to the unlinear gestation that gave birth to these chapters. Lovers of Aristotle for their part may feel short-changed, unless they keep before them the propaedeutic nature of the role in which I have cast him. So as not to retard the forward-looking impetus of the earlier chapters I have had to skimp on textual quotation. With some exceptions my compromise has been to quote only where the doctrinal importance of the relevant passage and the dialectical complexity or obscurity of its argumentation maximize. Elsewhere, for the purpose of verification I have offered the appropriate textual reference. It will also be of help to distinguish in my procedure three main phases, viz. paraphrase of what Aristotle says, reconstruction to clarify the intention behind what he says, and replacement by what I think the truth requires. These divisions are, however, somewhat fluid and hence uneven in execution. Thus in chapter 1 the reconstruction of his Special Theory of Being, i.e. his category doctrine, leans towards replacement. It serves as a critique of his apparent positions. Then again, in chapters 3 and 4 the reconstruction of his General Theory comes closer to paraphrase. Its function is to sharpen distinctions in terms of which that theory is assembled. Here, then, the need for the later replacement arises in part from flaws that the sharpening lays bare.

As earlier conceived the balance in this book would roughly have been two parts philosophical psychology to one part ontology. In the present version that balance is more than just reversed. At an intermediate stage in planning my ambition was for a more even distribution within the same two covers. Then a bit later I had settled for a two-volume work, the imbalance in each half to compensate for that in the other. Though most of the latter portion of that project is already in draft, I now procrastinate so as not to delay. My present commitment is to bring out a sequel to this book instead – one in which certain issues in philosophical psychology, too briefly covered here, will receive intensive treatment. However, the need for more background to my discussion of intention in chapter 6 has struck me as too glaring. Hence I have included in the form of an appendix part of a previously published article on that topic, the contents of which could not conveniently be fitted into the main body of the text.

The dedication to John MacMurray pays homage to a philosopher whose psychocentric stance won him a solitary distinction as yet not generally recognized. Two of his major themes, viz. the primacy of the self as agent and time's identity as the form of action (see *The Self as Agent*, volume 1 of his Gifford Lectures, *The Form of the Personal*, 1953–54) have played a decisive role in my rejection of Aristotle's ultimate and historically fateful turn towards a partly immaterialist ontology.

The Recovery of the Soul

CHAPTER ONE

The Complete Reality of Substance

1 . 0

In distinguishing between different categories of being, Aristotle has given some kind of primary status to the category of substance. Of the notion of the primacy, however, he has offered a rather confusing number of accounts. Here I confine myself to just three. Sometimes he claims that members of the secondary categories depend for their being or existence upon substance – i.e. that there is an ontological dependence. Sometimes, again, he contends that there is a semantic dependence of same sort, that the sense in which certain conceptually crucial terms apply to members of the secondary categories depends in some way upon the sense in which, or the fact that, these same terms apply to substance. Sometimes, finally, his claim is that substance alone constitutes complete reality, or that the substance of a thing constitutes complete reality – i.e. that a substance is an entelechy. It is possible that he thought that all three accounts amount to the same. I shall argue that they do not, and the third alone – at least on a certain interpretation – is correct.

For this purpose I proceed reconstructively. In 1.1 the need for category distinctions is attributed somewhat narrowly to the need to dispose of one specific problem. In 1.2 certain basic category distinctions are drawn *ab initio* from a precisely formulated principle of division. In 1.3 these distinctions are tested by application to the specific problem out of which the need for the theory arose. Finally, in 1.4, I arbitrate between the three accounts of primacy that have been enumerated above.

1.1 THE PLATONIC HERITAGE

Aristotle was the archetypal exponent of the periodic fresh start – so much so that the metaphysical problems to which he gave priority would seem to derive from, rather than correspond very closely to, the problems of his predecessors. Those that he placed in the forefront are primarily the creation of a set of complex conceptual distinctions of which he himself is the reputed author. Nevertheless, it is convenient, if possibly wrong, to assume that in first drawing these distinctions he had the resolution of two Platonic problems in mind, viz. the one-over-the-many (*Phlb* 15a–c, *R*. X596ff)[1] and Heraclitean flux (*Cra.* 439–40).[2] On that assumption we can best explain why a notion of substance is needed, and to meet that need what, exactly, substance must be. Here, however, I confine attention to the one-over-the-many alone.

Originally it seems to have insinuated itself in the following way. If there were no distinction between predication and identification, or between types of identification, the fact that we say of many beds that each is hard or that each is a bed would imply by symmetry of identity that one thing, i.e. that which each bed is, is identical with many things, and by transitivity of identity that each of the many is identical with the rest. Thus a dilemma besets us. Either the oneness or the plurality of particulars may be taken as axiomatic, but not both. If we postulate their oneness, then only the one thing that each bed is, i.e. hard or a bed, can be real – at least relative to the many beds that are it. The plurality of particulars must as such be illusory. Accordingly, to distinguish the unique status of the one thing that the many beds are, we might follow Plato by referring to it as the Hard Itself (or just Hardness) or the Bed Itself, and to the class to which such unique reality belongs as Forms or Ideas. Alternatively, if we postulate the plurality of particulars, and conceive their oneness as consisting of the partial identity of each with a Form (as distinct, say, from resemblance), then each bed participates in this way in Hardness or the Bed Itself. But then, as Plato himself says (*Prm* 131b–d), we can no longer represent the Bed itself as one and entire in itself. Instead it must be spatially dissipated over the many beds, and as many as they are. Hence the Bed Itself taken as the unity of the many beds would be unreal. However, in devising his Theory of Forms, Plato selected the first of the two horns. His solution to the dilemma lay in a wholesale, but one-sided, shedding of ontological commitment, an excommunication of all particulars that fall under Forms.[3]

Now admittedly it would have been less drastic to distinguish predication from identification more sharply than he did, and within the latter between different types. To say of many beds that each is hard or that each is a bed is not to identify many things with the same one thing. But the right to draw a sharp enough distinction has still to be earned; for, as Aristotle in effect has shown, at least two distinction-masking features (DMFs) make the notion of predication seem problematic.

DMF 1 In any predication of one thing of something, there would seem to be a twofold ontological commitment of the kind that the thing-language I am indulging in makes explicit. Thus, "Socrates is wise" entails "Something is wise" and "Socrates is something," and consequently "Something is something." Hence the question of the numerical sameness or difference of these things has to be in some way settled before the distinction between predication and identification can be properly understood.

DMF 2 Predication and identification have quite commonly been taken to consist of asymmetrically and symmetrically related terms respectively. By this criterion, then "This (man) is pale," "This is a man," and "This is Cairngorm" would quite commonly be taken as exemplifying predication to the exclusion of identification in the first two cases and identification to the exclusion of predication in the third. Yet the difference between the first and the second may not seem conspicuously less than the difference between the second and third. Thus the first precludes the substitution of "is identical with" for the copula, whereas the second and the third permit that substitution without loss or change of sense.

In short, then, to argue against Plato that the one-over-the-many is not to be taken for an aberrant exemplification of identity is more of an undertaking than one might casually suppose. That there is some alternative to, or specific form of, identity that the one-over-the-many could non-aberrantly exemplify has yet to be shown.

How completely Aristotle rose to the challenge is not entirely clear.[4] Indeed it is doubtful whether he would have been capable of formulating the problem in these sorts of terms.[5] He had, however, a remarkably adequate conception of the problem's complexity, and he offered the matrix at least of a satisfactory solution. To show what the latter should be it is advisable first to distinguish a special from a general theory of being, both of which with suitable reservations can be accredited to him. The Special Theory is special in the sense that on its own it deals specifically with just one of our two Platonic problems, that of the one-over-the-many. The General Theory is general in the sense that it incorporates the Special Theory for the purpose of dealing with flux as well and the further range of problems to which our two Platonic problems turn out to be basic. In this chapter we are concerned with the presentation of the Special Theory alone.

1.2 THE SPECIAL THEORY OF BEING

The Special Theory turns upon a distinction between two category lists. As Table 1 takes for granted, the categories listed are categories of things or existents. The distinctions of the lists became partly explicit in Aristotle's own category doctrine, though he gave more attention to category differences within each list than to cross-comparison. Indeed he may not have attached quite the same significance to their distinctness as I do here.

On the right half of Table 1, and in standard Latinate guise, the categories are all substantive. Any substance, quality, quantity, or relation can function as a subject, i.e. as that about which something is said or thought. On the left half we have predicative counterparts. Any member of these counterpart categories is something that in some way may be attributed to or predicated of a subject. Thus, courage, the length five feet, and equality are respectively cases of the other three substantive categories just mentioned, i.e. quality, quantity, and relation. Courageous, five-foot long, and equal to are cases respectively of the predicative counterparts.

Whether these cases, and cases of any other category in the same predicative list, have a claim to the status of thinghood at all — whether the predicative categories really are categories of things — may on this showing seem open to question. However that may be, certainly courageous is not properly a quality, nor is five-foot long a quality, nor equal to a relation.[6] If they are to be classed as things at all, then they are more aptly differentiated in terms that are closer in spirit to some at least of Aristotle's own than are the Latinate terms by means of which some of his translators render his sense. Thus courageous is more aptly categorized as an of-what-quality than as a quality, five-foot long as a how-much than as a quantity, and equal to — if we keep closer to the preceding coinage than did Aristotle himself — as a what-to than as a relation. So categorized, the predicative status of these cases is made more unmistakable.

On the question of thinghood Aristotle is not consistently forthright. Generally it seems he took cases of predicative categories to be related to cases of substantive categories as to counterparts. Thus

Table 1
the length 5 feet

Predicative e.g.		Existents Category	Substantive e.g.
		substance	Socrates
		substance	a man
		substance-species	Man
courageous	an of-what-quality		courage
5-foot long	a how-much	quantity	the length 5 feet
equal to	a what-to	relation	equality
		other?	

the predicative courageous[7] is what he called a paronym of the substantive courage (*Cat.* 1a12). By this he meant, at least on the surface, that the name for the former is derived from the name of the latter. Hence, by an extension of the same notion, we might regard anything falling under any predicative category as a paronym of some counterpart falling under a substantive category. To do so, however, is to take the counterpart categories, predicative as well as substantive, in each case to be categories of *thing*. It is courageous, not "courageous," that is the paronym of courage, for what makes it a paronym is that its *name* is derived from the name of the latter.

On two other occasions at least (*Cat.* 2a20–5; 2a30), however, Aristotle may seem to pursue a nominalistic line. Thus he argues that white is something that is present in Socrates, in the sense that it is incapable of existing apart from the particular it is present in, and that strictly it is not something that is "said of" Socrates. It is only its name, he says, that is said of the subject. This may suggest that predicatives in general are just names and that what they name are either particular substances, as "man" names Socrates, or substantive but non-substantial particulars that are existentially dependent upon, and particularized by, the particular substance they are present in. But then again, the point may simply have been that the colour white, i.e. whiteness, is an exceptional kind of substantive, viz. that it shares the same name with its predicative counterpart – i.e. it and its paronym are covertly paronymous.

There is, however, a more profound basis for the distinction I have been adumbrating than either an untempered intuition or an etymology can offer. The distinction evolves from the more fundamental distinction between two related types of existential framework (henceforth "E-frame"), both of a quasi-Quinean form (cf Quine, 1953), viz.

> Unqualified: There is one thing, viz. ...
> Qualified: There is one thing that one or more than one thing is (or is not), viz. ...

Here the first of the two E-frames is somewhat redundant in wording. It could end as appropriately after the "is" as after the "viz," i.e. with the designator-blank appended to the former rather than the latter. The purpose of the redundancy is merely to make the ontological commitment as emphatic in the first as in the second E-frame. But if the contrast between the two is to be syntactically sharp – not just a matter of grammatical complexity – what comes after the "is" in the second E-frame cannot be redundant. In other words, what fills the blank in that frame must be limited to expressions that would not fit syntactically into the blank in the first frame. It is, then, in terms of the contrast between the two frames as syntactically so delimited that the scope, composition, internal differences, and correspondence between the two lists are to be determined. Thus, while articles 1 to 15 below confirm the main results of the original Aristotelian doctrine, they also furnish these results with a sounder basis.

1 The names of what the substantive categories categorize – e.g. "Socrates," "a man," "Man," "courage," "the length five feet," and "equality" – all fit syntactically into the Unqualified E-frame. On the other hand, given the non-redundancy-limitation needed for the second E-frame to be exclusively Qualified, they do not fit syntactically into the latter.

2 The names of what the predicative categories categorize – e.g., "courageous," "five-foot long," and even "equal" – fit syntactically into the Qualified E-framework alone. By themselves they do not fit syntactically into the Unqualified E-framework. (Note, however, that for names like "equal" we have to add some further expression to the subordinate clause, e.g. "to something"). An equivalent rendering of the E-frameworks will confirm this limitation, viz.

> Unqualified: One thing, viz. ..., exists.
> Qualified: One thing, which one or more than one thing is (or is not), viz. ..., exists.

3 The non-parenthetical disjunction in the Qualified E-frame need not be interpreted truth-functionally. In other words, the dis-

junction can be interpreted as allowing for the possibility that all of a number of things are collectively and distributively, i.e. all and each, the predicative thing in question, unless qualifying expressions such as "uniquely" specifically preclude that possibility.

4 On either rendering of the two E-frames the complex name-frame

one thing, which one or more than one thing is (or is not), viz. ...

has a neutral status. It would seem to fit either of the two main designator-blanks as syntactically as the other. But may not this versatility invalidate our quasi-Quinean categorial criterion? Things may be either substantive or predicative. They may not be both. Yet by the criterion it now may seem that they can be both after all. There is, however, a simple solution to the dilemma. Notice that in some cases the occurrence of the name-frame in one or other E-frame is redundant and in other cases not, depending upon how the designator-blank in the name-frame is filled. Let us confine ourselves to non-recursive fillings of that blank, i.e. to fillings that do not employ a further application of the name-frame being filled. Thus where the name-frame is filled by a name that would fit in this non-recursive way into the Qualified E-frame by itself without any mediation from the name-frame, e.g. by "courageous," it occurs redundantly in relation to the Qualified but not to the Unqualified E-frame. Consequently, the complex name thus formed with its assistance is predicative in the Qualified and substantive in the Unqualified E-frame. By contrast, where the name-frame is filled by a name that would fit in the same non-recursive way into the Unqualified E-frame by itself without any mediation from the name-frame, e.g. by "Socrates," it occurs redundantly in relation to the Unqualified E-frame and not in any way at all in the Qualified E-frame, due to the non-redundancy-limitation we have imposed on the latter. Accordingly our quasi-Quinean criterion has been salvaged with the help of a minor modification. The distinction between substantive and predicative names to which it points applies in a twofold way. It holds partly within the class of names that are unmediated by a name-frame that would prove to be redundant in the context of one or other of the two E-frames. But it also holds between a non-redundant and a redundant use of the same complex name, i.e. between where the name-frame in question is not and where it is being used in a redundant way.[8]

5 The existential form of the E-frames guarantees that the predicative as well as the substantive categories are categories of *things*. Thus, wherever the application of the Qualified E-frame results in

a *true* proposition, the name in the designator-blank must name an existing thing. However, as the contrast between the two frames shows, substantive things alone can be things *unqualifiedly*. Predicative things, for their part, are only *qualifiedly* things. One rightly refers to them (e.g., courageous, five-foot long, and equal to) as *things* just as long as one explicitly or implicitly then employs the name-frame discussed in article 4, i.e. just so long as one understands of each that it is one thing that one or more than one thing is (or is not). In other words, we are entitled to refer to substantives and predicatives alike as different categories of things *without any ambiguity whatever*, despite their categorial difference, by virtue of the fact that the name-frame (as used above) has a non-redundant use in the Unqualified E-frame.

6 For every sentence generated by placing a predicative name in the Qualified E-frame there is a logically equivalent sentence generated by placing some substantive name in the Unqualified E-frame. Thus "There is one thing that one or more than one thing is (or is not), viz. courageous," entails and is entailed by "There is one thing, viz. courage." Presumably, then, it is the function of the substantive term "courage" to abbreviate the complex name that includes the predicative term "courageous" as above, thereby indicating that the including name-frame has a non-redundant role. This sort of disambiguating abbreviation, rather than mere etymology, may then be the basis for the relation of paronymy.[9] (See also article 11.)

7 For some sentences generated by placing a substantive name in the Unqualified E-frame there is no logically equivalent sentence generated by placing some predicative name in the Qualified E-frame. Thus, where "Socrates" fills the Unqualified E-frame, there is no equivalent sentence to be derived from a Qualified E-frame. Even if one were to coin artificially some predicative name such as "uniquely Socratic" and to suppose, for the sake of the argument, that it stood for a predicative thing, the sentence produced by plugging it into the Qualified E-frame would not entail the sentence produced by plugging "Socrates" into the Unqualified E-frame.

8 It is this difference between different substantive things that constitutes the difference between other substantive categories and the category of substance. Notice, however, that by this criterion "a man" as well as "Socrates" names a thing that belongs to the category of substance. Whether the species named by "Man" or any other species that takes substances as members would also belong to the category of substance by this criterion is not clear to me. If the notion of a species is extensional as well as intensional – e.g. if Man is just men and women, i.e. if the existence of a species implies that members of the species exist – then a species would be a substance, unless

it is treated not as one thing but as a plurality of similar substances. If, however, we allow for the existence of a species with no members, then species do not fall into the category of substance. Then it would be plausible to suppose that for any Unqualified existential stating the existence of a species there would be an equivalent Qualified existential referring to some collection of predicative things.

9 It follows that only those things that belong to the category of substance, and constructs of these, are basic to the category of substantives, i.e. of things that are things unqualifiedly. They are first-order substantives. Things belonging to other substantive categories are of some derivative order. That is because their existence is equivalent to the existence of predicative things, i.e. things that some more basic order of substantive is (or is not).

10 Likewise, predicatives that a substance could directly be are basic to the category of predicatives. They too, in their category, are first order. The paronyms of these first-order predicatives are second-order substantives. Predicatives that these substantives may directly be are second-order predicatives, and so on. Thus equality is a second-order substantive and symmetrical is a second-order predicative that such things as equality directly are.

11 On the assumption that members of the predicative categories are not things, nominalists sometimes try to show that all statements about members of the non-substance substantive categories are translatable exclusively into equivalent statements about substances and the predicative things that these substances are or are not. On exactly the same assumption realists, in contrast, claim to have shown that there are cases – e.g. "Courage is a virtue" – that are not amenable to this analysis or not obviously so (see Loux, 1976, and Jackson, 1977). Since the assumption is false – since predicatives are things, albeit qualifiedly – the issue is of little relevance to nominalism and realism. To forestall possible misunderstanding, it may be advisable to emphasize that my claim that for every Qualified existential there is an equivalent Unqualified existential is less ambitious than the claim that in *every* statement about a non-substance substantive the reference to that substantive can be analysed out.

12 When an Unqualified E-frame is appropriately filled, i.e. by a substance-name, the resultant sentence, if true, is only contingently true. To avoid tangential controversy, I am willing not to press the contingency-claim where the name is "God" or some equivalent.

13 When the Qualified E-frame is filled by a predicative name of the first order, then (in certain cases at least) the parenthetical clause can be interpreted as allowing for the possibility that there is no substance that is the predicative thing. In such cases in fact the resulting sentence is necessarily true. Exception to this principle can

be allowed in the case of predicative things the names of which make an essential reference to some primary thing or substance. Thus if, *pace* Kripke (1980, 54–6), "a meter long" makes essential reference to the object that is the standard metre (Wittgenstein, 1953, §50), then the truth of the Qualified existential within which it occurs depends upon the contingent fact that the object exists. For similar reasons predicative things that are relational properties have only a contingent existence, at least where the substantive component of the property is a substance. Another possible exception, one that would be more important, might be found in predicatives such as inflammable, elastic, soluble, intelligent, etc., which are paronymous with causal powers. Since natural kinds such as water, wood, etc., are essentially definable in terms of causal powers, this type of exception would include wooden, of water, and everything that Aristotle subsumed under the general predicative *thaten*, among other things. The existence of such predicatives, it may seem, depends upon the existence of one out of a number of possible specific systems of natural law, and the existence of any such specific system presumably would depend upon there actually being particulars that are thereby governed.[10] Thus every *thaten* would presuppose some that. However, it may be that at least some of the powers that are exemplified within one system of natural laws would have to be exemplifiable within any other. Hence, for a more certain type of exception than any so far provided, perhaps we should content ourselves with predicatives that explicitly relate to some contingently existing substance, e.g. hotter than the sun. The existence of these must be as contingent as the existence of what they relate to.

14   The substantive paronyms of those predicative things that have necessary existence must likewise have necessary existence. This is a further difference between them and things belonging to the category of substance (other, perhaps, than God) – an additional element in their P-primary status.

15   Categorial differences between things, apart from the broad categorial difference between substantives and predicatives and their respective orders, consist in the first instance of categorial differences between predicative things. The categorial differences between non-substance substantives depend upon these latter by virtue of paronymy. To draw the necessary distinctions with sufficient sensitivity between these predicative categories would be, however, a major undertaking. What follows is just an approximation.

(a) A predicative thing is a "what-to" if and only if its name qualifies as the occupant of the viz-gap in a variant of the Qualified form, viz.

There is one thing that one or more than one thing is (or is not) in respect of something, viz. ...

Here the gap might be filled in by "at," "in," "below," "upon," "to the left of," "between," "part of," "during," "for the sake of," and similar expressions. Paronyms of things so named are relations. According to this criterion, however, the things Aristotle listed as affections would count as relations. Thus the predicative thing named by "scorned by" qualifies for the gap.

(b) A predicative thing is a "how-much" if and only if where each of a number of things is it, then all taken together as a physical whole of some sort are some contrary of that predicative thing. Thus a number of five-foot-long rods lying end to end are together in length the length of each times their number. Paronyms of things meeting this condition are quantities.

(c) A predicative thing is an "of-what-quality" if and only if as well as being a predicative thing it is neither a "what-to" nor a "what-to" combined with one or more substantives (i.e. the paronym of a relational property) nor a "how-much." Paronyms of things meeting this condition are qualities.

(d) Predicative things belonging to other candidates for predicative category-status are reducible to predicative things belonging to one or more of the four categories consisting of substance, and the three predicative categories defined above. Thus a thing belonging to the category of a "where" is reducible to the category of substance and of a "what-to." What amounts to a reductive program can be found in Aristotle's *Physics*, particularly in his analysis of motion, place, and time.

1.3   PREDICATION AND
IDENTIFICATION

From the the Special Theory thus revised issues arise that I do not pursue. Instead, we now can come to terms with the three DMFs by which the distinctness of predication and identification has been obscured.

Beneath DMF1 lies the fact that the propositional form "Something is something" is entirely neutral. There is nothing in it to make it the form of a predication as distinct from an identification or conservely. By itself the copula "is" is incompetent to determine the issue (see also Lockwood, 1975, and Mates, 1979, for similar theses). But, contrary to a dogma currently enshrined in the canonical notation of contemporary symbolic logic, the incompetence has nothing to do with any ambiguity in that verb. Whether in predication or identification, its use is univocal. There is no distinction between an "is" of predication and an "is" of identification – or for that matter between either and an existential "is" – except of an extrinsic kind.[11] What establishes the distinction we need is just the broad category of each thing, substantive or predicative, to which each "something" indefinitely refers. Thus there is predication if one indefinite reference is to a predicative and the other to a substantive. Given that inversions are idiomatic, the order does not matter. There is identification, however, if both indefinite references are to substantives. This leaves room for categorially confused predications and identifications, which nevertheless are plainly one or the other – e.g. for "Wisdom is red" as well as for "Socrates is wise" as predications, and for "Socrates is wisdom" as well as "Socrates is Plato's mentor" as identifications. Intuitively that is as it should be. To sift well-formed from ill-formed assertions of either type is the business of the hierarchical orderings and other category differences internal to each list. Also left open is whether "Wise is wise" is a predication or an identification, or neither. Decisions on such matters have to be guided by context.

Likewise, beneath DMF2 lies the further fact that identification splits into two classes, definite and indefinite. The definite kind does not permit names with an indefinite reference as names of that to which they refer. It is in this class that "Socrates is Plato's mentor" and "The morning star is the evening star" – and other examples commonly cited as cases of identification per se – belong. The indefinite kind, however, contain at least one name that makes an indefinite reference to that to which they refer. Thus "Socrates is a man" and "A man is an animal" are identifications, for the noun-names therein are all fitting occupants of an Unqualified E-frame. All these names are of substantives. But the propositions are indefinite identifications into the bargain by the criteria I here propose.[12] Further, plural identifications such as "Socrates and Callias are men" and "Men are animals" are, more covertly, indefinite as well, for the former translates into "Socrates is a man and Callias is a man" and the latter into "A man is an animal."

As for DMF3 – i.e. the contrast between the convertibility of definite and inconvertibility of indefinite identification – that can readily be explained. It is, after all, only comparative. In definite identification, pragmatic grounds can arise for resisting complete convertibility. Stylistic or poetic inversion aside, "Socrates is Plato's mentor" might be a better way of presenting one of the many true answers to "Who is Socrates?" where "Plato's mentor is Socrates" is the better way of presenting the corresponding true answer to the question "Who is Plato's mentor?" Similarly, in indefinite identification there are pragmatic grounds for relaxing complete inconvertibility. Thus in response to the question "What (who) is an example of an ironist?" one might be as willing to say "An example of an ironist is Socrates" as the reverse. Obviously, then, since the latter is an indefinite identification, the inconvertibility of indefinite identification is only comparative, and the constraints that impose that inconvertibility are only pragmatic.

The distinction between predication and identification is now unmasked. Hence our right to challenge the Theory of Forms is in part already established. What seemed to Plato to be cases of a one-over-the-many are in some of his instances clearly not cases of that at all. Once indefinite identification has been recognized not just as identification but as an indefinite form of identification as well, what otherwise seemed to be an identification of many with one turns out to have been an identification of each with just one – if it was a case of identification at all. Thus where many, e.g. Socrates, Callias, et al., collectively are all men, distributively each is a man, i.e. one thing; but collectively they are not the one thing that each is, i.e. a man. Hence in its application to identification, even indefinite identification, the problem of the one-over-the-many is simply fraudulent.

How, then, does the problem of the one-over-the-many fare as applied to predication? Here indeed it is more on the level. Thus where many, e.g. Socrates, Callias, et al., are collectively all white, distributively no doubt each is white as well. But, unlike the case of indefinite identification, where distributively each is white, collectively all must be white too. Hence in predication there are genuine cases of one-over-the-many. But, of course, these genuine cases are not genuine cases of identification. Hence the trouble that the symmetrical transitivity of identity would otherwise have caused just does not arise.

Notice, however, that to dispose of the problem in this twofold manner, the distinction between predication and identification had first to be properly drawn. It would just not be good enough to say that the problem trades upon an ambiguity in the copula. That would suggest that the question of the identity of any one of Socrates, Callias, et al. with white could after all arise. But if it could arise, why shouldn't we use the copula in the alleged identificatory, instead of the alleged predicational, sense in saying that they are all white? Simply to avoid contradiction? But Plato claimed that function for his Theory of Forms. Hence this way of drawing the distinction is question-begging. Only by drawing it as we have in terms of the respective status of the things that copulate can it become clear that the question of the identity of a man with white can never arise.

1.4 THE PRIMACY OF SUBSTANCE

In Aristotle's scheme of categories the contrast between predication and identification does not fully emerge. He understood of course that his discovery entailed some kind of distinction between the things we copulatively assert or deny, but for lack of a sharp enough division within the scheme between substantives and predicatives he failed to see what, precisely, the distinction would have to be. On the credit side, he saw clearly enough that within his scheme the main distinction falls between substance and other first-order categories, and that the being of substance is in some way primary. Correctly, too, he saw that distinctions of category preclude any attempt to classify the categories thus distinguished in terms of genus and species. Being is not a genus of which these various categories are species. On the other hand, in the course of his persistent efforts at characterizing the primacy of substance, he misrepresented it in two distinct ways. It is this misrepresentation that we have now to rectify.

His first mistake was to construe substantial primacy in terms of a relation of existential or ontological dependence. Thus in certain passages (*Cat.* 1a20–8; 2a20–5; 2a30–5) he seems to suggest that the existence of any predicative thing or its substantive paronym depends upon the existence of just one substance, i.e. a substance that happens to be the predicative thing. What he seems to suggest is, in other words, that unless that particular substance had happened to exist, the predicative thing or its substantive paronym would not have existed either. Here his assumption may be that only the particular exists and that a predicative can be particular only by being present in a particular substance. In any case, what he seems to be saying should be taken in conjunction with a further claim of his about substance (*Cat.* 4a10–11), that, while remaining numerically one and the same, any substance is capable of admitting contrary predicatives as things that it is. The conjunction of these two claims yields the conclusion that predicatives are existentially dependent upon substances in an asymmetrical way. Substances must be independent and primary. Predicatives must be dependent and secondary.

Yet in many other places Aristotle himself seems as ready as Plato to treat predicatives and their substantive paronyms as universal, i.e.

as things that more than one substance can be or instantiate. And on this he surely was right. Perhaps, then, he should have selected an existential dependency of a slightly looser kind. That may, indeed, have been his intention (*Cat.*, 2b5–6). Should he not have hung the existence of any predicative thing simply upon there being at least one or more than one substance that is it? Thus, the possibility at least of more than one substance being the predicative would be recognized. Yet surely it remains every whit as true that the existence of any substance depends upon there being at least one predicative that that substance is. Hence it would seem on this alternative that any substance is no less dependent than any predicative, and that any predicative thing is no less independent than any substance.[13]

Apart, however, from that, the revised position has already been ruled out by article 13 of the Special Theory. By 13 (with the exceptions noted), neither a predicative nor its substantive paronym depend for their existence upon there being at least one instance of the latter.

Aristotle's second major mistake was to construe substantial primacy in terms of a relation of semantic dependence.[14] More specifically, he believed being to be homonymous, meaning by that that the name "being," and to this we can add "thing," does not apply to all that it names in the same sense. Thus, on this conception, the name "thing" in the Unqualified form means something not quite the same as the same name in the Qualified form.

Before we delve more deeply into this explication, however, we must first differentiate more finely. There are at least three distinct types of homonymy in terms of which we might choose to domesticate the Platonic one-over-the-many, viz. ontic, enumerative, and copulative.

1 An ontic homonymy of the kind he postulated would allow Aristotle to say that the sense of "thing" in which two things, e.g. Socrates and Callias, are things is not the sense of "thing" in which they are one thing, viz. white.

2 Enumerative homonymy would allow him to do much the same, but this time by concentrating upon (allegedly) different senses in which the name "one" instead of "thing" can be applied. Aristotle himself invokes this kind of homonymy in places (*Meta.* Γ2.1003b30ff; Δ6.1016b32–5; Z4.1030b10ff; Z16.1040b16) while failing fully to appreciate its distinctness from the ontic homonymy that he places in the forefront.

3 Copulative homonymy would allow him to say that the sense in which "is" and other forms of the verb "to be" function non-

copulatively (as in "there is ...") is different from the senses in which they function copulatively. It is, in other words, an existential sense. But more pertinently still, he might also say that there are at least two copulative senses, viz. identificatory and predicational. He could simply say that in predication the "is" has a predicational sense and in identification an identificatory sense. That would seem to explain why "Socrates is white" does not imply "Socrates is identical with white," whereas "Socrates is Plato's mentor" does imply "Socrates is identical with Plato's mentor." That would seem to be the method brought into vogue by Frege (1952b) and Russell (1926, 48–9). Aristotle, furthermore, does use a similar method in a polemic against the monism of Parmenides and Melissus (*Phys.* I, 3), though there his way of distinguishing senses of "is" is somewhat different.

Hence, given these options, the semantical explication is vulnerable to a preliminary criticism. If we were to base the distinction between categories of thing upon ontic homonymy rather than upon the distinction between Unqualified and Qualified E-frames, the inference would be that category distinctions are not indispensable. The three types of homonymy would seem to be independent, and each can do the same anti-Platonic work without assistance from the other two. Further, as already remarked in 1.3 with specific reference to ambiguity in the copula, each of the three semantical claims would do its anti-Platonic work in a question-begging way. Each would show the Theory of Forms – and also the other two types of homonymy – to be unnecessary, but that would not show the theory to be wrong. Only by going back to the distinction between E-frames can we do that.

But there is worse to follow. When taken in an unmodified form, an explication either in terms of ontic or enumerative homonymy leads to the conclusion that there is a plurality of realms of reality all on an equal footing, the reality and oneness of each realm being homonymous. Against this demotic pluralism Plato's élitist ontology appears to advantage. Hence Aristotle found himself compelled to accord a "focal" meaning (G.E.L. Owen's term, 1960) to one of his senses of "being" and apparently to one of his senses of "one" as well. Thus he held that the being of any substance and its oneness, or the oneness of the realm of substances, is primary in relation to members of other categories by virtue of their focal meaning.

To found focal or primary *being* and oneness in this way upon focal *meaning* is, however, to place the primacy upon an arbitrary footing. Thus, in terms of one of his two main illustrations[15] one might agree that "healthy" as applied to a person, as opposed to his healthy condition or diet or exercise, is applied in its primary sense, and that those other applications are all in various ways derivative. Probably it is because of their different connections with the healthiness of a healthy person that we have come in our culture to apply the adjective to these other things in the obviously different ways in which we apply it. Perhaps, indeed, some of the interconnections between the applications are *logically* implicit in some of them. But it is not difficult to imagine a different culture in which the present primary application would be derivative and one of the secondary applications primary.

Further, while recognizing that all the homonyms[16] we call healthy stand in the causal nexus responsible for our calling them so, there would be no *need* for us to call them all healthy, even though we do. It just happens to be convenient to use the same name, somewhat in the way that it is convenient to call a razor a shaver because it shaves. Though the one word reminds us of, or alludes to, the causal connection, fundamentally, at least, the causal is not a conceptual link. In contrast, it is in no way arbitrary that we call a predicative thing, i.e. that which can only be that which one or more than one thing is (or is not), a thing (see article 5). To call it anything else would conceal the conceptual link. To say that something is a thing *tout court* and to say that essentially it is only a thing that/..., etc., is to use the word "thing" in the same sense. If it were not, the necessary contrast between a thing that is unqualifiedly and a thing that is qualifiedly would be destroyed.

This completes my rectification of Aristotle's two major misrepresentations of substantial primacy. To summarize: what they misrepresent is simply that substances are those substantives (i.e., those things that exist unqualifiedly) that are not derivable from predicatives (i.e. those things that exist qualifiedly), where the contrast between these two modes of existence is to be understood in terms of that between the Unqualified and the Qualified E-frames. We shall see later (chapter 4) that his failure to render the primacy fully perspicuous contributed to a divorce in his General Theory of Being between two main applications of the notion of substance. One of these is to particular subjects, e.g. Socrates, of singular propositions. As such it is unintelligible, but immanent or sensorily available. The other is to what has complete actuality, i.e. to what in its perfect form belongs to the Prime Mover alone. As such it is intelligible but ultimately transcendental, or sensorily unavailable. However, as it now turns out, not only do sensorily available singular subjects of propositions exist unqualifiedly. Not only is their categorial primacy thereby perfectly intelligible. For good measure, their existing unqualifiedly entitles them to the status of *complete actuality*, or *entelechy*. It does so in the sense that thereby they presuppose the existence of qualifiedly existing things, whereas in contrast qualifiedly existing things (apart from the sort noted in article 13) do not presuppose the existence of unqualifiedly existing things. Hence, to that extent at least, being sensorily available as a subject of a singular proposition in no way precludes being intelligibly in possession of complete actuality.

CHAPTER TWO

Particularity, Reference, and Identity

2.0

If the Special Theory of Being is true, then its category distinctions are applicable only if the category of substance is applicable. Predicatives, indeed, exist by necessity – at least some of them – but that could not be unless, in a sense of "could" that should become plainer, substances could exist, even if they happen not to. Of course it is equally true that in the required sense substances for their part could not exist unless predicatives could, indeed *do*, exist. However, it is the applicability of the category of substance that is the more directly perplexing. It comes into question in two main ways. We may doubt whether the category is coherently applicable – and, more specifically, in a spatio-temporal way. Then again, should these doubts be removed, we may doubt whether its spatio-temporal applicability is non-arbitrary, i.e. whether the categorial structure within which substance is primary is intrinsic to the spatio-temporal reality it categorizes.

In this chapter the question of non-arbitrariness remains in suspense. It will register its impatience mainly from the wings, but works centre upstage in the chapters that follow. My immediate focus is on the *coherence* of application, whether that application be arbitrary or otherwise. More specifically I now will consider (1) whether anything in the category of substance is coherently identifiable, and (2) whether, if it is, it is also coherently reidentifiable through time. Only after these two questions have been investigated as far as independently they can be is the question of non-arbitrariness worth more intensive consideration.

2.1 THE QUEST FOR A DEFINITE REFERENCE

Either you know into what you inquire, or you don't. If you do, the inquiry is pointless. If you don't, inquiry cannot even start. This is how Socrates sharpens a dilemma posed by Meno (*Meno*, 80D). What is mainly at stake is the feasibility of the Socratic type of inquiry, and more specifically of that form of identifiability that consists in definability.[1] Right here my concern is with the identifiability, not of *notions* by means of definition,[2] but of *particular substances*, i.e. substances that are distinguishable from each other spatially or otherwise, even where they have properties in common. Nevertheless, there is a similar if more narrowly focused dilemma that makes the latter's feasibility seem as precarious. Its source can be found in the following three premisses.

P1 The epistemically most basic type of predication is singular in the sense that the reference to the singular subject is definite in some way, i.e. of a uniquely individuating kind.

P2 In the last analysis the securing of reference to, i.e. the identification of, a particular as the subject of either a predication or a further identification is through the agency of predicatives.

P3 In any basic predication the predicative is universal in the sense that any particular of which it is predicated is just one among an infinite totality of actual and possible particulars of which it might be truly or falsely predicated.

In P1 the notion of an epistemically basic proposition can be limited to the type that supplies the empirical basis of our empirical knowledge. To reveal my hand at once by pointing a finger, this premiss is yet another dogma that is taken for granted, or at least strongly suggested, by the canonical notation of symbolic logic. As for P2, it is meant to apply even where the reference is secured, not by overt description, but by the use of names and indexical terms. These secure reference to particulars through our awareness of various kinds of relation in which their referents stand to the context of utterance (or inscription) and thought, or to the utterance (or inscription) and thought themselves. They do so even though these relations need not be, and very rarely are, predicated in the propositional content for which such terms supply the reference. I believe P2 to be evident enough to be actually true. Similarly, I am committed to the truth of P3, for that is presupposed in the E-frames that differentiate predicatives as a separate category from substantives.

But now, whether we take P2 and P3 to be true or not, the point to notice is that with the addition of P1 they generate a chicken-and-egg dilemma not unlike Meno's. Were all three true, then in any basic predication some predicative, other than the one ostensively predicated, would have to intervene to indicate of which particular, or particulars, the original predicative is being predicated. Thus in the proposition "This square is red", where red is the predicative predicated, the predicative square helps to narrow down the referent. It performs, let us say, as a referential, as distinct from a predicational characterizer. Similarly, then, in the proposition "This is square" there must, it would seem, be some further predicative intervening for the same purpose. The result would then be is an infinite regress, in which chickens and eggs relentlessly vie for relative precedence. Though in order to predicate, a definite reference to a subject would have *first* to be secured, in order to secure a definite reference there would have *first* to be a predication.

In this section I consider whether one can evade either horn by promoting the other. Either alternative must rest on P1 and more specifically on the existence of uniquely individuating factors whereby a definite reference for epistemically basic propositions might be secured. But for one the sort of factor required must consist exhaustively in some sort of network of predicatives that would require no further reference to something outside itself. In brief this preference retains P2 as well as P1 while rejecting P3. Call it for convenience solution A. The other precludes P2 and is at least supported by P3. It identifies the unique individuating factor – without any mediation whatever from predicatives – with a bare particularity or, if you like, with a *haecceitas*.[3] Distinguish this preference as solution B.

Thus on solution A we can entertain an epistemically basic proposition only if we can recognize the referent independently by means of some set of properties that it uniquely has. On solution B, however, we can recognize or specify its properties, uniquely or otherwise, only if independently we single out the reference uniquely. Hence for solution A the recognition or specification of certain properties has to be logically prior to the securing of reference, whereas for solution B it has to be the other way round.

Now for solution A the network of predicatives might take the form of a unique individuating nature analogous to the species-differentiating nature or essence that distinguishes any actual or possible member of a species, e.g. Adam, from any actual or possible member of another, e.g. Pegasus. The critical difference would be that it has also to distinguish both actual and possible members of the *same species* from each other. The same analogy further suggests that the existence of an individual would entail, but not be entailed by, the existence of the unique individual nature, just as we may suppose the existence of a particular ball entails the existence of the property of approximate sphericity without the existence of the latter entailing the existence of any ball.[4]

Alternatively, a particular individual might be taken as *identical* with the uniquely individuating network of predicatives. In that case the analogy with species-differentiating natures would no longer hold. If the individual particular exists, it exists *unqualifiedly*. On the other hand, a mere set of predicatives (or their substantive paronyms), whether uniquely individuating or not, is a non-substantial thing. Its existence is underivatively or derivatively a *qualified* existence. Furthermore, the existence of any individual particular is a matter of contingent fact, whereas that of non-substantial things (other than the impure sort of predicative allowed for in article 13 in 1.2) is necessary.

Where, then, the network of predicatives is interpreted as a unique individuating nature, solution A must take the following more specific form. In the last analysis, to secure a definite reference for a singular proposition one must ascertain that *there is something* that is all the predicatives, i.e. has all the paronyms of the predicatives, which constitute a certain unique individuating nature. One must do so for there remains the possibility that there is in fact nothing that has all of them. In this interpretation, however, solution A is open to a number of damaging objections.

1 Surreptitiously it contravenes P1, i.e. one of the two premisses it was supposed to conserve. It presupposes that there is a proposition more basic than, and different in type from, the singular proposition for which the network of predicatives is meant to provide a unique reference. In so far as the proposition that there is something that is all of a uniquely individuating set of predicatives refers to anything, it does so indefinitely. This lapse might, however, be seen as in breach of the letter rather than the spirit of P1, for *ex hypothesi* the proposition has a singular character due to its predicatives, if not independently to any reference.

2 No intrinsic property or set of intrinsic properties could differentiate one actual or possible from every other actual or possible particular. Hence no such property or set could constitute a unique individual nature in the sense defined. In their intrinsic properties two particulars, a and b, might be exactly alike, i.e. in those properties that may belong to one particular without logically presupposing the existence of any other. They might be idealized cases of the proverbial peas.

3 No extrinsic property or set of such properties, either by itself or as a further supplement, could distinguish one actual or possible from every other actual or just possible particular. In other words, no property or set of such that consists in one particular's relation to one or more than one other particular can enter into a unique individual nature.

(i) Notice, first, that if a relation's relatum or relata did not exist, then the property formed by the relation could do exist either. That is what makes the property extrinsic. Accordingly, not just the actuality but the very possibility of the existence of the particular for which the property constitutes what is supposed to be a unique individual nature would depend upon the existence of the relatum or relata. Not just the actuality but the very possibility would entail the existence of the relatum or relata.

(ii) Suppose the relation to be many-one or many-many. Then more than one actual or possible particular could have the property, in which case it would no longer be either whole or part of a uniquely individuating nature.

(iii) Suppose the relation to be necessarily one-one (like that of a finger to a ring) or one-many (like that of a hand to five rings). Then indeed it can individuate any particular that actually has the corresponding relational property from any other actual particular, since only one thing can be in the relation to the particular relatum or relata at any one time. Nevertheless, even if it were not contingent that the relatum should exist given the existence of the referent, since the relational property is extrinsic, it has to be contingent that the referent has just that relation to some relatum.

(iv) While any particular may be uniquely individuated by its relations to others, that individuation is parasitic upon the individuation of at least some other particular. Hence, as so individuated it cannot function as the referent of an epistemically basic proposition. If that function could belong to any particular, it would have to belong to a particular or particulars by its relation to which it has been ultimately individuated. But it can only belong to any such if the latter can be individuated in a non-parasitic way, i.e. not by means of any extrinsic relational property.

(v) The two particulars a and b might be numerically differentiated by nothing further than their being in an irreflexive symmetrical relation R, e.g. the relation of being two diameters apart, to each other. There might be no other particulars for them to be related to. Hence in this case there could be nothing in the extrinsic property which each has in being in R to the other to distinguish the two, apart from the otherness of a and b. Their otherness would not depend upon their uniquely instantiating different relational properties. On the contrary, their uniquely instantiating different relational properties would depend on their otherness. Furthermore, even if they happened not to be the sole particulars, their relations to other particulars might be exactly matching (Black, 1952 and 1954). For any relation that *a* has to one or more than one of these, *b* might likewise have respectively to one or more than one. Hence there might be nothing but the otherness of the respective relata of these matching relations to distinguish the relational properties that these relations form. Notice what has been denied here: not that the otherness depends upon the *relation* between the particulars but that it depends upon the difference in their *relational properties*.[5]

Solution A can, however, take another form. A unique individual nature consists of a *set* of predicatives or their substantive paronyms. But the network in question might be interpreted instead, not just as a set, but as a *bundle* or collection.[6] Take for illustration three predicative things, viz. F, G, and H. To cast this trio in the specific role of a bundle, let us then make its existence as such depend upon the truth of a quasi-Quinean affirmation, viz. "There are three things, all of which collectively one thing is, viz. F, G, and H." In short let us stipulate that the existence of F, G, and H as a bundle is equivalent just to the truth of this affirmation.[7] Similarly, F-ness, G-ness, and H-ness, viz. the corresponding substantive paronyms, must belong to a bundle as well by virtue of the same truth.

Now the existence of any such bundle so conceived must be just as contingent as the existence of an individual. That is because the quasi-Quinean definiens is contingent, which in turn is because it does not contain the parenthetical disjunctive phrase "or is not." Otherwise the definiens would be necessarily true, and F, G, and H and their substantive paronyms mere sets, whose existence would be necessary too. But likewise the bundle's existence must be *un*qualified as well as contingent. Ontological commitment in the substantive existential "There is a fact, viz ..." is just as unqualified as in the equally substantive existential "There is a thing, viz ..." where one plugs the bundle-constituting affirmation into the first frame and "Socrates" into the second. What, then, is there to prevent one from identifying any particular individual substance with some such bundle or collection on the basis that what distinguishes the latter's existence is just as unqualified and contingent as that of the individual substance?

Well, if as we have already seen no particular substance need be one-to-one related to a set of predicatives or properties of the intrinsic kind, similarly it need not be so related to a bundle of such predicatives or properties as thus defined. As for extrinsic relational properties, these would seem no basis for bundle-uniqueness. Otherwise the existence of every bundle would seem parasitic upon that of some other.

As well, however, this second version of solution A fails for at least two further reasons. First, once again it runs counter to a premiss it aims to conserve. It presupposes that the most basic kind of fact corresponds, not to a singular proposition, but to a quasi-Quinean existential. Second and more damagingly, the stipulation fails to make the bundle's existence unqualified in the way in which the existence of an individual substance is unqualified. If the existence of the fact and the existence of the individual subject of the subordinate clause in the fact's propositional expression were the same, presumably the fact would be self-referring, for it refers to that individual subject. But self-referring it obviously is not.

The same type of objection applies, furthermore, if we reform the notion of bundling rather more complexly. We might have based it on a metaphysical distinction sometimes drawn between property-particulars and property-universals.[8] Examples of the former would be F-ness here now, G-ness there now, and H-ness here then, where of course here, there, now, and then are examples of a specifically locative kind of predicative thing. Now these property-particulars can be taken as bundles in more or less complex groups according to whether one or more than one shares the same spatio-temporal location. Thus F-ness here now forms a single-membered bundle and F-ness, G-ness, and H-ness, all three here now, a triplet.

But the existence of a bundle so conceived would seem to depend upon, indeed consist of, the truth of an existential sentence. Thus the existence of F-ness here now depends on the truth of "There is one thing which at least one thing is, viz. F, and there are two things *at* which at least one thing is that thing (viz. F), viz. here and now." Once again, then, the bundle's existence depends upon the truth of a sentence, and the existence of this truth is both contingent and unqualified. Yet, though the existence of the individual subject of the final subordinate clause is likewise unqualified, once again, for the same reason as before, it cannot be identical with the existence of the truth or fact about it.

The preceding group of arguments against the identity-alternative for solution A may be recognized as in part an allusive, if tacit, confirmation of current objections[9] against what is commonly referred to as the Bundle Theory. According to the latter a particular just is a "compresence" of properties, which in turn are conceived either as universals or as in some way more basically particular than the particular that is formed by their "compresence." It is this compresence that is commonly referred to as a bundle. But the agreement may conceal a fundamental difference of approach. The standard critique has been *ad hominem*. It may take a theory of Russell's (Russell, 1940, chap. 6, 1948, pt II, chap. 3) or some variant, discuss that theory in its own categorially somewhat confused terms, and by some *reductio ad absurdum* show *that* the theory is categorially confused rather than *why*. While establishing that the *analysandum* and proposed *analysans* are in some way categorially discrepant, it fails to clarify more exactly what the categorial relation underlying the discrepancy must be.

My procedure, in contrast, has been to postulate the categorial distinctions and relationships that have been drawn, and partly elucidated, in chapter 1. The intended effect has been to pre-empt the very formulation of the Bundle Theory in its terms by showing that the category distinctions are the basis for a further exhaustive distinction between *mere* property-sets and property-sets that are *also* property-bundles in the sense *I* have defined. Once these distinctions are drawn, the rest is plain sailing. A particular substance cannot be identical with a property-set, because the existence of property-sets (provided they exclude the exceptions for which I have allowed) is both derivatively qualified and necessary. That of a particular substance, on the other hand, is unqualified and contingent. Nor can a substance be identical with a property-bundle, for the latter is identical with a fact about a particular or particulars, and not a particular substance itself. But mere property-sets and property-sets that are also property-bundles are the only things into which properties can be combined, apart from some combination of the two. Hence there are no other ways in which particular substances could be identical with properties.[10]

Strengthened, then, by the failure of its more conservative rival to solve the paradox, solution B can now take up the challenge. Given that the unique individual status of the ultimate referent is not to be found in some network of predicatives or their substantive paronyms, does it consist of a bare particularity? Contrary to the second premiss from which the paradox stemmed, is the ultimate reference unmediated by any predicative? There are, in fact, two quite distinct accounts of how this might be.

1 In his *Tractatus* Wittgenstein seems to have held that the numerical otherness of the members of the totality of objects that constitute what he called "the substance of the world" is constitutive of each object. All such objects in their numerical difference and mul-

tiplicity are *internally* related. As a matter of fact each object stands to any of the rest in a specific relation, and these specific relationships are *external*, i.e. in no way constitutive of the related objects. But neither the existence nor the numerical otherness of objects is a mere matter of fact. They constitute the object's *logical form* – the logical space that consists of all the possible situations or external relationships in which the objects might participate. That the objects exist and are numerically different is, accordingly, something that a suitably articulate language must indeed show, but cannot state: for on Wittgenstein's picture theory of language the multiplicity of the world's substance is evenly matched by the multiplicity of the naming signs in the language, and hence on his conception of naming there could be no way of stating with sense either that this was or that it was not so.

Some doubt exists as to the category of being to which these objects are supposed to belong. Are any of them either properties or relations, as distinct from particulars? Are any of them particulars? But according to the more common interpretations, at least some are particulars, and bare particulars at that. In other words, intrinsically at least these particulars do not possess any properties whatever. Their intrinsic nature is exhausted in their logical form, i.e. in the internal relations to other objects. What properties, other than logical form, they may have are constituted entirely by their external relations to other objects, whether the latter consist exclusively of other particulars or otherwise belong to other logical categories. Hence, on this interpretation, the *Tractatus* view must be that the identifiability and distinguishability of each particular is intrinsic to that particular – though something that is shown through the referential role of names in a language without being capable of being stated.

The thesis that particulars not only are bare but also have an a priori necessary existence has, however, been determined or suggested by what in this context are an alien set of considerations. Wittgenstein's picture theory developed out of the Frege-Russell-Whitehead analysis of language, which in turn was conceived by its authors as instrumental to their logicist enterprise of reducing mathematics to logic. Their concerns, accordingly, and his as well, were rather more specific than those that gave birth to the notion of substance in chapter 1. Further, for reasons that have been rehearsed far too many times to bear repetition here, the picture theory, at least in Wittgenstein's version (whatever more exactly that is), is in itself incredible. Hence I shall continue to assume what I have already assumed in rejecting solution B, viz. that the existence of any particular is extrinsic to that of any other – as extrinsic as is the external relation between them – and that the existence of no particular is an a priori necessity.

2 But now, it may seem, this assumption still leaves one part of Wittgenstein's thesis unchallenged. Other philosophers (Bergman, 1964 and 1967; Allaire, 1963 and 1965) have held that the identifiability of any one particular, or its numerical distinguishability, is ultimately due to a bare particularity, though in a rather different way. For them the bare particularity is a potentially distinctive residue that remains as a constituent of each particular after everything in respect of which the particular could be the same as any other, i.e. after every one of its properties, has been discounted.[11] Contrary to the *Tractatus*, to possess this is not taken to preclude that a particular also possesses intrinsic properties, nor to presuppose the existence of all other particulars that exist, nor as an a priori presupposition of propositional sense. Thus, whether the particular of which it is a constituent actually exists is to be taken as a straightforward matter of empirical fact. But because of its bareness, they further hold, we take cognizance of this residue, not through any judgmental recognition of anything the particular may have – for anything it may truly be *judged* to have, others might be truly be judged to have as well. It is, on the contrary, through a prejudgmental, or purely referential, kind of empirical intuition, i.e. through what Russell and others have called "acquaintance."

One might wonder at this stage whether the bare particularity so construed can really be cast in the role of an intrinsic identifiability or distinguishability. How could it take on the function of numerically distinguishing both actual and merely possible particulars from other actual and merely possible particulars?[12] That basic objects have acquired an intrinsic distinguishability in the *Tractatus* should not distract us. In that work the classes of actual and possible basic objects conveniently coincide. But this part of the Tractarian doctrine has now been dropped.

Surely it is properties alone that are capable of making a numerical distinction that is irrespective of whether the particulars distinguished are actual or merely possible. That is because properties can, for the most part, have more instances than they actually do have, and certain properties are mutually incompatible, in the sense that they cannot be simultaneously coinstantiated by exactly the same particular in exactly the same respect. It follows directly from these two propositions that instances both actual and merely possible of one property must be numerically distinct from contemporaneous instances both actual and merely possible of any incompatible property. But *ex hypothesi* the bare particularity is not a property. Hence it cannot numerically distinguish either actual or merely possible particulars from merely possible particulars. Hence, for good measure, it cannot do so uniquely. Alternatively, to suppose that it could would be to treat it as a property.

Perhaps, then, it would have been altogether more fair to suppose that the bare particularity of the non-Wittgensteinian kind had never been intended by anyone to function as an intrinsic feature. But first, our main concern is with what the function could be. Second, Allaire (1965; see Loux, 1976b, 299 and 302) has stated that "Bare particulars are the entities *in* things accounting for the numerical difference *of* things," and further that they are "the entities which carry the numerical difference, the entities which ground the numerical difference of things." Apparently, then, at least for him, the otherness of any given particular from another is not just like the extrinsic relationship of being to the left of the latter, which it may also have, for that relationship is not grounded in any specific property of either particular apart from its mere spatiality. It would be more like the extrinsic relationship of being redder than. In other words, it is due to something in each particular, which is analogous to the intrinsic shade of redness that characterizes each particular in the case of the one being redder than the other. Further, I cannot see how Allaire could escape the inference that this kind of intrinsic entity must be the ground, not merely of the otherness of two actual particulars, but also of the otherness of an actual and a merely possible particular or of two merely possible particulars.

2.2   THE PRIORITY OF INDEFINITE REFERENCE

For its coherent identifiability a substance does not require the ultimate precedence of either reference or predication over the other. In more precise terms, it does not require that one of P2 and P3 should be false, where P1 is to be taken as true. On the contrary, as I shall now argue, P1 is false. Particulars are identifiable for the purpose of predication in an indefinite as well as a definite way, and it is indefinite identifiability that is epistemically basic. Hence there is no need whatever for reference and predication to compete for precedence. Predication can secure an indefinite reference for its subject. Reference can be secured and predication take place in one and the same act.

Notice that the present distinction between definite and indefinite forms of identification is not quite the same as the distinction in 1.3 in these same terms. There it lay between two kinds of proposition each of which identifies one thing with another. As such it coincided more or less precisely with a distinction between definite and indefinite noun-phrases that appear in the non-subject place of an identifying sentence. Here, however, we are dealing with identification of a more primitive kind, i.e. with identification that establishes reference to the subject of a proposition that either identifies or predicates. It is as a reminder of the difference that I sometimes specify the distinction as between two types of *reference* or *referring*, where dealing with identification of reference.

My thesis, then, is that to refer to, to think or write or talk about a particular, i.e. a definite particular, no unique or definite reference to that particular is absolutely essential, though possibly it might be had (see also Hall, 1961, 46–7; Chastain, 1975; Wilson, 1978; and Stich, 1984, chap. 6). Properties need not to be specified which that particular alone has. It may be quite enough that whatever is said by way of reference to that particular is truly said, provided it is perceived as truly said. But to determine more exactly how that is to be done, a number of distinctions need to be noted.

First, the so-called mass-nouns (e.g. "gold," "water," "garbage," "cattle") should be distinguished from the so-called count-nouns (e.g. "cow," "horse," "man"). To secure reference to something numerically definite by means of mass-nouns some individuating noun-expression has to be prefixed, as in "a nugget of gold," "a glass of water," "a pile of garbage," and "fifty head of cattle." To secure reference to something numerically definite as well as particular by means of count-nouns, nothing other than a definite or indefinite article or a number-adjective has to precede. The count-nouns may, of course, be preceded by certain noun-expressions in a manner analogous to that in which mass-nouns are preceded by individuating noun-expressions, as in "a herd of cows," "a team of horses," and "a gathering of men." But these have the converse function of amalgamating individual particulars into group particulars, instead of dividing something off from a whole.

Now the two types of noun correspond to two types of thing – though not exactly. Notice first that with or without an individuating noun-precursor many mass-nouns are syntactically as at home in the Unqualified E-frame (1.2) as any proper name or count-noun. Hence what they name must belong at least to the general class of substantive things. But unlike property-names, which name substantives as well, the things that they name have no predicative paronyms. Thus, "water" in "This liquid is water" is not an adjective like "white" in "This liquid is white." The former sentence, in other words, is just as identificatory as is "Socrates is a man." Hence certain mass-nouns, at least, are names of substances, not just of substantives. But others, e.g. "cattle," do not belong as comfortably to the Unqualified E-frame, if only because names that fit there name something singular, whereas these mass-nouns seem to be understood as naming something plural. Thus water *is* a liquid, whereas cattle *are* domestic animals. Accordingly, we have to distinguish things that, though numerically indefinite, are yet numerically many or individuated from things that are numerically indefinite, because they are conceived as not individuated. Both types of thing are named by mass-nouns, but the latter alone are named by a subclass, the so-called material-names. It is the distinction between the material-names and the count-nouns and between the corresponding types of thing for which the expressions respectively stand that interests us primarily here.

My next distinction is between two sets of adjectives and the corresponding properties. Certain adjectives like the colour-adjectives are such that, if they apply to each part of a whole, then they apply to the whole of that whole. Others, e.g. shape and size, are not of this type. It is adjectives of this latter type that denote properties essential to the individuation of particulars which count-nouns denote. Thus the adjective "spherical" stands for a property or predicative essential to the individual particulars denoted by the count-noun "sphere."

My final distinction rests upon these precursors. It falls between referring indefinitely to some *indefinite* particular and referring indefinitely to some *definite* particular. We may do the former either in speech, writing, or thought through the medium of existentials that contain mass-nouns or the former of the two types of adjectives, as in "There is water" or (as when we come to in the midst of a fog) "There is something white." Of course, we need not in all cases be referring to something indefinite when we refer indefinitely in this way. Some stress has to be given to the "may." "There is something white" may pick out something definite against a background of other colours. But we can also refer indefinitely to something definite in a less equivocal way, viz. by means of count-nouns or the latter of the two types of adjective, as in the existentials "There is a sphere" and "There is something spherical." To secure reference, at least for oneself, there may be no need to distinguish the referent from any other particular. The applicability of the count-noun or adjective may be enough.

Once more, however, some stress has to be placed upon the "may." Not all existentials have a referring function. Indeed, according to a current orthodoxy, none does. Hence it may seem to some that in giving certain existentials a referring function I have confused the existential "There is," which does not refer (or so they say), with a demonstrative "There is" which does refer inasmuch as the "There" indicates a location.

But first there would have been nothing to gain from this confusion, if it had not been a confusion, since if the "There" did function as a locative demonstrative, it would no longer be clear that the referring was indefinite and not definite. Second, when one takes unbiased stock of the situation, it should become clear enough that in a special, but prevalent, circumstance existentials do refer to particulars. This circumstance is partly reflected in a grammatical feature distinctive, if not exclusively so, of existentials that refer. Whether the existential refers indefinitely to something definite or to something indefinite, its present tense is not of either the tenseless or tense-neutral kind. It is the tense that contrasts the present with the past and future. It has to do this because the function of the existential is primarily to give expression to what is an immediate presentation to the consciousness of the speaker or writer or thinker. If you like, the tense functions demonstratively even if the "There" does not. But first the function of the demonstrative, if that is what it is, is not to select one particular that satisfies the further characterization from other particulars that might possibly do so as well. Second, the present tense, in so far as its function is to express the presentedness of presentation, is rather more primitive than any demonstrative. The use of any demonstrative would seem to presuppose that something or other is presented – before the speaker and the person addressed – *now*.

Granted that the existential gives expression to an immediate presentation, it refers indefinitely to something definite where the applicability of the characteristic for which the count-noun or count-adjective stands is enough to select the particular uniquely from other particulars likewise present. The characteristic selects rather in the way that a lock selects one key from a bunch of non-duplicate keys as the one to unlock it. There being no duplicates around, there is no need for any further principle of selection – something that would set up a distinction between a this and a that. The selection is a function of the interaction between the presented situation and the applicability of an individuating characteristic. Where a visually presented situation includes just one cow in a meadow, one's apprehension that there is a cow secures reference to that definite cow, without requiring an awareness of anything that distinguishes it from other cows.

Notice, further that this kind of indefinite reference need not be reference exclusively to just *one* definite thing. It may be to several.

Nor need the individuating characteristics involved be exclusively of the intrinsic kind. Ease of exposition required that we first attend to examples of a simple sort, but to correct our perspective we can vary our fare. Thus one may have reference indefinitely to two definite things as two, by recognizing that there are some things that stand in one irreflexive relation to each other. One may be aware of something red and spherical as being some distance apart from something that is red and spherical. Here, of course, there is a greater element of definiteness than before: for one is likewise aware of an individual distinctness. But this distinctness is only of a relative kind, and need not contribute any property intrinsic or relational to the one individual that is not shared by the other.

No doubt it might be difficult to be aware of one thing as red and spherical, or of two things as in some irreflexive relation, and of no other thing. It would be difficult not to be also aware that *we* are aware of it or them, and also of a more or less precise relation that what we are aware of has to us. Indeed, when we look at something, the relation may be more of an intentional creation than something to be discovered – and hence not something we ignore.

But *first*, that *we* are looking at something that is red and spherical, etc., may not attract our interest at all during the time that we are looking, even if it is to be conceded that self-awareness is always there. The focus of our attention may be entirely on the object, and not upon something, viz. ourselves, in relation to which we could give a more definite reference.

Second, even if the focus is on oneself in relation to the object, no unique or definite reference to oneself is absolutely essential. Each one of us is as devoid of a unique individuating nature as any other particular of which we may or may not be cognisant. Our self-knowledge, in the first instance, has not the definite self-reference of a Cartesian Cogito. At best it need only be to the effect that there is something that is aware of something, e.g. red and spherical, and that this same something (if we grant the self-referring nature of awareness) is aware that it is aware. To that extent our awareness is somewhat like the previously mentioned awareness that there is something red and spherical at some distance apart from something red and spherical. There is an indefinite reference to at least two things in relation to each other, not a definite reference to one thing in terms of its relation to something to which we have a definite reference – though admittedly in this case the relation is asymmetrical, and hence more discriminating.

Third, it is through our awareness of our cognitive and spatial relation to that to which we have indefinite reference in perception that – it would seem – we are able to acquire a more definite reference to ourselves. One acquires a more definite reference to oneself through one's reference, definite or indefinite, to what one perceives about one, rather than a definite reference to the latter through a definite reference to oneself. Even one's awareness of oneself as something that is aware, which we provisionally took as primitive in the last paragraph, is less than primitive. Through something becoming aware of the spatial relation to some particular, to which it has a definite or indefinite reference in perception, it acquires an awareness, not merely that *there is* an awareness of something but that it itself is something among other possible things that is aware.

The more general issue has, however, still to be fully exposed. Seldom, if ever, are we aware of a particular except as within a specific context, and seldom, if ever, does its relation to other things in that context fail to distinguish it uniquely from everything else therein. That, then, may seem to throw the occurrence of indefinite reference in doubt. But first, we cannot identify a context in relation to which we identify a part without first identifying parts, the relations between which make up the context. Second, even if that were not so, the same problem of securing a definite reference to the total context arises as originally arose for securing reference to an individual particular.

There is no need, then, to look for something to do the job that in 2.1 we found that nothing could do. To provide a reference for any predication that does not secure a unique reference for itself, there is no unqualified need to look beyond the predication for some simple or complex property that does. Nor if that task is abandoned need we look for some non-property that would do the job instead. In immediate experience, at least, any true predication identifies in the sense that it secures a reference, though not necessarily in a definite way.

Accordingly it follows that for definite reference there is a somewhat more limited and specialized role than philosophers and logicians commonly allow.

1 Its possibility is always dependent on other particulars if such are around, or if there are none, upon the fact that there are none. Hence it must be, in part at least, in terms of extrinsic as distinct from intrinsic properties. That a given particular in the *only* one to be F depends as much upon other particulars, if there are any, as upon the predicate F. The F-ness itself does not guarantee uniqueness, except perhaps in so far as it is an extrinsic property that involves reference to all other particulars as a totality. What, then,

if the particular happens to be the only particular *tout court*, as well as the only one to be F? Suppose there is a limit to the divisibility of particulars into smaller ones, and that only one such atom exists. But – here as well – that the atom is the only particular to be F does not depend upon its F-ness – at least not exclusively. It depends upon the contingent and extrinsic fact that there are no other particulars.

2 It is not just the definiteness of a reference that is dependent upon extrinsic factors in this way. More radically, it is the very need for the definiteness that is extrinsically conditioned. If there were nothing else around, the need would not arise.

3 But further, the presence of other particulars is no more than a necessary condition for the need. It is not sufficient as well. Thus, we have seen, to identify a particular as one of two there is no need for more than the recognition mentioned above, viz. an indefinite reference to both as things in an irreflexive spatial relation to each other. There is no need to recognize the one as possessing some intrinsic or extrinsic property not possessed by the other.

4 Typically the absolute need for definite reference will arise where it is impossible for one person to have a panoptic perception, current or remembered, of the field of particulars over which that person's mental discourse ranges, or where two or more persons in communication wish to refer to the same thing or things. In the latter case the need arises from the fact that one's perceptual field is nothing like panoptic or continuous in relation to the field of discourse over which one ranges in interpersonal communication, and that even if it were, the various personal perceptual fields stand in need of a mutual calibration, if communication is to be attained.

The chicken-and-egg dilemma is, therefore, avoidable. To secure reference it is unnecessary to secure a definite reference; for a characterization[13] – viz. a referential characterization – can adequately supply, albeit indefinitely, its own reference. Hence, further, in order to explain how a characterization can have reference to a subject, there is no need to postulate the existence of unique individual natures either in the form of unique conjunctions of properties or in that of bare particulars.

More could now be said on how definite reference by such various devices as definite descriptions, indexicals, and proper names is ultimately derived from indefinite referring. A fuller justice to that process here would, however, pre-empt some of the attention I must direct towards more pressing items on my announced agenda. Hence I terminate this section with a mere sketch.

In general the derivation is a process of anaphora of the sort (Chastain, 1975) that allows one to introduce a story with an indefinite reference, as in "There was something disgusting in my chocolate mousse," and then continue with a definite reference, as in "On further examination it (or the disgusting thing) turned out to be the embryo of a mouse." However, the principal problem lies in the further vindication of P2. In the case of several types of definite referring expression, e.g. in that of the indexical "I," there is no overtly specified reference-securing predicative. Hence one has to show further how the definite reference is indeed in all cases through the agency of predicatives.

Now in the case of indexicals that are commonly recognized as such there is little mystery as to how predicatives are covertly at work. Thus where "I" secures reference, it usually does so by virtue of an awareness, on the part of those between whom communication occurs, of who the particular communicator happens to be.[14] Yet quite obviously "I" cannot be explicitly defined as, say, "the communicator of this communication." That is partly because such sentences as "I am bald" and "You are bald" can be used to communicate what would normally be regarded as exactly the same thing, in spite of the fact that in the use of the second no reference overt or covert is made to the use of the first. But also, if one were to use "The communicator of this communication" in place of the "I," the communicative act or token in question would be morphemically different from the particular act or token through their consciousness of which the communicator and those to whom it was addressed both secured reference to the former (Rankin, 1964).

With proper names, however, there might seem to be more of a problem. They too can and, I believe, should be classified as indexicals.[15] But the specific nature of the predicatives whereby they covertly secure a reference is a matter of controversy. Here I shall merely remark that the very general account provided by Kripke (1980, 91–7, 163) and Donnellan (1974, 1979) of how proper names succeed in designating can be combined with their classification as indexicals.[16] In brief, where we succeed in designating by means of any such designation, it is by means of an awareness on the part of those between whom the communication takes place that there is some sort of causal chain or historical story connecting an original with the present use of the designator in question. However, that there is such a connection no more enters into what a proposition with the designator as subject says or predicates of the subject than does a statement in the first person say or predicate that its subject is identical with the person making that statement.

2.3 BACK TO THE PLATONIC APORETIC

The spatio-temporal applicability of the category of substance also hangs on a further and somewhat more narrow issue. Given that the identifiability of substance is above suspicion, is its reidentifiability equally so? More narrowly still, are *mutable* particulars coherently reidentifiable?

It is, of course, in this latter form that the narrower issue becomes the most patently crucial. Mutable particulars – as distinct from their histories – are not what I shall distinguish as EVENTS. In other words, they are not temporally continuous or discontinuous (spatio)temporal particular wholes. As so defined, EVENTS – whether continuous or discontinuous – need not be taken as capable either of change or of remaining unchanged. They may simply be the sum – ordered, partially ordered, or unordered – of continuous or discontinuous variegated or uniform temporal parts that belong to different times. Mutable particulars are, in contrast, capable as such of either changing or remaining unchanged. As such they are only associated, as distinct from identical, with EVENTS. Each change or abstention from change in a mutable particular completes a particular EVENT, which includes a particular EVENT completed by the mutable particular's immediately preceding change or abstention from change, if any. Each change or abstention, in other words, concludes a history, whole or partial, that extends a less inclusive history.

Misgivings about identifiability of the sort just dismissed apply indifferently to the mutable and the non-mutable type of particular. Further misgivings about reidentifiability, on the other hand, have had the compatibility of reidentification with the possibility of change as their traditional focus. Indeed, it is difficult to see for what further reason reidentifiability should be in doubt where possibility of change is ruled out. The reidentifiability of any EVENT is no more than the recognizability of separate EVENTS as different parts of the same more inclusive EVENT. All that the recognition requires is some principle of connection, arbitrary or otherwise, that determines the two as parts of the same more inclusive EVENT. Hence, for the present, I limit myself to the intelligibility of something remaining the same throughout change.

Plato sometimes refers to change as though it, too, were anomalously one-over-many. In this context, however, it could be more precisely described as a many-over-one. Its salient feature is that a number of predicatives flow over one particular substance (though, of course, each of these predicatives may be shared by other substances as well). Thus that the same one thing, e.g. a tree, is (say) initially short and later tall – the two predicatives to be counted here as absolute rather than relational – might be thought to imply, by transitivity of identity, that somehow through time one thing that the tree is, viz. short, becomes identical with another thing that the tree is, viz. tall, or that one property it has becomes identical with another property it has, i.e. that shortness becomes tallness. But no property can ever become another. Shortness can never become tallness. Hence, if one assumes that change as to predicatives is basic to all change, one might be led to infer quite generally that particulars, where conceived as at least subject to change, are just as Plato said, i.e. not completely real. And then one might follow him further by inferring that only predicatives really are real – that they, or rather their substantive paronyms, belong to a realm of eternal unchanging Forms – for in themselves they alone (with, perhaps, an exception for souls) are completely free from change.

The sophistry, no doubt, already seems blatant. To distinguish between predication and identification, as now we are entitled to do, is to allow that change may have either a predicational or an identificatory description. But neither type *need* imply any loss of identity. In the former, no identifications are directly or explicitly made (except in the securing of reference). Hence the transitivity of identity can do no damage. In the latter, however, though the transitivity can apply, its application need not lead to any conflict. Thus the same tree is at one time a short tree, if then it was short, and later a tall tree, if then it was tall. Likewise the short tree on the knoll becomes the tall tree on the knoll. But in neither the indefinite nor the definite example of identification does the tree undergo any loss of identity. Since that the tree is initially short and later tall is not contradictory, neither is the identity of a tree that was a (the) short tree with a tree that later is a (the) tall tree.

2.4   THE GENERAL THEORY OF BEING

So far, then, a solution to the problem of flux or the many-over-one would seem as much within the grasp of the Special Theory of chapter 1 as our solution to the converse problem of the one-over-many. Thus, as limited in 2.3, the wider issue of spatio-temporal applicability may seem less complex than its earlier limitation in 2.1 and 2.2. No fallacy other than category-confusion has had there to be scotched. Hence nothing as grand as a General Theory of Being would seem required. The issues of the one-over-many and the many-over-one have yet to appear sufficiently distinct.

Sometimes, however, a loss of identity through change actually does occur, i.e. with no connivance from category-confusion or other conceptual muddle. A log that begins as a cellulose package may through the course of aeons eventually petrify. With less delay Jeremy Bentham the man or person has transformed into Jeremy Bentham the headless mummy and college mascot. In either case it is no longer a matter of one thing changing from either of two contraries to the other while continuing to exist as the same. What now is at stake is a distinction between two sorts of change and the contrast between two sorts of property from which it stems. More specifically it is the distinction between change in *accidental* properties, during which what changes continues to exist, and change in *essential* properties, by the end of which what changes ceases to exist. Hence two lines of inquiry still lie before us.

We may take the notion of change for granted and then go on to ask why one should consider any change to be a loss or acquisition of an essence. Could it not as well be the loss and acquisition of one (or more than one) accident? Conversely, why consider any change to be a loss or acquisition of an accident? Could it not as well be the loss or acquisition of an essence? Indeed, might not all change amount to loss of essence, or alternatively loss of accident? More concisely, is there any non-arbitrary basis for the contrast between properties upon which the distinction between the two sorts of change depends? Might the essence-accident contrast be nothing more than just a matter of arbitrary choice determined by extraneous considerations of convenience? If a transition from cellulose to petrification is seen as a loss of identity, may that not merely reflect a change in our normal use for what undergoes the change?

These are comparatively conservative questions. But they also instigate a further and less conservative series. Whether we despair of a non-arbitrary basis for the essence-accident contrast or not, we may further ask whether there is any non-arbitrary basis for attributing a mutability of any sort. Might it not be equally, or more, appropriate to conceive of reality as consisting of EVENTS, i.e. of more or less variegated or uniform spatio-temporally or temporally cohesive wholes? Might there not be less of a subjective bias in this way of conceiving? Is our addiction to the alternative conception due to anything more than a limit to our knowledge of the spatio-temporally or temporally cohesive particular wholes that are there – to the fact, say, that our direct acquaintance with the remoter past, and to a greater extent with the future, is less detailed in some respects than our acquaintance with the immediate present?

Either line of inquiry may seem quite new. Each addresses a question of non-arbitrariness, whether as pertaining to a particular's reidentifiability throughout change or to its reidentification as mutable rather than EVENT. Hence each leads to the final question reserved in 2.0 as if quite distinct. If the essence-accident contrast is non-arbitrarily drawn, than the individual thinghood, i.e. the identifiability at any time as well as the reidentifiability through a succession of times, of that to which the contrasted properties pertain is non-arbitrary as well. If, furthermore, that contrast applies primarily to mutables and only secondarily (if at all) to EVENTS, then the mutability of substance is non-arbitrary as well.

However, the question of non-arbitrariness is not as distinct as 2.0 may seem to suggest. It is partly a question of whether the reidentifiability of a particular is not circumscribed by limits to its spatio-temporal unity (i.e. its continuity or other form of cohesion) of a sort that only a distinction of essence from accident can supply. Partly too, once we grant that spatio-temporal identifiability depends upon some essence-accident distinction, it is a question of whether the identifiability is indifferent to how the distinction is applied. Would the spatio-temporal totality or ensemble divide as coherently into individual particulars under one way of distinguishing essences from accidents as under any other? Finally, and even more deeply than these, there lies a further question, viz. whether even the spatio-temporal medium within which a particular is spatio-temporally reidentifiable is independent of that particular's mutable status. Is the spatio-temporality upon which a particular's identifiability depends indifferent to which of the two guises, that of mutable or that of EVENT, is the more basic?

It is, then, for answers to questions such as these that a General Theory of Being is mainly required. What we need is a more comprehensive theory of spatio-temporal applicability than what I have so far provided – one to which the Special Theory and earlier sections of this chapter are a mere prolegomenon. More specifically, what we have to determine is whether the essence-accident contrast and the mutability within which it applies has a non-arbitrary basis.

The General Theory I am about to offer is a causal theory. For a start it attributes a non-arbitrary distinction between essence and accident to a causal structure in nature, which if not entirely independent from us is at least something by which we, in how we apply the distinction, should be instructed. This theory is not, however, just any kind of causal theory but one of a rather distinctive type. It is a hylomorphic causal theory, and stands to Aristotle's hylomorphism or matter-form distinction much as the Special Theory stands to his category doctrine. The General like the Special Theory is in fact a reconstruction, but one of a different type. Both theories reconstruct to a greater or lesser extent by disambiguating certain ambiguities in Aristotle's original doctrine. But the ambiguities in Aristotle's hylomorphism are rather more conscious and deliberate than those in his category doctrine. Partly for that reason there will be in the sequel a more express parting of the ways on several points between the General Theory and its predecessor than has occurred in the unveiling of the Special Theory. Aristotle's failure to agree preveniently with all aspects of the General Theory cannot as easily be put down to inadvertance.

CHAPTER THREE

A Dynamics of Matter and Form

3.0

As a first approximation distinctions between matter and form can be taken as basic to a conceptual scheme the applicability of which is presupposed in the questions to which opposing empirical hypotheses or scientific theories give conflicting answers. This suits one contemporary view of how metaphysics and science may collaborate (cf Strawson, 1959, 9–11). So conceived, Aristotle's hylomorphic distinctions belong to a metaphysical inquiry of either a descriptive or a revisionary kind – or, if to neither, at least to an inquiry ancestral to either. Provisionnally, i.e. just for the purpose of this chapter, I connive with this viewpoint.

Less anachronistic is my further refinement of certain standard technical terms. While this sort of liberty has no explicit textual sanction, textually it is not unprovoked. Aristotle assembled his conceptual apparatus in a somewhat piecemeal, improvised, analogical, evocative, informal, and generally unsystematic way in the course of more or less independent, if convergent, methodological, physical, psychological, theological, and ontological inquiries. Through a consciously cultivated use of systematic shifts in the meanings of his technical terms, he is the master of an enviable, if irritating, facility for making its intricacies seem less bothersome than in fact they are. He moves from one application of the same term to others without missing a beat, in much the same way (to adapt one of his favourite analogies) as we ascribe health variously to persons, food, and appetites without confusion and yet without explicit display, or even adequate knowledge, of the rules by which this systematic equivocation is governed.

This procedure, if convenient, is not without peril. *We* do not need to spell out how "healthy" and "unhealthy" food or appetites are oppositely related to each other through their causal relations to healthy and unhealthy organisms. But more is at theoretical stake in his equivocal use of hylomorphic terminology. Furthermore, shift in meaning is a source of philosophical confusion. Even where the shift is deliberate, one may credit oneself with more control over its effects than one really has. Hence better avoid or circumvent it, even at the cost of consent to new-fangled coinage.

3.1 THE DUAL HYLOMORPHISM

Relations of matter to form are elusively complex and various. As the parallel lists in Table 2 are meant to emphasize, they comprise a whole nexus of analogously related relations. Various kinds of matter and of form can in this sense be described respectively as homonyms, i.e. as displaying the particular kind of homonymy that is based not on some quirk of natural language but on analogy. It may be noticed that textually the right-hand classifications are not as firmly rooted as those on the left. Some of the distinctions in the former are evoked by his examples rather than codified as such in his writings. Indeed, some of the examples that evoke these distinctions are either modifications of his (as in SR1) or not his at all (as in SR3), but seem needed to bring explicit and implicit distinctions into sharper relief. Even so, however, the list may be incomplete, partly because some of Aristotle's own examples are not easy to classify.

A further duality is tacit in the right-hand list. Synchronic matter-form distinctions belong in parallel to two distinct types of substance – artefacts on the one hand and natural substances on the other. This duality is, however, not in types of relation, but just in application; and in any case the artefact-examples play an auxiliary role. Their purpose is primarily to serve as models for the application of synchronic matter-form distinctions to natural substances. Aristotle's assumption in this is that nature acts like an intelligent workman. This further duality will here be given its due by being set to work in a similar way.

The left-right duality (see Williams, 1958, and Hintikka, c. 1977, chap. 5) is, however, rightfully the more conspicuous. It is as central to Aristotle's General Theory of Being as the comparable duality in his category doctrine has been to our Special Theory, and provides a key to other distinctions upon which the non-arbitrary application

Table 2
Hylomorphic Homonymy

Diachronic Relations (DR)	*Synchronic Relations* (SR)

1 In locomotion
  M. What moves
  F. Different places
	1 In combination
	  M. Materials (e.g. tin, copper)
	  F^1. Ratio of mix (e.g. 2:1)
	  F^2. Homogeneous character (e.g. of bronze)

2 In alteration
  M. What alters
  F. Different qualities
	2 In compounds
	  M. Materials (e.g. bricks, timber)
	  F. Mode (e.g. mortared, fitted, glued together)

3 In growth/diminution
  M. What grows/diminishes
  F. Different sizes
	3 In individuation
	  M. Indeterminate mass (e.g. of lead)
	  F. Different shapes (e.g. of lead shot)

4 In generation
  M. Privation of
  F. Positive character (e.g. what makes a man a man)
	4 In moulding
	  M. Definite quantum (e.g. of bronze)
	  F. Specific shape (e.g. of shape)

5 In dissolution
  M. Thing destroyed
  F. State of dissolution (e.g. that of a corpse)
	5 In species
	  M. Generic property of genus
	  F. Differentiae

	6 In functional structure
	  M. Specific structure (e.g. house, body)
	  F. Function (e.g. to shelter, live)

	7 In motivation
	  M. Physiological process (e.g. boiling of blood around heart)
	  F. Potency (e.g. anger as desire to hurt)

of the matter-form distinction depends. To turn this key more smoothly I will continue to abbreviate. For the purpose of more minute disambiguation the adjectives "diachronic" and "synchronic" will sometimes be curtailed to D and S respectively and then conjoined by hyphen to what they qualify.

3.2 DIACHRONIC HYLOMORPHISM

The diachronic matter-form relation is mainly *inter*categorial as distinct from *intra*categorial. In terms of the categorial distinctions of 1.2 it holds mainly between substances and predicatives, but now these categories submit to a further condition. Things within the category of substance are to be understood as open to change in respect of the predicatives they are (or the substantive paronyms of the latter that they have). Conversely things within the category of predicative (or the substantive paronymous forms of that category) are open to change with respect to the substances that are them (or have their substantive paronyms). In the case of the first three DRs both kinds of change are involved, i.e. both substances and predicatives change in their respective ways. In the case of DR4 and DR5, however, the change would seem to be primarily of the latter type. The generation and dissolution of substances would seem to consist, at least with respect to these substances as distinct from their parts, exclusively in changes in the substance-membership of the extension of certain properties. That generated substances do not exist before generation and that destroyed substances do not exist after dissolution requires that the sense in which it is *they* that change is somewhat extended.

Notice, however, that the diachronic matter-form relation is not uniformly that of an instance to the universal it instantiates, despite being for the most part intercategorial.[1] There are three reasons for this. First, in locomotion (DR1) the D-form is not in the strictest sense a universal – at least not if by definition a universal can have more than one instance simultaneously.[2] Here the form is place, and place to comply with Aristotle's definition must be snug. As the innermost boundary of the motionless container it can only belong to the particulars it places one at a time. Second, though in the case of dissolution (DR5) the D-matter is a substance, and as such an instance of some universals, those it instantiates do not include the relevant D-form. Third, in the case of generation (DR4) the D-matter is simply the privation of the D-form and in that capacity no more an instance than is the latter. It is for this final reason that the diachronic matter-form relation is only mainly intercategorial. In DR4 it is not between substances and predicatives or the latter's substantive paronyms.[3]

3.3 THE SYNCHRONIC HYLOMORPHISM

The synchronic matter-form relation is entirely *intra*categorial as distinct from *inter*categorial, at least so far as the two broad categories of substance and predicatives or their substantive paronyms are concerned. Hence, unlike the diachronic matter-form relation it is in no respect whatever an instance-universal relation – not even in any of its more specific forms. The distinction between the terms related can, however, be drawn in either and both of two ways:[4] as between two types of characteristic (e.g. being brazen and sphericity), irrespective of whether anything instantiates the two, and as between a particular inasmuch as it instantiates the one type and that *same* particular inasmuch as it instantiates the other (e.g. between a bronze sphere as brazen and the same thing as spherical). Admittedly this dual application has not been made very explicit by Aristotle, but it seems implicit at least where he explicitly refers to general or universal matter (*Meta.* Z7.1033a5ff; Z8.1033b24–5; Z10.1035b30; Z11.1037a5ff; Θ7.1049a20–7).

Some of his illustrations, either unmodified or as modified by me, may seem to belie this. Thus in SR1 materials, e.g. bricks and pieces of timber, are instances of properties, e.g. being brick or being timber, whereas the form, i.e. the mode of composition, would seem more directly to be a property, not an instance – unless we present it as, e.g., bricks mortared and pieces of timber fitted together rather than the being mortared or fitted together. Then again in SR2, once more the materials, e.g. tin and copper, seem to be instances of properties, whereas even more unequivocally than in SR1 the form is a property, e.g. the homogeneous character of bronze. All the same, it is only as instances of the properties by virtue of which they are material, *and* by virtue of the synchronically dynamic relations between these properties and formal properties, that the materials are materials.

Accordingly, the SRs do not coincide, not even in part, with the instance-universal relation. Instead, they cut across the latter, for both S-matter and S-form can be either particular or universal.[5] Hence, too, they do not coincide with the DRs, for the latter are coincident, at least in part, with the instance-universal relation. On the contrary, and more positively, the SRs fall mainly within the referential characterizations that are constitutive of D-matter in the first three DRs, e.g. within the characterization of the bronze sphere as such.

In sum, the matter-form distinction in its synchronic mode is a distinction between correlative forms of mutual abstraction and not between correlative categories. We have, however, still to pin down more precisely just what it is that distinguishes each of the two sorts of correlative abstractions from the other. What marks out S-matter as material and S-form as formal?

Notice, first, that these distinctions are hierarchically ordered. Hence, except at the scalar extremities, whatever these are, they are by no means absolute. Characterizations that are respectively material and formal in relation to each other may in conjunction be material to other characterizations, these others being formal in relation to them. Thus in a scale of artefact-substances there are at the lower end certain material substances, e.g. timber, stone, clay, water, tin, copper, etc., that lend themselves to compounding or combining by a workman or craftsman into something more complex. These material substances constitute the absolute matter (or instantiations of absolute material characteristics) in the workman's hierarchical scale. But he compounds or combines them into products that are themselves material (or instantiations of material characteristics) relative to some more sophisticated product.

Notice, second, that the scale would seem to divide absolutely into a bottom and top half, despite its hierarchical relativity. Items in the bottom half include both clay and water *and* mud, both tin and copper *and* bronze, despite the fact that in each trio the first two members are matter relative to the third. Items in the top half include both bricks *and* houses, both bronze links *and* chains, though in each pair the first member is matter relative to the second. As these examples suggest, some substances, those in the bottom half, are *mass*-substances. They are not individuated as countable members of a species by their constitutive characteristics. In this, then, they contrast with other substances, those in the top half. These are individuated as countable by their constitutive characteristics.

The division between S-matter and S-form consists, accordingly, of a combination of factors. Their purely relative position on the scale is determined by the asymmetry of the more specific relation in terms of which the sr list has been divided. Thus their relative position, over part of the scale at least, may be ordered homogeneously either by the relation of combination or by that of composition, or by some other. Alternatively, and certainly over more extensive reaches, it will be ordered heterogeneously by a connected variety of such specific asymmetrical relations. Yet in one half of the series, that containing the mass-substances, the constitutive characteristics are in a sense absolutely material, though among themselves they fall into a hylomorphic hierarchical relationship. Likewise in the other half, that containing individual substances, the constitutive characteristics are, with the same proviso, in some sense absolutely formal.

It is obvious, none the less, that without some further account of what gives a characteristic a constitutive or essential status this analysis of the division is not enough. One such account is, of course, implicit in the extensive use of artefacts as examples. In these the constitutive or essential status is determined partly by the technology of the craftsman and partly by the needs or interests of his customers or patrons. Certain types of thing are given absolute status as mass-substance because they only become of use to the craftsman after he has divided them up in certain ways. He conceives of water, clay, and timber as water, clay, and timber, viz. as masses, because he has to put the first into containers, divide the second into gobs, and cut up the third to put them to their typical use. Likewise certain collections or combinations of such units are regarded as individuals for similar reasons. A combination of pieces of wood is regarded as an individual thing, viz. a chair, because it is especially adapted to the anatomy of individual human beings. Here, however, the analogy between artefacts and natural substances begins to fail. Whereas the constitutive relationship holds as such in a somewhat arbitrary way for artefacts, for natural substances it must hold non-arbitrarily.

3.4   THE ESSENCE-ACCIDENT DUALITY

The matter-form duality has its essence-accident counterpart. The latter too has both diachronic and synchronic manifestations.

As a diachronic distinction it differentiates the last two from the first three DRs. Generation (DR4) and decay (DR5) have in common that they consist respectively in the acquisition and loss of an essence. Thus rational animality is the essence of a man, given that a man's generation consists in the first instance of the acquisition of animality and in the second of rationality. Locomotion (DR1), alteration (DR2), and size-change (DR3) for their part have in common that they consist in loss and acquisition of accidents. In this sort of application, accordingly, the essence-accident opposition has a distinctively diachronic role.

As a synchronic distinction the essence-accident opposition is less well defined and more complex in application. We have already observed how the synchronic matter-form relation falls between characteristics that at *different* levels are essential to substances that instantiate them. Thus the form that is distinctive of a man as a man, *beyond his merely being an animal*, is the S- as distinct from the D-essence of a man. Likewise, the form that is distinctive of an animal as an animal, *over and above what it has in common with plants*, is the S- as distinct from the D-essence of an animal.

However, it is not so clear what sort of characteristics are synchronically accidental. That in the first instance is because an S-essence is the more specific part of a D-essence. Thus rationality is more specific than animality in the D-essence that is rational animality. As a consequence we are left with a choice. One alternative is that the corresponding S-accident is the less specific part. In that case animality would correspond as S-accident to rationality as S-essence. In more general terms, the synchronic essence-accident and matter-form distinctions would coincide, accident coinciding with matter as well as essence with form. As one alternative to that the synchronically accidental might be identified with some contrary to or privation of the S-essence, e.g. with what is distinctive of an idiot as opposed to a rational animal, or of vinegar as opposed to wine. Another alternative again is that it consists of *all* the characteristics of a particular apart from its S-essence. These would comprise both its synchronically material characteristics and its D-accidents. Since Aristotle has left the duality of his hylomorphic distinctions somewhat tacit, there are no clues to how the choice should be made. Nor is the need for choice very urgent.

As a further complication, the synchronic essence-accident opposition is more complex than the diachronic, not just less well defined. Two distinct types of characteristic are sometimes allowed to count as the S-essence of a subject. In some contexts the S-form or essence of a house would consist, as in SR2, of the kind of structure that distinguishes, or further specifies, its material characteristics of being of bricks and timber. In other contexts, as in SR6, it consists of the *function*, i.e. to shelter people and their goods (*Meta.* H2.1043a15–17; cf also SR7 as in *De An.* 1.1.403a30–b1). As the same example can illustrate, these two types belong to a hierarchical order. At one level the former combines as S-form with a correlative S-matter to comprise a D-essence. At that level the latter, i.e. the function, does not enter as S-form. It enters instead as D-potency that belongs, by virtue of the D-essence, to whatever that essence characterizes. Yet at a higher level it too combines as S-form with a correlative S-matter. This time, however, the correlative matter consists wholly or in part of what was the D-essence at the lower level.

Table 3

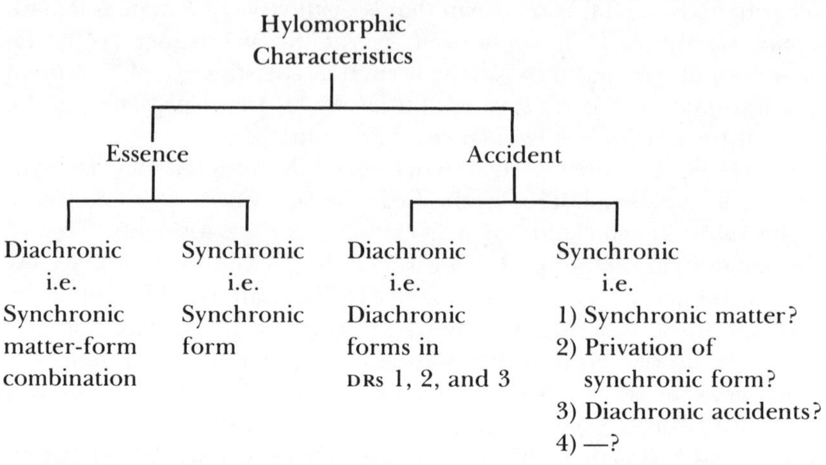

The schematic guide in Table 3 to some of these complexities may be of service. The branchings on the left under Essence indicate the dependence of D- upon S-essence. Likewise the branchings on the right under Accident serve notice of the comparative definiteness and indefiniteness respectively of the D- and S-varieties of accident.

3.5 DYNAMIC DUALITIES

The actuality-potentiality distinction has two sides as well. The actualities and potentialities[6] on either side are those of matter, but with a diversity that brings preceding distinctions into further play.

Diachronically the distinction pertains to a particular in its function as D-matter. D-actuality is the D-form for which a particular in that function has at some stage or other a potentiality – and that potentiality likewise is diachronic. Synchronically the distinction pertains to a particular in its more restricted function as S-matter. S-actuality is the S-form for which, as an instance of S-material characteristics, a particular has a potentiality – and this specific potentiality is synchronic.

D-potentiality is in some cases of an interactive kind.[7] Primarily in these cases it is passive, i.e. a power of a particular to be acted upon by something other, or by itself *qua* other. That is because the correlative actuality must be the result of interaction in that particular, i.e. the form that as matter it acquires. However, in other cases the potentiality is for *a natural state*, i.e. one towards which it would tend from some current contrary state, given no interference from anything other. As for S-potentiality, it is in no way interactive. It is merely a potentiality of a particular as an instance of a material characteristic for itself as a *simultaneous* or *continuing* instantiation of the the corresponding formal characteristic.[8]

I venture now into minuter detail than in all respects the texts themselves vouchsafe. In the case of the first three DRs, i.e. locomotion, alteration, and size-change taken separately or together, a particular as D-matter must have both a *general* and a more *specific* type of D-potentiality for D-form. The general type is respectively for certain types of place, quality, and size. This, however, is by virtue of its D-essence alone. Consequently, the particular retains this general potentiality throughout its lifetime, for on losing its D-essence it ceases to exist. The general potentiality is, one may therefore say, time-*unrelativized* or occasion-*loose*.

The specific type, in contrast, consists of specifications or particularizations of the general potentiality. These are for quite specific places, qualities, or sizes. As such they too belong to the particular by virtue of its D-essence, but only *in combination with* some or all of the D-accidents of forms that it has on the occasion of their possession. Consequently, they are time-*relativized* or occasion-*bound* to the times or occasions of the accident's possession. Furthermore, the corresponding actualities, i.e. the forms in which these potentialities are actualized, are time-relativized or occasion-bound as well — though to a time or occasion that is later.

That leaves generation (DR4) and dissolution (DR5) as still to be considered. For them the further detail is harder to decipher. These after all are limiting cases of change. To focus on the less complex of the two, in dissolution the particular has a potentiality for a D-form that, as the negation of its D-essence, involves the loss of the general type of D-potentiality that it owes to that essence. By virtue of what, then, does it have that dissolute potentiality? Presumably here, too, the D-essence is the source. Taken by itself it generates the potentiality as time-unrelativized. In conjunction with accidents the same potentiality's time-relativization or occasion-binding is a further result. Notice that for generation a comparable generalization would be harder to attain.

Consider next the *synchronic* side. Combination (SR1) and composition (SR2) contrast quite sharply with functional structuring (SR6). In the case of the first two the distinction between the material and formal characteristics that are constitutive of the particular is a distinction within the D-essence. In the case of the third the synchronic material characteristics coincide by themselves with that essence entirely.

The house, once again, can instruct us. As exemplifying composition, it is the general character of the house's material components that is the S-matter, and it is the architectural structure that is its S-form or S-essence. But as exemplifying functional structure, a combination of the general character of the materials with their architectural structure is the S-matter, and the function of sheltering (a D-power) the S-form or S-essence. To employ a preferential distinction that Aristotle reserves for the soul, the function of the house is the *first* actuality. As an actuality the form in which that function is fulfilled is merely secondary. Notice further that, whatever the type of case, for S-potentiality no distinction between a general type and particularizations would seem to arise. That is because it exclusively involves the constitutive characteristics of D-matter.[9]

3.6 DYNAMICS AND REIFICATION

If, then, Aristotle's hylomorphic system admits construal as a conceptual scheme, it must be with a proviso. In that role the system has more than a neo-Kantian sort of function. It is more than a transcendental sort of fish-trap from which, once caught inside, it is difficult or impossible to escape. On the contrary, as a package it includes the means for distinguishing its arbitrary from its non-arbitrary application. The non-arbitrariness of its applicability does not consist (just?) in an impossibility of rejecting the conceptual scheme without in the very act presupposing what one rejects. It consists, in the first instance at least, in a non-arbitrary individuation or separation of mutable substances as distinct on the basis of a non-arbitrary essence-accident differentiation, which depends in turn upon ownership of occasion-loose powers by virtue of the essences thus differentiated.

I do not preclude as a further *question* whether the whole inter-definable circle of hylomorphic dualities, *including the dynamic duality upon which the non-arbitrariness of the others thus depends*, is non-arbitrarily applicable. The suggestion might be that the attribution of non-arbitrariness here provided is hypothetical rather than absolute, i.e. that *if* the hylomorphic system is non-arbitrarily applicable as a whole, it supplies from within itself the means for determining which one or more of several alternative applications is or are non-arbitrary. But I reserve this suggestion for later consideration. Enough for the moment that it does not arise from within the conceptual scheme in question — at least not unless the description of the system as a *conceptual scheme* is allowed to stack the cards in the suggestion's favour. On the contrary, it is the product of a conceptual *meta*-scheme that imposes a tendentious Kantian or neo-Kantian interpretation on what sort of thing a conceptual scheme must be. It is one, furthermore, to which we shall later see that there is an Aristotelian counter.

In the meantime I broach a more pressing issue. If the non-arbitrary individuation of a particular mutable depends upon its essential properties being the basis of an occasion-loose power, then we must look for further criteria to determine whether any set of properties is that basis. Attributions of non-arbitrary mutable thinghood would seem, in fact, to depend upon criteria at three distinct levels. Possession of power, whether diachronic or synchronic, is first-level. Principles for the attribution of such powers on the basis of the properties that particulars are observed successively to have are second-level. Observation of properties under guidance from these principles is third-level. Accordingly, to understand more exactly how non-arbitrary thinghood is determined we have to see how these levels fit together, and more specifically how the second mediates between the third and the first.

Common to candidates for this mediating role is their assumption of a nomological constraint. To satisfy the first-level criterion, i.e. to own an occasion-loose power, the properties supporting that power must be such that under certain circumstances the owner behaves in certain specific ways. This constraint may be more or less strict, i.e. either *deterministic* or *indeterministic*. Thus the occasion-bound form of the power must consist in a causal *necessity* in the former case and in a causal *contingency* in the latter. In other words, the totality of accidental conditions specific to an occasion in conjunction with one or other occasion-loose D-power will in the former case *necessitate* and in the latter merely *make possible* a certain actualization on that occasion.

It is, then, under this constraint upon their mediation that the second-level criteria attempt to reconcile the data of experience. In the specific nature of the attempt, however, they vary. They may be either reductionist or non-reductionist, mechanistic or non-mechanistic, or teleological or non-teleological. Reductionism interprets apparent inconsistencies in the regularity with which particulars of a certain sort behave in terms of a greater consistency in the behaviour of the sorts of things that make up that sort of particular's parts. The failure of a watch to keep time with the regularity for which it is designed may thus be attributed to a regularity in the rate of fatigue in the spring. However, the mechanical nature of this example, coupled with the failure of the teleological interpretation in terms of design that it illustrates, is no guarantee that reductionist, mechanistic, and non-teleological interpretations all coincide. Might not the ultimate parts of things conform with a greater regularity to purpose or design than do any of the wholes of which they are parts? Then again, might not the wholes conform to a perfectly consistent non-purposive or undesigned regularity without further recourse to the individual behaviour of parts? In short, reductionism has a non-mechanistic as well as a mechanistic option. Conversely, mechanism has a non-reductionist as well as a reductionist option. Perhaps, then, we should allow that mechanistic and non-teleological interpretations likewise have options each for the contrary of, as well as for, the other. Here, however, I assume – with some encouragement, I believe, from traditional usage – that mechanistic and non-teleological interpretations exactly coincide.

Now second-level criteria of these diverse kinds may to a greater or lesser extent collaborate for their mediatory purpose. Hence different systems of dynamics, all hylomorphic, will result from differences in the extent of the collaboration. In the rest of this chapter I concentrate on one such result, viz. Aristotle's own elementalism, but with parenthetical allusions to classical atomism for the sake of comparison. Not surprisingly the hierarchical structure and duality of his hylomorphism is more thoroughly engaged in his specific combination of criteria than in any opposing coeval. My aim, however, is not merely to demonstrate this advantage, if advantage it is. More generally, in his specific combination we shall also find concrete instruction in how the non-arbitrary thinghood of mutable particulars can in principle be established, whatever the second- and third- level criteria may happen to be. Empirically, or at the third criteriological level, his elementalism and its rival coevals are somewhat underdetermined. Hence in them the underlying ontological and conceptual motivations are nearer the surface than in the scientifically more rigorous systems of today.

3.7 DIACHRONIC DYNAMISM

Space, for Aristotle, is finite and in no part void (as opposed to the infinite atom-punctuated void of Democritus and Leucippus). It differs from its contents merely as a geoconcentric structure of places, which are variable in what they enclose. From a quantitative point of view, as well as finite it is infinitely divisible. Hence Aristotle's all-pervasive plenum is infinitely divisible too (unlike the indivisibly solid atom). From the qualitative point of view, however, this totality is divisible into five elements or kinds. Four of these are exclusive to the sublunar core. They may be present together in any part of sublunar space, no matter how small. They may commingle, combine, blend, or homogenize in any such part, as distinct from merely compound (*GC* 1.10.328a6). But together or apart they are marked out uniquely by coupled properties one apiece from two pairs of mutually dilutable contraries. Heat and coldness make the one contrary pair, dryness and moisture the other. Thus while in purest form air is hot and moist, earth is cold and dry. While in purest form fire is hot and dry, water is cold and moist.

Now in each such qualitative coupling the elements also employ a distinctive set of D-powers. Indeed, the basic elemental properties may even be powers in their own right. Either way, apart from the infinite divisibility and mutual dilutability they have in common, their powers are fourfold in nature. First, as either hot or cold an element has active powers of association and dissociation. Heat associates the like and dissociates the unlike. Cold does the reverse. Second, as either moist or dry an element has a susceptibility or passive power. The moist is, and the dry is not, readily adaptible in shape (*GC* 2.2.329b25ff). Hence the complementary nature of the opposing pairs, i.e. that either of one pair has to accompany either of the other. This seems in intent nothing but the dynamic complementarity of the active and the passive, whereby what acts upon another thereby is acted upon. Third, each element in its parts has an alchemical power to transmute into parts of another by virtue of a cyclical exchange of basic properties or powers. This power is conceived holistically. Gains and losses to any element through transmutation are within upper and lower limits to variations in the quantity of the whole. Fourth, and finally, each element has a natural affinity to one of four concentric sublunar regions. Earth has its natural place directly round the cosmic centre, water next encircling that, air encircling that again, and fire in the remaining region below the shell of the innermost cosmic sphere.

Conceptual economy may tempt one to associate the third and fourth types of power as closely with the first and second as these with each other. Perhaps both the alchemical and the place-seeking powers are implicated in the associative/dissociative powers of the first type. Perhaps the two pairs of contraries require, either for their qualitative difference or just for their associative/dissociative function, both the cyclical transmutability from one element to another and the geometrico-dynamical anisotropy attributed to space. Perhaps, indeed, all four types of power function just as specifications of the infinite divisibility of the total plenum. Perhaps the mutual dilutability of contraries is nothing but a qualitative specification of that quantitative power. Perhaps the further identification of the contrary pairs and their powers is in turn nothing but a specification of mutual dilutability. But, however that may be, the role of these powers as essence-accident differentiators now becomes patent.

Through them as occasion-loose the four qualitative couplings have non-arbitrary status each as the D-essence of the element it distinguishes. Through its complementary unity and qualitative distinctness in turn each such essential coupling confers both a non-arbitrary qualitative simplicity and a non-arbitrary qualitative singleness or separateness upon what it qualifies.

Notice that this simplicity and singleness is not that of spatially delimited and separately localized particulars within the same class. That is because both are *qualitative*, not quantitative. (While comparable in function, they are unlike the quantitative simplicity and singleness its indivisible solidity confers upon the atom.) Their function is not even to distinguish the several particulars of one class from those of another – except in an incidental way. In so far as the four elements divide each other up at any one time they no doubt fragment into four qualitatively distinct classes of discretely configurated particular portions. However, these portions need not have a non-arbitrary individuation as substances in their own right. Certainly the configuration of each may linger on or transform continuously from one moment to the next. But, not unlike the industrially polluted Niagara Falls, it may do so only by continuous replenishment to compensate for loss, and while hosting various sorts of adulteration. In short, and more positively, elements (unlike atoms) have a non-arbitrary *massiness*. The configuration of an element's portions and their distribution in space at any one moment are *accidental*, and the basis of its occasion-bound rather than its occasion-loose powers.

So far, then, the attribution of D-powers in Aristotle's elementalism, as in its Empedoclean predecessor, has been reductive. Impressed by the observable fact that sublunar particulate objects are subject to generation and decay, Aristotle takes their instability to signify that they are spatially delimited complexes of qualitatively stable mass ingredients or stuffs. But his elementalism, unlike the Empedoclean, takes a further non-reductive turn. The hierarchical structure of his dynamics allows a non-arbitrary singleness or separateness to particulars that are non-arbitrarily complex, i.e. combinations or compounds of non-arbitrary simples. Some of these, e.g. blood and semen, are non-arbitrarily massy (at least if we take being a particular as distinguishable from being particulate). Their configurations and distribution just as such are accidental. Others,

e.g. organisms, are non-arbitrarily particulate. Their spatial delimitation is, within certain degrees of latitude, not accidental. But in
either case the non-arbitrary singleness in non-arbitrary complexity
results from the supervenience of further D-powers. These must be
more than mere compositions of powers that distinguish the elements in the complex particulars concerned. (Similarly in a non-
classical emergent sort of atomism a power, which is more than a
composition of the powers of individual atoms, may be attributed
to a complex of atoms.)

It is arguable – if commonly contested – that Aristotle's attribution
of powers is hybrid in one further respect, i.e. not in how it reconciles
data with nomological constraint but in the strictness of the constraint
itself. On this thesis it allows deterministic powers to all or most
things and indeterministic powers just to some. These latter are the
agents of voluntary action. They have an indeterministic power inasmuch as they are able to deliberate and choose between alternative
courses of action. (The Epicurean notion of random atomic swerve
serves a somewhat similar function.) But however that may be,
whether Aristotle's elementalism is singly or doubly hybrid, it is
absolutely pure in a further respect. The D-powers he attributes to
things are exclusively teleological.

Teleology is already conspicuous in the more primitive elementalism of Empedocles. There the running together and separating
out of elements are manifestations of Love and Strife. But Aristotle,
as the place-seeking proclivities of his elements already suggest, has
made a more specific commitment. More comprehensively still, he
conceives *all* natural substances – not just the elements out of which
others are put together – as seeking more or less directly to approximate as closely as they can to the immutable perfection of the
Prime Mover. The four sublunar elements do so through incessant
change and cyclical transmutation one into another. All living beings
do so in perpetuating their species through reproduction. Finally,
in regions beyond the sublunar, the ether or fifth element does so
as well. The heavenly bodies in which it is visible imitate the im-
mutability of the divine perfection through an eternal circular motion round the cosmic centre.

This teleological sort of behaviour is every whit as law-conforming
as non-teleological or mechanistic nomological behaviour (e.g. that
of the classical atom). But the rule or conditional sort of generality
to which it conforms is to be conceived on the model of the rule that
gives content to a general sort of desire, viz. the desire to behave (or
else that something should be done) in such and such a way under
such and such actual or possible circumstances. Thus the place-

seeking power of, say, the element of fire is to be likened in its occasion-loose aspect to the conditional desire to move in certain parts upwards to the appropriate region if in those parts (say as a flame in the hearth) it happens to be elsewhere. Similarly the occasion-loose orbital power of the sun is to be likened to the conditional desire to be at relatively westerly points on a certain circle round the earth if (indeed, whenever) it is at relatively easterly points.

We now have an understanding of two non-arbitrary features, viz. simplicity and singleness or separateness, that constitute the non-arbitrary thinghood of elements as mutable particulars (and, by analogy, of atoms as well). To recapitulate – elements are in non-arbitrary possession of these two by virtue of the non-arbitrary essence-accident differentiation effected by powers that are attributable on the basis of second-level criteria of a reductivist-cum-teleological kind. Another feature may, however, seem conspicuous for its absence from this list. The notion of non-arbitrary reidentifiability enjoyed some prominence in chapter 2 as due for investigation, but here may seem in eclipse. The neglect, however, is merely one of explicit reference. This third feature simply consists in the *continuous* instantiation of the sort of non-arbitrarily differentiated essence that confers non-arbitrary singleness or separateness throughout possible change in properties simultaneously differentiated as accidents. It is just the sort of continuity that gives evidence for the attribution of the D-power upon which the non-arbitrary essence-accident differentiation depends. The non-arbitrariness of the singleness or separateness, then, is just the product of the non-arbitrariness of the continuity, and hence of the reidentifiability. In a system like Aristotle's – where the essence may be purely qualitative or, if quantitative, only so in ratio – that continuous instantiation may not involve continuity either in spatial configuration or place, such properties being regarded as accidental. It need only be temporal. In an atomistic system, however, continuity in configuration and place through time is required, other properties such as relationships to other particulars being accidental.

3.8 SYNCHRONIC DYNAMISM

As a conceptual scheme – descriptive, revisionary, or ancestral to either – can Aristotle's hylomorphism serve any further useful function? What need is there for duality and, more specifically, for the S-component?

Two metaphysical procedures vie for our custom. Do we take a particular's non-arbitrary reidentifiability during a period of time to be a sufficient basis for its non-arbitrary identifiability at any instant therein? Or conversely, do we prefer the latter as a basis of the former? On the first procedure D-powers are without exception the ultimate non-arbitrary basis for the identity of particulars. On the second S-powers are (for the most part, at least) that basis instead or as well. Certain D-powers are taken to depend upon non-arbitrary constitutive relationships within each particular, and these relationships to depend upon powers that are *synchronic*. Now it is in his practice of this second procedure that Aristotle is most unique. He carries us, indeed, to a point at which the elementalist and atomistic executions of the first are diametrically opposed. But he goes beyond to where the intrinsic identifiability of a particular becomes the basis of its intrinsic reidentifiability.

Many of the things that are unstable by reason of complexity are not all that unstable. Nor is their comparative stability mere matter of chance. Nor, again, is this absence of chance non-autonomous. Their continuous unity is quite unlike the extraneous sort that certain cliff formations impose on Niagara Falls. To a more than negligible extent, where portions that are essential to the integrity and continuation of the whole are lost through wear and tear, they tend to be replaced in an autonomous fashion by new material with a similar function. Accordingly, we are faced by two sorts of question. First, in what does the autonomous sort of stability consist? Second, how can such a complex lose parts without a corresponding loss of identity?

As one answer to the first question we might compare the structure of the complex to that of some kind of club or society whose constitution provides, by procedures of appointment and election, for replacement of office-bearers and members who for one reason or another step down or depart. The organization may thus survive through several generations of membership. For particle theory, prior at least to quantum mechanics, this sort of comparison is congenial. It charges the biophysicist with the task of discovering how the members of a collection of discrete particles may operate so as to construct a self-renewing society.

However, any such solution lies open to an intuitively damaging objection. Certain kinds of complex, e.g. ourselves, have a more absolute sort of unity and continuity than that of a club. No doubt relations between statements about the latter's actions and statements about the individual actions of its members are logically loose. The club's relocation from Kuala Lumpur to Moscow might have been carried out by a subset of members other than the actual subset involved. Nevertheless we are reluctant to say that its actions are anything more than actions and forbearances of such and such individuals. The club just *is* a collection of individuals, united perhaps in their access to a certain property, who behave in such and such ways. But we, though materially complex, commonly credit ourselves contrariwise with a less reducible individuality. In short, the comparison between complexes such as ourselves and a club or society provides no satisfactory solution to the second question.

It is as an answer to both types of question that Aristotle's qualified reductivism comes into its own. His elements, perhaps, are not unlike the members of a club in one respect. When combined in certain ratios with other elements (as in flesh, or blood, or bone), or when then compounded in accordance with a certain structure (as in the anatomy of an organism), they do more than *just happen* to continue in a non-arbitrarily single complex. They further conspire that portions lost to that complex through wear and tear are replaced in ways that maintain the complex as an autonomously stable whole. They have a positive power for *maintaining* the instantiation of the D-essence by which the unity of complex's singleness is conferred.

Nevertheless, this sort of unity is quite unlike the reducible unity of a club. The elements are essentially masses or stuffs in the sense that their spatial configurations and apportionments are accidental, as we have seen, to their nature as elements. Hence a certain configurated complex of elements, such as one of us, need not be conceived as reducible to spatial parts that interact discretely with each other in certain complex ways. In so far as their parts can have any status as non-arbitrarily configurated particulars, that derives instead from their specific functions within a non-arbitrarily delimited complex whole. (The particles of quantum mechanics provide an analogue – at least on certain interpretations. Unlike those of the elements, their quantifiable properties determine their identity. Hence these properties are not *accidental*. Instead, they are *indeterminate* in ways that remain unresolved except in certain macrophysical contexts.)

For Aristotle, then, the answer to our two questions lies in the counterbalance between a reductive and a non-reductive dynamic principle. Nature for him is the product of the two. The reductive principle is enmassing or spatially undelimiting. The non-reductive is individuating or spatially delimiting. The enmassing principle consists of the D-potency of elemental apportionments to enmass or lose their current limitations, whereas the individuating principle is an S-potency that elements as thus accidentally apportioned have for the maintenance of certain synchronic formal characteristics. This S-potency is what gives a certain complex to which these apportionments belong its actuality or intrinsic identifiability as a reidentifiable individual.

At the same time Aristotle's S-dynamics has a more pervasive or universal basis, i.e. one that operates in more than combination (SR1) and composition (SR2). Like its D-counterpart S-potency is consistently teleological, though in a quite distinctive way. Aristotle holds that the works of nature, like those of a workman, conform for the most part to design. Thus the matter-form distinction in its S-application is more than a hierarchical ordering in degree of complexity. The proximate S-form of each substance, as the S-essence or that upon which the substance's actuality or intrinsic identifiability most directly depends, is also the proximate synchronic *end* or final cause in a series of such synchronic ends or final causes, unless it is the ultimate synchronic final cause. Similarly the proximate S-matter of each substance, or that most directly by virtue of which the substance has the S-form, is synchronically instrumental to that form and the remoter forms beyond, if any.

As ends, furthermore, S-forms are intrinsic to what they inform since they also constitute the actuality and intrinsic identifiability of the latter. The design to which the products of nature conform (or from which they sometimes fall short) is a *natural* design. One might indeed say – given that nature is the totality of its products – that nature is *self*-determining and *self*-designing.

However, though each type of dynamics is as teleological as the other, they are so in somewhat different ways. Aristotle makes an explicit distinction between two types of final cause. Type 1 is the beneficiary of an action, i.e. that for the good of which an action is done. Type 2 is the purpose of an action, or that at which it aims (*De An.* 2.4.415a22ff; 2.4.415b 20–1; *Meta.* Δ6.1072b1–4). Both types may motivate what he broadly calls movement. Hence both types function diachronically at least. However, type 1 alone can operate in the type of action that more narrowly is activity, which in turn he equates with actuality and at least the higher types of form.[10] Hence it alone may function synchronically.

Given, then, that nature acts like an intelligent workman, the synchronic mode of final causation can be conceived as functioning in natural substance somewhat as it functions in, say, a house. Taken at the level of SR2 the instantiation of certain material characteristics, e.g. jointly by stone, brick, beam, etc. strictly as such, is to be distinguished as particular S-matter from the instantiation of the house's structural characteristics as S-form. Here the basis of the distinction lies in the fact that the former instantiation exists for the benefit of the latter, which in turn is the beneficiary of the former. In other words, in the house the raison d'être for the matter lies in the form. Similarly, to transpose the same example to the level of SR6, the raison d'être of the S-matter (taken this time as the coinstantiation of the material and formal characteristics at the level of SR2), i.e. the raison d'être of the house, is a thing with the function of providing shelter.[11]

Similarly, then, with a natural substance such as an organism. Thus, in bodies such as ours, molars and incisors, as instantiating their proximate dental S-form, are beneficiaries of themselves as instantiating their synchronic material characteristics. But as bearing more remotely their respective interactive powers, those of grinding and cutting, they are beneficiaries of themselves conceived as instantiating the combination of what were the material and formal characteristics at the lower level. Likewise, at a more complex and comprehensive level, the body as constituted by molars, incisors, jaws, stomach, and other organic parts, each with its own specific role or interactive power in an interlocking set of such powers, is the proximate beneficiary of these components. Then, one further step up, the nutritive soul – conceived by Aristotle as a diachronic teleological potency for the ingestion of food – consists of the interlocking set of the interactive powers of the body's components, or of some of these powers, and as such is the beneficiary of the body (*De An.* 2.4, especially 415b 15–22, 416a 6–9, 416b 17–19).

Whatever the SR, S-matter is, accordingly, matter and S-form is form because the latter is the beneficiary of the former. That, too, is why the various SRs can connect the one hierarchial series, even though no one SR runs through from beginning to end. The teleological relation is transitive and asymmetrical (or, at least, non-symmetrical). Hence, despite the differences between SR2 and SR6, the beneficiary in SR6 may be a more ultimate beneficiary of the benefactor in SR2 than the proximate beneficiary in SR2. In more general terms, that which is instrumental to a proximate end is also instrumental to remoter ends.

Here, furthermore, is why S-form qualifies as essence, albeit distinctively of a synchronic kind. As the end of the matter it is essential to the substance in which the matter and form are synchronically combined. That matter, for its part, is in a manner accidental, or at least incidental, inasmuch as the end might have been actualized in an alternative way. Thus a house with a particular type of structure might be built out of stone, or brick, or concrete. Equally clear is why the nature of the synchronically accidental is relatively indefinite and hospitable. Thus that the D-matter should consist of one individual substance rather than another is accidental to the realization of the formal characteristics. You may spend the night as comfortably in one motel as in another. Again that the building materials should comprise a ruin, that their form should be the privation of the form that is their end, is in a similar teleological sense accidental to them. A further corollary presumably is that remoter beneficiaries are in a way more essential, and the intermediary ones correspondingly accidental – hence that teleologically there is something accidental about substances that are distinguishable by the fact that their S-forms belong to the class of intermediary beneficiaries.

3.9 TELEOLOGICAL ASSETS

The last two sections have been illustrative. They show in some detail how second-level criteria may mediate between first and third to establish non-arbitrary thinghood. They present Aristotle's natural philosophy as one attempt among others to reconcile empirical data (behavioural and morphological) with nomological constraints upon potencies, diachronic and synchronic, which confer that thinghood. At the same time, however, they show something more. Thanks to their teleological nature Aristotle's second-level criteria are endowed with two distinctive theoretical assets. These I shall later adapt and exploit.

It is tempting to say that potencies for Aristotle are primarily *desires* – or, where minus the cognitive ingredients of desire, at least something more rudimentary for which desire is paradigmatic. He himself is remarkably stingy or irresolute about making even the weaker commitment outright. As I shall later contend, his hylomorphism and his psychology are somewhat out of kilter. But in any case the manifestation of potency in behaviour is goal-seeking – and for the latter he explicitly takes purposive animal behaviour as standard.

Now that is enough to render his notion of a power or potency more effective as a touchstone for non-arbitrary thinghood. It becomes more than a disposable theoretical construct hypothetically imposed upon behavioural data for the purpose of a hylomorphic systematization. To the extent to which teleological powers have their paradigm in the introspective phenomenon of desire or purpose they are phenomenologically more available than powers of a non-teleological sort. Hence their attribution on the basis of behaviour testifies with more immediacy to the non-arbitrary applicability of the whole interdefinable nexus of hylomorphic concepts. Here, then, is the first asset. As commonly understood, on the other hand, the mechanistic or non-teleological sort of power is without the same advantage – at least when taken as antithetical, not just subsidiary, to the other. Typically its entire intelligibility is taken as deriving from the role it can play in the interpretation of nomological regularities observed in behaviour.

Mechanists, of course, insist that all powers are of the mechanistic type. Therefore their tendency has been to interpret desire, i.e. operative desire, and hence anything more rudimentary that might take such desire as its paradigm, in one of three ways. (1) They may deny that desire is any sort of power at all, regarding it instead as a causal condition that may mediate between the conditions under which an agent will seek something as a goal and the goal-seeking behaviour. (2) They may deny that desire is a mediating causal condition and allow that it is a power, on the supposition that attribution of a power is nothing but attribution of truth to some causal law-like conditional sentence. (3) They may allow that desire is both a power and a mediating cause, on the supposition that to conceive it as a power is nothing other than to conceive it in a functional role as a mediating cause. Where they take the first course it is usually with the assumption that desire is a phenomenologically patent introspectible datum. Where they take the second or third, that assumption is commonly rejected.

Against mechanism in any of these forms I eventually argue (chapter 6) that the teleological powers specific to animate life, or at least to its higher forms, do have a special dynamical status, but not as dynamically paradigmatic in the Aristotelian way. Not all powers are teleological. Some are mechanistic. On my thesis the two types of power are disparately interdependent. The teleological depend upon specific mechanistic powers for their specific nature. Yet they are *primary* and the latter *secondary*, for the latter depend upon the former for their status as powers.

The second asset is axiological. Through Aristotle's teleological dynamics, in both its diachronic and its S-form, being confers an intrinsic non-relativistic value. In the diachronic case the D-form for which the particular has the D-potency that determines non-arbitrarily its D-essence must be essentially attractive to and hence intrinsically good for that particular. In the synchronic case the ontological ordering in terms of the greater degrees of actuality that the remoter forms possess is likewise an *axiological* ordering in degrees of value, goodness, or perfection. Unlike the commercial value of an artefact, the value thus conferred does not depend upon anything as arbitrary as customer demand. Unlike the utility-value of the same thing, it does not depend upon human need. On the contrary, the form that confers being is essentially attractive and its value intrinsic.

In the tempered sort of teleology I propose I make use of this asset with comparable restraint. More specifically, I limit the sorts of conditions that are essentially attractive and have intrinsic value to those that affect the narrow class of particular to which I limit possession of teleological or primary power (see chapter 9).

A Doctrine of First Causes

4.0

Exponents of Aristotle tend to unburden in one or other of two distinct styles. They may present both his intercategorial, and his intracategorial distinctions as belonging to a kind of conceptual toolkit that is applicable within different fields of inquiry. Just to that extent he may seem to be placing all branches of science on equal footing without prejudging what sort of solution within any one branch should be preferred. Alternatively, they may treat these distinctions as theoretically more biased – not just as subjecting other sciences to a master science, or science of first causes, but also as prejudging within the latter what the first causes must be. Comparatively speaking, the former style is the more modern and the latter the more medieval.

That these two styles may alternate is not, of course, to be precluded. If I favour the former in the first half of chapter 3, is there no switch to the latter when I near the end? Aristotle's elementalism has come to the fore not just as one example of a hylomorphic system but also as singularly well suited to that system's synchronic mode. But need this bias have been absolutely decisive? Furthermore, and in any case, it affects the base of the hylomorphic structure. Might a similar bias determine the peak?

In this chapter I shall try to show that the same inter- and intracategorial distinctions do in a manner function as a conceptual scheme, but one in which the application takes a curiously reflexive turn as the summit and diadem of the structure that initially it helps to build. As we are about to see. It casts the very activity of application in the role of the closest approximation to the final form or first formal cause that we can experience at first hand.

4.1 THE PATH TO ENLIGHTENMENT – FIRST APPROACH

To reiterate the last point in more direct terms, for Aristotle the first or very final formal cause consists in its own contemplation. There is, he thinks, a consensus – general or informed – that contemplative thought is the most divine of things observed by us (*Meta.* Δ9). Elsewhere he mentions that happiness, defined by him in terms of an unimpeded activity in accordance with virtue, is the most profoundly present in that form of thought (*NE* 10.7). Now if one sort of contemplation is more noble than another, it is the sort that is focused exclusively on the noblest of objects, which, for the reasons just mentioned, is itself. Therefore, as so focused, it qualifies as no less than the first or very final cause. Therefore, again, as exclusively self-focused it or its contemplation is the objective of the theoretical activity that Aristotle distinguishes from all other sciences as first philosophy, or the science of first causes.

First philosophy qualifies as a science of causes, whether first or subsequent, for it deals with that *by virtue of which* something is something.[1] It is in this rather broad sense of "cause" that Aristotle distinguishes between four general types of cause, viz. efficient, material, formal, and final. An *efficient* cause is specifically an interactive cause. It is a substance by virtue of which, or by virtue of the behaviour of which, something other, or itself *qua* other, is in some state or undergoing some change. Alternatively, in what seems to be a secondary sense, it is the behaviour of that substance rather than the substance itself. A *material* cause can be either D-matter or S-matter. If D-matter, it is a cause in a somewhat attenuated sense. As that which undergoes change from one state to another, it is that by virtue of which it is one thing to which there is change, or that by virtue of which change is change and not just difference. However, if it is S-matter, the sense is less trivial. It is by virtue of having certain material characteristics that a particular has a certain S-form. A *formal* cause, whether a D-form or an S-form, is that by virtue of which the final causation of the respective type of final cause is mediated, unless it is the final cause itself. Finally, a *final* cause of either type is that by virtue of which a substance requires or has the respective type of mediating form.

First philosophy qualifies further as a science of causes that more specifically are *first* for at least three connected reasons. First, it is the science of being qua being, for being is more fundamental than anything else. It is concerned with that by virtue of which the members of some category have being. Second, it is concerned with that by virtue of which the members of the primary category of being, viz. substance, have being. It is concerned with that by virtue of which a substance is a substance, with the substance's substantiality, with what is the substance of a thing. Third, in the circumstance that the primary or ultimate cause of substantiality is mediated by subordinate or instrumental causes, it is concerned with the order of priority and above all with the identification of the ultimate or primary or unmediating mediated source of the substantiality.

Compared with first philosophy the other sciences fall short, for as Aristotle comments (*Meta.* E1.1025b2–16)

[1] while ... in general every science which is ratiocinative or at all involves reasons deals with causes and principles, more or less precise, all these sciences mark off some particular being – some genus, and inquire into this, but not into being simply nor *qua* being, nor do they offer any discussion of the essence [the what is it] of the things of which they treat; but starting from the essence – some making it plain to the senses, others assuming it as a hypothesis – they then demonstrate, more or less cogently, the essential attributes of the genus with which they deal. It is obvious, therefore, that such an induction yields no demonstration of substance or of the essence, but some other way of exhibiting it.

To elaborate further or interpret: if we confine ourselves to the various physical sciences, at least as conceived by Aristotle, various types of particular are classified therein as indefinitely identified in terms of referential characterizations that make both a general and a specific assumption. The general assumption – whether the particular is identified as air or earth or ox or raven or dogfish or beetle, etc. – is that essentially the particular is mutable. The more specific assumption is that acquisition and loss of these specific referential characteristics respectively constitute cases of generation and dissolution as distinct from other sorts of change. In short it is assumed that these characteristics in their referential or identificatory capacity have a non-arbitrary basis without its being specified.

On this understanding the activity of the first philosopher is indeed as Aristotle further describes. It is, in the first instance, a definitional activity. Primarily, of course, its concern is with essences, especially those of substances, or of things that are primarily real. Furthermore, in so far as its concern is specifically with D-essences, the definitions or formulae it discovers are primarily *per genus et differentiam.* As such, however, they provide more than mere verbal equivalencies of meaning. Otherwise their province would remain within the special sciences. We have seen that the D-essence of any substance is the product of a dynamic relation between S-matter and S-form. Only as such does it hold the first philosopher's interest, but even then, not entirely for its own sake. The discovery of its formula is more in the nature of a gift from the definitional activity to some special science. It is a spin-off from the discovery of the S-essence, which at one level or another the uncovering of the dynamic relation between S-matter and S-form must bring in its train. The discovery of the S-essence is the more ultimate goal.

Guidelines for this sort of inquiry are to some extent implicit in the network of distinctions set out in chapter 3. How close Aristotle comes to abiding by them is, however, still at issue. As he further conceives of the inquiry, the distinctions begin to seem over-refined. The critical passages occur in *Meta.* Z3. Quotations [2] and [3] between them pose the problem. Provisionally I omit the argument that connects them.

[2] We have now outlined the nature of substance, showing that it is that which is not predicated of a substratum, but of which all else is predicated. But we must not merely state the matter thus; for this is not enough. The statement itself is obscure, and further, on this view, *matter* becomes substance.
[3] If we adopt this point of view, then, it follows that matter is substance. But this is impossible; for both separability and "thisness" are though to belong chiefly to substance. And so form and the compound of form and matter would be thought to be substance, rather than matter. The substance compounded of both, i.e. of matter and shape, may be dismissed; for it is posterior and its nature is obvious. And matter also is in a sense manifest. But we must inquire into the third kind of substance; for this is the most perplexing.

These conjoin to form the major metaphysical crux on which Aristotle now hangs before us as some sort of witness. For the moment, however, I overlook [2] and focus on [3] as if it were alone.

In isolation, and at a pinch, [3] might be taken to say little more than that S-form confers separability and *this-ness* on a particular more directly than the particular's S-matter, and hence that the substantiality, reality, or being of the particular lies not in its S-matter, nor even in the union of S-matter and S-form, but in the latter alone. Indeed, whether this is what Aristotle has in mind or not, it gives a cogency to his subsequent account of the first philosopher's program that would otherwise be lacking.

The definitional activity, as he further describes it, is just the implementation of the Path to Enlightenment (see my Introduction). It takes off from the initially more known to us with the purpose of comprehending the known by nature (or in its nature), so that ultimately the former terminates in the latter. More specifically, if somewhat evocatively, it might be called a process of sublimation whereby S-form is purged of all necessary association with S-matter.

As a paradigm, or perhaps the end achievement of this process, Aristotle elects the sublimation of the soul – or at least of one of its faculties. That he should might, then, suggest that D-potencies qualify quite generally for the role of the sublimated type of S-form that most eminently is a thing's substance. The soul as he defines it is an analogue of the occasion-loose D-potency of an axe to cut or of an eye to see (*De An.* 2.1). It is with reference to these objects and powers that he elucidates his statement that the soul is the first actuality of an organized body with the potentiality for life. The potency to cut and to see are respectively the first actualities of the axe and the eye, whereas the second actualities are the active processes or activities of cutting and seeing.

More generally, then, when we refer to something as a man or an ox or a fish, the referential characterization in such terms would seem to involve an undifferentiated and indefinite amalgamation of descriptive properties, the possession of which is more or less immediately ascertainable by the senses, with certain modal properties, the possession of which is not immediately ascertainable in that way. It is in such cases that reference is to a substance as it is initially more known to us. It is not until we discover the formula of the D-essence of such things that we may directly designate a modal property as the differentia – as when we define a human as a rational or a grammatical animal. Alternatively we may select the differentia from among the non-modal properties for the reason that it functions as the *basis* of the thing's most distinctive modal properties, or at least as a reliable criterion for the presence of this basis[2] – as when we define a human in terms of a certain neural structure or, less ambitiously, as a featherless biped. In either case there would seem to be a sublimation of a D-potency, as a result of which we progress, as the Path to Enlightenment enjoins, to what is known by nature or in its nature.

In less evocative language the process of purging would, then, seem nothing more than the intracategorial abstraction of certain characteristics from others. Furthermore, what Aristotle offers at times as a sort of model or analogue for the process apparently confirms that interpretation. Primarily the configurative property of snubness can attach only to particulars that qualify as noses. The property of concavity, however, which he takes to be the configuration whereby noses are snub, can attach to things other than noses.

In that respect, then, the detachment of concavity from snubness and the process I have described as sublimation are comparable. Here I am of course assuming that the same sort of D-potency conceived as S-form may have more than one sort of S-matter as basis. Now Aristotle holds, at least tentatively, that concavity and mathematical properties in general are mere abstractions incapable of existing independently from matter. Hence the analogy suggests that the process of sublimation or purging is merely the abstraction of one property from a more complex property.

4.2 THE PATH TO
ENLIGHTENMENT —
SECOND APPROACH

Quotation [3], however, should not be taken in isolation. It must cohere with [2]. Under that constraint, accordingly it acquires a quite different significance. The connecting passage puts this beyond doubt (*Meta.* Z3.1029a10–26).

[2–3] For if this [sc. matter] is not substance, it baffles us to say what else is. When all else is stripped off evidently nothing but matter remains. For while the rest are affections, products, and potentialities of bodies, length, breadth, and depth are quantities and not substances (for a quantity is not a substance), but the substance is rather that to which these belong primarily. But when length and breadth and depth are taken away we see nothing left unless there is something that is bounded by these; so that to those who consider the question thus matter alone must seem to be substance. By matter I mean that which in itself is neither a particular thing nor of a certain quantity nor assigned to any other of the categories by which being is determined. For there is something of which each of these is predicated, whose being is different from that of each of the predicates (for the predicates other than substance are predicated of substance, while substance is predicated of matter). Therefore the ultimate substratum is of itself neither a particular thing nor of a particular quantity nor otherwise positively characterized; nor yet is it the negations of these, for negations also will belong to it only by accident.

Quite clearly, then, whatever else it is, matter as mentioned in [3] has to be the ultimate subject of predication that [2] identifies as a substratum, or sort of underlying residue. It is as thus identified – and for the reasons that [2–3] advances – that [2] finds matter ontologically substandard.

Now to allow to one sort of matter the subject-role is, of course, perfectly legitimate. It is precisely as subjects that the sorts of D-matter in DRs 1, 2, 3, and 5 operate. To conceive that role as that of a substratum is less legitimate. Here lies the apex of a double cone of darkened counsel. Balanced above is a confluence of errors against which my first three chapters both forewarn and forearm. Draining below is a diffusion of nonsense that carries right through to the present day.

One confluent strand is the failure to place distinctions between substance and other categories on a sound enough basis. Aristotle has failed to see that substantive things in other categories are related to the substances to which they belong as higher to first-order substantives. Their relation is not of the sort that the bits and pieces suspended in a soup have to the suspending fluid. The substantive things in other categories cannot be stripped off from a subject in some way other than simply by being in their predicative aspect denied of the latter. That is because they are but paronyms of predicatives that can only be stripped away by denial. To strip by denial is not to deprive something literally of its possessions or properties, despite the insinuation of our current technical terms. In denying any predicative of a subject (or in stripping away the substantive paronym) we thereby imply a complementary affirmation of some other predicative (or compensatory gift of its substantive paronym). We don't leave the subject to that extent more indeterminate – not even where the substantive is essential as distinct from accidental to the subject. Thus the justification for denying that something is any longer a plant lies in some such fact as that it is now a fossil. In contrast to that, when you strip a man of his shirt he is not automatically clothed in or otherwise endowed with something else.

A second strand is epistemological and complements the first. It is the tendency to think of the most basic form of knowledge as a non-judgmental, purely referential sort of intuition or awareness in which we are merely confronted by objects. This tendency goes back to Plato. It is betrayed in his initial oversight of the existence of judgmental or propositional knowledge, and then in his later comparison of the syntactical structure of singular propositions to the spelling of words. Thus he eventually thought of a true proposition as if it were a complex object, and of judgmental as distinct from the putative non-judgmental knowledge as conscious confrontation with that sort of object. In similar vein Aristotle pictures the relation between a singular subject and its accidental predicates in terms, however metaphorical, of the presence of something in the subject. But the relation between a complex and its parts is extrinsic, in the sense that one part can exist independently, at least for a while, from another. The relation between an unqualifiedly and a qualifiedly existing thing is, on the other hand, a specification of a relation that is internal to the categorial kinds to which the relata belong, in the sense that any member of the former kind (e.g. Socrates) cannot exist independently of being some member of the latter kind (e.g. wise) and any member of the latter kind can only exist as something that, possibly, some member of the former kind is or is not. Hence any immediate awareness of a member of either categorial kind as present to one must have a syntactical structure to match this internal relationship. In short, it must be judgmental.

To do him justice, Aristotle does deny (*Cat.* 2) that the relation of *being present in* is a relation of part to whole. He insists instead (misleadingly, as I have argued) that it is merely an inseparability of something from the subject. Nevertheless he continues to traffic with a picture of the relation as *basically* within a complex of extrinsically related substantival things. I emphasize "basically." Though he recognizes that the components of the complex are categorially distinct, he appears to compromise that recognition by deriving what I have distinguished as predicatives from non-substance substantives (*Cat.* 5.2a30–3: *Meta.* Θ7.1049a30–4), instead of the latter from the former.

As a third strand there is his imperfect control over conscious equivocation. In conjunction with the first strand this leads to a confusion of D-matter with S-matter, and negation or denial with abstraction. In other words, he confuses something from which something can be stripped by negation or denial with what *results* from something being stripped from something else by abstraction. Certainly an S-form can be stripped from a D-essence leaving an S-matter. Certainly, too, if pushed far enough this results in something more indeterminate. It entails, furthermore, no complementary sort of compensation – but only because it is a process of abstraction, not of denial or negation. As an elementalist it was, no doubt, easy for him to mistake the ultimate kinds of D-matter for kinds of S-matter. After all the elements are just one qualitative whisker away from being completely indeterminate. The length, breadth, and depth of any of their portions are accidental to the qualitatively separable mass-substances so apportioned. Nevertheless, mass-substances, whether elemental or composite, are not S-matter.

Possibly, and finally, as a fourth strand there is a failure to recognize that definite reference to anything definite depends in the last analysis upon indefinite reference to something definite (see chapter 2). Wrongly construed, the dependence may lead, by a sort of hypostatization of the indefiniteness of the ultimate referring, to the supposition that the ultimate referent must itself be something indefinite.

For those caught up in these toils the options are three, with minor variations. First, the notions of substance, subject, and substratum may be equated without any further reservation of the sort that Aristotle has required. Descartes and Locke align themselves thus in the cause of their respective epistemologies. To give epistemic priority to reason Descartes likens a physical substance to the passer-by hidden from upstairs observation by hat, cloak, and other accoutrements. Less metaphorically he takes the substance to be nothing but a highly plastic non-sensible and purely intelligible spatial extension. To transfer the priority to experience Locke, for his part, portrays substance as an I-know-not-what-support of properties – an epistemically anomalous ontological surd. Secondly, substance may be equated with substratum, but not with subject. That is how empiricists more radical than Locke proscribe it. Thus for the numerous exponents of the bundle theory nothing is there over and above the Cartesian clothes, and these usurp the status of the wearer. Latent in both these positions is the curious assumption that substantives other than substance are, or include, the most basic referents of sense perception. Finally, subject may be equated with substratum, but not with substance. With some further qualification this is the option declared in quotation [2].[3]

Why, then, did I ever pretend that [3] might be anything less than a sequel to the latter? And, more to the point, why did I foist a rectitude on Aristotle to which he never completely conforms? I began by doing so for two reasons – first, to give him some credit for the degree of rectitude towards which he reaches; and second, to show how far on the basis of that alone his account of first philosophy could take us. But now for a while let us restrain him no further. Profounder distinctions beckon obscurely through the medium of these initial confusions. For a while, then, give our pilot and mentor his wayward head.

Let us, for a start, distinguish a substance's distinctness from something or other from its individuality as an object of reference. Then we can identify that distinction with Aristotle's between separability and *this-ness*. Initially, if tacitly, I have assumed these two marks to be implicit in our notion of particular thinghood, and along with the latter as a sort of given. This was tantamount to taking the first philosopher's problem simply to be one of determining how such marks non-arbitrarily apply. Thus where Aristotle amplifies the question "What is substance?" by the further question "What is the substance of each thing?" (*Meta.* Z3.1028b33–5), I have taken the *things* under scrutiny to be substances in their own right. I have assumed that individual mutables such as Socrates still have the primary status as substance they first acquire in *Cat.* 5, in contradistinction to the secondary status at the same time accorded to species and genera. But this assumption, if not utterly wrong, is far too simple.

Given his deficiently differentiated interpretation of a mutable particular as a union of matter and form, what makes its thinghood non-arbitrary becomes only part of a wider problem. The extent to which that thinghood (or separability and *this-ness*), even if non-arbitrary, is *intrinsic* to the particular is also taken as moot. It is put to a test more stringent than the categorial tests we have so far encountered.

4.3 SEPARABILITY

Consider first distinctness, or separability, as a criterion of substance or thinghood. For Aristotle it has both an exoteric and an esoteric sort of satisfaction. Exoterically it is satisfied in the spatial or the mere qualitative discreteness of mutable particulars. But there is a hint of a more esoteric satisfaction as early as in *Cat.* 5. There he distinguishes substantive things that are present from those that are not present in primary substances, i.e. in particulars. The former include the properties he eventually distinguishes as accidents. The latter are properties, such as manhood, that determine the extension of the species and genera to which primary substances belong. Accordingly, given that *presence in* is to be understood as *inseparability from*, these latter properties must in some sense or other be marked by separability.

Now it is in this second mode that separability is cited in [3], but as further amplified. It attaches not only to the sort of form I interpret as S-form. As well it detaches from whatever it is that is now conceived as the ultimate subject. The half-explicit rationale is somewhat as follows.

The first- and second-strand errors insinuate that accidental substantives are inseparable from individual particulars in that their particular *instantiations* are parasitic upon the particular substances that instantiate them. At the same time this dependence is seen as a mere *presence in* because the instantiation of no such accidental substantive exhausts the particularity of the particular substances that instantiate it. In other words, these very same substances can instantiate the contrary substantives without loss of identity. But differentiae and essential properties, for their part, do exhaust the particularity of particulars. In other words, the latter cannot without loss of identity instantiate the contrary of these properties.

Why, then, should properties with the fully exhaustive type of particularity be regarded, unlike accidental properties, as *separable from* something or other? Shouldn't the relevant difference be that they are wedded *even more* firmly than accidental properties to the particulars in which they are rooted? Yes, indeed – but the third- and fourth-strand errors insinuate a further distinction. Aristotle apparently believes that, even as fully exhaustive of the particularity of particular substances, these properties are predicated of something further yet. It is of this something further that their particularizations are not fully exhaustive. The reason is not that in this residue there is some further particularity that they fail to capture – quite the contrary. The residue is non-particular and absolutely indeterminate.

Hence with a marginal infringement upon their original primary status, mutable substances embrace two quite distinct types of component. To the one (identified without further qualification as form) separability (and hence thinghood or substance) is *intrinsic*. To the other (identified without further qualification as matter) it is *extrinsic*. As for the *exoteric* separability of qualitatively discrete mass substances on the one hand, and of spatially discrete individual substances on the other, that is legitimized as child of the embrace. It remains non-arbitrary, but thanks entirely to the intrinsic factor in its composition.

Matter and form are now on the lurch towards destinies Cartesian and even more dire. They precipitate into an existential division within the category of substance itself – but not yet as between two independent pretenders to that status. First, the distinction between the material and the formal remains relative except at the scalar extremes. Second, these extremes, even though absolute, are not yet on par. The existential status is intrinsic in the formal extremity alone.

Thus the formal extremity is not as identified in 4.1. There it became home to the soul. But even were that quite right, its separability does not lie in the soul's abstractability, i.e. not in the fact that different kinds of proximate matter may be instrumental to one and the same sort of D-potency. The vegetative soul (i.e. the mere capacity for species-preservation through reproduction and for self-maintenance through ingestion of food) and the animal soul (i.e. the further capacity for self-locomotion, desire, and sensation) are separable, i.e. abstractable, in that way. However, they are not *existentially* separable. They are actualizable only through movement or change in their proximate matter.

If, then, the formal extremity *were* to be home to any kind of soul, that kind would have to be quite different. And given that any kind of soul is a sort of D-potency, what the difference would be can be further determined. All D-potencies are actualized in movement or from a whence to a whither. For some, however, the whence and the whither fall under the same sort of determinable. The D-actuality is of the same sort as the state from which it was actualized. Call these "sidelong potencies." Thus the potencies of locomotion, alteration in temperature, and size-change are all alike sidelong. In the first, the whence and the whither are both some definite position or other; in the second they are both some definite temperature or other; and again in the third they are both some definite size or other. Contrariwise, for other potencies, the whence and the whither of the actualization may fall under different determinables. The D-actuality may not be of the same sort as from what it has been actualized. Thus the potencies of sense-perception and of understanding are of this type. While actually seeing something you may, indeed, have the potency of seeing other things precluded from your field of vision then. In that case, no doubt, the whence and the whither are alike visual. But you may not have had any visual experience at all. You may have been asleep. The whence, in other words, need not have been any kind of experience. In general, then, the specific nature of the state from which the actualization of this type of potency is a change, if change it is, may be only incidental to the nature of that actualization. Call this type of potency "upward."

It now is more clear why the sublimation of S-form should have its paradigm in the cognitive faculties. As powers the latter are upward. Their D-actualities are of a different sort from the properties by which their bearers at least *may* be informed prior to actualization. But might not their actualities depend upon the prior sort? Aristotle held that, for the faculties of sense, indeed they do – that there is a dependence upon the organism, and hence upon matter. As he acutely observed, intense sensations impair our immediately subsequent ability to experience sensations of the same type. Presumably, then, some physiological mean has first to be restored before sensitivity is properly regained. Of the intellectual faculty, however, he held the contrary, on the basis of the same sort of test. Thought about a highly intelligible object facilitates the thinker's immediately subsequent ability to think about objects that are less intelligible (*De An.* 3.4.429a31–429b4). The intellect, therefore, has no special organ.

If, then, any sort of soul really were at home in the formal extremity, it would have to be the soul as mind, i.e. as intellect. The intellect alone of all the faculties would seem to qualify absolutely for S-form separability. Like the navigator to his ship, it is related (pace Descartes) to the body in a twofold way. Not only can it and the body exist apart, but the body exists for its sake, just as by ordinary standards of seafaring commerce his ship exists for the sake of the navigator (*De An.* 2.1.413a8–9).

It would seem, however, that it is only as a link between the formal and the material that the intellect is properly a potency at all. Considered as completely separable it resolves into its possible activities. It is these, rather than the intellect itself, that occupy the formal extreme. Were the intellect a sidelong potency its activities would be D-formal rather than S-formal. But as a potency that straddles an ontological divide, the distinction between the D-formal and the S-formal for its activities suffers collapse. Accordingly, it is both the existence and the value of the activity, as distinct from the potency, that is of the intrinsic sort. This alone is the absolutely final cause. This alone is, or is closely akin to, the source both of being and value in all else.

But is this conclusion not, perhaps, premature? Separability from the body is one thing, separability from matter yet another. Might the intellect not depend upon matter in some other way? To consider how Aristotle does or could meet this suggestion, I turn now to *this-ness*.

4.4 EXOTERIC THIS-NESS

For Aristotle, *this-ness* likewise is both exoterically and esoterically satisfiable. Likewise, again, its exoteric satisfaction is conjointly intrinsic and extrinsic. Its esoteric satisfaction is, in contrast, exclusively intrinsic. The following quotation (*Meta.* Z10.1036a1–9) begins to show how.

[4] But when we come to the concrete thing; e.g. *this* circle, i.e. one of the individual circles, whether perceptible or intelligible (I mean by intelligible circles the mathematical, and by perceptible those of bronze and of wood) – of these there is no definition, but they are known by the aid of intuitive thinking or of perception; and when they pass out of this complete realization it is not clear whether they exist or not; but they are always stated and recognized by means of the universal formula. But matter is unknowable in itself.

To elaborate and interpret, whether something is more knowable to us or more knowable by nature, its mode of *this-ness* is its mode of knowability. The mode of knowability is internal to the thinghood of the thing known. In the exoteric mode of satisfaction, which faces us now, the *this-ness* of either a sensible or intelligible individual particular combines matter and form. The *this-ness* is extrinsic to the matter, since the matter is that in the object to which the cognition immediately refers that is other than the cognition itself. By implication and in contrast, the *this-ness* is intrinsic to the form, since the form is that in the object to which the cognition immediately refers that coincides in some yet-to-be-stated way with the cognition itself. In short, to have the *this-ness* of concrete particularity, whether sensible or merely intelligible, is to be an object to which some cognition refers non-reflexively by also referring reflexively to itself. It is further suggested that in relation to the extrinsic *this-ness* of the matter the informing form is a universal. It functions as the *such* in a *this-such*. Only under scrutiny through definition is it completely purged from the material. Only then is it revealed (see *De An.* 3.4.429b13–14) as the *this* in which matter is a *this*.

The fuller and more definitive account of cognition in the *De Anima* confirms this interpretation, though in a somewhat complex and possibly equivocal way. In view of the separate location and probable time of composition, we need not insist on perfect fit. Aristotle deploys somewhat impressionistically a series of analogies whereby similarities and differences between our more important cognitive faculties are signified. The two that pertain to sense perception will in the meantime suffice. One refers to the signet ring in relation to sealing wax (*De An.* 2.12.424a16–24), the other to the hand in relation to tools (*De An.* 3.8.432a1–2). Can two such dissimilar relations really represent the same thing? I attach some importance to the fact that they fail.

That the impression on the wax conforms to the signet on the ring is meant to model not only our sensing of the common-sensibles (i.e. movement, rest, size, figure, and number). Professedly it represents a conformity of the special senses to their special objects (e.g. colour, sound, and flavour) as well. Yet it would seem appropriate to the sensing of the common-sensibles alone. What informs the signet informs it independently of whether it is transferred to the wax or not. Similarly the movement or rest, size, shape, and number of physical objects quite typically belong to these objects independently of their being sensed. Furthermore, the wax-impression may *misrepresent* to some extent what informs the signet. Similarly the sensing of common-sensibles may misrepresent these properties in the objects sensed. The special senses, in contrast, conform in neither of these ways.

Consider sight and hearing as special-sense paradigms. Whether we count Aristotle as an early representationalist or not, initially he presupposes a representationalist type of distinction. He distinguishes between a *potency* or modal property in the independently existing physical object (i.e. the perceivability of the object having a special sensory quality, e.g. colour) and the *actualization* of that potency or modal property (i.e. the actual perceiving of the sensory quality). That he locates the latter in the sense-organ specific to that quality (e.g. in the case of colour, in the eye) is an oddity, but not enough to weaken the apparent representationalism of the distinction.

More idiosyncratically, however, Aristotle assimilates each of the two paradigms to the other. A typical representationalist assimilates the perception of colour to that of sound as ordinarily conceived. The immediately sensed quality of colour is thereby ascribed to an *effect* of the independently existing object (which possesses the modal property of colour conceived as a potency) just as the immediately sensed quality of sound is popularly ascribed to an *effect* of an object's behaviour, or at least to something the object makes or does, as distinct from the object itself. Aristotle is no foe to this ascription. He assimilates in the same direction, while apparently subscribing to the same popular conception of sound. But more impartially he assimilates in the reverse direction as well. For him the immediately perceived quality of sound pertains directly to the sounding object, just as the immediately perceived quality of colour is conceived by the naturally or studiedly naïve as pertaining directly to the coloured object.

Each special object of sense would seem, on Aristotle's view, to fulfil conjointly an activity-in-perceiver and a quality-in-object role. The object with the colour-potency *colours*, as the colour is seen, just as an object with a sounding-potency *sounds*, as the sound is heard. Likewise an object is *sounded*, as sound is heard, just as an object is coloured, as it is seen (*De An.* 2.7; 3.2.425b18–25).

Therefore, what previously passed off as representationalist now looks more like the marriage of two types of non-representationalist theory. It is a form of naïve realism in so far as it ascribes the sensory quality that arises in the sensing directly to the physical objects sensed. It is also an adverbial type of theory in so far as it also regards the sensory quality as characterizing the mode of sensing. In any case, though on Aristotle's theory the special quality informs the object sensed, it does not inform that object *independently* of informing the sense that senses. Likewise, a mismatch between the informing of the object and of the sense cannot arise. The actualization of the object in acquiring the quality coincides with the actualization of the sense in sensing the object so actualized just as – to use another of his analogies – the activity of teaching on the part of the teacher coincides with the activity of learning on the part of the pupil. That is why Aristotle insists that the special senses are not open to error.

In sum, if the sensitivity of the special senses is at all like the malleability of sealing wax, and any special form they acquire in sensing at all like the sign that informs a signet ring, then that same ring must surely embody the very latest state of the art. Perhaps it is the gizmo of some Macedonian superspy. It must acquire and retain its distinctive form only while actually impressed on the wax.

By comparison, the hand-tool analogy is in the same context more adaptable. For this we can thank three factors:

1 The activity of a diversity of tools is instrumental as such to the activity of the hand.
2 The activity of a diversity of tools coincides as such with the activity of the hand.
3 Therefore the different jobs done by the diversity of tools are simultaneously all jobs done by one thing, viz. the hand.

Hence, just as the hand is the tool of tools, so then, according to Aristotle, the senses are the forms of sensible things. The relation between the sensibility of any special sense and the perceptibility of physical objects sensed by that sense is like the relation between the skill of the hand and the utility of its tools, as presented in 1, 2, and 3. In short, it is a relation between D-powers respectively of organisms and certain objects with which these organisms interact.

One discrepancy is of little import. Aristotle regards the faculty of sense as passive and the potency of being sensed as active. For him the object sensed acts on the sense rather than vice versa. Yet with the skill of the hand and the utility of the tool it is surely the reverse. To that extent, then, the adaptability of the hand is analogically less apt than the malleability of the wax, for the latter potency is definitely passive. But this does not seriously impair what is central to the likeness, viz. that in sensing, as in manipulation, the actualizations of complementary D-powers coincide. Furthermore, by way of compensation, the object sensed, though actively empowered, is otherwise like the tool in being *for the sake of* the sensing – sensing being in Aristotle's estimation an intrinsic good – just as in factor 1 the tool is for the sake of the manipulation.

Now in so far as either analogy can stand on its own, that of the hand and its tools is more adequate to exoteric *this-ness*. It does more justice both to the extrinsic and the intrinsic aspect of the latter.

As addressed to the extrinsic aspect, it alone can portray how matter is indeterminate independently of being sensed. Admittedly, the kind of indeterminacy in question would seem in respect of properties that are accidental rather than essential, at least in so far as these properties are merely those of colour and sound. However, the implication may merely be that only through the mediation of the special senses, and of the accidental properties they determine, can matter attach to essences, even if these essences themselves do not depend on any sense special or common.

As addressed to the *intrinsic* aspect of the exoteric form of *this-ness*, the hand-tool analogy is likewise superior. It alone seems able to represent the dependence of that aspect upon sensory self-reference.

Aristotle explicitly argues for the self-reference of sensing (*De An.* 3.2.425b11ff). His initial assumption is that our awareness of any special sense must be attributed to some special sense or other. The reason, presumably, is that if we are non-inferentially aware of our sensing, when a special sense (e.g. sight) is active, our awareness must include an awareness of the special object sensed (e.g. colour). From that he then infers that our awareness of the special sense must be provided by the special sense itself. If it were by another special sense, it would *per impossibile* have to include among its objects the special objects of the special sense that it senses. Hence it could no longer be a special sense. Further, an infinite regress would then ensue, for each special sense that senses a special sense not itself would itself have to be sensed by a special sense not itself. Therefore it is by each special sense that we are aware of that sense.

But if a special sense really does sense itself among its special objects, just how does it do so? The hand-tool analogy once again suggests an answer. Typically utility belongs to a tool under two aspects. It derives from the manipulative skill of the hand, relative to which the tool is passive, in conjunction with the susceptibility of the objects upon which the tool can work and relative to which it is active. Accordingly, given that the hand is the tool of tools, and therefore has utility as well, it is both active and passive relative to itself, i.e. self-utilizing and self-utilized. To put it another way, the hand both reflexively determines and is determined by its own constitutive activity. Similarly, the special senses both reflexively determine and are determined by the constitutive activity peculiar to them, i.e. that of cognitive referring. Notice further, for its own self-use one hand is enough. It is not a matter of the one hand being a tool for the other. Similarly Aristotle is no party, not even in germ, to black-box freakery. For him our awareness of our senses does not consist in one part of a mechanism scanning another. Their *this-ness* in short is truly intrinsic.

Even so, however, can the hand-tool analogy render all that Aristotle must require? The utility of the hand whereby the hand is self-utilizing does not exactly coincide with the utility of any of its tools. The latter sort of utility is merely constitutive of the former. Contrariwise, the colouring in the eye whereby the sense of sight becomes aware of itself is supposed to coincide with the colour in the concrete particular that is seen. At least it is coincidence that gives the simplest explanation of how the reflexive, and hence intrinsic, *this-ness* of the form that qualifies the cognitive activity is likewise to belong to the form in the particular that is sensed. Perhaps, then, we should settle for a less simple explanation by allowing the latter form to depend for its intrinsic *this-ness* upon its being merely constitutive of the reflexivity of the sensing.

4.5 ESOTERIC THIS-NESS

To keep in contact with Aristotle on his journey to enlightenment is in the final stages like plumbing the profundities of some cosmic black hole. As the conclusion to 4.3 already suggests, the more sharply focused hylomorphic distinctions may begin to collapse rather in the way in which the geometry of space and time is supposed to transform or homogenize when, under the stress of an intense gravitational field, light turns in on itself.

It is therefore not so strange that in the final stages Aristotle's style of exposition is even more metaphorical than before. For this he has the precedent of Plato's Sun. Line, and Cave at a similar crux in the *Republic*. Altogether he brings as many as four distinct types of image to play. One of these is the hand-tool analogy yet again. The other three are place (3.5.429a23–9), the writing tablet (3.4.429b29–430a1), and light (3.5.430a14–17). None of these are easy to construe. That the first is applied both to the senses and the intellect, despite the uniqueness that the second, third, and fourth stake out for the latter, is a symptomatic difficulty. Furthermore, the intermediate faculty of understanding or judgment may seem barely acknowledged. I economize by confining myself to the first and fourth of these images, though the second and third are almost as beguiling.

That the activity of the intellect is its own terminal object is the underlying theme. Its knowability by nature is ascribed to a particularly stringent reflexivity or self-preoccupation. The latter confers a *this-ness* that is intrinsic with no extrinsic blemish. Intellectual activity, at least in its ultimate stage, is (unlike sensing) entirely coincident with its objects. However, these latter, as well as being somehow nothing but the activity itself, must be the essences (i.e. S-essences) of things as well. Examples specifically given are *the what it is to be* or essence of magnitude, water, and flesh. It is, after all, in its concern with the like that the intellect is superior to other faculties. Accordingly, that its activity can actually be identical with such objects adds the final touch of mystery that makes the esotericism of its intrinsic inwardness quite peerless.

Consider my previous conclusion that the ultimate S-essences of things are D-potencies, and more specifically potencies that are sidelong. By identity with any of these an activity of the intellect would be as much involved with matter as they are. In short, we are back to square one, i.e. our first approach to first philosophy and the Path to Enlightenment.

Perhaps, then, the essences in question are something else. Indeed, Aristotle stipulates (*De An.* 3.4.419b17–23) that they stand to essences that involve matter much as, say, two-ness to the continuity of a straight line or to straightness, and therefore to whatever line is straight. But, given his non-Platonic conception of abstract mathematical entities, two-ness in relation to straightness – like concavity to snubness – does not really exemplify the type of sublimation from matter that he would seem to require. It has no certain claim to existential independence.

Could Aristotle, then, be using the already postulated independence of the intellect from matter, and more specifically the body, to explain how something abstract might at the same time be existentially dependent? Is he claiming that exclusively as an object of the intellect, and thus as identical in part at least with some intellectual activity, something like two-ness or concavity has the absolute independence from matter that in itself, or in the nature of things (*de re*), it does not have? Is this how abstract objects become abstract?

But if so, he must reckon with a dilemma. He can postulate separability for abstract essences to establish separability for the intellect, not just from the body but from matter in general. Alternatively, he can do the reverse. He can postulate a separability of intellect from matter in general to establish separability for abstract essences. To try to do both, however, is self-defeating. By postulating separability for the intellect to elucidate that of abstract essences, he precludes himself from postulating separability for abstract essences to elucidate that of the intellect. And that is surely excessively frustrating, for up to this point he has offered no argument, good or bad, for the separability of the intellect from matter in general as distinct from just the body in particular.

Furthermore, it is difficult to see how there could be any abstraction from sidelong D-potencies comparable to two-ness from straightness, or concavity from snubness. Are we to suppose that Aristotle surreptitiously subscribed to a form of Pythagoreanism whereby for every unsublimated essence there corresponds some mathematical entity? Alternatively, is the abstraction not *from* the sidelong potencies? Instead, is it *of* the potencies themselves *from* something less abstract, e.g. *of* rationality *from* the being human? Has mathematical abstraction of one sort or another just been used here as an analogue for this? But sidelong potencies presuppose materialization even more directly than mathematical abstractions, as I have argued.

As if the identity of its activities with their objects were not enough of an enigma, that of the intellect itself with its *possible* objects (*De An.* 3.4.429b5ff) is even more so. The activity-object identity would make the intellect's possible objects identical with its possible activities. But, since all of its possible objects are limited to the essences of things, they must likewise all be actual. Hence each of its possible activities must likewise be actual. But, then, unlike other faculties, the intellect must consist not just of the possibility of each of its possible activities but of the actuality of all of them into the bargain. Apparently its home is a Megarian world in which the possible collapses into the actual, or the actual expands into the possible. Its world must be the best of all possible worlds, for all these worlds are one and the same with each other and with the actual.

Somehow, furthermore, the collapse of distinctions must leave his contrast between a lesser and an ultimate fulfilment of intellectual activity intact. Penultimately the intellect is realized in the first philosopher and in the contemplation of abstract essences that the definitional activity of the latter finally achieves. Though not the function of any organ – for that form of contemplation has no organ – it associates with physical organisms of certain specialized types. These, like others, are spatio-temporally limited and numerically diverse. Hence, in association with these, the intellect is likewise limited and numerically diverse. However, that is not its ultimate realization. The latter is in the Prime Mover and the Prime Mover's activity, the two being the same. Here there is no such association with any limit. The realization is an eternal all-encompassing numerically non-diverse activity.

From an internal point of view the contrast, no doubt, is in its fulfilment to some extent minimized. In either case any act of contemplation that is a simple act has a simple object, since it is its own object. Hence the object must, according to Aristotle (*De An.* 3.6.430b14–15), occupy a simple non-composite time. Admittedly this simple time must reflect the character of the self-intimating types of act by which it is accepted. Admittedly, then, in the one case it must be eternal or temporally all-encompassing, and in the other ephemeral. Nevertheless, the simplicity of the self-intimating acts cannot allow them to appear to themselves in the context of a wider time, even if there is a wider time. Hence both types of act, the ephemeral as well as the eternal, must appear to themselves eternal.

I now revert to the hand and its tools. In the further application of the relationship, as the hand is the tool of tools, and as the senses are the forms of *sensible things*, so the intellect is the form of *forms*. Does this give us more of a purchase on these puzzling identities? Perhaps up to a point. The skill of the hand imposes a unity on the utilities of the diversity of tools that the hand may possibly use, for all these utilities are constitutive of, as complementary to, that skill; and consequently the skill transcends what is required for any one of its possible applications. Similarly, perhaps, the intellect may unify a set of D-powers, given that the latter are in some way constitutive of, as complementary to, the former. Suppose for simplicity that the hand can only use one tool at a time. Similarly, then, we may suppose that through the intellect we sublimate only one essence or D-power at a time. Yet the intellect would still be a unifying factor in, because constituted by, essences other than whichever one we sublimate at any given time. In short, its identity with its possible objects would consist in this asymmetrical unifier-to-constitutor relationship.

The limit to the likeness lies in the fact that the manipulative skill and the instrumental utilities are functional properties that determine the extention of respectively a less and a more inclusive class of particular. From the members of these two classes they are inseparable except by abstraction. Hence they are correlative rather than merged into identity. If the skill could be conceived as existentially separable from the hand, then it would represent the intellect more perfectly. Somehow it might be seen as detaching, through its function of unification, the utilities from the diversity of tools that have them. Taken separately, we might suppose, each utility is merely abstracted, while taken as unified by the skill they become existentially independent as well as abstracted from tools. Another blemish is that the manipulative skill is nothing more than the mere possibility of each of its possible applications. It can provide no model for a faculty that supposedly would consist in the actuality of all its possible activities. Nor can it parallel, in any way that I can think of, what distinguishes a first philosopher's sort of contemplation from that of the Prime Mover.

Too often, of course, a minuter scrutiny of features to which an analogy owes its charm is as stultifying as over-proximity to an impressionistic painting. In our effort to see more clearly what appears to be there, we lose sight of the appearance. Some similar disenchantment may affect us now. That an analogy should sometimes prove less than completely reliable may not detract entirely from its value. Even to create the illusion of a parallel may allow us to focus on what the parallel is supposed to signify. Nevertheless, we may have hoped for more.

Does, then, the analogy of light extend more promise? Certainly it is more flexible and suggestive as a parallel, or illusion thereof. In effect it relieves the tension between some of the requirements that the intellect has to satisfy. It shares them out between different realizations of what, with the aid of the analogy, is represented as none the less to some extent the same thing. Though it is notoriously cryptic, I quote the passage (*De An.* 3.5.430a10–20) that hints at this procedure.

[5] Since [just as] in the whole of nature there is something which is matter to each kind of thing (and this is what is potentially all of them), while on the other hand there is something else which is their cause and is productive by producing them all – these being related as art to material – so there must also be these differences in the soul. And there is an intellect which is of this kind by becoming all things, and there is another which is so by producing all things, as a kind of disposition, like light, does; for in a way light too makes colours which are potential into actual colours. And this intellect is distinct, unaffected, and unmixed, being in essence activity.

While the comparison here deserves its reputation as obscure, Aristotle took some pains to prepare for its introduction. Indeed, his antecedent disquisition on the nature of light and its cosmic basis (*De An.* 2.7.418b4ff: cf *De Sen.* 2.439b17–439b14; 6.446b27) may seem to us physically so preposterous as to have more appeal as a parable. In any case, it is not how we regard light, but how he regarded it and its cosmic basis, that holds the key.

Light for Aristotle is not something that travels through space from a source. It is simply the actuality of whatever is potentially transparent. Among instances of the latter are air and water – media through which things are seen once these media become transparent. Without the existence of such media there could be no such thing as light. Nothing could be seen in a vacuum. Light in a sense is the colour of these media, a property that pertains to something, notwithstanding which, unlike colour in the strict sense, it is not visible in itself. It owes its colour to the colour of other things – those things it renders visible.

Of air and water Aristotle goes on to assert that they owe their transparency to a nature that they share with the uppermost shell of the physical cosmos. Elsewhere he identifies this further substance with a fifth element, viz. ether (*De Cael.* 1.3). Besides being somehow associated with transparency, it is distinguishable from the other four elements in a number of cosmologically significant ways. Its natural motion is circular, whereas theirs is rectilinearly upwards or downwards. Hence it is neither light nor heavy. Further, it does not coinstantiate properties selected from complementary pairs of opposites as they do. Hence it is subject neither to generation, nor dissolution, nor transmutation, nor growth, nor diminution. It is indeed eternal, and above all divine.

How more exactly air, water, and similar media are supposed to change from a potential to an actual transparency may not seem obvious all at once. Aristotle attributes the change to fire, or to something that resembles ether. But of course, in bringing about change this factor cannot function as source. This seems to follow not merely from Aristotle's conception of light as a property of a substance rather than as an emanation, but independently also from his more detailed description of fire. Some things are visible only in the presence of light, viz. colours. Others are visible only in the absence of light, viz. the phosphorescence (e.g. of rotting flesh) that is visible in darkness. Fire he distinguishes from these as visible both in light and in darkness. By implication, then, fire does not illuminate by transfusing the surrounding medium with light. Instead, the medium imitates the fire in its resemblance to aether by becoming transparent, much as the ether itself imitates the eternal unchanging nature of the Prime Mover through untiring circular motion.

Let us now apply this highly structured account as an image and in totality. My suggestion is that its application in part is best taken within the context of the whole. Thus understood it portrays the relationship between three distinguishable types of intellectual activity. That the transparency of the medium, the incandescence of fire, and the unsurpassable luminosity of the ether all reveal something or other qualifies them as analogues of the cognition of objects; that *ex hypothesi* they are all manifestations of a single, if triune, nature qualifies them as analogues of a diversity of cognitive activities that are in essence the same; and finally that they are manifestations in unequal degrees of fulfilment of the one nature (roughly, and in reverse order, as Light the Father, Light the Son, and Light the Holy Ghost) enables them to portray significant differences between cognitive activities that are in essence the same.

In first and most developed stage the analogy lends a specious legitimacy to a hylomorphic collapse. In one aspect the tranfusion of media by light is primarily a case of alteration, i.e. D2. It is primarily a change of one unitary and continuous thing (D2-matter) from opacity or darkness to transparency (D2-form). Likewise, if we take darkness to be the absence of any colour, it is a change in which that continuous thing acquires an internal differentiation in colour and shape, e.g. through its interface with the individual surfaces revealed. In the other aspect, on the other hand, it is primarily a case of generation, i.e. D4, for colours or coloured shapes have now to represent objects. It is primarily an emergence of something new, i.e. these colours and shapes, which through the acquisition of their constitutive D4-form are not identical with anything from which they have emerged. In the combination of these two aspects of the analogy lies the clue to part of our puzzle, i.e. to the intellect's mind-boggling identity with its *possible* objects. It allows the intellect in changing from its passive to its active mode to remain one and the same thing, with loss neither to unity nor identity as D2-matter, while at the same time losing both by becoming many things in the second mode with which it was not identical in the first.

For the rest of the mystery there is a similar, if more elaborate, anodine. Each of the three major manifestations of light in Aristotle's physics is, in what it reveals, self-revealing. As one of them, however, transparency is the least fulfilled. Not only is its self-revelation the least direct, for colours reveal the transparency to itself only in the course of the transparency revealing their colour. In addition, it is implicitly faulty. Quite typically the transparency of the potentially transparent is flawed either by impurities or by shadow. Furthermore, it waxes and wanes with distance from fire or ether or with the intensity of the former (that of ether being invariant). Hence, the colours seen, though truly seen, may give no reliable indication either of the colours that the same objects may appear to have at other times or of the translucence of the medium. Contrariwise the incandescence of fire and the unsurpassable luminosity of ether reveal themselves directly and, we may suppose, for exactly what they are. Yet fire is as inferior to ether as transparency to fire. Since the four sublunar elements are inter-transmutable, fire may be generated in many discontinuous places, and is ephemeral in any of its portions. But the ether and its luminosity are, for their part, continuous, all-encompassing, and eternal.

Now in all three of these forms the self-revelation of light is matched by the self-reference of a corresponding intellectual enlightenment. Thus in the self-revelation of transparency its limitations resemble those of an intellectual sort of activity for which Aristotle would otherwise seem – despite his explicit recognition of its existence – to have no particular representation. I refer to the activity of judgment or understanding. This activity has a distinctive place in his list of cognitive faculties, at least inasmuch as he recognizes that its objects are propositional, composite in some way, and thereby capable of being either true or false. Take, then, the possibility of defect in the revelation of the objects in which transparency reveals itself to signify the possibility of our misjudging the essences that the referents of our judgments may happen to instantiate. In other words, take defects in the revelation of colour to signify these defects in judgment – or if that sits too awkwardly with the incorrigibility that Aristotle confers upon colour-vision, take the defect to be in the revelation of potentialities for colour instead.

At this stage, however, we remain at a loss for the answer to a more salient part of our problem. How more exactly can the intellect qualify for a sublimated status? The essences that are objects for judgment or misjudgment are such as universals, and as still attached to the particulars to which these activities directly or indirectly refer. Hence to that extent the activities must be attached to particulars likewise. Here, then, is where the incandescence of fire and the unsurpassable luminosity of the aether become analogically pertinent.

Not only is fire directly self-revealing. What it reveals, particularly when in a penumbra of darkness, is quite separate from what transparency in the media reveals. Nevertheless, inasmuch as transparency is of the same nature as fire, albeit as a lesser fulfilment, what fire reveals as separate is to that extent identifiable both with the transparency and with the objects through revealing which transparency reveals itself. In other words, these objects – in quintessence at least – are more fully assumed into the self-revelation of light where the latter assumes its incandescent form. Inasmuch as the fire is one, they too are one, and one with the fire. Accordingly, as the analogue of the intellect and its activity only in one of three distinguishable phases, fire sheds an illusion of lucidity on the requirement that the intellect is separable from matter, on the one hand, while identical with essences that in one aspect are *inse*parable from matter, on the other.

Ether, likewise, is as separate from the transparent media as fire, only more so. In fact it is as separate from fire as the latter from the transparent media. Hence fire and ether have a further analogical role to play, this time not as in contrast to the transparent media but as in contrast to each other. Both, in so far as they directly reveal themselves, reveal a simple undifferentiated object, and in this way they are alike. Fire, however, has to represent the spatio-temporally limited and numerically diverse sort of intellectual activity that is specific to the first philosopher. This consists in the contemplation of abstract essences, which the latter achieves in the culmination of the definitional activity. In a sense these essences are still the same as the essences cognized in the course of judging or misjudging. But now they have achieved an existential independence and unitary simplicity through their presence in, and identity with, an intellectual activity that is as ontologically removed from their bearers as fire may be spatially removed from what it illuminates. Sometimes this activity accompanies, indeed causally elicits, the inferior contemplation in the teleological way in which fire elicits transparency in a medium. Sometimes it may occur without such accompaniment, somewhat as when fire is visible in the absence of light. Ether, on the other hand, represents a spatio-temporally all-encompassing intellectual activity that is just as obviously identifiable with the activity of the Prime Mover. Besides being eternal, it is as ontologically removed from the first two manifestations as the supralunar cosmos is spatially removed from what it encloses.

If these interpretations are nearly fair, there is a close symbiosis between some of Aristotle's analogies and his hylomorphic equivocations. Or, if you prefer a coarser buzz, the two types of device are in cahoots. The craft of the one is front for the other – the phosphorescence of a deliquescent decay. Aristotle's ascent to first causes both begins and ends in a confusion and collapse of the distinctions over which he equivocates. His analogies, on the other hand, give countenance to the equivocation by disguising the confusion and collapse.

4.6 THE INTEGRATIVE PROGRAM

In a pivotal and much-debated passage Aristotle identified first philosophy as either physics or theology, without at that point declaring which. Thus he writes

[6] But if there is something which is eternal and immovable and separable, clearly the knowledge of it belongs to a theoretical science – not, however,

to physics (for physics deals with certain movable things) nor to mathematics, but to a science prior to both. For physics deals with things which exist separately[4] but are not immovable, and some parts of mathematics deal with things which are immovable, but presumably do not exist separately, but as embodied in matter; while the first science deals with things which both exist separately and are immovable ... If there is no substance other than those which are formed by nature, natural science will be the first science; but if there is an immovable substance, the science of this must be prior and must be first philosophy, and universal in this way, because it is first. And it will belong to this to consider being *qua* being – both what it is and the attributes which belong to it *qua* being   (*Meta.* E1.1026a10–32).

It is of so small consequence that this identification follows almost directly after quotation [1] (see 4.1). He has barely finished distinguishing first philosophy from the special sciences. Yet now it may seem he has identified it with one or other of two sciences each of which has an arguable claim to being special. Physics is a science that deals with being *qua* mutable. Theology is a science that deals with being *qua* divine (or eternal and immutable). How, then, can first philosophy be either physics or theology, while yet being the science of being *qua* being? We have Aristotle's assurance that if a science is a science of first causes, as either physics or theology must be, then it must also be the universal science of being *qua* being. But does this settle the matter? Can what it assures be anything more than a shotgun wedding between inherently discrepant criteria for scientific priority?[5]

The answer to these questions surely is that the criterion for a science's being special upon which they so selectively focus is relatively superficial compared to the criterion announced in [1]. There a science is classified as special if it takes the sort of essence that is within its purview as a datum, on either an inductive or a hypothetical basis, i.e. if it neither demonstrates the essence nor proves that anything with that essence (i.e. anything for which what is postulated as an essence truly functions as an essence) actually exists. By implication, therefore, the science of being *qua* being is qualified as such by supplying what the special sciences in this way withold. Why, then, assume that a science that deals with being *qua* immutable, or else with being qua divine (or eternal and immutable), must be deficient in the way that special sciences are deficient and in which the science of being qua being is not? To do so not only dismisses Aristotle's express assurance. It also seems to ignore what is central to the first philosopher's enterprise. The aim of the latter must be to establish the intrinsic thinghood of those things that have it by showing that that thinghood has an adequate dynamic basis.

If, then, first philosophy amounts just to physics, physics cannot be a special science as it otherwise would be. It would not start from the general mutability and the more specific essences of the particulars of which it treats. It would go further back by demonstrating the intrinsic thinghood of things that are mutable and to which these essences are conceived as pertaining. It would establish both the non-delusory and non-arbitrary nature of their sortal characteristics.

Aristotle, furthermore, makes explicit provision for leaving open, at least temporarily, the question of whether physics has this latter and more searching function. Apparently the science he has in mind when he refers to physics is one in which the sublimation of the substantial form of mutable particulars has been carried through. Thus he says quite explicitly that physics deals not just with the mutable, but with the mutable that exists separately. Here, as the context seems to suggest, the separateness must be a separateness from *matter*. The sublimation must then be of the most refined type that the sublimation of the substantial form of physical things can possibly be. Presumably, therefore, the form he has in mind as such is the intellectual activity of which wise men are capable. As we have seen, for him this activity has strictly no *material* basis. Yet it remains strictly *physical* for in at least one sense it is not immutable. The contemplative thought to which certain humans can attain is of an intermittent character. It is to this extent, then, that physics has certain pretensions, at least, to the status of first philosophy. As the final physical cause, the sublimated but mutable form that is identifiable as human contemplative thought provides a dynamic basis whereby the empirically identified essences, which differentiate between the mutable particulars we perceive, can be regarded as conferring intrinsic thinghood upon such things.

If, however, first philosophy amounts to theology, then theology cannot be a special science. In fact Aristotle seems to imply that in any case it cannot be a special science, given that it deals with the eternal and immutable. For him the only question to be raised is whether it is *a science at all*, or more directly whether the eternal and immutable does indeed exist. Given that it does, the claim of physics to be first philosophy is most certainly superseded, for the sublimated form that is the final teleological cause is then not mutable, but immutable.

However, whichever of the two sciences wins the prize, notice that it thereby acquires a dual sort of status. As the master science under which the special sciences are subsumed and thereby integrated, it establishes the scientific validity of the latter in *more than one sense.* It establishes the non-arbitrary nature of what on inductive grounds or by mere hypothesis they take to be essences, both by demonstra-

tion and by constitution. In other words, what it thus effects is simultaneously an ontological as well as a theoretical subsumption or
integration, given that the contemplative activity in which the master
science culminates is itself the ultimate dynamic factor, or a close
approximation thereto, upon which the non-arbitrary status of the
specialized essences depends.

To do full justice to its more distinctive features we may take this
ontological-cum-theoretical integration as involving, or the product
of, four interlocking principles. In their theoretical aspect these principles simply are theses. In their ontological aspect they are operative
factors. In short, as applied to them the word "principle" is equivocal
(e.g. as it sometimes is in phrases like "the principle of the division
of labour"). At present, furthermore, their formulation will be deliberately vague, so as not to beg questions as yet unanswered.

The first of the four is a *reificatory* principle, viz. that what confers
non-arbitrary being, thinghood, or substance is a certain kind of
form, and more specifically a form with the attributes of intrinsic
separability and *this-ness*. The second is a *psychocentric* principle, viz.
that this form is, or is akin to, a type of soul or soul-activity. The
third is a *modal identification*, viz. that the soul in question is, at least
in certain of its aspects or kinships, a faculty or potency. The fourth
is an *axiological* principle, viz. that the reifying, psychocentring form
functions as an ultimate end and good that is absolute. This end and
good is ultimaté and absolute simply because allegiance to it is the
only ticket or title to intrinsic thinghood or being. In sum, then, it
is by identifying itself reflexively as the reificatory, psychocentring
absolute good that the activity of first philosophy fulfils both its
ontological and its theoretical integrative role. It both constitutes or
confers *and* demonstrates the non-arbitrariness of the essences with
which the special sciences are or should be concerned.

Now, as we are already well aware, it is finally to theology that
Aristotle gives the prize. He ultimately held that a non-physical, non-
sensible, immutable substance – one that is divine – does indeed
exist. Furthermore, he identifies the reifying, psychocentring, absolute good with this transcendent being. Hence, to complete the
Integrative Program that he has been pioneering he has one further
task of integration to discharge. He has to establish the immanence
of the divine in the teeth of its transcendence. Conveniently, however, his cosmological type of proof for the existence of the transcendent serves this further purpose equally well.

For one part of his proof he offers a unified theory of motion –
both motion in general and locomotion in particular – of the type
then in vogue. On this theory the cosmos is finitely structured as a

geocentric system of nesting spheres. While each of these rotates eternally on an axis of its own, it also shares in the rotation of the sphere, if any, in which it directly nests. Accordingly, the motions of everything included within the outermost sphere become in principle explicable, whether mechanically or teleologically, in terms of the rotation of the latter.

For the rest of the proof Aristotle relies more or less explicitly on three aetiological assumptions. According to the first, the causes of motion cannot be infinitely regressive. According to the second, the all-encompassing rotation of the outermost sphere itself stands in need of causal explanation. Since, then, motion takes place beyond doubt, it follows from the unified theory in conjunction with just these two assumptions that there must be an Unmoved or Prime Mover with a unity to match its immediate effect on that outermost sphere.

The third assumption specifies the nature of the causation thus involved. Aristotle holds that only what moves other things as the ultimate object of their admiration, and hence as divine, can move without itself being in motion or moved. From this he infers that as the most perfect sort of motion possible the outermost sphere's all-encompassing rotation is directly imitative of the eternal perfection. As for the natural motions of all other things, they imitate that paradigm as well, though less directly, in manners appropriate to the hylomorphic status of their natures. Indeed, the very natures, or essences, that these motions manifest are part of the structurally differentiated approximation of nature as a whole to the divine. To allude to his semi-apt metaphor, a kind of Alexander-syndrome is here at work. Nature is imbued with the actuality of the transcendent somewhat as the members of an army are imbued according to their interdependent functions and rank with the spirit of a charismatic general.

Epistemically, of course, the unified theory and the three further assumptions are of different origin. The former draws on what is more knowable to us, for cosmology and astronomy fall into that category. The latter draws on what is more knowable by nature, or our closest approximation thereto. We may reasonably suppose that the intellectual activity of the Prime Mover serves as a paradigm that determines the conceptual constraints upon causal explanation that these assumptions lay down.

Consider, more specifically, the third assumption. Presumably it is by an extrapolation from their own intellectual activity that first philosophers become aware of the divine nature as the eternal self-engrossed activity of contemplation that it is. The ectypal activity, no doubt, is evanescent and numerically diverse, like the incandescence of fire, whereas the archetype is eternal and single, like the refulgence of ether. But despite the difference, they have much in common. Both are separate from matter, both have intrinsic *thisness* due to reflexivity, both are self-determining as providing their subject-matter from themselves, both occur within a simple time without internal subdivision or passage, both are wholly satisfying, and both are wholly good.

Similar extrapolation will, then, give insight into how the archetype moves in the sense of causes. Here again the differences are quite radical. The ectype is identical with the essences of the natural substances it investigates, though only as separate from these substances. Hence, inasmuch as these essences function as teleological causes of their enmatterment, so does the ectype. The archetype, however, is other than essences of natural substances. Its function as a teleological cosmic cause is less direct. The outermost sphere mimics the eternal self-engrossed activity of the archetype in two modes — both diachronically, through eternal rotation, and synchronically, through the all-encompassing aethereal rotundity that that rotation manifests. Aside from the ectypal activity of the first philosopher, this diachronic-synchronic bifurcation is nature's closest approximation to the correspondingly monolithic actuality of the archetype. Nevertheless, despite these differences, the influence of both ectype and archetype is teleological. Hence, through the insight that the former has into its own more direct immanence in matter, it has similar insight into the less direct immanence of the transcendent.

Some further words of caution. To analyse the ontological-cum-theoretical integration in terms of the four interlocking principles is to view the function of first philosophy from a somewhat fractured perspective. That a science of first causes should simultaneously concern itself with being, mind, and value is at the very least consistent with a tradition that goes back to Anaxagoras if not further. By Aristotle's time these concerns had not yet properly fallen apart. Hence for him his integrative task presumably would be to render in more detail the nature of connections that he and many of his contemporaries were already willing to presuppose. However, my ultimate interest in the Integrative Program as seen by him is in its capacity as a sort of model for the conduct of further inquiry in the following chapters. It is therefore expedient to make clear to ourselves what he is after in terms more appropriate to our less integrated *status quo ante* than to his.

CHAPTER FIVE

The Doctrine Confronted

5.0

This chapter dismantles the hylomorphic system that came together in chapters 3 and 4, but with a conservative purpose. It will allow chapter 6 to relocate those constituents that do not fall by the way into a hylomorphic system of a somewhat leaner kind. In this further transformation the General Theory of Being remains as psychocentric as ever, but minus some of its previous commitments. At no cost to the Path to Enlightenment and Integrative Program, it will shed Aristotle's anthropomorphism, reform his psychology, and dispense with or sideline his transcendentalist theology. It is with the need for, or propriety of, these remedial measures that I am in the meantime concerned.

5.1 ARISTOTLE'S ANTHROPOMORPHISM

The term "anthropomorphism" is used to impugn. It signifies the scientifically questionable or illegitimate application of expressions appropriate to the description of human beings, or to explanations of their behaviour, to the description or explanation of phenomena of a more general kind. Even so, however, its use may be more or less strict. The questionable extrapolation is either from the exclusively human or from something broader. Thus it may be from other forms of animal life with properties close enough to the human. Consequently in some contexts "zoomorphism" might be the more appropriate term, were it is convey the same censure. Some of Aristotle's doctrines or assumptions would, indeed, be more accurately labelled thereby. As it is, however, retention of the term "anthropomorphism" for their evaluation is prudent, with the proviso that in this context its use may be more or less strict.

Aristotle's anthropomorphism is of two main sorts, geometric and dynamic. While the two are entwined, the former is the less central. It represents space as a vectorially differentiated totality of places, and three-directional oppositions as intrinsic to the totality's three dimensions. These are the up/down, right/left, and before/after oppositions. To elaborate, an intrinsic upwards runs radially from the centre of the cosmos towards the periphery of the shell, and an intrinsic downwards counterwise. This first opposition is a geometrico-dynamical constituent of the natural spatial ordering of the four sublunar elements. Similarly, the before/after[1] and right/left oppositions are equally intrinsic (*Phys.* 4.1.208b9–22), though in just what way is left a bit unspecific. Presumably they coincide respectively with the east/west and north/south alignments, thereby respectively determining in an equally geometrico-dynamical way the diurnal and seasonal motions of the sun and firmament of fixed stars.

All three geometric assymetries correspond more or less directly to asymmetries of the human anatomy. Here lies their anthropomorphic indiscretion. Nevertheless, in declaring that they are intrinsic to space, i.e. absolute, Aristotle is equally insistent that their anatomical counterparts are relative just to us. Hence his geometric anthropomorphism is merely quasi-anatomical. The censure it deserves is more for just being false than for being anthropomorphic as well. Indeed, as anticipating in principle the geometrico-dynamic conception of space now in vogue – the thesis that cosmic forces are a function of cosmic geometry – it even earns a slight genuflection.

More, however, than geometry is at stake. The dynamics as well may be tainted. For Aristotle both the natural behaviour and the natural structure of all natural substances are teleologically determined. Thus the quasi-anatomical assymetry of space is presupposed in the teleological behaviour of the most basic stuff. As the most basic D-matter, the elements *seek* their natural places in the up/down dimension, and conversely the natural places, as D-form, *attract* the elements. From a structural point of view, furthermore, nature in general acts like an intelligent workman. Any natural substance is invested in its S-matter for the sake of, or in order to have, the proximate S-essence. As invested in flesh, blood, and bone animals generically are for the sake of their organization into living bodies. As invested in organized bodies non-human animals are specifically for the sake of their faculties of sensation, appetite, and locomotion. As invested additionally in these faculties men and women are for the sake of their more distinctive human faculties. Indeed, not only are the natural substances designed; they are likewise *self*-designed

(*Phys.* 2.8.199a27–31), for it is by a teleological potency intrinsic to each by virtue of its S-matter that it has its constitutive S-form.

Now, given that the geometry is merely quasi-anatomical, may the like not be true of the dynamics? Is the latter more than merely quasi-teleological? Well, certainly physics does not feature for Aristotle as a branch of psychology any more than it does as a branch of anatomy. Quite to the contrary. In his system of classification the subject-matter of the natural sciences belongs to a hierarchically ordered hylomorphic continuum. On this conception it is the continuum as a whole that is the subject-matter of physics proper, i.e. of the study of nature. The respective subject-matters of the more special sciences, e.g. anatomy and psychology, are mere segments. Contrariwise, the psychological segment does play a superior role within the hierarchy. In particular, the activation of ensouled substances by ends that are objects of desire – or of the sort of desire (if there is another sort) that involves the imaging or conscious projection of its object – provides a paradigm for the activation of the natural behaviour of natural substances in general. Likewise, the potency that certain types of ensouled substance have for being attracted to, or activated by, these ends serves as a paradigm for the hylomorphically more primitive potencies of other natural substances as well.

Aristotle's dynamics, accordingly, is more than just quasi-teleological. He claims more than that natural substances other than those that are ensouled behave, or merely in some respects are, *as if* they were attracted by ends. Were that not so, he would have had to have had the possibility of some non-teleological account of natural behaviour and natural structure in mind. Thus he might have supposed the seemingly teleological behaviour of natural substances to be reducible to mechanistically determined behaviour of their more basic parts. But there is no evidence that he toyed with any such possibility. First, his differentiation between four types of cause, material, efficient, formal, and final, is between factors that work in conjunction with each other. Thus in particular the operation of an efficient cause is not conceived of as independent of some final cause, i.e. as mechanistic rather than as towards an end. Second, in his system there is nothing more basic than the elements, and their behaviour is just as teleological as anything less elemental. Third, in that system likewise the relatively more complex natural substances are not exhaustively determined either in behaviour or in structure by the ends that are specific to the constituent elements.

True, he is willing to deny that rain is something sent by Zeus in order to make the corn grow, and to agree instead that it comes of necessity (*Phys.* 2.8.198b16–20). But here his concern is to distinguish what in part is just coincidence from what is determined by an end. That the rain happens to fit in with the farmer's plans is not why it occurs. Nevertheless, the necessity by which it occurs is consistent with its being determined by some end, if not by one that is agricultural. Indeed, rain for Aristotle is just a phase in the cyclical transmutation in which the elements strive as best they can towards the nature of the Prime Mover.

Even so – even if his dynamics is truly teleological – need it on that count be anthropomorphic? Is it only through the mediation of desire in conjunction with the imaging or conscious projection of ends that behaviour or structure can be truly teleological? Surely certain teleological descriptions or explanations of non-conscious structures and behaviour are perfectly legitimate. The heart really does beat in order to maintain a flow of blood through its chambers and to supply nourishment to other organs; the teeth really do have the formation they have to enable the animal to chew; and so on. Apparently, then, one should distinguish between two types of teleological phenomena, i.e. the functional and the purposive (Woodfield, 1976), on the basis that consciousness, desire, and volition are specific to the latter alone. If so, may Aristotle not have made, at least implicitly, the same distinction too?

At one point (*Phys.* 2.8.200a15–30), indeed, it may seem that he did. His general analysis of teleological determination is in terms of a notion of necessity – and hence, it may seem, in topic-neutral terms that are free from all anthropomorphic taint. More specifically, it may appear to be in terms of causal interrelationships between certain factors without any apparent indication whether any of these factors is psychological. What comes before as a means is, on this account, necessitated by the end that comes after, just as the antecedent hypothesis that the sides of a given triangle are straight necessitates the consequent that the sum of the interior angles is equal to two right angles – *only in reverse*. In scholastic jargon, determination by ends is *a fronte* as opposed to *a tergo*.

Understood, however, as a general analysis in topic-neutral terms, this account is glaringly defective. Perhaps with suitable provisos it could be interpreted as giving a sufficient condition of what it is for something to behave or to have a certain property for an end, but it does not give a necessary condition. It fails to acknowledge that behaviour or design that is for an end may in some cases not fulfil its purpose. Consequently, Aristotle's account is inadequate at least as an analysis of the purposive form of teleology.

Nevertheless, as taken in the context of his whole hylomorphic system his notion of necessity is, I submit, far from topic-neutral –

or if it is indeed topic-neutral, then so is that of the soul and its desires. In other words, the necessitation is not some sort of skeletal Humean-type relation extrinsic to the factors it connects. It is, on the contrary, something that coincides in its more completely fulfilled or least mediated realization with the sort of desire that operates in upper echelons of the hylomorphic scale. In this region it is not a connection between one term, i.e. an end, and another, e.g. an action, when mediated by a third, i.e. a desire consciously directed at that end. On the contrary, the connection *is* that desire. His mathematical analogy confirms this interpretation. The relation between the straightness of the triangle's sides and the sum of its interior angles is internal to that relation's terms. Comparably internal, then, for Aristotle is the relation between an action and its end. While the former relation may be more binding than the latter, the important point of similarity is that, due to the internality, the latter no more than the former is topic-neutral.

The distinction between functional and purposive forms of teleology may, perhaps, suggest an alternative interpretation. Implicitly, at least, may Aristotle not have taken the functional non-purposive form to be merely *quasi* purposive? Well, unless one means to allege that some discontinuity in his hylomorphic continuum is intended, there is no harm in supposing that he did. In other words, the supposition might be regarded as consistent with my thesis that his lower echelon is just a lesser realization of his upper-echelon dynamics. Otherwise it seems mistaken. It would credit Aristotle with the belief that some non-teleological form of dynamics might underlie the quasi-purposive form. For this, as I have already remarked, there is no evidence whatever. Furthermore, it would seem to suggest that he was merely pointing to certain superficial similarities between truly purposive behaviour and the behaviour of certain non-conscious natural substances. But so far as I have been able to determine Aristotle offers no such behavioural criteria. If he had, they would presumably have to consist of, or include, the behavioural criterion sometimes described as plasticity (Braithwaite, 1956). Thus, that a sunflower does not rigidly face in one direction but normally turns towards the dominant source of light, from whatever quarter that may come, is taken to indicate that it is facing in a certain direction in order to receive the maximum possible light. However, Aristotle can attribute no such plasticity to the celestial motions. He regards these as necessary, and yet he regards them as for ends.

In no part, then, is Aristotle's dynamics merely quasi-teleological. On the contrary, it envisions a sort of teleological continuum within which the operation of consciously directed desire serves as the fullest but not the sole realization of purposive determination. That strikes me, at least, as the most plausible interpretative hypothesis. Accordingly, by the standards of current scientific orthodoxy as set by particle theory, molecular biology, and Darwinianism — if the vexatious question of the anthropic principle is set aside — the charge of anthropomorphism against his dynamics appears just.

Nevertheless, why not concede the benefit of doubt? There are admittedly very few passages in which Aristotle makes quite explicit attributions of desire, soul, or life to the lower-echelon natural substances. Richard Sorabji dismisses these as "most of them no more than conscious echoes from the phrases of his predecessors, rather than independent formulations of his viewpoint" (1980, 164). I maintain, on the contrary, that even if *in toto* the scarcity and manner of these attributions were to bear this interpretation, they jibe as well with mine, viz. that what operates in the lower echelons is a less complete realization of the teleological causation that operates at the conscious levels. On neither interpretation should they be taken quite at face value. Nevertheless, and once again, why do I not give Aristotle the benefit of the doubt? In part because I want to give him credit for something else.

There are two opposing attitudes towards the notion of causation. Which comes to the fore depends upon whether the primary interest is or is not in that notion's epistemolgical role. One may limit oneself to inquiring how the notion can underpin the rational conduct of such epistemic activities as inference, expectation, prediction, generalization, and explanation. In that case one may be driven, like Hume, to analyse the notion either in terms of the criteria for its application (e.g. constant conjunction) in these activities or in terms specific to the activities themselves (e.g. feelings of expectation). The tendency of certain commentators, of whom Sorabji is one (see also Charlton, 1970, xvi and 101), to elucidate Aristotle's four types of cause in terms of their explanatory role is an example of this limited approach, particularly in the second of its two alternative forms. But causes are also determinants of behaviour and structure as well as bases for the explanation of what they determine. In this aspect they have an ontological as well as an explanatory, i.e. an epistemological, role. In other words they have a role as constitutive in some way of non-arbitrary thinghood or being. Now, while wearing his hat as a first philosopher or metaphysician as distinct from a zoologist or botanist, this is the role that Aristotle is primarily concerned to investigate. Thus while dealing with teleological causation he is dealing with ends as determinants as well as, through not to the exclusion of their also being, providers of explanations. Hence, the teleological continuity throughout his hylomorphic continuum must be a continuity in manner of determination.

Given, then, that Aristotle's anthropomorphism affects the determining as well as the explanatory aspect of the notion of causation, what redounds to his credit is the interesting implication that causal determination is something of which we are directly aware in our consciously directed purposive behaviour. It is presumably true that the causality manifest in that behaviour is not related to the causality manifest elsewhere in the way he took it to be. As, however, we shall eventually see, that need not prevent the two from being related in some other way that is consistent with our awareness of causal determination in general through the immediacy of our awareness of it in ourselves.

5.2 ARISTOTLE'S
SOUL-ARCHITECTURE

Aristotle's views on psychological structure are fundamentally misleading. That he broadly ascribes a type of soul to botanical as well as to zoological or other biological species can perhaps be condoned. True, it poses a dilemma – through one he could hardly anticipate. Let us suppose that human intelligence and self-control can be well enough simulated and even surpassed by the capacity of some construct of silicon chips or laser beams, etc. Are we then to deny psychological faculties to such machines on the ground that they are lifeless or to say that they have life on the ground that they have psychological faculties? That, however, is a relatively piddling issue. If by definition, or by the linguistic convention of his time and place, psychology and biology are made to coincide, we can only quarrel with the convenience of that identification.

More contentiously, his structural analysis in terms of faculties puts into question the unity of the soul – at least at the higher biological levels. The soul, no doubt, is in some sense a congeries of faculties – and particularly at the zoological level – if only because faculty-language and talk of soul-parts is overtly or covertly too deeply embedded in how we distinguish between various psychological activities to be either completely nonsensical or conveniently exorcised, if exorcism were otherwise desirable.[2] If under one interpretation the customary language is misrepresentative, then perhaps we should try harder to interpret it more aptly. In fairness to Aristotle, furthermore, that is exactly what he set out to do. Soul-partitioning was far from being his invention, if it is an invention at all. For him as for us it had already insinuated itself as a customary mode of representation – a mode, indeed, of which he was explicitly mistrustful. He evidently saw that unity in the soul is in some way more intimate than in certain other types of whole, that the diversity in the one is quite unlike that in those others; and his effort to vindicate that insight is at least instructive.

It is, of course, to some degree doubtful whether anybody's soul is a complete unity. As Aldous Huxley has astutely remarked (1952), on the basis of the seventeeth-century view that the soul is indivisible the hysterical behaviour of the Ursuline nuns of Loudon could only be understood by their contemporaries as either faked or the result of demonic possession. I discuss the sort of issue this raises more fully in chapter 7. Here, however, it is not particularly relevant. While it would be correct enough in some sense to say that the nuns were not completely in possession of all their faculties, my present concern is with what unites those of one's faculties one does happen to possess. Altogether two features of this unity have to be reconciled. On the one hand, the faculties are part of the soul. On the other, they belong as directly to the individual form of life that the soul ensouls as the soul of which they are the parts. How, then, can this be?

The main emphasis of Aristotle's answer is on a vertical stacking of faculties in a one-way relation of functional dependence. Within this stacking each member is conceived as a power. Powers that by themselves constitute the vegetal soul of plants, i.e. the nutritive and reproductive, combine with other powers, i.e. those that are specific to the capacity for self-locomotion, to constitute the zoological soul of animals. It is likewise with the faculties that are specific at one or more levels to the capacity for self-locomotion, i.e. with the faculties of desire, sense, imagery, and memory. These combine with the ratiocinative to constitute various capacities for rational conduct, particularly as in the human species. The latter, then, in turn from a basis for the purely theoretical faculties that culminate in the final contemplative faculty of the first philosopher. In sum, the powers that ensoul the higher forms of life are functionally dependent on those that ensoul the lower. Hence both the soul and its parts belong directly to what is ensouled somewhat as a column of cups may rest on the same saucer.

As it stands, however, this account is incomplete. At different stages in the vertical stacking certain same-level or horizontal combinations of faculties intervene. These faculties, too, Aristotle regards as distinguishable powers. But of these it is equally true that their components belong as directly to what is ensouled as to the soul that horizontally combines them. What explanation, then, can Aristotle give for that? Unfortunately nothing very explicit.

One tempting construction is that he took the relation of the soul to the faculties it horizontally combines to be that of S-form to S-matter. Thus the capacity for self-locomotion involves a complex relationship between members of the two sets of powers that I have earlier (see 4.3) distinguished as respectively sidelong and upward. The self-locomotive capacity as such is a sidelong power, i.e. the state *from* belongs to the same sort of determinable as the state *to* which it is a power for change. Nevertheless, it is constituted even at the very lowest zoological level by upward faculties or powers, i.e. at least by those of desire and sense. As powers these faculties are upward inasmuch as their bearers, e.g. when asleep or in a coma, need not be in any desiderative or sensory state at all. Perhaps, then, for Aristotle the sidelong power of self-locomotion is related to the relevant upward powers as S-form to S-matter.

The same sort of construction could also apply at the rational level. The constitutive upward faculties at the non-rational level do not go beyond those of desire, sense, imagination, and memory. At the rational level, however, a syllogistic and deliberative ability to apply rational formulae to particular cases supervenes. These formulae, according to the purpose of desire of the being empowered, can be applied in any of several opposing ways that lead respectively to different courses of action (*Meta.* Θ2.1046bff). Thus the doctor, though effectively qualified by his ability to apply the rational formulae supplied by the medical art for the purpose of healing, is thereby equally well qualified to secure a patient's more rapid demise.

Consequently, at this level, and with the addition of this deliberative power, the upward powers qualify as S-matter to a superior type of self-locomotive capacity, viz. the rational capacity for choice. Deliberation creates the condition for and necessitates choice through the discovery of means to ends. These ends, at least typically, are determined by the agent's non-rational desires. But in the rather limited number of situations in which any one of these desires could operate and be satisfied without deliberation, e.g. as thirst by the Duke of Clarence in his butt of Malmsey wine, the action thereby motivated is merely *voluntary*. Where, in contrast, deliberation does take place, the action actualizes the superior power of deliberative choice. For Aristotle, of course, that does not imply that the non-rational desire plays no part in the motivation. But the additional component of deliberation brings it about that it is only as one among a company of at least possible competitors that the non-rational desire is satisfied. Even if the chosen action is determined by the dominance of a non-rational desire, it is deliberation that unites the totality of an agent's desires into the sort of community within which one desire can dominate.

I am not put out by the consideration that, on Aristotle's more official view at least, the cleavage between sidelong and upward powers seems to run in the contrary direction. The upward power of the intellect plays the role of form in relation to characteristics such as the various powers for movement in the role of matter. To the detriment of coherence, as we have earlier seen, Aristotle imposes an absolutist or semi-Cartesian conception of the matter-form distinction upon one that is relativistic. More detrimental to the reconciliatory construction is a further consideration. Whether we characterize the unity of faculties at the one level in hylomorphic terms as just proposed or not, on the assumption that these faculties are distinct types of power their unity would have to be one of functional *interdependence* between powers. But, as I am about to argue, the relation of functional interdependence is even less adequate for the purpose of faculty unification than that of one-way functional dependence.

Consider first the diversity of powers or functions that pertains to the components of a house or a state taken as a unit or whole. This diversity too is, at least in part, same-level or horizontal, and its unity as such consists of a functional interdependence between component powers. However, the powers or functions thus diversified all pertain more directly to the separable parts of the unit than to the unit as a whole, e.g. to bricks, mortar, beams, and joists, etc., in the house, and to artisans, tradesmen, merchants, clerks, doctors, lawyers, and teachers, etc., in the state. Notice, furthermore, that parts such as these all possess a certain measure of existential independence. A brick need not be in a structure. A citizen may survive as a Crusoe. Hence in these two models the requirement that the several powers that are unified horizontally under an umbrella power belong as directly to the whole as does the umbrella power itself is not met.

The Platonic conception of the soul as writ large in the state had a slightly different application from the one I consider here. Plato was as much concerned with the disunity as with the unity of distinguishable soul-components, and more particularly with the relation between different types of desire. Nevertheless, it is instructive to note that even in this slightly different application the analogy of the state is inadequate, and for the reason we have already encountered. Even when our desires are at odds with each other they belong as directly to us as does the soul of which they feature as constituents.

Take, then, a living plant as an alternative model. Up to a point, indeed, this is more than a model. For Aristotle it is in its own right a case of ensoulment. But can it serve as model for same-level unity

at the more elevated biological levels? At the purely botanical level
the nutritive and the reproductive faculties contribute in their interdependent way to the power of vegetal life belonging to the plant
as a whole. The organs upon which these faculties are specifically
dependent, e.g. the roots and the flower, are organically interdependent, though not quite as neatly as, say, heart and stomach in
animals. The reproductive depend on the ingestive and digestive
organs for their continued functioning, and the ingestive and digestive organs depend on the reproductive organs, at least for their
reproduction in subsequent members of the same species. Here
again, however, these separate powers belong more directly to parts
of the plant than to the plant as a whole. The reproductive functions
belong to the floral structure and the nutritive to the roots. Of course,
in so far as these parts are to some extent dependent for their
existence on each other, a power that is specific to a part might be
said to belong directly to the whole as well. But this difference between the parts of a biological whole and the parts of a house or a
state is no more than one of degree. Each part could exist without
the other for a while before succumbing to atrophy or decay.

I conclude, accordingly, that with one exception the interdependence of distinguishable faculties at the same level is not the functional sort of interdependence between interactive causal powers.
Indeed, what I have classed as upward powers cannot be powers at
all. If they were, their interdependence would be of the functional
type. The exception is the interdependence of the nutritive and
reproductive faculties at the vegetal level. That is indeed functional
and between interactive causal powers, but then for that very reason
it is not between soul-faculties at all.

For Aristotle, however, this exception is no exception. Instead it
belongs to the lowest level of a set of horizontal interdependencies
that differentiate different soul-levels. Hence my conclusion, that
the interdependence of soul-faculties at the same level is not the
functional sort of interdependence that holds between interactive
causal powers, runs counter to what he at least strongly suggests.
Furthermore, it runs counter to contemporary forms of function-
alism, which give that suggestion its further longevity. One can give
functionalist descriptions of parts of the brain and their activities.[3]
Indeed, such descriptions are likely to be more useful and explanatory than any attempt at more refined description in more ultimate
microphysical terms. But these descriptions, just because they describe the interdependent functions of parts within a total ensemble,
are not psychological descriptions. Conversely, psychological descriptions of the activities of our various psychological faculties are

not functional descriptions, because the activities they describe are not realizations of interdependent causal powers that belong to different parts of that which is ensouled. On the contrary, and to repeat, they belong as directly to the conscious being as does the soul of which in some sense they are part.

The rest of this section is more constructive. To see what the above-mentioned sense might be, let us look more attentively at some of the ways in which our psychological faculties divide. These divisions include

1 desires as opposed to sense, memory, imagination, and even thought;
2 sense, memory, and imagination as opposed to thought;
3 judgment or understanding as opposed to deliberation;
4 deliberation as opposed to desire.

Between the faculties thus divided there are very intimate connections indeed. But, as we are about to see, this intimacy is one of internal relationship, viz. logical rather than causal.

As I have already insisted, there is an essential connection between desire and conscious or imaginative projection. It is upon this projection that the teleological directedness essential to desire depends. But further, any desire that has a practical bearing upon the here and now, any present desire that might motivate action in the present, must surely require sensory perception for its essential reference to the current situation. The desire is for some imaginatively projected state relating to some *this*. Then again, desires that are for the repetition or avoidance of some past state of affairs must invoke memory. Likewise, desires that are quite general, that provide us with some rule for how to comport ourselves in a variety of situations or to control the variety in which we successively find ourselves, require fairly abstract thought. Such are the desires for pleasure, or health, or knowledge in general, as opposed say to the desire to suck this popsicle, or to recover from this cold, or to find what is behind this door.

But the internal relation between desiring and the cognitive faculties is even more intimate than this sort of consideration has yet suggested. That in part is because cognitive faculties are intimately connected with each other. In its epistemically most basic form thought, conceived as the faculty of judgment or understanding, is the sensing of sensible objects as characterized in certain ways either referentially alone, or predicationally as well.[4] Likewise the sensing of sensible objects is an activity of judgment or understanding in its most basic form. One sees or hears or feels that the horse is in the stable. Furthermore, this sensory referential characterization involves, at least typically, the ascription of powers to the object sensed. Therefore the sensings *as* must be more or less fused with the retention of past experiences on the basis of which these powers seem ascribable, and also with a conscious (if hypothetical) imaginative projection of the future, i.e. of what will happen by virtue of these powers under certain conditions. Hence to this extent desire is internally related to the various cognitive faculties, not just severally but in a lump, for these faculties are internally related to each other through the understanding.

These somewhat sketchy comments have been evoked by the first pair of distinctions. More would no doubt emerge from a more intensive scrutiny of that pair on its own. But rather than delay, let us extend the inquiry. A study of the second pair will reinforce our conclusion by showing that desire is internally related, not just to judgment or understanding, but to deliberation as well.

Judgment or understanding may occur where deliberation does not. That is because the latter is an inferential process, whereas the former need not be. Or perhaps, more cautiously, the latter is a thought-process that typically involves inference, whereas the former, though a form of thought, need not be a process at all. Deliberation, for its part, cannot occur without judgment or understanding. Thus, if we accept from Aristotle that it is a more or less explicit process of a syllogistic kind, it would typically require (1) a casting around for relevant premisses, (2) the entertainment of or commitment to some of these, (3) the seeing what conclusions follow therefrom, and (4) the entertainment of or commitment to a conclusion. Hence some kind of process takes place in the first and third step, whereas in the second and fourth there may be none. Yet what takes place at every stage is a form of judgment or understanding.

Now, that desire in its occasion-bound form is internally related to some judgment or understanding of a situation to which it is bound would seem relatively uncontroversial. Without such judgment, we have seen, the desire could not have the focus it requires directly to motivate action. This focus will result either from deliberation or immediate judgment, though the distinction between the two may not always be easy to draw. With desires that are occasion-loose, however, the issue may initially seem more open. Aristotle's syllogistic conception of deliberation may suggest that such desires are externally related to judgment or understanding, at least in its deliberative form. Just as believability is transferred from an independently believable major premiss to a conclusion with the help of an independently believable minor premiss, so likewise attractiveness or desirability is transferred from some independently attractive end set by some independently desiderative potency of a general kind to a situation that the conclusion indicates as currently practicable.

Thus, from a primary major premiss that dry food is healthy, in conjunction with the secondary major premiss that chicken is dry food, the discovery as a minor premiss that this hapless fowl is a chicken leads to the conclusion that the consumption of it will promote health. Given, then, that to be healthy is for you a general end, i.e. that you have an occasion-loose desire for health, this conclusion may in the absence of countervailing considerations seal the chicken's fate through a valetudinarian choice. An occasion-bound desire to eat the chicken may have dominance over any other occasion-bound desire that might compete for execution.

However, a syllogistic inference may be employed in its purely theoretical aspect either as a method of proof or as a component in a hypothetico-deductive process of discovery. In the former case the ultimate premisses are taken as axiomatic. In the latter they are not taken as independently believable. Rather they are confirmed or disconfirmed to some degree by the eventual believability or otherwise of the conclusion. Something similar is true for the process of deliberation in its teleological desiderative aspect. The attractiveness of certain general states of affairs may be discovered through the discovery of the practicability of their realization on given occasions and the attractiveness thereof.

Thus the general principle that dry food is healthy is not just confirmed by the results of eating the chicken. Indeed, in the deliberative context the confirmation of such major premisses is not to the point. Rather, it is through the discovery of general prescriptions – aesthetic, medical, educative, social, political, etc. – that are practicable because of their generality on a variety of occasions, if not immediately applicable in every situation, that we are able to form and give focus to occasion-loose desires of the corresponding kind.

Distinctions between types of desires depend, obviously enough, upon distinctions between types of end. But the latter depend very much upon what external circumstances on different occasions allow or preclude as conjointly realisable.[5] Hence the community of potentially competitive desires to members of which a person may give allegiance may vary according to geography, climate, prevalent technology, and, more generally, social culture. Thus at one time or other such activities as horse-riding, sailing, archery, and fencing functioned primarily as applications of a technology directed at military or mercantile or other ends. Now that more efficient technologies have been developed towards these same ends – or perhaps, we should say, towards contemporary counterparts of these same ends – such activities may linger on as ends themselves, i.e. as sport. Indeed, it would be more accurate to say that, to some extent at least, with the development of new technologies, new types of distinctions between means and ends arise. The conservative soldier may lose interest in battle once the horse is phased out by the tank, or the tank by some remotely controlled robot. Likewise, for the merchant seaman the demise of the clipper may have taken the soul out of trade.

It is true, in a way, that one does not desire exclusively within one's means in a sense. Desires are not governed exclusively by considerations of immediate or even eventual practicability. What, however, these preceding considerations would seem to show is that a certain persistent constancy in the repertoire of our desires is inseparable from a constancy in the type of external circumstance in which a desire's possessor is typically or quite regularly to be found. That in turn brings out the internal relationship between having the desire and understanding external circumstances, whether the desiring and the understanding are occasion-loose or occasion-bound.

Nor again, is it to be denied that certain types of desire are more independent of external circumstance than others, and that these are to be had occasion-loosely. No matter how varied the time, clime, or society, people seem to have them. Examples are the bodily appetites such as the desire for drink, food, and sex. These appetites or desires are in fact innate, and their occurrence or recurrence is largely the product of rhythms of the metabolism. They are due to a less extent to promptings from outside.

None the less, it is also true that the bodily appetites have evolved in the course of generation upon generation of interaction between species of organism and their environments. Hence, though their occurrence and recurrence are to a significant extent independent of the environment, they presuppose genetically a certain constancy therein, e.g. the prevalence of food, drink, and sexual partners. Furthermore, the appetites in themselves are the basis of desire rather than desires in their own right. They are malleable and comparatively directionless cravings that acquire their focus upon such ends as the consumption of food and drink and sexual activity through learning. We have to discover those fairly constant or recurrent features in our environment in the interaction with which the physiological bases of our appetites have evolved. In lower forms of life the response to such recurrent features may be instinctive and unlearned, but then we have no basis for supposing that it has any conscious focus at all. In our case, in contrast, though an appetite is more dependent on metabolic rhythms of the body for its arousal than is any other type of desire, the very distinguishability of one appetite from another would seem dependent upon the organism's ability to make discriminatory and conscious responses to an environment's discriminable features. Thus, presumably, the baby at its mother's breast has still to learn the distinction between thirst and hunger – a distinction that it will later learn only in the course of making discriminatory responses respectively to liquid and solid nourishment.

I shall return to the subject of the internal relationship between faculties in chapter 6, but in the meantime one caveat. I have not denied that the faculty of desire, or any other psychological faculty for that matter, is a causal power when taken in its variable conjunction within a complete quota of faculties. In other words, I have not denied that the soul, as consisting of a complete quota of psychological faculties, is a causal power of a sort. I have merely been arguing that the relation between faculties within the soul is not between interactive or functionally interdependent causal powers.

5.3   THREE METHODS ON TRIAL

In 2.3 the normal view of substance as mutable found absolution from an ancient slur. Thanks mainly to the Special Theory of Being, as revised in chapter 1, the charge of incoherence was rebutted. Then in 2.4 a more complicated and controversial issue took over. This came in two parts. Its first concern was whether there could be any non-arbitrary basis for the essence-accident sorts of contrast upon which the identity of mutable substances depends. Its second concern, given that basis, was whether that sort of contrast would be ontologically mandatory as well, i.e. whether reality is inherently mutable in at least some of its components. My purpose for the moment is not to settle this issue but simply to place as briefly as possible three methods for doing so on probation. One method is pragmatic, a second is transcendental or Kantian, and the third conforms to the Path to Enlightenment and Integrative Program as initiated by Aristotle. I hope eventually to redeem what is exemplary in his initiative from its compromising flaws.

Of the two concerns, clearly the second is the more crucial. One might find a non-arbitrary way for drawing the essence-accident contrast, and hence for identifying subjects of change, without convincing oneself either that the contrast was mandatory or that basic particulars of reality are inherently mutable. One might perhaps subscribe to the hylomorphic dynamics of chapter 3 without feeling obliged to make the further ontological commitment. However, the same does not hold for the doctrine of first causes in chapter 4. True, it makes no explicit distinction between the question's two concerns. But it does make – at least in principle – the further commitment the dynamics may seem to avoid.

To bring the issue into sharper focus, consider the distinction between a mutable substance and its mutations and non-mutations, i.e. its distinction from events (for our present purpose the term "event," its equivalents, and congenors are to be used where necessary with ontological neutrality). If we set aside mass-substance, mutable substance is characteristically conceived as spatially extended in a fairly definite way. Or at least – not to preclude the possibility of spiritual substance prematurely – the definiteness of spatial extension can be taken as a paradigm. Events, for their part, are indefinite in spatial extension (Kim, 1966; Hacker, 1982) – at least where conceived as the mutations or non-mutations of mutables. They borrow whatever definite spatial extension they have from that of the mutable substance they involve.

This difference depends on a more profound, or more abstract, difference between the ways in which mutables and these events are respectively propertied at any point in time. (The greater abstractness leaves room for spiritual mutables, if you want them.) In a sense mutables instantiate properties thickly, whereas events instantiate them relatively thinly – if they can be said to instantiate properties at all. In other words, a mutable has to coinstantiate at any instant some complete quota of logically and physically complementary determinables, e.g. volume, shape, mass, colour, etc. These determinables would seem to be complementary in the sense that it is physically and logically impossible for matter to instantiate a determinate under one of the determinables without coinstantiating determinates from all the rest. Events, on the other hand, may just consist of the successive instantiations of the same or contrary determinates specific to the same one among a set of complementary determinables.

Thus the successive instantiation by an object first of s^1, then of s^2, where these are contrary shapes, is enough to constitute an event. Likewise, the successive instantiation by the same object of v^1, then of v^2, where these are contrary volumes, is enough to constitute an event distinguishable from the first, even where s^1 is coinstantiated simultaneously with v^1, and s^2 with v^2. The successive instantiation by the same object first of s^1, then of v^2, or first of v^1, then of s^2, is not enough, however, to constitute an event. Now since the spatial extent of anything consists both of its volume and shape, it would seem that the two single events in our illustration have spatial extention from instant to instant only indirectly, i.e. through the coinstantiation from instant to instant of determinates of these two complementary determinables by the same mutables. The two events do not have definite spatial extension in themselves.

There are, of course, more complex events than these. Some consist of the conjoint behaviour of more than one mutable. Others, in some ways simpler, are of more concern here. They consist of the successive coinstantiation of complementary determinates that together are sufficient to fall under the determinable of spatial extension by the *same* mutable. One example of the latter kind would be the changes that occur as a deflated inner tube assumes through inflation the volume and shape of the supporting walls of an outer tire. In some cases, as in this one, there would seem, furthermore, to be non-arbitrary grounds for regarding such events as single, albeit complex. Thus the tube-inflation has an assignable unitary cause, i.e. the pumping of air into the tube, and an assignable unitary result, i.e. the supporting of the outer tire's walls. Accordingly, it would seem that there are cases, after all, of single events that have a definite spatial extent from instant to instant in their own right. Indeed it would seem conceivable that some events directly instantiate properties just as thickly as does mutable substance.

None the less, one must insist that such events are complex in some way even while single, and also that the complexity is no more arbitrary than is the singleness. They have to be conceived either as complexes of concurrently successive instantiations of simple determinates of at least two complementary simple determinables, or as successive simple instantiations of complex determinables, or as both, if here we have a distinction without a difference. More briefly, they have to be conceived either as complex event-tokens composed of simple event-tokens or as simple event-tokens instantiating complex event-types, or as both. Thus, to make a definite choice for our example, the inflation of the inner tube seems to be the more perspicuously conceived as a complex of event-tokens. The reason is that not merely do the changes in volume and shape have a common cause, but the change in the volume is the more direct cause of the change in the shape. Surely the effect of an event-token must be a separate event-token from its cause.

But whatever analysis we give to the complexity of such events, the non-arbitrary nature of the complexity has to be granted. It would be idle to distinguish within the more comprehensive determinable of spatial extent between volume and shape were it not that a difference in the spatial extent of things may constitute a difference in their causal properties according to whether the difference is in volume or in shape or in both. Thus two things of the same shape but different volumes will displace different volumes of water, whereas if they had been of different shape but the same volume they ordinarily would not. Likewise changes in the spatial extent of a thing will yield different results according to whether the change is in volume or in shape.

Accordingly, the contrast between mutable substance and events in terms of a relative thickness of instantiation still holds. A mutable substance instantiates properties thickly whether it is simple or complex – though the type of property it can instantiate may depend upon its degree of complexity. Events, on the other hand, if they instantiate thickly at all, do so only if they are complex.

The superiority in spatial definiteness that thus results for a mutable substance is, however, the complement of an inferiority in temporal definiteness. The reason will not fully emerge until 8.1, but connects with two factors we can already mention.

Inherently in the substance at any instant there is no more than a potency for a subsequent history of any specific period of time, for its subsequent history depends in part on extrinsic conditions. Thus the potency of a descending missile at any given instant to terminate explosively at some particular later instant may partly depend upon its position at the earlier instant relative to the target at which it is aimed. Further, no antecedent history of any very definite period of time is required as the condition for the mutable's potency at an instant for a specific subsequent history. Thus the missile's potency at the earlier instant for exploding at the later is conditioned by the angle and velocity of its fall at the earlier instant. That it should have been launched so many seconds or minutes before from a certain location is not essential.

The fairly definite period of time that pertains to some mutable is, then, on par with the fairly definite extension in space that pertains to an event. Temporal definiteness is borrowed by the mutable from the totality of events that form its history, just as the spatial definiteness is borrowed by events from the mutables they involve.

Finally, to complete these comparisons, the indefiniteness of a mutable's temporal duration has a consequence for the durational definiteness of an event. The fairly definite period of time that pertains to an event is conceived not just as fairly definite but (except in the case of change at an instant) as being completed in successive stages. Events are ordinarily conceived as things that happen or occur or take place; and their happening, etc., is just this cumulative, stage-by-stage completion, until in the fullness of time they have happened. Thus the unsegmented line in Diagram 1 (b) only represents the fairly definite temporal extension of an event, whereas the segmented line in (a) represents the further cumulative stage-by-stage manner in which the event is characteristically conceived. Here the segmenting arrowheads indicate both the inclusion of one stage in later stages and also the direction of time.

That, characteristically, events are so conceived would seem due to our characteristically supposing that, at any instant in an event, what remains of the event thereafter is merely a potentiality of the mutable substance involved, whereas that which has gone before is to some extent that which determines that which is then potentially thereafter as potentially thereafter. There is, in contrast, nothing comparable in the structure of the fairly definite spatial extension that constitutes mutable substance.

We now are ready to pose the crucial question with more precision than before. Characteristically substance is conceived as mutable, and thus distinguished from events or from what mutable substance does or undergoes. In other words it is conceived characteristically as fairly definite in spatial but not in temporal extent, except in the latter case indirectly, and as thickly propertied, even in its simplest form. As such it is distinguishable from events, for the latter are characteristically conceived in the simplest form as fairly definite in temporal but not in spatial extent, except in the latter case indirectly, as thinly propertied, and as cumulatively structured in their fairly definite temporal extent in a way with no spatial analogue. But why not conceive substance instead as combining all the more determinate aspects of mutable substance and of events? Why not conceive it as fairly definite in its own right both in spatial and temporal extent, as thickly propertied, and as not cumulatively structured, not even in temporal extent?

Thus we might no longer think of the most basic particulars in terms of some mutable object M being engaged in a number of simple concurrent events e^1, e^2, e^3, etc., by becoming or remaining simultaneously s^1 (a shape-predicative), v^2 (a volume-predicative), and c^5 (a colour-predicative), etc., at, say, t^3, where s^1 and v^2 are holistic predicatives that M has to be as whole, and c^5 a non-holistic predicative that M can be in part of itself alone. Instead we might think of the most basic particulars as exemplified in a composite non-mutable entity NM (call it, if you like, a space-time worm or an EVENT, as distinct from an event), which is not subject to the characteristic restrictions. This entity NM, let us suppose, is likewise s^1,

Diagram 1

(a)   (b)

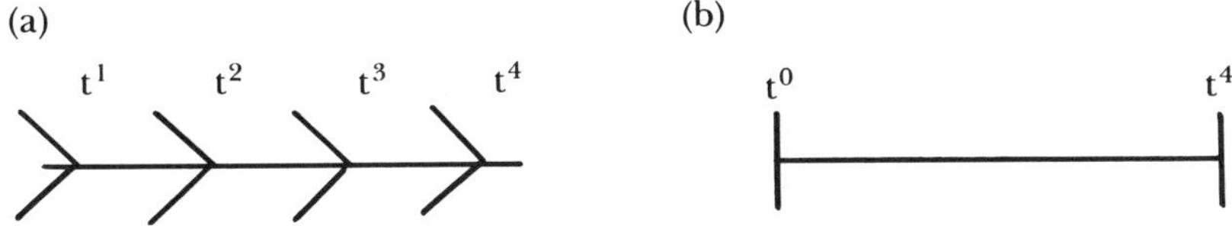

v^2, and c^5, etc., at t^3. Here, however, the being s^1 and v^2 are no more holistic relative to NM than c^5 is relative to M, and t^3 is not the terminus of any stage. On this way of conceiving NM, its being s^1 or v^2 at t^3 is analogous to M's being c^5 at a place p^3 on its surface, but with an important difference. M's being c^5 at a place p^3 is relativized to some time or other such as t^3. NM's being s^1 and v^2 at t^3, in contrast, is not relativized to any further time or to anything, etc., but is timeless. Hence the non-mutability of NM.

This amalgamation, of course, can only be achieved by discounting in some way the applicability of the notion of potency upon which the distinction between mutable substance and its behaviour depends. Perhaps, however, a discounting of that applicability may seem in order. According, at least, to the deterministic variety of mechanism or of teleology, the occasion-bound potency of mutable substance at a specific instant must amount to a necessity. In other words, what exactly the mutable does or undergoes after that instant must happen, given what it and other mutables as well have done or undergone beforehand. In fact the whole of history has been determined from whatever time you can care to take as a start. Furthermore, from the point of view of the most rigorous form of determinism, what any mutable does or undergoes before is just as strictly determined by what it and other mutables do or undergo after. Accordingly, on such premisses neither the temporal indefiniteness characteristically attributed to substance nor the cumulative structure characteristically attributed to events will seem attributable to anything that is basically real. These limitations we impose upon substance would have to be extrinsic in some way, e.g. mere limitations upon what we can know about basic particulars at any particular instant of time.

Given, then, that there is such a thing as temporal substance, it would seem that either:

H1   the basic substance-particulars are inherently mutable; or
H2   they are inherently EVENT-like; or
H3   they are inherently neither one nor the other.

Which, then, of these three hypotheses, if any, is true? With this in clarification of our test-question, let us now compare some ways in which we might try to solve it.

The pragmatic method of justification relies on such criteria as consistency with environmental input or empirical data, self-consistency, explanatory comprehensiveness, and simplicity. Thus, in vindication of mutable particulars it might draw attention to the incremental nature of our perceptual knowledge or the empirical data we acquire from what happens in time – in short, to the fact that time is experienced as becoming. The emphasis here is upon consistency with immediate experience. Alternatively, in vindication of EVENTS it might rely upon the Minkowskian interpretation of the theory of relativity, for which reality is a four-dimensional spacetime structure. The emphasis here is upon the criterion of explanatory power or the comprehensiveness of the theory in question. However, theoretical structures that are built and justified on the basis of such criteria are beset by a well-documented failing. They are underdetermined by their evidential support. Even the incremental nature of experience might be discounted as due to an innate epistemic limitation. Alternatively, even if the theory of relativity is held sacrosanct, its Minkowskian interpretation might be questioned.

Consider next the so-called transcendental or Kantian method of justification. The first of these descriptions does little more than commemorate the opacity of the method's Kantian origin. The suffix *-al* adds something to the adjective "transcendent" the full chemistry of which is not quite certain. Furthermore, the attribution of the method as now so described to Kant is a bit misleading. Kant's method strikes me as more of a half-way house between this second method and the third.[6] But in any case, whatever its connection with Kant, this second method works in a negative way. It seeks to show that the contradictory of the theory it sets out to justify is self-invalidating, i.e. that any attempt to refute or cast doubt upon that theory presupposes the latter's truth. As a contemporary example take Putnam's recent (1981) counter to a referential form of philosophical scepticism. He argues that if we were just artificially stimulated brains in a vat it would be logically impossible for us even to entertain the thought that that is just what we might be. Apparently, then, this second method is exempt from the defects of the first. The self-invalidating nature of a theory would seem justification enough of what that theory contradicts.

For better or for worse transcendental arguments these days win very few friends. For some, to box anyone at any time into a logical corner runs counter to the spirit of the Fifth Amendment. Others less pure in heart can also complain that all too often the corner leaves enough room between the ropes for your opponent to duck outside. The compulsion that the method exerts typically depends upon too many presuppositions that the theory under attack can disown. I, for my part, cannot devise a sufficiently compelling application in this particular context. If it were simply a matter of refuting H2, viz. that reality is inherently EVENT-like, the task might be comparatively simple. But, even were H2 shown to be false, H1, viz. that reality is inherently mutable, would not follow, for H1 is the contrary, not the contradictory, of H2. So far as I can see from my own abortive efforts, which I here suppress, the elimination of H3, viz. that reality is inherently neither mutable nor EVENT-like, as well as H2 would have to depend upon analyses of the notions of cause and time of the kind that I give in chapter 8. These analyses themselves require justification, and whether their justification could include transcendental arguments seems to me highly uncertain.

It is, however, on a different sort of complaint that I here want to fasten. It takes its cue from the method's Kantian antecedents. These suggest that what the transcendental method seeks to conserve is a conceptual scheme conceived as a sort of network spread over things-in-themselves as opposed to things as they appear to someone or other through that or some other network. As thus interpreted the conceptual scheme provides the structure of doxastic systems that are representative of an independent reality in a manner that is entirely *extrinsic* to the latter. Hence, all that the method is alleged to demonstrate at its best is the difficulty of dismantling such a scheme from inside. On this interpretation it cannot demonstrate the impossibility of some completely alternative equally extrinsic system of representations. Injudicious use may merely confirm the more deeply entrenched prejudices of some cultural establishment. Now whether these charges are well enough founded is not to my immediate point. What I here wish to emphasize is a deficiency that the transcendental and the pragmatic methods share, when left to their own devices. Neither on its own seems equipped against interpretations that discredit the evidence-providing cognitive activities upon which they depend.

Has Aristotle, then, anything better to offer? On the specific sort of question that he puts to the first philosopher I think that he has – at least, almost. For Kant the notion of a thing-in-itself is primarily epistemological rather than ontological. For Aristotle, however, it is more the reverse. If we first draw a distinction between the non-arbitrarily and the arbitrarily separable, his notion of a thing-in-itself is a notion of something within the former that is intrinsically as opposed to extrinsically separable. However, this ontological notion of his is not without an epistemological aspect as well. The existence of something, e.g. of enduring three-dimensional basic particulars (Strawson, 1959) or of brains in reliably sensitivized bodies (Putnam, 1981), is justified in the transcendental way by attempting to show that any contrary hypothesis is self-invalidating. For Aristotle, in contrast, the existence of what is intrinsically separable is justified in a more positive way by attempting to show that as a hypothesis it is self-validating or self-grounding. As we have seen, his way of doing this is to identify what is intrinsically separable with what has an intrinsic *this-ness*, i.e. with what is knowable by nature. In other words, what is intrinsically separable is the object of a reflexive awareness, by identity with that reflexive awareness.

At first sight, perhaps, Aristotle's customary procedure may seem closer to the pragmatic method of justification as outlined above. His investigations, particularly within first and second philosophy, take the deliberate form of a dialectical refinement or synthesis of the opinions held by the many and the wise. In this process all that he may seem to be trying to achieve is a coherent system that reduces the friction between these opinions to the minimum. To that extent, then, a premium seems to be placed on the pragmatic criterion of internal consistency or coherence.

Were that all, however, the method would fall to the obvious objection that the criterion of coherence merely checks one opinion or belief against others, without attention to whether any are independently worth epistemic respect. Of course, so long as the dialectical method is mainly applied where observational data are not in dispute, this objection loses some of its force, but only some. True, one need only count to determine which are the beliefs of the many, but there still is the further question of how to recognize among the few who hold the remainder those who are wise.

For Aristotle I believe the answer is that truth, if earnestly sought, will out. Given that some things are knowable by nature, these at least will make themselves known or declare themselves, if only one casts around. Seek for the ultimate reifying factor and, by a negative feedback sort of logic, ye shall eventually find. His basis for this assumption is his conception of the ultimate reifying factor as not merely intrinsically separable but also as a self-intimating activity that consists entirely in the contemplation of the sort, or of something akin to the sort, of activity that leads to its discovery.

On its own recognizance, then, this method of justification has an advantage over the other two. Left to their own resources they could offer no guarantee that their evidence-providing cognitive activities might not in some way be *misrepresentative* of what that evidence is evidence for. They tend to assume, or to permit the assumption, that the activity in question, whether it involves immediate experience (e.g. of temporal becoming) or the coherence of a set of beliefs or the restrictiveness of some conceptual scheme, is *extrinsically* representative of what it purports to represent. The Aristotelian method, in contrast, takes its evidence-providing cognitive activity to be *intrinsically* representative – at least if it makes the questionable assumption that cognition is primarily representative in function. In the final discovery of the ultimate reifying factor, the act of discovery or the contemplation of what it discovers is what is discovered.

That self-validation or self-grounding as thus conceived can ever be of much theoretical use may seem, however, none too clear. After all, the ultimate reifying factor is for Aristotle an immutable substance, i.e. the Prime Mover. Unlike any sublunar mutable this being comprises a definite temporal whole, viz. eternity. Unlike any EVENT, on the other hand, it is an activity in the sense that it is complete in any part of that eternity. But more to the immediate point are two distinctive cognitive features. First, its existence is given as an immediate datum only to itself. Second, the existence of nothing else would seem to be given, or even of interest, to it. Accordingly, the self-intimation of this sort of datum may not seem much use to us. Furthermore, the self-intimation of the ultimate reifying factor, whatever that factor may be, would seem to be of a purely referential and non-judgmental sort. Thus it may seem to present a bare datum with no further information about what the significance of that datum might be. In particular it may seem to do nothing to confirm the hylomorphic dynamics and doctrine of first causes that have led to its interpretation as first cause. Hence it may seem to contain no answer to our test-question, i.e. whether there really is anything inherently mutable.

In mitigation, however, the activity whereby men of science or first philosophers contemplate the essence of mutable things is an approximation to the self-intimation of the immutable's intrinsic thinghood. As we have seen, the former approximates as closely to the latter as in their various degrees the transparency of air or water and the incandescence of fire approximate to the eternal luminosity of the ether. Furthermore, my earlier exposition of these same analogies suggests that for Aristotle the referential sort of awareness to be found in the reflexive activity of intellectual contemplation is far removed from the quotidian sort we direct at the particular referents of, say, our perceptual beliefs. On the contrary, it is a higher or more refined or quintessential form of the activity whereby the first philosopher interprets being in terms of the hylomorphic dynamics and doctrine of first causes. Accordingly, as thus interpreted it lends its authority to the presuppositions of that dynamics and doctrine. Among other things it confirms the existence of inherently mutable things for the mutations of which it functions as first cause.

5.4 ARISTOTLE'S TRANSCENDENT COGITO

At this point a tribute is due. If not clearly the first to conceive or devise the more positive form of validation, Aristotle at the very least was the most level-headed and pragmatically accountable of its early practitioners. His dialectical sifting of the opinions of the many and the wise shows very clearly that the method of self-validation must defer to pragmatic criteria as well. Accordingly, it may seem a little churlish immediately to add, as hindsight and his accountability require, that in a historically fateful way his promotion of the procedure has failed by these criteria.

I have no quarrel with his locating the substantiality of all manner of substance in a form of a psychological nature. That much is basic to his method. Indeed, had he limited himself to identifying that form as the soul, and the latter as simply a potency of the body, I would be less grudging with praise. What that form would reify would have to be mutable, for only mutables have potency. That, then, would be enough to settle the question I have been posing as a test. As well, however, he associated the reifying form more abstractly with one *faculty* of the soul, viz. the intellect, by identifying it more narrowly with that faculty's activity. Then, to compound the mischief, he conceived it as immaterial, not just univocally in the innocuous sense that it is formal, but in the more portentous sense of being separable from the matter it informs – i.e. incorporeal and a substance in its own right.

When self-validation re-emerged as a method in the modern era, it was under the handicap of these presuppositions. To this extent the self-intimating subject of the Cartesian Cogito took the Aristotelian Prime Mover as prototype.[7] The difference mainly lay in a number of adjustments inspired by the physics of the time and Christian theology. First, for Aristotle the material/immaterial opposition is primarily a transcended/transcendent one, with the psychological functioning as an attenuating link. For Descartes it is primarily a physical/psychological opposition that subsumes the transcended/transcendent opposition as a somewhat border-line case. Second, for Aristotle what sustains the link is a teleological dynamics. For Descartes what connects the poles is a form of mechanistic interaction of which the creative act of the Christian God can perhaps be taken once again as a borderline case. Third, for Aristotle what qualifies the knowability of the knowable by nature as the light of nature is primarily the self-intimating character of the Prime Mover and of beings that in their nature approximate the closest to the latter. For Descartes what qualifies the sort of self-intimation exemplified by his Cogito as the light of nature is conceived rather more Platonistically in terms of its being innate. More particularly it is something implanted by the Deity rather than a manifest approximation to the latter's nature. Fourth, for Aristotle the light of nature is exclusively intellectual. For Descartes it involves a partnership between the activity of the intellect and the operation of free will.[8]

My next chapter will place the light of nature or self-validation as a method on a different basis, in which the material/immaterial opposition and the first three Cartesian adjustments are dismissed out of hand. The fourth will survive as fit for further cultivation.

CHAPTER SIX

The Doctrine Rectified

6.0

Thanks to its anthropomorphism, Aristotle's ontology is fundamentally psychocentric. But need a psychocentric theory be anthropomorphic? Thanks to its soul-architecture his specific account of the soul as a differentiated unitary power is confused. But need that discredit the underlying thesis that the soul is a power both unitary and differentiated? Thanks to its transcendence and abstraction the status of his transcendent Cogito as an ontological and epistemological foundation must be challenged. But need that prevent the soul from fulfilling that foundational function instead? In particular, to find that temporal substance is intrinsically mutable, have we very much further to look? Some rectification of his Path to Enlightenment and Integrative Program will indicate the contrary. More particularly, the four principles that pave the path and present the program, viz. the reificatory, modal-identity, psychocentric, and axiological, will be revised. In 6.1 to 6.8 inclusive I assign specific sorts of modal identity to the soul and its various activities. Then in 6.9 I show that the soul and its activities as thus identified have the primary, if not the only, reificatory function, i.e. that reality is psychocentric in a non-anthropomorphic way.

6.1 THE SOUL AS AN OPEN PHYSICAL POWER

The soul is not a substance of any kind or at any level. Instead it is a power, viz. a D-power, from which certain types of material particular directly derive their unity and status as mutable substance. As a D-power it is, in other words, constitutive of its bearers in the way in which S-form is constitutive of what it informs. To this basic doctrine I now shall add that any D-power is exclusively a power for physical behaviour. Hence, contrary to Aristotle, in none of its faculties is the soul a potency for some non-physical or immaterial sort of state. Indeed, there are no such potencies, i.e. no upward powers.

But if the soul is a power indeed, then what kind of power can account for its unique nature? The answer to this question lies in the ability we have had on certain occasions to act otherwise on those occasions than we actually were about to and later in fact did (for short, the O, i.e. otherwising, ability). The soul is nothing but the occasion-loose (OL) form of these various occasion-bound (OB) abilities. It is what qualifies you as an agent, or as a being that is liable to be responsible for what it does on certain occasions in a primary way, even while you are asleep, or comatose, or otherwise temporarily incapacitated.

On that basis, then, the soul is unique in at least one respect. As an ability or power it has an *openness*. In other words, unlike other types of OL-power, it is in its OB-instances no more than *just* an ability. When other types of power such as solubility and elasticity are bound to an occasion, that binding results in their bearers then behaving in a causally necessary way. They *necessarily* dissolve or stretch, etc.[1] An occasion-bound ability to act otherwise (an OBO-ability), however, is such that (ostensibly at least) the totality of conditions under which it is occasion-bound do not necessitate whatever course of action is the outcome. In short, relative to that totality the outcome is causally underdetermined.

But if this causal underdetermination is no mere appearance, is the identification of the soul with the O-ability really enough to account for the soul's being unique? The quantum-mechanical underdetermination of microphysical particles is commonly cited as a reason to the contrary. Particles behave indeterministically. Yet surely they are not ensouled. However, the quantum-mechanical underdetermination of particle-behaviour is quite unlike the causal underdetermination of an agent's acting in certain sufficiently relevant respects. Three kinds of datum, viz.

1 spontaneous emission and absorption,
2 complementarity, and
3 pair creation and annihilation,

will suffice to show this. As orthodoxly interpreted these exemplify the conceptual anomalies peculiar to the microphysical sphere.

In themselves, i.e. independently of their impact on some recording instrument, electrons are considered to have no definite location.

But, further, the definite sort of dependent location which that impact may confer is somewhat singular. Thus, as determined instrumentally, the change in location when an electron jumps from one orbit around a proton to another, in accordance with 1, is instantaneous in time and discontinuous in space. Again, if it has a definite location, then by virtue of 2 it does not have an equally definite momentum, and likewise the other way around. Furthermore, since it is qualitatively indistinguishable from any other electron, indeterminacy of location carries with it an equal indeterminacy as to whether one or more than one electron is in a certain vicinity. Lastly, when it emerges from a gamma ray in partnership with its antiparticle a positron, or where the two collapse into the ray, as in 3, the same phenomenon is amenable to description as just one electron moving backwards and forwards in time and discontinuously in space.

In sum, there are two distinct levels of physical indeterminacy. One is quantum-mechanical and microphysical as just described. The other is macrophysical and consists in the causal underdetermination of any of the courses of action between which on some given occasion an ensouled agent has a choice. In the former the normal conditions of synchronic and diachronic identity are impaired, and the behavioural causal underdetermination is associated with this impairment. In the latter, by way of contrast, the synchronic and diachronic conditions of identity for the agent being what it is are not similarly anomalous, even if in some sense an agent is an assembly of anomalous entities. Hence the OLO-ability that this type of causally underdetermined action realizes is to this extent sufficiently unique to be identified with the soul.

6.2 THE OPEN POWER'S INTENTIONALITY

As a physical power for physical behaviour the O-ability is unique in yet a further and perhaps more obviously relevant way. It is an *intentionalistic* power in the most comprehensive sense, and for two main reasons.

The first can be found in a qualified logical equivalence between the modal and the hypothetical sentences

M "He can do otherwise" and
H "He is about to do otherwise, if he intends" (chooses, decides, tries, has a dominant desire to, etc.)

where the possible performance of some action by an agent is therein being considered. Accordingly, given this equivalence, the O-ability can only belong to beings who are capable of some sort of volitional, i.e. intentionalistic, activity.

As it stands, of course, the claim of equivalence is vulnerable to diverse counter-examples and objections directed both at the M-to-H and H-to-M entailment (See Chisholm, 1964, and Lehrer, 1966: for a qualified defence see Rankin, 1980). Thus, as Austin (1961, 166) has indicated, I may remain convinced that I could have holed a very short putt in one, even where the fact that I have tried and missed gives the lie to the claim that I would have so holed it if I had tried, etc. Retrospectively, then, I would have to reject at least the M-to-H entailment.

But here the entailment's failure can be traced to either or both of two somewhat special kinds of circumstance for which provision can easily be made. The capacity or skill, an OL-power, that is one component of my "all-in" OB-ability to achieve as required on the green may have a statistical character. Indeed, what we most commonly ascribe as capacities are in some way stochastic, particularly in relation to those tasks in the performance of which these capacities are being taxed to the full. The occasional falling below par on our part is not allowed to count as a temporary loss of capacity, and hence as determining the absence of the "all-in" ability of which the capacity is a necessary component. To this extent, then, an element of convention has crept into the ascription of the ability. But second, the lack of entailment may occur because the choosing or trying leads to my doing some relatively basic act in order to perform a relatively less basic act. That in turn allows for the possibility that I may not choose or try in the right way. Perhaps I forebore or neglected to recite a fail-safe mantra while addressing the ball. In sum, then, the M-to-H entailment holds only where neither the statistical nature of capacity nor misjudgment about means is a relevant factor.

Nor should the polemical context in which examples of this sort were first elicited go unexamined. The dominant assumption has been that H is a *causal* conditional, i.e. that the volitional sort of activity its antecedent specifies functions as a *causal* condition of the action to which the consequent refers. It was on this chosen ground that certain warring factions came to collude and collide. Hence they agree on a common principle of inference, viz. that if M really does entail H, then it cannot entail the causal underdetermination of the action to which it refers – at least not if the converse H-to-M entailment holds as well. They took the first entailment to require that the action open to the agent has a volitional activity as part of a sufficient proximate causal condition, and the second not to preclude sufficient causal conditions antecedent to that.

Guided, then, by this principle and with the equivalence as premiss, one such faction, viz. some compatibilists, concluded that our possession of OBO-abilities is perfectly compatible with determinism. Guided similarly, some of their opponents cast around for examples to show the equivalence, in its unmodified form, to be faulty. The significance of such examples thus became overinflated. Given that possession of an OBO-ability implies a causal underdetermination, it would be more to the point to deny, as I am about to, that H is a conditional of the causal sort.

One further example does, none the less, deserve immediate and special attention. It indicates directly the second way and a broader sense in which the O-ability is intentionalistic. This time, however, the entailment about to be countered is H-to-M. (For other counter-considerations see 6.7.)

To have the O-ability one must be aware that one has it. One must be aware at least to the extent to which one is aware of the doing otherwise as a project that one does not conclusively believe to be impossible. Thus as you are sitting in your chair, given that you are not paralysed, etc., it might be thought that you have the ability to stand up instead of remaining seated. Certainly H is true. You will stand up if you intend, etc. Nevertheless a principle of *teleological inertia* is here at work. Given that the circumstances are normal, e.g. no electric shocks are administered, you will inevitably remain seated, unless it occurs to you to stand up. The O-ability, provided it is complete or "all-in," requires that the agent have a certain minimum of current perceptual beliefs and conditional predictive beliefs pertaining to the occasion to which the ability is bound. In short, in occasion-bound form the ability is self-intimating.

This projective occurrence is, of course, more than a mere thinking about doing something. Let us suppose that while convalescing from temporary paralysis, you think wistfully about standing up, e.g. wish you could. However, as long as that is your only mode of thinking, then, other things being equal, you will inevitably remain seated. This will be the case even were your recovery just at that point enough to allow you to stand up should you "put your mind" to it. Alternatively, it may occur to you that there may come a point when you can stand up. Perhaps, indeed, that you can do so has already occurred to you before that point, in consequence of which you then "put your mind" to standing up, only to meet with failure. You may, therefore, have become increasingly pessimistic about the prospect of your ever standing up again. Nevertheless, the entertaining of the project as a possible project, which is presupposed in your trying – and even in your not trying by reason of pessimism – would seem to be different from your merely thinking about standing up when you have resigned yourself to the conviction that you cannot stand up.

6.3 MODAL IDENTITY

I have attributed the soul's uniqueness as an ability to the openness and intentionality that distinguish that ability's occasion-bound forms. However, these two features are not independent. What distinguishes an OBO-ability is not just an openness with intentionality stuck on. The connection is conceptual, not logically contingent. Thus the openness expressed in M is conceptually dependent on intentionality in the form both of volition and of self-intimation.

This link, by the way, in no way detracts from the phenomenological immediacy with which volitional and cognitive activities of the mind are introspectively intimated, nor from the privacy of that intimation. My premonition is that unless this caveat is italicized, doubly underlined, triply asterisked, quadruply exclamation-marked, and printed in all the colours of a mandrill's snout, my thesis will be misconstrued. By a quirk of a perverse tradition the recognition of the phenomenological immediacy of these activities, and of the privacy of their intimation, is commonly assumed to be specific to some sort of mind-body dualism. Yet the Modal Identity Thesis is a form of Physicalism. Not only are OBO-abilities powers. Without presupposing that there is any other general sort of power that any sort of power conceivably could be, the thesis identifies them with powers that are physical as well.

But rather than wrest attention by shocking the eye I will merely remark that in linking intentionality conceptually to an open sort of ability, and in thus giving it a modal status, I am not into the business of a one-sided or *reductive* kind of analysis, i.e. of translating the putatively more in terms of the putatively less obscure. What I am into is nothing like, e.g., a Rylean analysis of mentalistic in terms of dispositional characteristics, where the latter are already understood reductively in the manner of Hume. In other words, it is not a form of logical behaviourism. Nor again is it yet another of these attempts to reduce mental processes to processes of the sorts of thing that it conceives the mind as reifying. It is hostile to the various kinds of topic-neutral analyses of psychological reports that have been proposed (Smart, 1958; Lewis, 1966; Armstrong, 1969; Putnam, 1967; Fodor, 1968) for the purpose of facilitating a contingent identification of the processes reported with processes of the central nervous system or with more holistic organic processes.[2] It is equally opposed to the alternative attempt to represent these same reports as theoretically negligible or superfluous or replaceable – in principle at least – by physiological reports of some kind (Feyerabend, 1963a, 1963b; Rorty, 1965). It refuses to treat them as epistemically delinquent in either of these two ways or in any other. Instead, it provides a non-reductive integration. As an integrative analysis of a non-reductive kind it aims at conceptual reciprocity. It deals even-handedly with two systems of concepts, respectively psychological and causally modal, that have become opaque in complementary ways by virtual segregation.

On the one hand, it accounts for the immediate and privileged nature of one's access to one's own mental states at any moment by interpreting these states as necessarily revealing themselves in the self-intimating abilities of which they are the intimating aspect. They are as unique to the one person as are the self-intimating abilities of which they are this aspect. Hence, so must be their reflexive self-revealing. On the other hand, the same analysis allows to these abilities, and hence to the mental states in which they intimate themselves, a specific form of the public sort of manifestation more generally inherent in the possession of any kind of causal modality. Thus for *you* whether or not I at this moment am here or over there, whether or not the attitude of my various sensory receptors is alert, whether or not I am sound in every limb, whether or not I wear a basebal cap and chew gum, whether or not my bank account is overdrawn, etc., all necessarily constitute reliable, though defeasible, inductive evidence as to the particular OBO-ability unique to me right now.

The soul, however, as an ability is not just a unity. More particularly it is a complex unity of diverse faculties. Hence, to bring the integrative type of analysis nearer to completion I must show in some detail how these faculties fit into that ability's unitariness. My brief will be that the activities of our various mental faculties are just conditional forms of the powers that we have for action on particular occasions. They are powers that we have on condition that we have the capacities or skills and the opportunities that we think we have. They are, in short, conditionally modal. Likewise their implicit reflexiveness, the indefinite iterativeness with which they intimate themselves, is simply the non-vicious iterativeness implicit in the modality that they conditionally are, e.g. the necessity of the necessity, and so on, of the possibility of each of a limited number of mutually exclusive courses of action. I will amplify this thesis in sections that follow with particular reference to the faculties of understanding, desires and the will.

6.4   UNDERSTANDING

Given that the O-ability is self-intimating in any of its occasion-bound forms, the activity of self-intimation would seem to be identifiable the most directly with understanding. The agent must be aware of the situation – he must have an awareness that such-and-such, through one or more of the senses; and any action that is open for performance must be entertained by him, however tentatively or sceptically, as an immediate project. This degree of understanding is a logically necessary but insufficient condition for the equal OB-possibility of several incompatible courses of action. That you un-qualifiedly can do otherwise than you will do in the situation logically entails that tentatively at least you think you can do it. Consequently the activity of the understanding, at least as thus exemplified, turns out to be a *conditional* form of an OBO-ability. In other words, if you have this understanding you have an OBO-ability, provided you also have the capacities of bodily or other forms of control and the opportunity for carrying out the project. Here the use of the word "understand" with its implication of freedom from error may mis-lead. It may seem to imply that these other requirements for a proj-ect's realization are indeed fulfilled, and hence obscure the conditional nature of the identification. To that extent, then, "judg-ment" in place of "understanding" would be preferable, as providing for the possibility that error is being entertained.

Activities of understanding take, however, several forms. They may be relatively near-sighted with a relatively narrow focus upon the present. Alternatively, they may be spatio-temporally more far-ranging. In other words, they may oversee the possibilities of action for a period of time from the present into a more or less indefinitely remote future, i.e. the permutations and combinations of types of eventuality that can be realized successively within that period. In short, these activities are sometimes more and sometimes less delib-erate.

In their less deliberate forms, distinctions between the various forms of cognition (i.e. between imaging, remembering, and sensing, or again within the latter between its various modalities) are the least in evidence. Given that the cognizer has a sufficient history of ex-perience, they are *recognitions* in a synaesthetic sort of way of things as referentially and predicationally characterized, and therein as lending themselves to such-and-such projects. You recognize the glass of water on the table before you as such, and as available to you for drinking. Here your recognition might certainly be said to involve perception (e.g. through sight), memories of past encounters (monitored at different past times variously, e.g. by sight, touch, taste, and hearing) with the same or similar objects, and imagined projects (e.g. through visual or tactile imagery) of subsequently drinking the water. But qualitatively the actual experience would typically be much more homogeneous than this analysis might seem to suggest.

It is where there is a more deliberate engagement of the understanding that the separation of sensory modalities[3] and of the various cognitive faculties or their respective activities is likely to become phenomenologically articulate. This seems likely to occur when the situation by which the agent is challenged is less stereotyped in nature, or where its stereotyping is being resisted. Here the critical factor is to be found in the acquisition of certain general principles, e.g. Aristotle's dietetic recipe, that furnish the basis of deliberative inference. I have already argued that it is through our commitment to principles of this sort that we become susceptible to the specific attractiveness of certain general types of end and motivatable by the corresponding types of general desire. But the same commitment must lead to other types of psychological distinction as well. Thus it involves a reference to a certain data-base presented by past experiences of the testimony of experts. This data-base is likely to be largely independent of whatever past experiences are immediately involved in the recognition of any situation immediately at hand. You may bear the maxim that dry food is healthy, and part of its data-base, in mind before you confront any chicken in the market. Similarly your imaginative projection of some such situation as your eating dry food may not be immediately achievable in what you experience at the moment. Finally, in determining the realizability of the general end by some course of action you may immediately initiate, you have consciously to project, perhaps on the basis of past memories, yourself as doing such things as going to the market and listening above the din for chicken-cackles, looking at the chickens when you trace the source, and probing what you look at to find out how much flesh it has. In general the implementation of general recipes requires the acquiring of information about particular situations, which involves various kinds of muscular motion that bring into play separate forms of sensory modality.

The contrast between the more and the less deliberate activities of understanding reveals, accordingly, the distinctive roles that the more specific cognitive activities play in our ability to act otherwise. All these activities, despite their distinctiveness, are ingredient in their various ways in occasion-bound forms of the ability, or conditional forms of the latter, as is understanding in general. The more articulated their heterogeneity the more ramified and time-encompassing are the abilities in which they are ingredient.

Simultaneously, however, the contrast poses a problem. Deliberative understanding consists of a process, and in some cases of a process that is purposive. Sometimes the process just happens to occur. Sometimes we set out to assist it or create conditions that favour its occurrence. Yet the O-ability is not a process at all. How, then, can activities of the understanding, comprising as they do both the more and the less deliberative kinds, be identifiable with the ability even in just a conditional form? The answer surely is that they cannot, at least not without further qualification. It is only the *outcome* of a deliberative process of understanding, i.e. a judgmental commitment that is alert to the rational basis the process provides, that is thus identifiable. As for the process itself, that has to be identified with the *acquiring* of a conditional OBO-ability. Once again, as such it may just happen, or it may itself constitute one of the alternatives the possibility of which belongs to some second-order OBO-ability to acquire OBO-abilities. Thus, by withdrawing for a time from the pursuit of immediate goals, one can *make* oneself reflect.

6.5   UNDERSTANDING AND
DESIRE

The intramural relations within understanding between the more specialized forms of cognitive activity no doubt merit more extensive exploration. But enough has emerged to allow us to move to an adjacent topic, viz. the relation between understanding and desire. Until that relation is further clarified, the modal affiliation of neither will be fully apparent.

As we have already seen (5.2), desiring as an actual activity (as distinct from a latent mental disposition) cannot take place without some form of cognitive commitment. Desires rely upon some specific cognition for their focus. If they are of a general type, their differentiation from other desires at the same level is tied to understanding of general ways and means, or of laws determining the compossibility of non-compossibility of general types of event. Then again, if they focus on particular occasions, sense perception will play a more dominant role. In neither case, however, is the converse linkage (wishful thinking aside) quite so tight. While cognition determines the specific nature of the desire to which it is linked, desire does not determine the specific nature of the cognition. To what we are partial we might conceivably be averse. Hence to that extent activities of the understanding are teleologically neutral or uncommitted. The same understanding can intimate to the agent an ability to promote any one of a number of incompatible ends.

Nevertheless, the activities of the understanding teleologically are not totally detached. In its constitutive determining of the possibilities for the future, possibilities that are latent in the circumstances in which one finds oneself, one's judgment is not separable from some kind of attitude of attraction or aversion. It is internally related to their being some such attitude. While understanding of a certain general kind is involved in the differentiation and articulation of our more general desires, the converse is equally true. The existence of desires as thus differentiated gives focus to the agent's constitutive understanding of the range of possibilities that a particular situation on a given occasion lays open. Different agents, e.g. the race-goer, the music-lover, and the bookworm, with radically different sets of desires, will see the range of possibilities for the future that pertain to the same circumstance, e.g. a public holiday, in radically different ways. Hence, because of the constitutive nature of their insight, the range of possibilities will indeed be radically different for each from that of the other.

Evidently, then, while desires attach more tightly to cognitions than cognitions to desires, both participate in the self-intimation of our OBO-abilities. These abilities intimate themselves as desiderative or teleological powers. Hence it may seem, as indeed I shall argue, that desires as well as cognitions are analysable as conditional forms of that sort of modality, their respective differences as such simply being determined by this asymmetry in tightness. Desires are nothing but conditional potencies for ends, the qualifying condition being that our abilities and opportunities are what our understanding of our situation takes them to be.

At the same time, however, these two forms of mental activity differ in another important respect. Each of several desires may belong directly to the same person as a whole while yet conflicting with some of the others. In the case of cognitions, however, conflict is not so acute. No doubt we often hold contradictory beliefs, but the conflict cannot hold our attention without becoming in one way or another thereby resolved, whereas the conflict between our desires agonizingly can. Hence desires raise a problem both for the unity of the soul and for the explanation of that unity in terms of O-ability, which cognitions do not.

6.6 DESIRE AND INTENTION

To show how each of several desires may belong directly to the same desirer as a whole and yet conflict with some of the others, I define desiring in terms of the notion of intentionality in the narrower volitional sense. Postponing some necessary modification, I define desiring of a general kind, e.g. your desire to go overseas during each summer vacation, as a certain *conditional* form of intending. It is, on this approximation,

> an intention to bring about a situation of a certain general type, if (whenever) circumstances other than the agent's other intentions allow, *unless* that bringing about prevents in these circumstances the fulfilment of another intention of the same agent to bring about a situation of another general type, *if* (whenever) circumstances including the agent's other intentions allow.

In line, then, with this approximation, a desire for some particular instantiation of a general type of situation at a particular time, e.g. your desire to go overseas *next* summer, can also be defined. It consists of

> an intention to bring about a certain general type of situation on a particular occasion (e.g. next vacation), if circumstances other than your other intentions allow, *unless* that prevents in these circumstances the fulfilment of some other intention you may have to bring about a situation of another general kind, *if* the same circumstances with the addition of your other intentions allow.

In these two definitions the conditions imposed by both the unemphasized and the emphasized conditional clauses provide for the intention's not being realized in every or in any situation. That in part is what distinguishes desiring from willing. An act of will consists of a *categorical* intention and commits itself to the assumption both that the conditions for realizing the intention are fulfilled and that the fulfilment is consistent with every other contemporary *categorical* intention of the agent – unless the latter looks upon himself as schizoid. But further, the emphasized clauses provide that the two conditional intentions specified in each definition are in a certain sense *defeasible*. The first can be superseded by a categorical version of the second, and the second by a categorical version of the first.

Consequently, these two definitions accomplish what they set out to do. Not only do they distinguish desiring from willing. They also are the basis for an explanation of how desires, that might be said to conflict, nonetheless are to be attributed directly to an agent as a whole rather than indirectly through direct attribution to soul-parts or bases of soul-parts. To see more precisely how, consider the nature of the conflict more closely.

Typically the possibility of conflict arises from the interplay between two types of desire. The first approximates to the synchronic type of teleological potency that in Aristotle's system a thing *qua* instance of material characteristics has for itself *qua* simultaneous instance of formal characteristics. More closely still, it approximates to the teleological relation in that system between the body and the soul. With this notion of teleological potency two things, however, are wrong as it stands. First, it is only as ensouled that anything can have a desire. Hence we have to represent the soul as in some sense self-desiderative. Second, no teleological potency can be strictly synchronic. Current desires, unlike current wishes, are for some state that is or may be future. Accordingly, the self-desiderative nature of the soul can only consist of the desire that something constitutively ensouled has for the continuation of that ensoulment – i.e. for the continued possession, occasion-loosely or otherwise, of an O-ability. While this type of desire is typically the more dominant, it is also more open than the second type. The second type consists of those more special desires the respective objects of which serve to differentiate the possibilites for action that a particular occasion may determine for the possessor of an O-ability by giving the possibilities for the future their respective focus.

In the interplay between the first and second types of desire, and also within the population of the latter, there is a considerable degree of mutual indulgence. Thus to continue as a being who experiences desires of both sorts is the actual objective of the first. Furthermore, the satisfaction of the second sort, e.g. of desires for food, drink, and clothing, may be more specifically instrumental to the satisfaction of the first. In a more general way too (and in a somewhat weaker sense), any two desires, even if merely of the second type, are *per se* mutually indulgent. That is because one's desires owe their individual character to the sort of situation one projects as desirable, and because in what one so projects there is in principle an implicit if unspecific *deference* to other desires, as long as it is merely desire as opposed to decision that is in play.

How, then, can conflict arise? Typically, or perhaps the most dramatically (if we exclude for the moment the topic of moral conflict), it arises between desires of the first and of the second sort. The first in some way inhibits some of the second, and vice versa, where satisfaction of the latter diminishes qualitatively or quantitatively the continuation of ensoulment either by restricting the scope and nature of the agent's future opportunities or capacities, or by leading prematurely to death. But once again, neither this kind of desiderative conflict nor any internal to the second type can arise between desires *per se*. That it because the emphasized conditional clauses pertaining to the conditional intentions specified in my analysis impose conditions that are merely sufficient and not necessary. However, the categorical intentions into which the conditional intentions that constitute two desires have to be translated on a given occasion, if on that occasion any action in favour of either desire is to be taken, may conflict. Due to the specific nature of the occasion these two categorical intentions may logically preclude each other. But notice that, though in these circumstances the agent can conjointly have both desires and one of the two corresponding categorical intentions without any logical inconsistency, he cannot unless schizoid have both categorical intentions. Hence there is no reason why the desires and categorical intention that he does have should not be together directly attributable to him as a whole.

On closer scrutiny this reconciliation of soul-unity with the diversity of the soul's desires and their potentiality for conflict may seem unconvincing. How can desires be definable in terms of intentions, even with the stipulation that these intentions are of a certain conditional kind? On four types of count, viz. deliberateness, emotive commitment, defeasibility, and ascendancy, it may seem that they cannot.

1 Deliberateness.   Intentions whether categorical or conditional may seem too deliberate to be identified with desire. To intend either categorically or conditionally is, as it were, to lay out the future in a specific plan. To have a desire even of a general kind may not, however, to require anything like the same clear-headed excogitation. Typically are not our hankerings, both singly or collectively, of a rather fuzzy-minded kind?

2 Emotive Commitment.   The spirit in which one forms one's intentions may be relatively cold-blooded. Thus our intentions may even be accompanied by an attitude of indifference towards what we intend. Surely, though, the objects of our desires have to attract, i.e. seem attractive.

3 Defeasibility.   Certain of our desires at least do not seem defeasible in the way required. Extreme pain seems inseparable from the desire to remove it, and if sufficiently prolonged or iterated can eliminate the sufferer's ability to resist trying to remove it.

4 Ascendancy.   As count 3 already suggests, desires would seem to determine intention rather than consist of a certain class thereof.

Where they compete we may seem, indeed, to enjoy a certain autonomy in how we intend. Otherwise not. At this moment I could knock over my desk lamp in the sense that I would if I intended, but I won't because in the absence of an immediate audience before which to clown I have no desire to – while yet having no positive aversion against the action.

However, the analysis of desire in terms of defeasible intention has, as I have already insisted, been no more than rough. What these four counts indicate is, accordingly, a need for modification rather than rejection.

On count 1. Intentions as such in the standard sense are indeed far too deliberate for the definitional purpose, but only to the extent to which intentions are too deliberate to explain in all cases what constitutes the intentionality of all intentional action. Not all actions done intentionally are preceded or accompanied by any quite so explicit planning. The comments we make spontaneously in reply to what is said to us in conversation are one kind of illustration. It does not seem that we first intend to say something and then say it. Likewise in some of our habitual actions, as when we return home from work: we don't plan beforehand to turn right at the next corner. But these examples serve equally to show something else as well, i.e. the nature of the undeliberate form of consciousness upon which the intentionality of the action depends. Thus normally in conversation we don't just hear and understand what is said to us, but hear and understand it as to be replied to in such-and-such a way. Likewise, in returning home we don't just see the next corner, but see it as to be turned to the right.

Accordingly, we need only stipulate in response to count 1 that in our analysis of desire the term "intention" is so used as to allow intentions to have an implicit as well as an explicit form. Thus an intention may be implicit in our immediate understanding of a situation as opposed to explicit in a more deliberate appraisal thereof. This distinction between the implicit and explicit occurrence of intention can then be extended to intentions of the conditional kind employed in our analysis as well as applied to those that are categorical, saving us thereby the labour of changing the wording. Thus an intention of the relevant conditional kind would be present where we hear a comment as to be replied to in such-and-such a way *unless* there is a question of our aiming to avoid trouble, or again where we see the next corner as to be turned to the right *unless* there is a question of our being about to get gas. This is enough to give our immediate experience the somewhat disturbing edge of something's being at stake, which on my analysis is distinctive of desire *per se*.

On count 2. No doubt intentions may be formed in an attitude of indifference or even exasperation towards what is intended. Nevertheless, where that is the case there must be some compensating intentional commitment of a more positive engrossing kind or tendency thereto. With his wife in labour a man may be in a position to take her by either of two routes to the maternity ward. Provided each will get him there in the same time as, and with no greater inconvenience than, the other, he is unlikely to care which he takes. Here it is easy to see how the indifference is the product of a more ultimate commitment and of the commitment's intensity. Or, to take a quite different type of case, the victim of accidie or boredom may be quite indifferent to the outcome of any issue that affects the relatively remote future. In so far as he is motivated in any direction at all, it may be only by the importunities of his currently active appetites, of which he cannot get rid. However, the weaker his inclination to concern himself with issues affecting his remoter future, the stronger must be his inclination to terminate his existence before any such issue comes up for final decision. That he hesitates to take this irrevocable step must be due to a stubborn if ailing intentional commitment to self-continuation that persists despite its failure to be sustained by comparable commitment to any of the various mutually discrepant ways in which that commitment might be attended to in the remote future.

Therefore, to adjust to count 2 we need once again only qualify. Desires are analysable as intentions of a certain defeasible or mutually deferring kind, provided we stipulate that what is intended therein is intended for its own sake and not entirely (if at all) for the sake of something else. To intend to bring something about not just (if at all) in order to bring something else about is to desire the bringing about of the former.

On counts 3 and 4. "However, to adjust to count 2 in this way may make its successors seem all the more poignant. Instead of identifying desires with defeasible and mutually deferring intentions that have the required degree of ultimacy, should they not be identified independently as that which confers upon something we intend for its own sake that ultimate status? Should the desires by which we potentially are moved not be regarded as a kind of pragmatic datum on the basis of which we form our intentions and without which these intentions cannot be formed?

To a certain extent I have already challenged the interpretation of desire as a kind of pragmatic datum in 5.2 by arguing that desire can only acquire its essential focus upon some specific end .in the course of our coming to understand the sorts of thing that can be done in the sorts of situations in which we find ourselves. That claim, however, is comparable to a more familiar one, viz. that we can only understand the significance of, and indeed identify, the facts which experience brings to our attention against a certain background or theory or theoretical assumption. Now that much one might concede, while yet reluctant to relinquish some kind of foundationalist approach, however vestigial, to epistemology. One might still insist that experience provides us in some way with data upon which the activity of theorizing may then get to work. Similarly, then, one way have a comparable reservation against denying the role of pragmatic data to desires.

But further, we are not really in a position to decide whether desire determines our ultimate intentions, or whether it is just a conditional kind of ultimate intention, or indeed whether these two hypotheses are in conflict, until we have clarified more exactly what intention is. Let us therefore reserve judgment until then.

6.7 INTENTION

For brevity I focus on categorical intending at the executive moment of action. Once that notion has been properly clarified the modifications required to account either for forms of intending prior to the executive moment, or for conditional intending, or for the more implicit intending, can be left tacit as being in principle provided for.

Categorical intending, like the various activities that comprise understanding and desiring, is a conditional form of self-intimating modality, i.e. potency. Like these other mental activities, furthermore, it is the intimating part of the modality of which it is the conditional form. However, the modality or potency in question is not that of OBO-ability. In different ways it both presupposes and is presupposed by the latter. None the less it is closed where the latter is open. It is a conclusive and determinate potency.

As the intimating part of this kind of potency a categorical intention can be viewed as a type of belief distinguished by three factors, viz. the future-tense, the self-intimating, and the residual.

1 The future-tense factor. Intentions are first-person future-indicative beliefs appropriately expressed in some such form as
   S. I am about to X at t.

This is because the potency they intimate is just an agent's being about to do one of the things for which he or she has an OBO-ability.

2 The self-intimating factor. Intentions differ from (more ordinary) predictive beliefs, projections, or anticipations expressed in the

same grammatical form (e.g. "I am about to sneeze") in that the belief (what is believed) *logically* entails that the believer believes it. Thus
S logically entails "I believe S";
i.e. the belief-content *logically* entails the existence of the intending.

This is because the sort of potency that the belief declares, i.e. the agent's being about to do something (the futurity of the action), differs from forms of futurity not based on OBO-ability in being self-intimating. The logical entailment is, of course, not to be confused with one of a pragmatic and more trivial kind. In a typical speaker-listener situation the assertion of any statement entails, implies, or presupposes that the assertor believes what is asserted (Moore, 1942, 540–4; Austin, 1962, 48–52).[4] But that entailment merely derives from the fact that a belief-disclaimer on the assertor's part would interfere with the *purpose* of the speech-act if it accompanied the assertion. What the disclaimer asserts in no way contradicts what the speech-act asserts. Here, however, the entailment holds independently of the purpose of any speech-act.

3 The residual factor. (a) Where one has an OBO-ability to perform what one intends, then at the executive moment of action one's intention to perform that action forthwith is nothing but that part of one's *being about to* perform the action that is not based on the underdetermining but on the total causal conditions upon which one's OBO-ability is based. (b) Where one does not have an OBO-ability to perform in some part what one intends, then at the executive moment of action any intention to perform that action forthwith is nothing but that part of what would have been one's *being about to* perform the action that would not have been based upon what would have been the underdetermining, but total, causal conditions of one's performing the action had one had the OBO-ability to perform it. In short, in both cases (a) and (b) an intention is a non-causal dynamical residue.

This is because to have an OBO-ability to do any one of a number of equally possible actions entails three things: viz. that one is about to do one or other of them intentionally; that whichever of the actions one does is conditioned by its being intended or intentional; and that the performance of whichever of the actions one does is causally underdetermined.

Elsewhere I have deployed a lengthy series of comparisons in further clarification and vindication of these three factors (Rankin,

1972). These deserve and are due for re-deployment as part of a more intensive study of intentionality in general, which I reserve for a subsequent volume (but see Appendix). Here I restrict myself mainly to showing how the analysis of intention they support fits into the present context. Accordingly, I now return to intention in relation to desire.

If categorical intentions are nothing but non-causal dynamical residues, then there can be nothing that predetermines one's intending to do one of two possible incompossible actions rather than the other. Hence, though desires may pre-exist the intentions to satisfy them, their pre-existence cannot predetermine the occurrence of the intentions. Thus, where one's intending something categorically arises from pre-existing desires, the implication is that it does so merely as resolving a situation in which one out of a number of mutually deferring defeasible conditional intentions has to be given precedence over the rest. But is intention really related to desire in this way? Two reasons may suggest it is not. The first points to a positive predetermining effect of the presence of desire upon an intention's presence, and the second to a negative predetermining effect of the absence of desire upon an intention's absence.[5]

First, to cite counts 3 and 4 (i.e. defeasibility and ascendancy) once more, many of our desires or aversions do seem to predetermine our categorical intentions. Thus aversion to pain, fatigue, and boredom (or desires not to undergo these forms of discomfort) seem severally to give little deference to any sort of project outside those set by others within their own group. Hard on their heels for recalcitrance come avarice, greed, lust, and ambition. Perhaps we can withstand their clamour for a while, but where members of either group persist in engrossing our attention, the probabilities are that sooner or later we will succumb to them unless they hold each other at bay. It may seem that I am lapsing from psychological analysis into ethics by labelling some of the second group in terms that they only acquire and deserve in situations in which for extraneous reasons their satisfaction is to some extent untoward. Nevertheless these same terms correctly suggest the recalcitrant presence in us of certain native or acquired desiderative tendencies *not* to defer in the way that my analysis of desire has required. Finally, to these two groups certain pathological kinds of compulsion have also to be added. These latter are equally desiderative and even more recalcitrant.

Now where we capitulate to these various types of motivation, we certainly seem to be acting intentionally, and if the capitulation has been reluctant, the intentionality is of a fully deliberate kind. How, then, can we deny that the intention, and the action that fulfils it, is simply some kind of causal outcome of some pre-existent of acquired factor in the agent's constitution? How can it be the sort of non-causal dynamical residue that we have claimed it to be? How can we say that the agent could have acted otherwise if by that we mean that the action was causally underdetermined?

Second, let us consider once again the project of felling my desk lamp. I will knock it over if I intend to. But although the action now occurs to me as a project, and though I may find in myself no particular aversion to knocking it over or the more direct consequences thereof, I have absolutely no desire to knock it over. Hence I won't intend to knock it over. In these circumstances can we really say that I am able to do otherwise than leave it upright? Can one really say that the missing intention is just a non-causal dynamical residue?

For the beginning of a reply to the first objection, i.e. to evaluate the positive predetermining effect of desire, let us focus on pain and pathological compulsion. This will discount an otherwise attractive hypothesis. One might have argued that the lack of deference shown by some of our desires to others does not preclude that they are intentions of some sort but merely precludes that they are of the conditional mutually deferring sort. Why should they not be categorical intentions instead?

The trouble with this suggestion is that one person can sometimes inflict the experience of intense pain upon another and that this experience would seem to be inseparable from the desire to have it removed. Contrary, then, to my indeterministic analysis, if such a desire to the extent to which it is non-defeasible were a categorical intention, intentions could be made causally inevitable. Likewise, if the non-deferential nature of psychopathic compulsions were to be explained by identifying them with categorical intentions as well, the conclusion would be the same. Presumably the whole point of labelling these compulsions as such is to represent their psychological presence as a causally inevitable consequence of physiological factors or psychological traumata.

My counter-proposal employs a perceptual analogy. The intentionality with which one gives in to pain or to a pathological compulsion is spurious in the way in which the perception we have within the visual blind spot is spurious. Normally the visual field is not experienced as including a blind spot. The spot is filled in as if you were seeing something within its limits. Its presence is inferred from the fact that things you do see disappear when they occupy the part of the visual field. Now this filling in is dependent on your genuinely seeing outside these limits. With no experience outside, there would be none inside. Similarly there is a range of non-intentional behaviour that is quasi-intentional. It appears as intentional only because it occurs within the context of behaviour that is genuinely intentional. The self-intimation of this apparent intentionality as such is parasitic upon the self-intimation of the genuine intentionality of other parts of the agent's behaviour.

By extension this explanation also applies to morally more interesting types of motivation, e.g. to those that belong in Plato's classification to the oligarchic, democratic, and tyrannical types of soul. In all three types the individual is represented as the slave of his desires, the difference lying in whether the slavery is to a few, many, or just to one. Are many of us, then, helpless in the most characteristic of our actions? If so, do these actions have a quasi intentionality that depends upon the genuine intentionality of actions that belong to the morally less critical parts of our lives?

With the help of an Austinian distinction (Austin, 1962b, 22–5), the perceptual analogy is once again apposite. *Delusion* is here to be understood roughly as non-veridical experience that represents the non-existent as existent or the existent as non-existent in a convincing way. Thus the blind spot may represent what actually does exist in the region it covers phenomenologically as non-existent by representing it as something quite different, and in a way we cannot discount. *Illusion*, in contrast is here to be understood, once again rather roughly, as non-veridical perception that represents what exists – e.g. the whirling firebrand, the oasis over the horizon, the arms of the Müller-Lyer figure, etc. – as existent in a misleading way by which we have (or have acquired) a tendency not to be misled.

Now the intentionality of some of our acts is very like the representativeness of delusion as above defined. It is a mere appearance that conceals an absence of what appears to be there, i.e. genuine agency, or the presence of which appears not to be there, i.e. causal necessitation. It may, of course, appear to the pain-succumber or to the psychopath that some agent within his own skin with whom he cannot completely identify has taken over. Even so, the analogy with delusion is present. Thus the experienced victim of delirium tremens, while unable to prevent himself from gagging at the abomination that seems perched on his lap, may very well realize or suspect that no such thing is there. If in the one case the agency is one from which the agent feels to some extent alienated, so in the other case there is a conviction from which the person convinced feels alienated.

In contrast, the intentionality imparted by importunate but quite normal desires might be likened to the representativeness of perceptual illusion. Whether these desires be timarchic, or oligarchic and necessary, or unnecessary and spendthrift – if we borrow these Platonic classifications at least provisionally – they are not completely non-deferring, just as illusions are not completely misrepresentative. They belong to narrower or wider, more or less exclusive coteries within which mutual deference takes place either on the basis of equality or in accordance with some principle of weighting. Thus our various self-regarding desires may not brook much opposition from ethical impulses of an altruistic kind – they do not defer to the latter – where social pressure is insufficient to bring the two types into line. To that degree we lack the strength of will to keep them in control, but at least they show some mutual respect within their own coteries.

It was with consternation that I first found myself stumbling into the Pelagian controversy and siding with the saintly (Bettenson, ed., 1950, 73–83). Augustine was right, the doctrine of original sin well founded. Complete freedom of will is indeed an ideal condition, which we fail fully to realize. Only in that condition is the mutual deference of an agent's desires unlimited. Yet the notion of a will whose desiderative promptings are without limit mutually deferring comes very close to the notion of a good will. How close will be left to chapter 9 to determine, but surely close enough to warrant my initial shock. Suppose that only the good will is free. Then, on the assumption that responsibility entails free will, how could agents who will evilly be held responsible for so doing? Yet surely we do hold them so responsible.

I shall leave further discussion of this difficulty to chapter 9, for the second objection to my analysis of desire is more pressing. How are we to account for the negative predetermining effect of desire's absence? With greater despatch. My apathy towards upsetting my desk lamp should be placed in context. We must remember that normally we are in mid-course of carrying out some project that we have already initiated. The apathy is attributable thereto. Upsetting the lamp would be too digressive from projects to which I am already in part committed. To put the point in somewhat exaggerated terms, I have already decided to do certain things such as thinking about the significance of my not intending to upset the lamp. If, though, I lived more from moment to moment, with the question "And what shall I do next?" continually renewing itself in my febrile mind, upsetting the lamp might indeed seem quite appealing. As it is, earlier intendings predispose me against it.

6.8 VINDICATIONS

The mental activities of understanding or judgment, desiring, and willing or intending require more intensive study than they have captured here. Enough, however, has been accomplished already for the purpose in hand. They have been identified either as or as implicit in various internally related complementary aspects of the intimating core of self-intimating OBO-abilities. With the exception of willing or categorical intending, participation in these activities is nothing but the conditional possession of these OBO-abilities. What distinguishes the categorical from this conditional possession is just the further possession both of certain capacities of control, e.g. bodily skills, which vary from one species to another, and the actual opportunity to act that the intimating core discerns as present. These, of course, may fail to be there. As for willing or categorical intending, it likewise is nothing but the intimating core of a self-intimating OB-power. This power, however, is of a quite determinate kind, viz. the actual *aboutness* (see also chapter 8) to do an action rendered possible specifically by possession of an OBO-ability to do it. To will or intend to do something *tout court* is nothing but coming into conditional possession of this determinate power. What distinguishes the categorical from the conditional possession of this same power is just the same as what distinguishes the categorical possession of the OBO-ability upon which it is based from its own intimating core.

As rendered here, the Modal Identity Thesis may seem to have been overlong in exposition and overshort in proof. If so, that is at least partly because in integrative analysis the line between exposition and proof is a bit fuzzy. What is presented as exposition in one sort of didactic accent can be presented as proof in another. In the one accent the emphasis is on the content of an explanation, in the other on the explanation's comprehensive power. However, any impression of imbalance can now be partially countered. As an indeterministic or incompatibilist type of theory the thesis has at the very least the intuitive sort of backing to which traditionally that type of theory lays claim. Our intuition is that at times we have an O-ability such that what we are about to do at these times does not follow inevitably from the total conjunction of what obtains both at and prior to these times. Appeals to intuition are, no doubt, notoriously open to subjective bias. If not mere statements of prejudice, they may involve mistaken interpretation or conflict with claims that ostensibly have similar status. In the Modal Identity Thesis, however, provision against that sort of failing is to some extent already implicit.

In the first place, it refines the intuitive basis upon which incompatibilist theories traditionally depend. It identifies the ability to which these intuitions supposedly attest with a self-intimating ability. It thereby relies not merely on intuition but also accounts for the fact that the intuition both occurs and attests to what it attests. The intuition attests to what it attests, i.e. the possession of a certain kind of power, as to something that is knowable by nature or self-attesting, and hence to its own testification of the latter. As in the Aristotelian mode of validation discussed in 5.3, the intuition has been firmly ensconced in a theoretical or explanatory framework that itself it confirms. Hence it can no longer be attributed merely to prejudice or to arbitrary interpretation.

Secondly, in a further extension the Modal Identity Thesis reconciles two intuitively based claims that traditionally have been treated as opposed. It shows that the incompatiblist interpretation of the O-ability is perfectly consistent with the qualified equivalence of statements M and H. This qualified equivalence is now attributed to the self-intimating nature of the power that is the agent's being about to do some action that he has had the OBO-ability to do. Intentions, etc., so far from being causal conditions, in these circumstances, of the agent's being about to do some action, are nothing but the necessary intimating part of that being about to. They are a logically necessary condition of the being about to whereby the futurity or imminence of an action intimates itself to the agent in a partly non-inferential way. Hence in the Modal Identity Thesis we are absolved from having to make an apparently arbitrary choice between competing claims that apparently are evenly matched in intuitive appeal.

In this way, of course, the main burden of proof or support has finally descended upon our analysis of intention. More specifically, the most critical thesis would seem to be that an agent's intention to act in a certain way is a non-causal but logically necessary condition of that agent's being about to act in that way. But though the restatement of my main defence for that position has had to be postponed to a later occasion (see Appendix), certain supporting considerations can without duplication be introduced here.

Notice first that the agent who intends to X, and who thereafter has X-ed, is one and the same agent. Nothing like this is uniformly the case for causal conditions that are critical to the realization of compatibilist potencies. The star that emits light, the brick that administers shock, the fire that ignites, and the water that encloses a translucent brittle inflammable soluble object are all different from that object. In other words, the agents of the activities that are the causes are in these cases different from the object that is caused by these activities to be the agent of further behaviour, e.g. to transmit light, fall to pieces, burn, and dissolve. Given, however, that an agent's intending, etc., is nothing but a non-causal dynamical residue, the sameness of the agent has been accounted for.

Furthermore, the intention is specified in the same way, as are both the preliminary and the final potency. The intention to X, the ability to X or to Y or to Z, and the agent's being about to X are all to be specified at least in terms of X. But causal conditions that are critical to the realization of compatabilist potencies do not have to meet this constraint, as our previous examples already amply illustrate. Nor does the mandatory specification end there. The intention has to be an intention at some particular time to X *at some other time,* e.g. immediately thereafter. The specification of that other time belongs every bit as much to the specification of the intention as does the specification in terms of X. In contrast, the event that is the causal condition critical to the realization of a compatibilist potency is not essentially specified in terms of the time of that realization but only in terms of the time at which it itself occurs. Given the hypothesis that an intention is just a non-causal dynamical residue, the essential nature of the specification is explained. An OB-potency is specified essentially in terms of the type and time of the action that it is a potency for.

The time-specification of intention in particular has a further corollary. The transition from forming the intention to X at t and the actual X-ing at t is a non-transposable form of change. In other words, it could not take place the other way around. You could not first do an action at a particular time and then later intend to do it at that time unless you were in some confusion over the relation between the time of your action and the time at which you intend. Similarly, the transition from being about to X at t and later actually X-ing or having X-ed at t is non-transposable. There is, of course, a manner in which a causal sequence of events may be non-transposable as well. Non-transposability seems to hold where the causal sequence is conceived uniformly as a sequence of processes rather than wholly or partly a sequence of states. The impact of the brick that breaks a pane could not conceivably occur immediately after the breaking, for there would be no pane with which the brick could make impact. But the sequence could be transposed in the manner depicted by a film of the sequence run backwards. The pane might integrate out of shards and propel the brick from its surface. The transition from intention to action, in contrast, does not seem transposable in this way. An intention, like potency, is not a process.

These arguments may seem a little too simple-minded and swift to be wholly convincing. To be won over by them we have to be ready to take our ordinary descriptions of intending at their face value. But some may suspect that – not unlike many of our ordinary descriptions of causal factors, e.g. burning, dousing, cutting, etc. – these descriptions are merely a theoretical kind of cosmetic that conceals a logically contingent causal connection between actions and their antecedents that could in principle be described in theoretically less or differently laden terms. I believe, however, that we should take things at their face value until they give us good reason to suppose that thereby we have been defrauded. The subversive truth may be that at this point in history in matters that most concern us, such as who we are, the best sort of evidence need not carry a megabuck price-tag. One further argument, this time of an ethical kind, will contribute to this creed in its present application.

For some of the acts for which one is accountable, that accountability is not derivable from one's accountability for any preceding action. Such actions are fully intentional on one's part. For others, e.g. acts of carelessness or incompetence, one's accountability is derivable from an underivable accountability for preceding omissions or commissions, e.g. acts that have made one a careless or incompetent person. One is accountable for them thus, despite their being to a significant degree unintentional, either in themselves or in their results. However, one is just as underivatively accountable for *intending* to do certain things for which one is underivatively accountable as for later doing or having done them. This is most patent when one intends to do something disreputable and yet through no merit of one's own, but through incapacity or miscalculation, fails to do it. Yet despite that, one's intending is not the sort of thing that can be intentional, or for that matter unintentional, on one's part — or at least not directly so. In this it is rather like one's getting conceived. Kant, so the story goes, planted his handkerchief at the other end of his study to compel himself now and then to walk across to get it. Hence, perhaps, his frequently intending to walk across was just as intentional on his part as his frequently walking. Nevertheless, it was not something he directly intended to intend. He merely placed himself in the sort of situation in which the consequences of not walking across, and hence of not intending to walk across, would be unpleasant, without giving up the option of not walking across and hence not intending to do so. To account for one's accountability for intending by supposing the intending to be directly intentional would lead, in fact, to a Rylean type of regress. That which makes one's intending intentional would also have to be intentional, if accountability were to be preserved, and so on *ad infinitum* (Ryle, 1949, 67).

Obviously, then, one's intending to do the action must be in a radically different category from one's acting, despite one's accountability for both. Thus is cannot be identical with, or epiphenomenal upon, some pattern of electrochemical discharge in the motor regions of one's brain. Anything one might learn to do intentionally, e.g. the intentional individual twitching of certain muscles one could not intentionally twitch before, is something one could conceivably do intentionally. Now through biofeedback one might learn to bring about certain patterns of electrochemical discharging in a directly intentional way. Hence such discharging could conceivably be directly intentional. Indeed, even if there are certain neural activities in one's brain that one could not learn to bring about in a directly intentional way, it would seem that one conceivably could.

On the dynamical-residue thesis, however, both one's accountability for one's intending and that intending's non-intentionality can be explained. One's intending to X is nothing but that part of one's being about, if one really is about to X in excess of one's equal ability beforehand to X, Y, and Z, etc. (these being mutually exclusive possibilities). One is just as accountable for being about to X as later for X-ing or having X-ed. Further, one is particularly accountable for such part of one's being about to X as does not simply depend upon what equally enables one to do X, Y, and Z, etc., just as later when one has done the action one is particularly accountable for that part of having done it that did not depend upon what equally enabled one to do any one of those actions. On the other hand, to be at t^1 about to do something immediately thereafter is not in itself to do something at t^1. Hence it is not to do anything that is intentional or unintentional. Perhaps one can be at t^1 about to be from t^1 to t^2 about to X immediately after t^2. But that cannot constitute the second *being about to* as something intentional, for it simply collapses into being at t^1 about to X immediately after t^2.

Arguments in support of the residue account of intention and other components of the Modal Identity Thesis should not, however, deflect attention from what the latter can accomplish as a whole. Its most remarkable asset is, perhaps, that it is a genuine, and not a pseudo, psychological theory. It does not deal with its topic by shifting to another. A genuine psychological theory must be capable as a minimum requirement of representing the nature of the soul as conceptually coherent without pretending that the soul is anything other than it is. More specifically, it must among other things permit us to recognize the unity and diversity of the soul without requiring us to pretend that the soul is not made up of diverse parts. This as a minimum is what the Modal Identity Thesis can accomplish.

As we have seen, it accounts for the unity of the soul by identifying the latter with the OLO ability. This ability can be attributed to some degree or other to a variety of ensouled species (e.g. canine, feline, simian, cetaceous, or human) as S-form. On that attribution the various occasion-loose overlapping auxiliary capacities or competencies that differentiate one such species from another count as proximate material characteristics (S-matter), which variously constitute a basis for the S-form that all these species have in common. As for the diversity of soul-parts, that has also been seen to. As already remarked (5.2), a number of superficially attractive models have failed to show how diverse elements could all belong as directly to an ensouled being as does the soul itself. The Modal Identity Thesis, in contrast, does not apply an alternative model. Instead it identifies the soul with something that is sufficiently unique to allow the required kind of unity in diversity to be realized.

In part the diversity is found in the diversity of desires that a being with a soul can simultaneously have. For an explanation of this we had, however, to resort to a more specific analysis of desire. With the necessary qualifications, desires are mutually deferring conditional intentions of the kind we specified. Hence the difference between them is not a difference between separate motive powers that divide the soul as between factions. But then again, in part the diversity of the soul is found at a broader level in the diversity of soul-faculties, and here is where the more general analysis directly applies.

We can say that each of the various faculties is the OLO-ability *minus* something. Thus, say, the faculty of understanding is identifiable with the OLO-ability *minus* by virtue of being specifically realized in one type of component of the OBO-abilities in which the OLO-ability as a whole is realizable. The various faculties are distinguished from each other by being realized respectively in this way by different types of such component, and they are internally related to each other by virtue of the internal though variable relations between these components. Though the Modal Identity Thesis does not apply a model, a partial model can help to clarify the type of internal relationship within which the differentiation between faculties takes place. The notion of each of the ontological categories – e.g., at the most general level, substantives and predicatives – is just the notion of a state of affairs *minus* something. Here a state of affairs is conceived as consisting of a number of parts internally related in a variable way. Thus substantives could not exist without predicatives and predicatives could not exist without at least the possibility of substantives. This categorial or syntactical model is, however, only partial, for it illustrates the internal nature of relationships between faculties alone – not how the faculties belong to their owners as a whole as directly as does the soul. That can only be explained by the further identification of the internally related faculties with internally related parts that are more specifically parts of an OLO-ability.

6.9   MUTABLE PRIME MOVERS[6]

To possess the O-ability in some measure and at some time is at the very least necessary for responsibility, and for anyone's being subject to praise and blame. Some further refinement in formulation is no doubt needed to free this principle from certain ambiguities (see chapter 9). For the moment, however, the present formulation will do. Recognition of what it attempts to capture has fed the debate between those who wrangle over whether human beings are responsible at least in part for what they do. Nor has the principle been challenged by a shift in focus to a further question, i.e. to whether free will or the O-ability is compatible with the deterministic conception either of the whole universe or, more narrowly, of human nature.

Regrettably, however, the recognition has too often been filtered by a pair of more dubious assumptions. These gravely affect the principle's interpretation. The first takes the crucial notion of causal underdetermination to be conceptually too skeletal to account by itself either for the ability's intentionality or for the responsibility that the ability confers. Causal underdetermination is viewed at best, if at all, as merely necessary for the possession of these two features. Intentionality is seen as supervening extraneously as a further factor upon which the ability and responsibility depend. For the second assumption, furthermore, the notion of agent-responsibility is more than intentionalistic. It is primarily a causal notion as well. Supposedly, the agent of an action is, in some way variously specified, the action's cause.

On the basis of this second assumption just on its own it has frequently been alleged that if the O-ability's actualizations in actions were causally underdetermined, then they would be random, chance, accidental, or (for good measure) mere products of whim – in short, the very antithesis of actions for which an agent has a primary responsibility (Hume, 1739, bk 1, pt 3, §§ 1 & 2; Hobart, 1924; Bradley, 1927). But the same assumption conspires with the first to prompt an almost as common collusive reply. To make up for the alleged deficiency of causal underdetermination just on its own, many libertarians conjure with a supervenient causal factor. They argue that an agent may exercise a quite unique intentionalistic type of causation that is distinct from the, in this case, incomplete nomological type. This unique type they commonly label "agent-causation" partly to signify that the cause falls within the category of mutable substance rather than of state or event (Chisholm, 1966; Taylor, 1963–65, 1966; Thorp, 1980).

While these two assumptions seem mutually supportive, neither is well founded. The first flies in the face of the principle of teleological inertia to which I have already appealed. What this principle shows is that the causal underdetermination specific to O-ability is inherently intentionalistic in nature. The skeletal conception of causal underdetermination is, in fact, a philosophical figment. As for the second assumption and the standard anti-libertarian objection it has inspired, these result from a mere equivocation. There is indeed a sense in which actions that are chance, accidental, or random are actions for which the agent can have at best only a diminished responsibility. But their fortuitous nature is in no way due to causal underdetermination. Quite to the contrary. If you accidentally collide with a power-line while aloft in a glider, your responsibility for the power-outage is no doubt of a diminished kind. It is certainly not of the same magnitude as if you had deliberately courted the collision. But this diminishment has very little to do with causal underdetermination or some other absence of causal connection. Indeed, given the specific nature of the thermal currents or the condition of the glider at the time, that the collision took place may well have been causally inevitable. The diminishment in responsibility simply lies in the fact that the interruption of power was on your part unintentional (Cranston, 1953, 169ff; Foot, 1962; Rankin, 1961, chap. 1). More generally, the nexus of concepts to which those of responsibility and accident, etc., are central is of a homonymous kind. They have both an explanatory and a narrative application.

Thus the impact of a brick on a glass window is responsible for the latter's shattering. Here the brick and its contact with the window are each, in Aristotelian terminology, an efficient cause of the fact of the shattering – the former in a primary and the latter in a secondary sense (*Meta.* $\triangle 2$, 1013a 29–32). Accordingly, the notion of responsibility here has an explanatory application. The responsibility of the brick and its impact on the window can thus be distinguished as a *result* or *explanatory* responsibility. Suppose, however, the window to have been of some resilient material that shatters if and only if exposed to a strong magnetic field. That it shattered when struck by the brick would then have been the work of a strong magnetic field. Provided they did not function as some sort of trigger for the field, the brick and the contact would not be responsible in any sense for the shattering. On the contrary. That the window shattered upon impact from the brick would be accidental, etc., in the *explanatory* sense. Here then the notions both of responsibility and of accident belong to the same explanatory nexus.

Where, however, *you* heave the brick or *you* break the window by heaving the brick (the window here being of ordinary glass), you are responsible, if you are responsible, for *so doing* in another sense. You are not the efficient cause of your heaving the brick or even of your breaking the window. (Here the precise wording needs close attention). You are not any kind of cause of your *action* at all. At best *you* or *your heaving the brick* are the efficient cause of the *window's* breaking or being broken. Accordingly, here the notion of responsibility has a narrative application. Your responsibility for what you do can be distinguished as an *act* or *narrative* sort of responsibility, for it is for your actions. Suppose, however, that you had been under the impression that there was no glass or nothing solid in the window-frame. In that case your breaking the window would be unintentional, and at the least your responsibility for breaking it would have to be diminished. The action indeed would be accidental — but here the notion of the accidental belongs, like that of the responsibility it negates, to the narrative nexus (Rankin, 1961, chap. 2).

To interpret an agent's responsibility as consisting in the exercise of an agent-causation is, then, to succumb to the very same confusion as underpins the objection to which the interpretation responds. It is to place the narrative type of responsibility and accident within the explanatory nexus. Those who do this, when pressed to explain what your being the cause of your actions could possibly be, sometimes concede that it consists in nothing more remarkable than in its just being you who does whatever you do or in your doing it (Taylor, 1963–65, 52; Thorp, 1980, 103).[7] Yet in this attempt at clarification they contrive to ignore that the emperor, if not exactly naked, no longer wears what supposedly were his robes of office. On the one hand, the notion of agent-causation is introduced in compensation for a supposed deficiency attributed to causal under-determination — where the latter is ascribed on the basis of the agent's having the O-ability upon which his responsibility as agent depends. On the other hand, the sort of responsibility for which causal un-derdetermination would indeed be inadequate as a basis is of the *result* or *explanatory* rather than the *act* or *narrative* type. In short, the notion of agent-causation was introduced specifically to attend to an imagined need to give or complete an explanation — notwith-standing its admitted incapacity to do the job of explanation in any circumstance in which an agent may have to choose between two ultimate ends that fall within his power to realize or to determine which to make ultimate.[8]

But once the relation between you and your actions is purged from explanatory pretensions, what more exactly it is may still seem enough of a puzzle. What does distinguish the emperor from those in attendance? What is so different about you in your relation to your heaving of the brick or your breaking of the window, on the one hand, and the brick in its relation to its hurtling through the air or its breaking the window on the other? What makes the former

Diagram 2

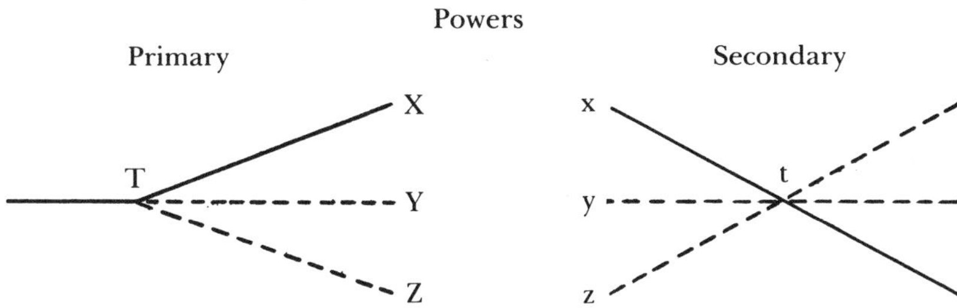

of these two types of substance-event relationship more exemplary as a type of narrative responsibility or of agency than the other? We can, of course, point to the intentionality that pertains to the former and not to the latter type of case. That leads to the important consideration that intentions can be controlled by ascriptions of responsibility, inducements, and threats of punishment. But to ascribe responsibility to an agent entirely on the basis of his or her susceptibility to such manipulation is dubious, and in any case the intentionality of intentions has been identified above as just the non-causal dynamical residue left over by the agent's O-ability as conceived in terms of causal underdetermination.

But once the non-explanatory nature of the responsibility in question has been seriously considered as a feasible hypothesis, the sufficiency (not just the necessity) of causal underdetermination as its basis becomes evident. The narrative responsibility that is distinctively an agent's is nothing but the intrinsic thinghood that is distinctive of the sort of mutable particular that is intrinsically such. The O-ability that pertains to that agent by virtue of a causal underdetermination of his action is the distinctive sort of power from which that intrinsic thinghood derives. Other mutables, if they bear other causal powers of a sufficiently fundamental kind, are things non-arbitrarily, but in an extrinsic as distinct from an intrinsic way.

More specifically, the O-ability is the primary sort of power. Other sorts of power may be fundamental in the sense that they are constitutive of simple natural kinds of mutable particulars. These, however, derive their status as powers through being constitutive of the O-ability. Diagram 2 will show this contrast more clearly.

In quite different ways each diagram contrasts one actual with several possible but non-actual stretches in the history of a mutable particular before and after a time, i.e. in its history as an instance of intrinsic and extrinsic properties. Thus on the left the branching of a continuous line at T into one continuous and two hatched extensions indicates the branching of a stretch of actual history at a time into one actual and two non-actual continuations. On the right, in contrast, the continuous and hatched lines are to be looked upon as intersecting rather than as each branching at t. This represents the coincidence of one actual and two non-actual stretches of history in the same place at a time. Notice finally, that T and t may or may not be the same time, and that (regardless of that) the mutable particular involved on the left may or may not coincide with that involved on the right.

To conceive the particular involved in each diagram as mutable is to suppose that it can or could exist throughout actual and non-actual stretches such as those represented without loss of identity – that in the non-actual stretches it might very well be the same particular as in the actual. Likewise, to conceive the stretches as strictly stretches of history is to conceive them as consisting of the temporal changes or absence of change in some mutable particular as just described. A mutable particular cannot, therefore, be identified with the sum of the parts of its history – not even of those parts in their correct temporal order. In each case the merological conditions of the particular's identity are more relaxed than that.

In each case, furthermore, the basis of the relaxation and of the consequent mutability is of a causal and hence of a non-arbitrary kind. It depends upon the non-modal constitutive properties of the particular thing being such as to make more than one history subsequent to a time of their instantiation in some sense causally possible. In that lies the constitutiveness of these properties, or their essential nature, and the non-arbitrary thinghood of their instances. Apart from that, however, the causal possibilities that the two diagrams respectively depict are quite different in type.

On the left, alternative histories subsequent to times such as T may all be causally possible in an occasion-*bound* way. Their causal possibility is occasion-*bound* at any time such as T, given that relative to the totality of conditions that prevail at that time, none of them are causally impossible, i.e. all are causally contingent. On the right, however, all alternative histories subsequent to times such as t cannot be causally possible in an occasion-bound way. Relative to certain constitutive properties that as such the particular instantiates at all times of its existence, and without reference to the fulfilment of the rest of the conditions that prevail at any of these times, all the alternatives may indeed be causally possible. But this possibility, of course, is merely occasion-loose. Relative to the *totality* of conditions prevailing at t, only *one* of the subsequent alternatives can be causally possible in an occasion-bound way. That, furthermore, is due to the fact that its causal possibility exceeds itself by being an occasion-bound causal *necessity*. As for the others, they are occasion-bound causal *impossibilities*.

There are, then, two distinct types of occasion-loose power that a mutable particular may possess by virtue of its constitutive properties. Each is a non-arbitrary basis for the identity or thinghood of its bearers through the mediation of these properties. Nevertheless they determine that non-arbitrary identity in two quite different ways. This becomes evident when we try to conceive a world in which the right-hand type of power alone would hold sway, and then compare the result with another world in which the two types of power reign in tandem.

In the world on the right, there would be no basis for attributing an intrinsic mutability to spatially delimited particulars nor, perhaps, for attributing an intrinsic spatial delimitation or separability to particulars either. The three incompatible histories x, y, and z of the one mutable particular would more basically resolve into continuous stretches of three incompatible possible worlds. These would conform to the same nomological structure in their mutually disparate ways. But, without reference to one or more of the rest, none in itself could contain mutable particulars. That the possible world that is actual, viz. x, consists of a history of a mutable particular could only be attributable to something extrinsic to that world, viz. that some other possible worlds with the same causal structure[9] intersect (in some sense of that verb that could benefit from further analysis) with the actual world at t and other times.

On the assumption, then, that our world is basically like the one just described, the fact that we normally view its inhabitants as mutable would be entirely attributable to a supposedly purely subjective limitation, viz. that at no time are we very certain which of the several possible worlds we can represent to ourselves happens to be actual. One might even doubt whether any particulars of a spatially delimited kind could intrinsically be so in such a world. Assuming, however, that they could, they would have to be spatio-temporal (as distinct from spatial) and determined by more stringent merological constraints than those that depend upon causal powers. Thus in a parasitic way we might take them to be determined by exactly the same spatial limitations that are intrinsic to mutables on the basis of the latters' causal powers. But in any case they would also have to be determined by the same sorts of temporal limitation that determine the total actual *histories* of these mutables. They would, in other words, be space-time worms or EVENTS with spatio-temporal conditions of identity such that they are logically capable neither of change nor of rest. Nor, of course, would they be capable of bearing causal powers, as distinct from having causal connections, for powers are powers for changing or remaining the same.

By contrast, in a world in which the two distinct types of power were in partnership, a similar fragmentation into possible worlds would be prevented. This can best be appreciated by applying the left diagram to the right to form a composite whole. Take t to be a time subsequent to T and allow the branching histories X, Y, and Z to contact their counterparts (x, y, and z respectively) at some intermediate time. Then the composite will represent either a number of ways in which one mutable may act on another, viz. an agent upon either a non-agent or an agent, or the number of different situations and their consequences in which an agent by acting at an earlier time may become involved later. What then becomes evident is that x, y, and z no longer resolve into different possible worlds. Respectively they have become later segments of the more extensive histories Xx, Yy, and Zz. The latter in turn become histories truly, because the succession of possibilities they severally comprise all belong to the one world – at least relative to T and before. All alike grow out of the one common stem that branches at T, and that common stem represents *ex hypothesi* what is actual. That they should be regarded as actual or possible histories of a mutable particular can no longer, then, be regarded as something extrinsic to the world in which whatever is actual takes place. That world thus becomes a world of mutables.

Hence, in summary: the power portrayed on the left is primary, while that on the right is secondary. The status of the former as a power is intrinsic, since the disparate possibilities that constitute it are all bound in their occasion-bound form to the actual world. Contrariwise, the status of the latter as a power is extrinsic, for its resolution into extrinsic relations between actual and non-actual possible worlds is only prevented by the fact that these "possible worlds" are extensions, or constitutive, of possibilities that in their occasion-bound forms are bound at a particular time to the actual world. Consequently the mutable particulars that the primary powers determine non-arbitrarily through the mediation of constitutive properties are intrinsically such. Contrariwise, the mutable particulars that the secondary powers determine non-arbitrarily in the comparable way are merely extrinsically such. In the latter class things depend for non-arbitrary thinghood upon the non-arbitrary thinghood of the former class of things.

Which, then, is the actual world? Just the one on the right, or the two together? If the latter, then the substance of the world is intrinsically mutable. Otherwise not. For some time now this question has awaited my final answer. What that answer would be may have been predictable, but now at last its basis is clear. The actual world is the conjoint world, for the latter is the world to which we belong. Each one of us takes over the function of Aristotle's Prime Mover in more than one way. Inasmuch as we possess the O-ability, i.e. inasmuch as some of our actions are causally underdetermined, we move other things without ourselves being moved. More significantly, however, the actual world is a psychocentric world. As bearers of the primary power we as substances are intrinsically mutable and the source of the less exclusive extrinsic non-arbitrary mutability that we share with other things. It is to this conclusion that the Integrative Program, as duly rectified, finally leads.

Further, as likewise rectified the Path to Enlightenment corroborates. The knowledge of the more knowable to us originally centres on things encountered in our environment, i.e. mainly upon things that are reified by secondary powers. Since these powers, like the utility of tools in relation to the skill of the hand, are constitutive of the primary power that reifies us, it is through the knowledge of them that we come to know ourselves. Finally, it is in this knowledge of ourselves alone, i.e. of ourselves as bearers of the O-ability, that we become aware of what is knowable by nature, i.e. of something the intimation of which is self-intimation. This, then, is an assurance that our awareness of mutability is not the product of some subjective limitation that hides our future just as faulty memory hides our past.

CHAPTER SEVEN

The Incomplete Immanence of Intrinsic Thinghood

7.0

To detranscendentalize the Prime Mover, to transfer its ontological role to ordinary souls or minds, and to identify these with O-abilities that confer the status of substance upon the spatially individuated mutable particulars in which they are embodied, all belong to one sort of theoretical enterprise. It is no part of that sort to maintain that the soul or mind as thus identified is ever completely realized in its ontological function. In fact within our experience the intrinsic thinghood conferred by ensoulment upon spatially individuated mutable particulars is never completely immanent. Indeed, conceivably it could be even less immanent than so far within our experience it actually has been. We stand to our intrinsic thinghood as approximations to an ideal that is ontologically mandatory in the sense that our approximation to it is constitutive of whatever individual status we have as intrinsically distinguishable.

In support of this claim I will now consider in turn some very normal, some highly abnormal, and some futuristically imaginary ways in which the psychological experience of human beings has been, or conceivably might be, affected. In so doing I abide by the implications of preceding chapters. I shall assume that the spatial unity and temporal continuity of the body is a necessary condition of personal identity throughout time. Not, however, as an epiphenomenalist might claim. More particularly, not as a proponent of what Strawson has named "the no-ownership theory" (1959, chap. 3, 95–8).[1] On that theory the mental processes of the one person owe their unity as such to a unique causal relationship to one body. On mine, to the contrary, the one person's body owes its spatial unity and temporal continuity as such to the unity of the mind instead, i.e. to the O-ability, which it embodies.

7.1 SLEEP AND COMA

Asleep or in coma a person is yet a person, and has a soul or mind by virtue of an O-ability of an occasion-loose sort. But the possession of this occasion-loose ability thus is little better than the possession by water-sodden paper of inflammability or by a frozen elastic band of elasticity on the basis that the sodden or frozen states are under normal conditions somewhat temporary. I say "little better" rather than "no better" advisedly, at least in the case of sleep and even perhaps in that of coma. Both falling asleep and waking up are part of the normal function of an agent. They are processes whereby our abilities are maintained; and the same is also true for coming out of, if not the falling into, a coma. Nevertheless, during these states – if we set aside dreams – it cannot occur to one that one has any of the O-abilities that, by virtue of the opportunities provided by the circumstances and of one's other abilities, one otherwise would have.

Accordingly, there is a distinction to be drawn between two different kinds of occasion-looseness that possession of the O-ability may have. The first is more inclusive, for it includes the occasion-looseness in sleep or coma. The second, in contrast, consists just of what is common to all OBO-abilities, whatever they may be, in so far as they are all instances of the same general sort rather than of other sorts of ability. Strictly, it would seem, it is the possession of this narrower sort alone that constitutes the intrinsic thinghood of a particular that has intrinsic thinghood. This would seem true even though particulars such as ourselves have in sleep or coma the power of coming out of these states into the narrower occasion-loose possession of the ability.

7.2 COGNITIVE ERROR

Cognitive mental states belong to the self-intimating component of our O-abilities. But what are we to make of those that mislead us about the nature of those abilities or the circumstances by which they are constrained? Do they, like sleep and coma, constitute a defect in the basis of our intrinsic thinghood?

What to make of simple ignorance – the non-occurrence of a piece of information or a thought at times when it would be germane – is perhaps the most obvious. Errors of that type can be construed very simply as restricting O-abilities either of first- or higher-order types in accordance with what I have proposed as a principle of teleological inertia. Of course, the restriction may not lie in the range of the immediate possibilities that our understanding partly determines for us. It may only impinge at some later point or node by constricting the range of less immediate possibilities that branch out from the more immediate. It may thus deprive some of the more immediate possibilities we do envisage either of an attractiveness, or of the lack thereof, that they might otherwise have had by virtue of some of our more long-standing or general desires. Nevertheless a restricted O-ability is still an O-ability. Hence in the case of simple ignorance a basis for intrinsic thinghood may still be retained.

What to make of more constructive ignorance – the occurrence of misinformation or misleading thoughts or beliefs – may seem less clear. States of that kind can to some extent be interpreted as similar to simple ignorance. Not only do we not have quite the O-abilities that our delusions lead us to believe we do. As in the case of simple ignorance, these delusions may determine that inherently our O-abilities are specifically more restricted than they need otherwise have been. An explorer may mistake a distant salt-pan for a frozen lake. That will determine not merely what he mistakenly *supposes* to be the range of possibilities before him but the actual ones as well. Thus he may assume that he can get water over there by digging or melting, or that it might be dangerous to try to get to the other side by walking directly across. Such assumptions will determine globally his latest set of O-abilities, partly by precluding the occurrence of thoughts or projects through which he would acquire O-abilities, which as it is he does not have, partly be leading him to dismiss certain projects that do occur to him as simply "not on." Even if a project occurs as such to an agent, unless it occurs as sufficiently feasible – as more than wishful thinking – he is not able to carry it through in a sufficiently "all-in" sense of "able."

To some extent, then, simple nescience and the more constructive sort of error can be treated as alike. Nevertheless, there is an important difference. Constructive error is more akin to dream experience than is simple nescience. Indeed dream experience is just constructive error in its most extreme and total form. Except to a negligible extent it cannot be regarded as the self-intimation of any O-ability at all. No doubt in dreaming one does have the potentiality to innervate certain efferent neural paths that would lead in a waking condition to various motions of one's limbs, etc., and thereby to various interactions with objects in one's environment that might or might not be the objects one dreams about. But it is not of these truncated sorts of potencies that the dreaming can be regarded as the intimating part. Not only does one not have the self-intimating potencies that the dreaming appears to intimate, but the potencies one does have through the dreaming are not self-intimating. In dreaming, accordingly, there is a radical lack of correspondence between what we believe, or are inclined to believe, and actual facts – a lack, moreover, to which our modal identification of cognitive states has yet to adjust.

Now at first it may seem that the only possible adjustment should be total collapse. If there is some kind of constructive error that fails to intimate any O-abilities, how can that kind be the self-intimation of such abilities or any components thereof? How can it have the modal status that I have attributed in general to cognitive states? But if it cannot, how can any kind of constructive error, indeed any kind of constructive cognitive state in general, have that status? Surely all forms of constructive cognitive state, erroneous or otherwise, must have the same kind of categorial or ontological status.

Against this kind of objection we are, however, already armed. One's total cognitive state on a given occasion is to be construed as a conditional OBO-ability. It is the OBO-ability of which it is representative – which really is as intimated – given that one's ancillary competencies and one's opportunities on the occasion to which it is bound are indeed as that total state intimates. In dreaming, accordingly, the radical lack of correspondence between what we believe, or are inclined to believe, and actual facts simply consists of the further conditions, which if satisfied would render the conditional OBO-ability unconditional, happening to a large extent to be unfulfilled.

Nor need we be at a loss how to answer the further question that now may seem to arise. Surely, it may seem, this conditional OBO-ability is an unconditional OBO-ability in its own right. Surely it is based upon the activity of exactly the same neural structures in the agent's brain as the putative unconditional OBO-ability of which it is a component would be, if that unconditional ability were to obtain. Why, then, does the dream experience intimate the unconditional OBO-ability of which it is the putatively conditional component rather than more directly the sort of neurological potency that it is in its own right? Why is the agent, whether dreaming or awake, not aware simply of certain neural structures and their potentiality for different kinds of innervation? A dispensation of this sort would at least exempt us from our susceptibility to immediate forms of delusion of the sort that we experience in dreams.

To deal with this question it is enough to remember that the sorts of abilities of which our cognitive states are the intimating components are abilities for interaction with other things. In this reminder, however, it is not my intention to propose a distinction between two classes of OBO-ability, i.e. between interactive and non-interactive forms. On the contrary, it is central to my thesis that OBO-abilities confer the status of intrinsic thinghood upon their bearers just because they are abilities for interaction. The otherness of their bearers from that with which these bearers interact is non-arbitrarily intrinsic because of the interactive nature of such abilities.

For that reason, then OBO-abilities are not to be reduced, with or without extra trimmings, to abilities of their bearers to innervate their internal neural structures in diverse ways, except in so far as – and contrary to any reductive intention – it is understood that such innervative abilities are but interactive abilities *manqués*. Here we may adapt a proposal made by Armstrong (1968, 260–5) in a somewhat similar context.[2] These innervative abilities must find their realization in a closed causal circuit. The output of the innervation in which the internal innervative abilities are realized must extend more or less directly to the source of the input, i.e. to the body's sensory receptors and their positions relative to sources of sensory stimulation. Without this kind of causal closure, to have innervative abilities is not to have any OBO-ability at all, except in a strictly conditional form. But it is just the absence of this circuit closure that marks the innervative abilities of the dreamer, or of someone under a similar form of radical delusion. Hence these innervative abilities are not OBO-abilities in their own right.

If that is granted, one can then go on to explain why dreams are delusory in just the way they are. The innervative abilities of the dreamer do not form part of any actual unconditional OBO-ability. Indeed it is only as conditional forms of OBO-abilities, which otherwise do not obtain, that they properly count as abilities at all of which the organism as a whole is an intrinsically unitary bearer. Hence the dream experience in which these innervative abilities are intimated mimic the experience in which an actual unconditional OBO-ability would have to intimate itself if it were to obtain.

Our modal identification of cognitive states has, accordingly, been saved from the threat of collapse. But a different kind of adjustment to the existence of constructive cognitive error is still required. One can certainly be said to exist as a person while dreaming – and not just because one had O-abilities before one fell asleep and will come again into possession of such when one wakes. Even in sleep, while one dreams one still is in possession of that type of ability at least in conditional form. Yet one's claim to intrinsic thinghood under these conditions is at least impaired. It can only be as a bearer of unconditional O-abilities to interact with other particulars that one enjoys the status of something that is intrinsically a particular and as such that one can be the source of the non-arbitrary extrinsic thinghood of those particulars outside one's genus with which one interacts.

The dreamer as a dreamer is intrinsically a thing only in a conditional and parasitic way.

7.3 COMMISSUROTOMY AND SOUL-UNITY

The Modal Identity Thesis does not contest that the central nervous system is the most immediate basis both of the human soul and of our O-abilities. That, however, raises certain questions about the traditionally vaunted unity of the human soul or mind. Is the human soul really a single simple entity? Or, if the Modal Identity Thesis is granted, do the O-abilities that on any one occasion all pertain to somebody or some body form just one simple unitary set? These questions arise in part at the purely psychological level with particular reference to unconscious or subconscious behaviour and the phenomena of split personality. However, the issues raised by recent investigation into the results of commissurotomy are particularly central, for there the evidence for psychological disunity is the least ambiguous, due to our knowledge of its physiological basis.

The efferent and afferent interchange of neural impulses between the central and more peripheral parts of our nervous systems is largely, if not exclusively, cross-lateral. By and large sensory receptors on one side of the body communicate the most directly with the hemisphere that is on the opposite side of the brain. Likewise that hemisphere controls the most directly the neurally controlled movement of the body on the side it opposes. Here the qualification "the most directly" allows for the fact that each hemisphere communicates with the other through the corpus callosum and anterior commissures, to say nothing of the brain-stem common to both. It is to the severance of these same connections that certain problematic behavioural discrepancies are due (Sperry, 1964, 1966).

Some of the most striking turn on the fact that the neurological speech centres of the normal speaker are located in the temporal lobe of the left hemisphere. Thus after commissurotomy a word that is flashed tachistoscopically on the right visual half-field can be read out loud by the subject, but not if it is flashed on the left half-field. Likewise, if an instruction is flashed on the left half-field it may be executed by the left hand, even while the subject declares ignorance of what it was. A slightly more complex variation is where the word is composite, e.g. "key-ring," and flashed at the centre of the subject's binocular field of vision (Marks, 1981). The dissociation of experience is then betrayed partly by his verbal response (a left-hemisphere function) and left-hand gesture (a right-hemisphere function) when questioned on what he sees, and partly by the actions he performs with his right and left hands in obedience to an injunction to select from an undercover assortment of objects those named by the word he sees. Here, however, is not the place to detail all the observed consequences of severance, or even to vouch for the conclusiveness of the evidence. Already we have matter enough for the sort of "conceptual bafflement" to which Thomas Nagel (1975) has compendiously confessed.

Nagel sets out to test the hypothesis that at any one time any such subject must be in possession of a definite number of minds, i.e. either one or two. As it stands this appears to leave open a limited number of possibilities, each one of which he proceeds to dismiss.

Suppose, first, that there is just the one mind during the whole period of testing. In that case it derives its contents either (1) from the left hemisphere alone or (2) from both. If (1), the responses from the non-verbal right hemisphere would have to be either (a) those of an automaton (not expressions of conscious mental processes at all) or (b) expressions of isolated conscious mental phenomena that are not integrated into any mind whatever. As Nagel remarks, however, neither (a) nor (b) seem true. The right hemisphere may be less competent than the left. Yet it is competent enough to justify attribution of a sufficiently unitary and personal consciousness to a subject whose left hemisphere has been destroyed. Accordingly, (1) must be rejected. As for (2), even with the concession that the contents of the one mind it postulates are rather peculiar and dissociated, the observed dissociations are in Nagel's estimation too radical to make it plausible.

Suppose, alternatively, that there are two minds, either (α) all along or (β) only in the experimental situation that yields the problematic results. Nagel dismisses (α) on the ground that "information from the two sides of the brain can be pooled to yield integrated behavioural control."[3] Outside the experimental situation the behavioural discrepancies disappear. Ordinary walking for the subject is not like a three-legged race is for us. But (β), i.e. that the single mind splits in two and reconvenes after the experiment is over, is no better. There is nothing about these situations that could occasion such a fundamental change in the patient — "it produces no anatomical changes and merely elicits a noteworthy set of symptoms." Furthermore, the subject's integrated responses are not clearly separated in time from those that are dissociated.

My own impression is that Nagel's difficulties originate in the more specious of two discrepant themes in Aristotle's philosophy of mind. For this theme, the non-arbitrary thinghood of the sort of thing that we are is attributable to the presence in us of an in-principle separable ingredient to which thinghood is intrinsic, an ingredient that in our case is identifiable with the mind. On this assumption, accordingly, there is a natural tendency to interpret introspective associations and dissociations of our conscious states in terms respectively of the singleness and plurality of such ingredients. The simultaneous togetherness of mental states within the same introspective field[4] is taken to attach them to the same ingredient somewhat as the spatially conjoint instantiation at any one time of physical states attaches them to the same physical particular. Here it makes little difference whether we interpret the type of ingredient in question as so-called immaterial substance or as some sort of neural complex located in the brain.

The Model Identity Thesis, for its part develops what I commend as the more promising of Aristotle's two themes, viz. that the mind or soul is a constitutive sort of power the possession of which makes a body a person. It represents the mind of a commissurotomized subject, like that of anybody else, as just an OLO-ability. Likewise it represents the relation of that mind to the subject's conscious states as just the relation of the OLO-ability to conditional OBO-abilities in which the OLO-ability is instantiated.

Accordingly, the oneness of the commissurotomized subject as a person and the unity of his mind is beyond question, despite the occasional disunity of his conscious states. He is just one bearer of the OLO-ability – not two – inasmuch as at all times he is such that in certain sorts of situation, or parts thereof, his body as a whole is the bearer of unconditional O-abilities that are bound to these situations or parts. The various possibilities of co-ordinated movement of arms and legs allowed by a situation in which none of the limbs is confined – as in walking or other activities involving the whole body – constitute OBO-abilities of this sort. Here practically the whole of the patient's voluntary nervous system may become involved. The self-intimation of these abilities will not involve any mental disunity.

Yet, while bearing the OLO-ability, the subject is such that, in certain situations of the sort that Sperry et al. have investigated, he is the simultaneous bearer of two dissociated conditional OBO-abilities bound to these situations. These two abilities are merely *conditional* inasmuch as both to some degree constitute error. Thus, where the instruction "key-ring" is on the screen, they are intimated respectively by the words "key" and "ring" in each case just on their own. Thus the sort of opportunity they appear to announce as there, e.g. that of response to someone's wishes, is in fact only apparent.

But they are also *dissociated* in the sense that the sorts of opportunity required to fulfil the conditions under which both abilities would be absolute are not conjointly *realizable*. In this case, if the compliance with the wish expressed were that of searching for a key, it could not be that of searching for a ring and likewise the other way round.[5]

Unity of mind is, accordingly, a matter of degree. Commissurotomized persons, if otherwise normal, have unity of mind, but less of it than others. Remember, however, that it is primarily upon OBO-abilities rather than upon the OLO-ability instantiated therein that the actual intrinsic thinghood of a person depends at any time. Hence, despite the unity of a commissurotomized person that depends upon unity of mind, one has to conclude that the intrinsic thinghood of that person as one thing is at some times somewhat fuzzy,[6] viz. particularly at those times at which the person is the bearer of OBO-abilities that are not merely conditional but dissociated as well. Finally, we may further surmise that the same conclusion also applies to physiologically less well-understood and behaviourally more complex cases of mental disunity.

7.4   THE DOUBLE-TAKE
TRANSFERENCE STORY

Variations on the theme of the Prince and the Cobbler latterly abound. Often their model is science fiction rather than mere fable. Nevertheless they are similar in purpose to the Lockean original. In diverse ways they usually attempt to dissociate the identity of a person across time from the survival of any particular organism at some functional level. Let us, however, begin with a more equivocal specimen. From it most of the others have taken their cue.

Bernard Williams (1973, 1975) has shown how the same set of circumstances when considered from different perspectives provoke different identity-verdicts. In the first presentation two people, A and B, are due for surgery that they believe will induce a memory interchange. They believe that the post-operative A-body person will no longer have A's pre-operative memories – that instead he will have B's. Likewise they believe that the post-operative B-body person will no longer have B's pre-operative memories – that instead he will have A's. On that basis each is then prevailed upon to choose between two further outcomes. On one option the post-operative A-body person will experience acute pain and the post-operative B-body person some unmitigated delight, when they come to. The other option will reverse these results. Then after the interchange

– however else one may describe it – has been successfully completed, it would seem plausible to expect their complaints or self-congratulations to indicate that the A-body person identifies with the pre-operative B and the B-body person with the pre-operative A. One would expect this whether post-operative outcomes fulfil the pre-operative choices or otherwise. Thus should A pre-operatively have chosen gratification for the post-operative B-body person, and should the latter then undergo pain instead, then in all likelihood the latter will feel entitled to complain that that was not what *he* had chosen.

Williams examines exhaustively other permutations and combinations of pre-operative choices and post-operative dénouements. All would seem to demonstrate the same point. But now we can turn to the second presentation. Suppose that the pre-operative A were to receive item by item the following five shots of information: that he is about to be tortured; that antecedently he will have lost his memory; that what purport to be the memories of B will be substituted for those that he has lost; that B in turn will lose his memories; and finally that B will receive those lost by A. Here, Williams persuasively argues, A's reaction to the first three shots will be one of progressive alarm about *his* future. Nor are any of the subsequent shots, i.e. about what happens to B, likely to allay his worries. In other words, A continues to identify himself with the post-operative A-body person throughout.

For the moment I shall contend, as others indeed have, that the retrospective point of view is less decisive in its slant than initially, if not finally, in Williams's telling of the story it may seem. In memory what we remember is quite often some fact that is without specific reference to the epistemic source of our information, i.e. to the act or acts of perceiving whereby the information was originally acquired. In the story, however, the remembering provides information with specific reference to epistemic source. Indeed, in the latter case it may seem that one does not use memory to *determine* that one is the person who witnessed some happening that one now remembers. That one remembers *presupposes* that it is one who witnessed – or so it may seem. In other words, one's identity with the witness may seem to be a pre-condition of its being a memory that one now has rather than a mere imagining.

Too much weight, however, should not be placed upon this consideration. Even if we confine ourselves to memory with specific reference to perceptual source, the necessity of the identity of the rememberer with the witness can be questioned. It is reasonable to suppose that it is in the perceiving rather than the remembering that the identity of the perceiver is given. One views a certain episode in the sitting room from one's position in the doorway. One feels the angular shape of a Rubik's cube with, i.e. from the tactual perspective of, one's right hand. In one's awareness of what one thus sees or feels one is likewise aware of the perspective from or in which one sees or feel it. More generally in one's perceptual awareness, first, one is aware of one's perceptual awareness; secondly, this awareness is an awareness of the perspectival characteristics distinctive of the perceptual awareness; and thirdly these perspectival characteristics identify the perceiver with something in a particular position at the time of the awareness. What this may suggest is that, when you remember a perceptual act, you identify the perceiver in the same way as the latter does, i.e. through the act of perception that you remember. On this supposition, then, any further identification of the perceiver as thus identified, e.g. with yourself, must be made on the strength of considerations external to your remembering that act of perception. Thus your memory of later perceptions may allow you to assume that there is a spatio-temporal continuity between the place that determines the perspectival characteristics of the original act of perception and the position you perceive yourself as occupying at present. That you remember a perceptual act does not on this supposition *presuppose* that the perceiver was you.

Accordingly, on the basis of their memories alone it is not unequivocably clear that the post-operative persons have to believe that it is they who made such-and-such pre-operative choices. Not even their complaints and self-congratulations need compel this conclusion. What each would remember is certainly that a differently embodied pre-operative person made the choice. However, on this basis alone they could still complain or congratulate themselves over their actual allocation of pain or pleasure, even if it were only in the way that the owner of a cat-home may complain if the bequest of some cat-loving benefactor were overturned, or rejoice should it finally be probated.

Williams himself allows for some such alternative in his concluding remarks. He concedes that the retrospective identification would seem less natural under circumstances less neat. Thus the memories of each one of the pre-operative persons might have been transplanted into more than one differently embodied post-operative person. That would create more than one post-operative candidate for identity with just the one pre-operative predecessor. Such less neat arrangements, and others even messier, become the theme of the three more recent proposals to which I now turn.

7.5 FISSION, FUSION, ET AL.

For all three proposals direct or indirect relations of psychological connectedness (e.g. through memory or through intentions) between temporally sequential conscious states function as their criteria. For two, however, these relations are without qualification criteria of personal identity. Both for that reason are relatively conservative. Thus, according to Lewis (1976), should the relevant relation link just the one pre-fission body with several post-fission bodies (no two of the latter being residence of, or direct contributors to, the same individual conscious states),[7] then the pre-fission body must be an embodiment of as many persons as the post-fission bodies conjointly embody. In fact, each such pre-fission person must be identical with one of those post-fission persons. For Nozick (1981), contrariwise, where there is fission in psychological connectedness, a pre-fission body only embodies the same person as any post-fission body where one of the latter is the *closest continuer* of the former, that one alone embodying the same person as the former. Here closeness of continuation consists of closeness of psychological connectedness, as determined by several criteria, between the conscious states that are housed in different bodies. Where there is a competitive tie between all the post-fission bodies, none embodies the same person as the pre-fission body.

While relatively conservative, these two proposals allow identity, whether of a synchronic or a diachronic kind, to depend upon extrinsic circumstance in a not so very conservative way. For Lewis, how many persons inhabit the same body at a given time would seem to depend not upon anything that is intrinsic to the psychological states that pertain to the body at that time but upon whether fission will take place and the number of separate bodies that will through their psychological states be connected with that body thereafter. For Nozick, contrariwise, whether a given embodiment of a person embodies the same person as a previous embodiment does not depend entirely upon anything intrinsic to the conscious state pertaining to the embodiments at the respective times but rather upon whether there is any other embodiment of a person that constitutes a closer continuer of the earlier embodiment.

Neither proposal, accordingly, is all that conservative, for paradigmatically and contrariwise identity is not conceived as depending upon anything extrinsic to what is being considered for identification. Both, however, are conservative at least in a sense that engages us once more with the transference-story. Both conserve the hypothesis that the retrospective point of view has initially been taken to commend, that two persons have exchanged bodies; for both modify the notion of identity to the point that psychological connectedness through memory can establish identity in both the neater and the messier types of case.

The third proposal is Parfit's (1975, 1976, 1984). Like Nozick, he recognizes that issues of identity may have no very determinate or non-arbitrary solution. Consider the case of the Hashound Harriers. This group originated as a cross-country running club in Kuala Lumpur towards the end of the post-war Emergency. More recently it achieved world press headlines on having its activities confined by the Moscow police to Gorky Park. Now were the latter really dealing with the same group as the one with which I occasionally puffed and panted in my Far Eastern expatriate days? Instead of proposing criteria for settling this sort of issue as far as possible, Parfit demotes the importance of identity where persons as well as groups are concerned in favour of a notion of survival. Here the sense of "survive" upon which he focuses is not that in which a man survives an operation but rather that in which his wife and children survive the man should he not survive the operation. For Parfit's purpose this sense requires some further broadening to allow (1) for a self to be survived by descendent selves who, unlike a man's wife and children, are in direct or indirect psychological connection with the former self, and (2) for a blurring of the identity-distinctions that would hold between those candidates for connected selfhood that are the most directly adjacent in the sequence of psychological awareness.

In keeping with these measures Parfit also adjusts the notion of psychological connectedness. For his purpose psychologically connected conscious states do not need to be states of the same person or self. The connections are made more generally be quasi-memories (q-memories) and quasi-intentions (q-intentions), and similar congenors, rather than exclusively by memories and intentions proper. Q-memories have to meet all the conditions that memories are commonly supposed to have to meet, with one exception. They have to depend upon actual past experience in the way that memories do, but the person remembering need not be the same as the person who had the past experience. Likewise, q-intentions have to meet all the conditions that intentions are commonly supposed to have to meet, but again with one exception. If they are fulfilled in later actions, these actions must depend upon them in the way that normally intentional actions depend upon intention, but the person acting need not be the same as the person who originally intended. Furthermore, in this system of classification memories are to be treated as just a subclass of q-memories, and intentions as just a subclass of q-intentions.

These provisions have enabled Parfit to deal with psychological connectedness in all sorts of messy cases, e.g. bodily fission, fusion, teletransportation, and combinations thereof. Here we need only pause to illustrate the first two.

In its corporeal aspect one might liken fusion to a Miltonic copulation where two angelic bodies unite into one. Presumably, however, even in the ecstasy of their total interpenetration the congress remains as between two distinguishable centres of consciousness. Consequently, to remove this barrier, suppose that at the climax there is a psychological collapse into the chaster solitude of a unitary if expanded consciousness. Physically, then, there will be a compromise between the discrepant characteristics of each body. If the union is heterosexual, perhaps a hermaphrodite will result. Psychologically a comparable cancelling out of disparities in character traits, ambitions, and plans will take place, together with a pooling of beliefs after an elimination of the grosser inconsistencies. In fission, for its part, the process both in the physical and psychological aspects goes in reverse. Foremost, however, let us suppose that in either case psychological connectedness is maintained.

Bafflement in the face of the conceivability of such cases can, then, be avoided by witholding any application of the concept of identity on the basis of psychological connections, except in some consciously arbitrary or else some extremely limited way. For the moment, however, our concern is with their application to the neater arrangement as first envisaged by Williams and the retrospective aspect of his story. Whatever the complaints or self-congratulations of the post-operative persons, there would appear to be no more need for them to suppose that they had interchanged bodies than for each to count himself as only a survivor of someone previously embodied in the other's body. That the relation of psychological connectedness that links the two bodies happens to be one-one rather one-many, many-one, or many-many is irrelevant.

7.6 PRAGMATIC FIT
AND TELEOLOGICAL
CONTINUITY

My response to these complex fictions applies the conclusion of chapter 6. It appeals to the versions of the Reificatory and Modal Identity principles for which that chapter argues. On my version of the former principle, personal identity throughout any period of time is nothing but the continuous instantiation of OBO-abilities throughout that period. Then again, on my version of the latter, one's awareness of one's personal throughout the period is in the self-intimation of this reifying continuity. With this as my basis I now shall argue that in their various ways the various fictions we have just been considering all involve novel and – as yet, one presumes – imaginary forms of discontinuity in instantiations of OBO-abilities.

For a beginning notice that the psychological connections in which the continuous instantiation of the reifying ability intimates itself are logically inseparable from that continuous instantiation. Not only do they reveal the continuity of instantiation. Simultaneously they partly fulfil, make up, or constitute it as well. This has a twofold implication. First, it confirms a principle that debate on these issues has for so long been trying to assimilate, viz. that personal identity throughout time must involve forms of continuity that are of both a psychological and a corporeal kind. Second, it lays two restrictive conditions on such forms of psychological continuity as both reveal and partly fulfil the sort of reificatory continuity required. These forms display both a pragmatic fit and a teleological continuity. It is in the fulfilment of these two conditions that the specific nature of the reificatory continuity lies.

Pragmatic fit relates the retrospective and prospective aspects of the successive points of view of a person who has continuously embodied OBO-ability. This fit reveals and partly constitutes or fulfils the fit between the situation that the person who embodies an ability is in and those possibilities for the future to which the ability as bound to that situation leads. Through the retrospective aspect of your present point of view you understand where you are, and through the prospective aspect, on the basis of that understanding, what is open for you to do.

As for teleological continuity, it is more specific to the prospective point of view. It lies in the cognisance a person's purposes for the earlier future can take of purposes to which the fulfilment of the earlier purposes could later lead. We all tend to behave in a more or less provident way. In pursuing our immediate projects we keep a wary eye on the future that lies beyond. Thus we maintain a certain degree of teleological continuity in the OBO-abilities we acquire consecutively through our lifetime. This continuity may depend upon teleological connections of a relatively short-term character. We may realize one of our possibilities just for the purpose of realizing something that becomes a possibility only through our realization of the former, while also at the later stage realizing some consonant possibility just for the purpose of realizing something that becomes a possibility thereby, and so on. Sometimes, however, we may have long-term ambitions. The ultimately worthwhile end may be realized only through a series of possibilities each of which, except for the last, is realized only for the sake of bringing about and realizing those that come later. However, teleological continuity may also lie in nothing particularly deliberate. It may consist, at least to a large extent, in our acting in such a way as to leave ourselves with a generous set of options for consideration at later junctures in our lives.

What more exactly these two conditions require may be more evident in their breach than in their observance. In any case, it is this negative sort of illustration that our various imaginary scenarios provide. Consider first the case of teletransportation as in some ways simpler in principle, if not technically, than the others. We are to suppose that in the course of your dematerialization on one planet information is beamed to a replicator on another which duplicates your body atom by atom exactly as it was at the instant of dematerialization. In the absence, then, of some technical hitch, we are to assume that the person who emerges from the replicator has at least the memories of the person who was dematerialized. But here *ex hypothesi* the instantiation of OBO-ability is discontinuous and, despite psychological connectedness, this discontinuity would be reflected in the consciousness within which these abilities intimate themselves. Unless certain specific arrangements were made, there would be an absence of pragmatic fit between the q-memories of experience just prior to dematerialization and the first experiences of the replica, though no doubt the replica could be prepared for this lack of fit through further information inherited from you, which would include that a teletransportation had been scheduled.

The teletransportability of intention, furthermore, brings teleological continuity into question. An intention formed on an earlier occasion to X on a later occasion is not quite the same as the final executive intention to X on that later occasion. It involves, usually in an implicit sort of way, intentions to do things that lead up to the situation in which X can be done by the person who forms the earlier intention, or at least to forbear from doing things that would prevent that situation from arising. Since, then, the intention on the later occasion is not the same as the one on the earlier, it does not resemble the teletransportation of memory. In fact it is difficult to see what its teletransportation could amount to.

If, however, we waive that difficulty, it is still not clear how it could enter into your intention on the pre-transportation occasion that it is you who would finally intend to X and actually X on the post-transportation occasion. What basis would you have for thinking that it is you that the replicating person would embody? As an answer one might suggest that the latter would have a memory of your intention implanted in him. But even if your replica identifies himself with you on that basis, that is not enough to explain how antecedently you identify yourself with him. And unless you do so you cannot form the intention that the replicating person is supposed to remember.

Again, if intentions are non-causal dynamical residues, as I have earlier argued, i.e. causally underdetermined potencies for future action, they are quite unlike memory traces. No doubt the performance of any intentional action originates in some neurological occurrence within the brain. But, as a non-causal dynamical residue, what the intention is in its residual way a potency for includes along with the action the neurological occurrence in which the latter originates. It is not to be identified with any such occurrence, nor does it have any such occurrence for a basis.

That may not preclude the teletransportability of *memories* of our most recent intentions, but let us compare these with transportations of a more normal kind. On a transcontinental flight you may resolve before falling asleep to make a phone call immediately you arrive. Then when you arrive and fulfil that intention, it does not seem to be a case of just having remembered that you had such an intention. In some cases you may remember that you had an intention without any longer feeling any commitment to it, now that the time for its implementation has arrived. Nor need your fulfilment of the intention be a case of having remembered that you had the intention and then of reaffirming it. If that were the case, I don't see how one could intend sometime beforehand to do something later. It would be more a matter of leaving a memo for consideration at some later time. When at the proper time you implement an intention formed some time in the past, it would seem to be a case not of remembering having formed an intention but of remembering to do something, or better still of not forgetting to do it. Now how, or whether, this not forgetting is teletransportable is at least unclear.

Next consider a more complex but perhaps a technically less ambitious form of teletransportation, viz. psychological exchange. This type of case will involve the breach of pragmatic fit and teleological continuity alike. For the sake of the argument, however, let us continue to waive preceding qualms about intention-transportation. Pre-switch Quilty has just been surprised by Humbert Humbert in bed with Lolita. Then the switch occurs, i.e. just before the aggrieved lover can wreak vengeance upon his supplanter. The pre-switch Humbert Humbert body in its vengeful pose, hands reaching for its rival's throat, is invaded by the psychological states, including alarm and malicious glee, animating the Quilty body just before. Likewise the pre-switch Quilty body in the bed is invaded by the most recent psychological states, including jealous fury, that had previously animated the Humbert Humbert body. The point to notice here is that the most recent memories of the two post-switch bodies, if they could impress themselves as memories, would be entirely inappropriate to their situation and to the opportunities for action to which they thereby are objectively confined. Neither body, whether in its active or passive role, can be omitted from what was constitutive of the intentions that the pre-switch persons were forming just prior to the switch. Hence through neither body can these intentions be implemented after the switch.

For each no doubt the situation is very like something more ordinary, as when we awake from a dream. Hence, as in the more ordinary situation, the two post-switch persons, or their descendents after subsequent switches with which the story may be tediously embroidered, may come to adjust their lives to the psychological interruption. Indeed it would be in the spirit of the Nabokovean paradigm to suppose that the original Quilty and his descendent selves had engineered such switchings for the greater torment of Humbert Humbert and his descendent selves, just as one might induce dreams every night by taking certain drugs. But this comparison with the ordinary fails to establish the presence of the sort of pragmatic fit and teleological continuity I have claimed to be absent, for neither in our ordinary lives is a continuous identity completely realized.

We now can turn to other scenarios, viz. those of fusion and fission. One well might doubt whether the person or persons involved could in either process have any point of view at all precisely at the time of so radical an organic disruption. But supposing they had, the psychological connectedness that would extend across the moment of either crisis would not suffice either to guarantee pragmatic fit between the retrospective and prospective aspects of their point of view or to guarantee teleological continuity. There is no way in which there could be a continuous change from the OBO-abilities pertaining to two or more bodies at one time to those pertaining to one body at a later time, or reversely from those pertaining to one body at an earlier time to those pertaining to two or more at a later time. That is because it is just to its possession of OBO-ability that the embodiment of a person owes its unity as intrinsically a mutable particular at any moment. Consequently there is no way in which there is going to be pragmatic fit or teleological continuity in the self-intimation of the OBO-abilities involved in either of these two forms of transition.

To concentrate for a while on pragmatic fit, what distinguishes uniquely the OBO-ability of an agent from that of any other agent at a particular time – even if implausibly the two were as like as they could conceivably be without being one – are the particular locations of the agents at that time. It is the spatially unique character of any OBO-ability that is reflected in the unique perspectival character of the ability's self-intimation. More specifically, it is reflected in the fact that as an agent one is aware of one's present situation as from a particular place, or occupant of that place, and that those of one's memories that are the most immediately critical to one's awareness of one's ability are likewise of similarly perspectivally characterized awarenesses. Consequently, whether the self-intimations of a sequentially related set of OBO-abilities are psychologically connected or otherwise, they must reflect the continuity or discontinuity of the sequence.

Admittedly some technique is conceivable whereby many persons could voluntarily or involuntarily merge into one or one into many. Admittedly too, some psychological adjustment could in the course of time be made to whatever lack of pragmatic fit obtained between what goes immediately before the transformation and what comes immediately after. Assuming that through the technique the transition from many to one or one to many takes place in a sufficiently regular and predictable way, plans for action or the actions of the descendent selves could be based upon the experience of the selves from whom the latter descend.

Nevertheless, the later selves would in their psychological relation even to their most recent predecessors be somewhat as one who has just recently recovered from acute meningitis. They would be as someone whose powers of short-term memory are absent and whose current experiences are pragmatically incongruent with his most recent memories, because the latter are of the relatively remote past. The memories might be lively enough to include reflexive information about the epistemic source of the more objective information that they furnish. However, this reflexive information would fail to establish the linkage upon which their current reflexive knowledge of who they are and where they are at depends. Furthermore, on the basis of whatever degree of pragmatic fit pertains in such situations there would have to be at least a potential lack of co-ordination in the OBO-abilities of the selves concerned, and a corresponding

Diagram 3

fuzziness in their thinghood, that would be somewhat similar to what pertains through commissurotomy.

To pursue the point further, consider a case of fusion. Reflect on the strange experience of two pilgrims who have been journeying, one from the East, the other from the West, to the Sacred City of TOT. Their paths converge towards the end of their journey at the entrance to a Y-shaped gorge, where for the first time, if only literally, the meaning of life becomes fully transparent to each. As they come to the point of convergence they examine a plan of the way ahead translucently displayed on a perspex panel by which as yet they are divided. What, however, still is hidden is that this display has both a surface and a deeper meaning. As imbued with the latter it is a mystic symbol that signifies that their final objective is all things to all religions and denominations thereof. It consists of nothing more than a symmetrical Y with "TOT" inscribed horizontally at the end of one of the arms. Thus one of the pilgrims – a Buddhist from the East – reads the sign as on the left half of Diagram 3, whereas the other – a Christian from the West – reads it as on the half to the right. Inspired, then, by the surface significance of what they see, they press on into the shaft of the gorge. But there because of the narrowness of the path, their competitive jostling, and a one in trillion to the trillionth chance, or else by the miracle-inducing influence of the city ahead, they fuse appropriately enough into one solitary outsize Hindu. Finally the latter arrives at the Y-junction itself, where he is faced by another sign that reads laconically:

To TOT – proceed as per view of previous sign.

Now most signs are so arranged as to make it immaterial from which viewpoint you view them – so long as they remain visible. Not so here. Furthermore, for our composite pilgrim it is not merely a matter of being faced by an equivocal instruction. Attuned to the deeper significance of the previous road-plan, our Hindu is of course fully competent to deal with that. The more intriguing feature of the situation will lie in his inability to summon up both views simultaneously, at least in one unitary consciousness. Here, then, we have a case where a potential lack of psychological co-ordination has actually been realized.

With some further variation the same example might be further exploited in diverse ways. However, to accelerate the process of illustration I shall confine myself to fission as my final scenario. I also drop the topic of pragmatic fit for that of teleological continuity, and examine the application of the latter as a criterion in more cursory, because more general, terms. Suppose, then, that a person is facing the prospect of splitting voluntarily or involuntarily into two descendent selves. Suppose further that each of these future selves is psychologically no less a survivor of the person than in a unilinear life is the self who wakes up in relation to the identically embodied person who fell asleep. Nevertheless, and potentially at least, there would have to be a lack of teleological integrity in the pre-split self, for in current action the latter may have to give preferential treatment to one post-split self in situations where the two post-split selves have to compete. Just as potentially in the case of fusion there are memories of the same situation that can neither be entertained nor acted upon simultaneously, so potentially in the case of fission there would be intentions to intervene in a given situation which would be incapable both of conjoint formation and conjoint implementation.

Finally, I now re-emphasize what at various points I have already indicated. Bizarre though the preceding illustrations of breach of pragmatic fit and teleological continuity may appear to be, the breach of these conditions of personal identity across time need not be abnormal. I do not unreservedly claim that personal identity has ever been fully realized throughout the complete conscious life of the one body. By the strictest of criteria, personal identity across time should be regarded as something that is realized in a relatively patchy way. We are not in continuous possession of OBO-abilities for the whole of our lives. That we periodically fall asleep is one case of interruption. There are, however, a number of considerations by which the strictest of criteria can be tempered.

First, in sleep we are in possession of OLO-ability in the wider sense. In other words, at that time we at least have a potentiality for OBO-ability the basis of which consists in our having a sufficiently healthy nervous system – e.g. if shaken we would wake up. Strictly this potentiality is only of the secondary kind. As such, however, it confers at least a non-arbitrary extrinsic thinghood. Furthermore it is a secondary potency of a rather distinctive kind, since it is a secondary potency for primary potency. Second, through control of our bodies we can to a large extent ensure, before we fall asleep or become otherwise incapacitated, where our bodies will be when we wake up or recover.

7.7   THE MANDATORY IDEAL

I now return to the double-take in Williams's transference story. Obviously the psychological connections that story recounts fail to meet the criteria of pragmatic fit and teleological continuity. That, however, cannot entirely account for the double-take. We have already seen that their post-operative point of view does not require the post-operative persons necessarily to identify with those who pre-operatively were differently embodied. Even in their complaints or self-congratulations they have the alternative of regarding themselves as descendent selves who survive (in Parfit's sense), rather than as reidentifiable with, the selves from whom they descend. What, however, may not yet be evident is why in the second presentation the worries of the pre-operative subject should run counter to the complaints or self-congratulations of the post-operative persons in the first. The answer to this problem will help to clarify the difference between Parfit's account of personal identity and mine.

Both accounts allow for psychological connections that are less stringent than those that in part make up a person's reidentifiability. For Parfit, however, those that are sufficiently stringent would seem merely to count as limiting cases of the less stringent. They are, furthermore, connections that only hold within a very limited period of time. In consequence he commends that where the claims of a present self and its descendents conflict, we should not be over-provident. We should regard the less remote satisfaction of the former as requiring as much consideration as the more remote satisfaction of the latter, if the only significant difference between these satisfactions is in degree of remoteness. In weighing the conflicting claims we should cultivate the attitude of impartiality that we reserve particularly for the conflicting claims of others. For my part, I have advanced the connections of pragmatic fit and teleological continuity as more than a limit, rather as an ideal, though in a sense that requires some further clarification.

There are two sorts of ideal. One amounts to no more than an ideal limit, i.e. something to which a number of things approximate but never quite attain. Suppose that the shape all potatoes deviate from and yet approximate to is that of a sphere. Then the ideal limit to the shape of a potato would be the shape of a sphere. However, that most potatoes, perhaps all, are non-spherical would not in any way detract from their potatohood. Pragmatic fit and teleological continuity, however, are ideal in a further way. While they may function as a limit, there is something mandatory about them as well. Only in aspiring to their requirements can a thing have a non-arbitrary thinghood of an intrinsic and primary kind.

To return, then, to the double-take story in its second presentation, the implications of Parfit's analysis for this issue are somewhat equivocal. It would seem that, to the extent to which the subject at the moment of surgery can be regarded as merely a descendent or survivor of the pre-operative subject for whom the operation is scheduled, the anxiety of the latter is to be regarded as not entirely well founded, or at least as no better founded than our anxiety for someone else. However, it remains as a presupposition of this form of consolation that should the pre-operative person really be reidentifiable with, rather than a mere precursor of, the subject under surgery, his alarm would be appropriate. This seems to be taken as just a datum. No attention has been given to why one should be concerned now about what will happen to one later, given that it is really to one rather than to a survivor that it will happen. Why should the anticipation of an unpleasant later state be accompanied by worry merely because the state of anticipation and the later state are states of the same thing?

Given, however, that one owes one's identity to a continuous instantiation of the sort of reifying ability the self-intimation of which meets the standards of pragmatic fit and teleological continuity, what Parfit's form of consolation takes for granted can now be explained. Not only are these reifying abilities self-intimating. They are also self-desiderative. In other words, their possession at any one moment necessarily involves a desire in the persons thus reified for the continued instantiation of that sort of ability. This desire is, indeed, a controlling factor in the teleogical continuity that pertains to these abilities' self-intimation.

From this explanation something further also follows. It shows why the pre-operative and post-operative attitudes of the subjects to the same sorts of surgical intervention must be out of kilter. The surgical procedures, as detailed to the pre-operative subject, must strike him as a radical interference with the pragmatic fit and teleological continuity in which his continued instantiation of the reifying ability would be partly realized. Furthermore the desire to avoid this interference is an essential component of his pre-operative being as a person. In contrast, for the post-operative person the radical interference is over. Since it is in the past, it is no longer a threat to the fulfilment of any present desire, and more particularly no longer a threat to the fulfilment of the desire for the continued possession of the sort of ability by which they are presently reified. Hence the attitudes of these persons towards the interference can be markedly different from that of any pre-operative predecessor.

Notice, furthermore, that the discontinuity in the instantiation of the reifying ability brought about by the interference is very different from the more normal discontinuities that we suffer more ordinarily with equanimity. I have already listed the factors that mitigate the sort of discontinuity brought about by ordinary sleep. These factors are absent in the scenario of the story. That is enough to explain the difference between the equanimity with which we turn in at night and the pre-operative alarm. However, it is easy to forget, or else to make light of, the fact that as children we were less reconciled towards sleep than we came to be later. Taking sleep in our stride is something we have had to learn.

We should also remark that, despite the contrast between the more and the less normal attitude, the latter submits to no succinct classification as a type of alarm. It is, for instance, nothing as simple as a straightforward alarm at the prospect of death. That is partly because of its somewhat divided focus. At the first shot it is aroused by the prospect of imminent torture – which of course involves the victim's not being dead. Then at the second shot it is augmented by the prospect of antecedent memory loss. As thus augmented the alarm, once again, cannot be aroused by the prospect of death. Suppose, however, that the first two shots were in the reverse order. Then the alarm at the prospect of subsequent torture might not augment the alarm at the prospect of antecedent memory loss to the same extent as the latter originally augmented the former. In fact, the alarm at the prospect of antecedent memory loss might approach more closely to an alarm at the prospect of death, though I very much doubt whether it could wholly become the latter. However, none of this need surprise. It merely results from the fact that the various conceivable forms of discontinuity exceed the number towards which we have developed standard reactions.

7.8 PRIMITIVISM

According to the Butler/Reid/McTaggart sort of approach to issues of personal identity, that notion is too simple or conceptually primitive to admit or require further analysis. From this position the source of the pre-operative person's alarm would simply be that he has been led to think of himself in the first person as the subject of all the impending visitations. Now I have already dismissed in chapter 2 the doctrine that the particularity of a thing consists in some unique individual nature – either in one that can be defined descriptively or in one that consists of some undefinable residue after all the particular's characteristics have been sloughed off. The above solution would seem to be no more than that doctrine in the second of its two versions, with specific (perhaps exclusive) reference to persons. On my view what distinguishes particulars, including particular persons, from each other – after we discount all characteristics in which they could conceivably be alike even if they are not – lies in their extrinsic spatial characteristics. To that extent, then, I have already disposed of this type of classical approach.

However, there is one argument recently employed by Madell (1981, chap. 4), in support of his application of the doctrine I have dismissed, that deserves consideration before I conclude this chapter. Its purpose is to show that one's identity cannot consist in any sort of characteristics (whether intrinsic or extrinsic) that one may happen uniquely to have. He contends that one can easily imagine oneself being some historical figure, e.g. Napoleon, or that historical figure being oneself. In other words, one can imagine that certain persons, oneself and others, satisfy significantly different sets of descriptions, either intrinsic or extrinsic from those they do satisfy.

What this argument fails sufficiently to distinguish is the difference between a lunatic and someone who is sane. When a lunatic imagines that he is Napoleon, he really believes that he is fitted out with characteristics that perhaps, before going insane, he believed Napoleon had. What enters into the intentional content of his imagining is not, in other words, that he is not himself but Napoleon. In contrast, when the sane man imagines sanely that he is Napoleon, the intentional content is explicitly that he is not someone whom he actually identifies as quite distinct from Napoleon, i.e. himself, but Napoleon instead. In the imagining the lunatic believes that he is Napoleon, whereas the sane man believes that he is not. Once this difference is appreciated, it becomes evident that sane imagining that one is someone one is not in no way implies that one is not identified by certain characteristics, bodily or otherwise, for what one sanely imagines in imagining that one is not oneself is that one has not those characteristics upon which one's identity depends.

CHAPTER EIGHT

Time and Modality

8.0

We found in 6.9 that two types of power were quite distinct in how they reify. One type is primary and the other secondary. Variations in the secondary powers of the things we encounter are mainly responsible for variations in opportunity conditions, and variations in these conditions in turn are what mainly determine the occasion-bound variability of our primary powers. Hence the secondary powers are constitutive of the primary. However, it is the openness of the primary powers that confers upon these constitutive secondary powers the status of power. Given then the reifying function of power, the non-arbitrariness of the thinghood conferred by the primary and secondary types of power are respectively intrinsic and extrinsic.

I now draw attention to a further aspect of this complementary relation. It is not merely their status as powers that the secondary owe to the primary in this way. More profoundly it is the very passage of time that both they and the primary powers require for their operation. The openness of the primary powers, on the one hand, and the successive divisions of time into increasingly inclusive pasts and decreasingly inclusive futures, on the other, turn out to be conceptually interdependent. Thus one's primary powers at successive instants condition, through pragmatic fit and teleological continuity of possibilities, not just one's reidentifiability in the time ahead of each such instant. They condition as well a salient feature of the very time itself across which both one oneself and the things one encounters are non-arbitrarily reidentifiable.

8.1 TWO THEORIES OF TIME

What I am thus proposing qualifies as an A-theory of time. A brief account of that somewhat cryptic title's origin will explain why. The story goes back to McTaggart's (1908, 1927) provisionally plausible distinction between two temporal series A and B. As he viewed it the distinction falls between two serial orderings of temporal *positions*, as distinct from the occurrences therein positioned. That is worth bearing in mind. Positions in the A-series are those that run "from the far past to the near past to the present, and then from the present through the near future to the far future or conversely" (1927, §306). Each such position can therefore be labelled "an A-determination," for it temporally determines whatever occupies it. Likewise the differences between degrees of pastness and futurity can be labelled "A-relations." Positions in the B-series run, for their part, "from early to later, or conversely" (ibid). Consequently the relational properties of being temporally earlier than and of being temporally later than some position or what occupies it can be termed "B-determinations," and the relations that constitute them as "B-relations."

Notice in passing that the two relations of simultaneity and non-simultaneity that complement each other belong no more to the ordering of the B-series than to that of the A-series. That has sometimes gone unnoticed, perhaps in some public place by myself, if I could bear to look, and certainly by others (e.g. Gale, 1966, 150, to whose work I am otherwise indebted). Properly speaking neither of these two relations are relations between positions. On the contrary, they are relations between things that are positioned by virtue of having or not having the same position in the A-series or the B-series. Perhaps where t^1 is earlier than t^2 or in the past when t^2 is present or will be future, etc., the two positions might be said to be non-simultaneous. But by that we mean simply that they are not the same position rather than that they are not at the same position.

Notice again that positions in either series would seem to require for their identification therein some kind of unit of temporal measurement, e.g. that of an hour, or day, or month, or year. In both cases these units will typically consist of the interval between the recurrence of some temporal phenomenon, e.g. some solar or sidereal spatial disposition, or (what amounts to the same) between two positions of time that are identified neither by A-determinations nor by B-determinations but by their positioning such recurring phenomena. In both cases, furthermore, the members of a series of recurrent phenomena will have to be identified further, typically by reference to some origin of the series. There has to be some means for distinguishing one of those recurrent phenomena from the rest other than by its relative position in the whole series. But in the case of the A-series alone, can one such recurrent phenomenon be identified by means that are intrinsic to the series? The origin is the instant of a recurrent phenomenon that is present, and degrees of pastness or futurity are measured from there. In the case of the B-series, however, the further identification of at least one such recurrent that is required has to be by means that are extraneous to the series. Thus we can identify such positions as 10/12/80 and 11/12/80, as distinct from merely being able to tell that the first date precedes the second in time, only because we can identify the first day of the year 1 as supposedly that on which Christ was born. And even then, for us at least, the identification would seem to be incomplete. To identify a definite locality in space we have to have some kind of information about its spatial relation to here (or where in space we are). Similarly, to identify with sufficient definiteness the date of Christ's birth we need to know how many days it was before today.

With the help of this terminological clarification we can now distinguish between two opposing theories of time, in at least an approximate way, according to whether they assent to or dissent from the following claims

1 B-determinations are reducible without remainder to A-determinations
2 A-determinations are reducible without remainder to B-determinations

where it is understood in both cases that the reduction may depend upon temporal determinations of neither type, and in some sense possibly may be eliminative or merely explicative rather than analytical. Thus an A-theory might be defined as any theory that assents to claim 1 while dissenting from claim 2. In that case a B-theory might be defined as any theory that dissents from claim 1. Alternatively a B-theory might be defined as any theory that assents to claim 2 while dissenting from claim 1. In that case an A-theory might be defined just as any theory that dissents from claim 2. McTaggart held an A-theory that satisfies the former definition. Thus for him that 10/12/80 is antecedent to 11/12/80 is reducible to such facts as that 10/12/80 was past when 11/12/80 was present. In this I believe he can be shown to have been correct, provided one remembers among other things that terms like "when," "while," and "simultaneous" are series-neutral. Here, however, it is the sort of A-theory that satisfies the latter definition that I shall the most actively uphold, i.e. a theory that is principally aimed at the refutation of claim 2.

What precisely is here at stake requires, however, some further clarification. For a start let us reflect upon the structural significance of certain sentential contrasts.

AB1 Jack will have left and Jill will be about to arrive.
AB2 Jack is leaving now and Jill will arrive.
AB3 Jack has left and Jill is now arriving.

or otherwise

AB1′ Jack's departure prior to Jill's arrival is future.
AB2′ Jack's departure prior to Jill's arrival is present.
Ab3′ Jack's departure prior to Jill's arrival is past.

All three sentences are recognizably *referentially* definite. They all (if we ignore the question of whether anything in the future can be the object of definite reference) refer definitely to particular activities of particular people.[1] In this they are unlike, for example, "The plebs are rioting in the streets." They are not to be simultaneously used without change of meaning to refer to one set of particular activities or particular people in one context and another set in another context, such that in the one context they might be true and in the other false. However, the same sentences are all *temporally* indefinite. In other words, when used at different positions in either the A-series or the B-series, while retaining the same meaning and referring to exactly the same particular activities as the other two, each sentence is true at some position or positions and false at others in the following sort of systematic way.

	t^1	t^2	t^3
AB1	1	0	0
AB2	0	1	0
AB3	0	0	1

1 = true

0 = false

Yet despite their time-dependent variable truth-value the same sentences would seem to suggest a time-independent truth-value constancy, for they all agree on an order in which the actions to which they refer are positioned. This contrast between variability and constancy is attributable, furthermore, to their simultaneous involvement of both the McTaggartian types of temporal determination. In the three ABs (not the AB's) each sentence refers the more directly to mutable particulars rather than to what these mutable particulars do. Hence the A-determinations of the two particular activities are indicated by the differences between three main types of tense. Contrariwise, the AB's (not the ABs), the most direct objects of reference, are event-particulars or the activities themselves. Here the A-determinations have been indicated by a combination of the present tense with three contrasting adjectives. It is, then, to these three contrasting A-determinations that have been expressed in these two ways that responsibility for the variable truth-value goes. In addition, however, throughout the change of tense or of adjective there is some constancy in B-relations between the two definite activities of the two definite people to which all the sentences in each trio refer.

Now whether A-determinations are reducible without remainder to B-determinations must ultimately depend upon how this constancy of the latter through the variability of the former should be conceived. Is the constancy of the one in some way detachable from the variability of the other? In other words, is there some sort of temporally definite sentence (i.e. one that is true at all times, if true at any time) by means of which a B-relationship could be ascribed, which is not translatable into temporally indefinite sentences that ascribe A-determinations? The answer to this question, and the issue of detachability, depends as we shall see upon the distinguishability of a number of types of present tense.

Uncontroversially distinguishable are the contrastive, the acontrastive, the non-contrastive disjunctive, and the non-contrastive conjunctive present – alternatively the tensed, the tenseless or detensed, the tense-neutral, and the sempiternal. Thus the tensed use of "is" in "He is forty today" points to a possibility of a contrast between what something is and what it was or will be. The tenseless use as in "3 is before 4 in the series of natural numbers" points to the irrelevance or inappropriateness of any such contrast. The tense-neutral use avoids commitment by functioning as shorthand for a disjunction of past, present, and future contrastive tenses. As for the sempiternal use, it recognizes the relevance of tense-contrast likewise. As well, however, it forestalls competition between differently tensed claims by functioning as shorthand for a conjunction of past, present, and future tensings of the same verb, as in "The flash is before the bang."

Of these four kinds of present tense it is evident that the tense-neutral or non-contrastive disjunctive alone could give expression to the sort of temporally definite sentence in which a B-determined constancy could be affirmed. Thus we might employ in a temporally definite way some such formulation as "Jack leaves before Jill arrives" or "Jack's departure is prior to Jill's arrival" to express the content that is common to the ABs or the AB's. Here the present could not be the tensed or contrastive present; otherwise the sentences would be temporally indefinite. Nor could it be the sempiternal or non-contrastive conjunctive present, for we are not talking of recurrent arrivals and departures but of particular ones. Nor could it be the tenseless acontrastive present identified as such above. The mere fact that what we are looking for is how to convey a B-determined constancy throughout an A-determined variability indicates that the contrasts drawn by tenses cannot be considered irrelevant or inappropriate to the ascription of B-relations in they way in which, as our example showed, it is inappropriate to relations of a mathematical kind.

Consequently we now impinge upon more controversial ground. On the basis of our classification of present tense, the tense of the temporally definite sort of sentences that express B-constancy could only be the tense-neutral or non-contrastive disjunctive. On that supposition, however, these sentences are reducible to disjunctions of temporally indefinite sentences that ascribe A-determinations. Hence we must further consider whether our fourfold distinction has been sufficiently sensitive for its purpose. Thus one might argue that while tensed ascriptions of B-relations are significantly contrastive, the contrast to which they point is accidental or extrinsic to the B-relationships ascribed. More specifically the claim might be that tense-contrasts are between what we might, rather impressionistically, describe merely as temporal perspectives from which the B-relationship is being viewed.

For this position, then, one must distinguish between two kinds of tenseless present, where before we recognized no more than one. First, there is the acontrastive type we previously acknowledged. This type cannot apply to B-relationships for the reasons just given. Second, there is a type that ignores as purely accidental to these relationships the contrast between temporal perspectives from which they can be viewed. For the opposing position, however, there is no such tenseless present as the latter, for A-variability is not accidental to B-relations. The variability may indeed be accidental to *which* B-relation holds between two non-simultaneous events, but not to their being B-relatable. Hence A-determinations are not reducible without remainder to B-determinations, and temporally definite sentences which ascribe B-relations must be exclusively tense-neutral.

What I shall show in subsequent sections is that this latter position, i.e. an A-theory, is correct. For this purpose my procedure will be primarily constructive. Many philosophical theories, particularly those we have been encountering, tend to fall into two complementary if sharply opposed camps. While some appear initially plausible but eventually unintelligible, their opposites seem more abidingly intelligible but initially implausible. Thus indeterministic or incompatibilistic accounts of voluntary action are in their common thesis one sort of example of the initially plausible type. Absolutist accounts of value are another. The variations upon the common thesis arise quite often from their respective attempts to overcome the unintelligibility in which that thesis may seem ultimately to result. Determinist or compatibilist theories, on the other hand – and relativistic theories of value likewise – tend to acquire support mainly from the putative unintelligibility of the thesis that in common they oppose. Variations upon their common thesis arise quite often from their respective attempts to mitigate its initial implausibility. No doubt considerations of an empirical kind may also have a part to play in swinging support from one side to another, but at the level of theoretical generality to which such issues belong these considerations make no conclusive impact, and in any case any assessment of their relevance cannot be sufficiently divorced from perceptions of the intelligibility of the theories upon which they might bear. Accordingly, the most useful sort of vindication for any theory that may be temporarily relegated to the former of these two classes is simply one that renders it intelligible rather than one that refutes the antithesis. Other procedures tend to be as counterproductive as the unco-ordinated decapitation of the Hydra's heads.

Now the sort of unintelligibility in which an initially plausible theory may seem eventually to be engulfed is sometimes the product of addressing our problems piecemeal. Thus the apparent unintelligibility of indeterministic attempts to reconcile freedom with responsibility has been largely the result of failure to connect that problem of action with problems about mind, and both with the more basic problem of being. What has been wanting has been the integrative sort of analysis by means of which the indeterministic theory of action has been incorporated into a modal-identity theory of the mind-body relation and both into the understanding of agent-responsibility as intrinsic thinghood. Similarly, then, with the dispute between our two theories of time. To vindicate the A-theory it will be more useful to render it intelligible than to refute the B-theory more directly. It is convenient, furthermore, that not just the general but the more specific method turns out to be the same as in the examples just given. Indeed we are about to see that the vindication is merely by an extension of the integrative analysis in which theories of action, mind, and being have become united.

8.2 TIME AND ITERATION

In McTaggart's own initial rendering – or at least in my initial paraphrase – the essential nature of the A-series has been somewhat misrepresented. Primarily, as properly understood the A-series is not a series of diminishing degrees of pastness and increasing degrees of futurity with the present featuring as a midway zero. It is only with the assistance of some temporal metric that it can at all plausibly be so conceived. McTaggart himself had, however, a profounder insight into what gives the A-determinations their serial ordering, though one that he proceeded to misapply. To see where it leads, let us consider a parable (for a fuller version, see Rankin, 1981, 337).

Conceivably a Sophist and his establishmentarian respondent might set to as follows:

Soph.   Reality is unreal.

Est.   Really? Why so?

Soph.   Truth and falsity are incompatible determinations. Yet of any proposition p it is both true and false that p (i.e. 1p and op).

Est.   Not so. If 1p then, no doubt o~p. Likewise if op, then 1~p. Hence either (a) both 1p and o~p, or (b) both op and 1~p. But neither (a) nor (b) imply both 1p and op or both op and 1p.

Soph.   But don't you see that if you try to avoid the contradiction implicit in p in that way, the contradiction is iterated one step back. Thus not merely o~p, if o~p, but also 1~p. Not merely 1~p, if 1~p, but also o~p.

Est.   Not so again. If o~p, that entitles you to claim among other things 10~p. Likewise if 1~p, that entitles you to claim among other things oo~p. Hence in the one case both o~p and 10~p, and in the other both 1~p and oo~p. But neither of these conjunctions either implies both o~p and 1~p or both 1~p and o~p.

Soph.   But now don't you see that in hour further effort to escape contradiction you are initiating a vicious regress that will lead to infinity? Either you must rest at some stage with the contradiction or else you must proceed incessantly to a further stage. There is no *via media*. Hence, since reality is what is true or the case, and alethic predications turn out to be implicitly incoherent, reality is unreal.

Here what the issue principally turns upon is in part the connection between the alethic operators, on the one hand, and the functions of affirmation and negation performed by non-negated and negated verbs such as the copula "is" on the other, and in part again upon the logical property of iterativeness, which the alethic operators share with other sets of correlative operators. Iterativeness is the result of one member of any set of correlative operators, e.g. "true" in the alethic set, making more explicit or confirming what is already implicit in just the verb in some predication, and in the other member or members, e.g. "false," either cancelling or otherwise qualifying what would otherwise be implicit in the same verb, though in the latter case the same effect could be had by altering the form of the verb or qualifying in some way, e.g. by "not."

But that being granted, who are we to say has won? Well, with a modicum of intelligence, the establishmentarian must see that from the manner in which the debate began he has been forced into the position of regressively begging the question at issue. Polemically the fact that what he says is sound common sense, even true, is no remedy for that. As long as he regressively begs the question by regressive iteration, the regressiveness of the iteration can be made to look like the regressiveness of an attempt to suppress a contradiction that after each suppression must always re-emerge. What does save the situation for him in no way redounds to his credit. From start to finish the Sophist's position is blatantly self-refuting. To claim that any statement whatever is both true and false applies to and refutes itself.

Now McTaggart is the author of a notorious paradox, the proof of the unreality of time, to which our proof of the unreality of reality bears a remarkable resemblance. His two least controversial premisses,

1 that the three main A-determinations, viz. past, present, and future, are mutually incompatible, and,
2 that all three belong to any one event

already show that. They are comparable to what our Sophist maintained about truth and falsity. To these he then adds a more controversial premiss,

3 that without A-determinations there could be no temporal determinations at all,

in which the resemblance is maintained. It is comparable to our Sophist's less controversial, though tacit, assumption that without a distinction between truth and falsity there could be nothing real. Then by a similar flight of (or from) logic he takes 1 and 2 by themselves to demonstrate that the ascription of A-determinations to any event or moment is ineluctably incoherent, and in conjunction with 3 that time is unreal.

But his argument, like its parallel, does not stop there. He is fully alive to the need to defend the logical flight against an establishmentarian objection. With a greater exhaustiveness than I here need emulate, he articulates the principle of iteration that that flight most obviously violates. If we confine ourselves to the instance of just one A-determination, viz. the past, then this part of the principle requires

> that if an event *is* past, then it *has been* future and then present in that order.

In short, no event is ever simultaneously past, present, and future (in any sense of "is"). Hence there is no essential incoherence in the ascription of A-determinations to events.

To this objection McTaggart, however, has an embarrassing, if sophistical, retort to which for the moment I shall give a different formulation from his. To assert the protasis of the principle of iteration would be to assert effectually

> that the pastness of the event is present.

Likewise, to assert the apodosis would be to assert effectually

> that the futurity and presentness of the events are successively past.

But by 2 all three A-determinations belong to any event, including the higher-order sort of event that consists of an event's being past or present or future. In other words, by iteration or its tensed equivalents the establishmentarian has eliminated contradiction in the ascription of A-determinations to events of the first order, only to let it leak out in the ascription of the same determinations to events of the second order, and if he were to apply the same device to suppress it therein, he would reintroduce it at the level of third-order events, and so on *ad infinitum*.

Accordingly, as in the proof of the unreality of reality, the attempt at rebuttal has been forced from the start into the position of regressively begging the question in such a way as to make the regressive iteration of A-determinations appear indistinguishable from the regressiveness of an attempt to suppress a contradiction that after each suppression re-emerges. But, in contrast to the earlier proof, in this case the establishmentarian protaganist can at least be saved from his embarrassment by the exposure of a more radical flaw than the one he tried to indicate. The claim that time is unreal is not self-refuting, or at least not so obviously so as the claim that reality is unreal. No doubt one might avoid McTaggart's conclusion by rejecting premiss 3, but in so doing one would seem to concede by default the validity of the logical flight from premisses 1, 2 and 3 to the conclusion. It would be like avoiding a conclusion that reality is unreal just by denying the Sophist's assumption that without a distinction between truth and falsity there could be no reality. There is, however, a less ignominious alternative. One can vindicate the principle of regressive iteration that the flight of logic violates by means of parody. Because the procedure in the proof of the unreality of time is essentially the same as that in the proof of the unreality of reality, it becomes clear that if it were to prove anything it would prove too much. Hence it does not prove anything.

But the major purpose of my parody has not been to refute but to highlight a contrast. While McTaggart's procedure in essence has been the same as that in the parody, his actual wordings are further instructive. In his own presentation, to assent to the protasis of the principle of iteration that he supplies for consideration would be to assert effectually

the event to be past *at a moment of present time.*

Likewise, to assent to the apodosis would be to assert effectually

the event to be future and present *at successive moments of past time.*

Here then lies the contrast. An alethic determination directly qualifies another with narrower scope and in so doing either cancels what it qualifies (as 01p cancels 1p) or redundantly reinforces it (as 11p reinforces 1p). Similarly an A-determination may directly qualify another with narrower scope, and in so doing either cancel what it qualifies (as the pastness of the presentness of an event cancels the latter's presentness) or redundantly reinforce it (as the presentness of the pastness of presentness of an event does). But the qualification by one A-determination of another is relativized in a way in which

Diagram 4

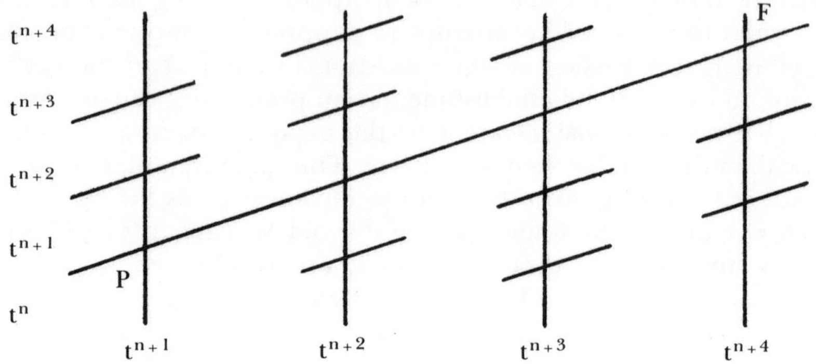

qualification by an alethic determination of another is not – or at least need not be – i.e. to a moment of time.

Now it is here in the relativization to moments of time that the seriality of the A-series appears at its most distinctive. To make this the more evident I shall, however, first depart from McTaggart's and my own previous practice. Let us represent the present not just as an intermediate if minimal compartment of time between past and future, but as constituting or constituted by a past/future (P/F) cut, i.e. *the* P/F cut. It is thus to be conceived as one among a set of moments, and that moment just as the bisection that renders one continuous set of events past and the rest future. But not only does that bisection separate past events from future. It also separates past moments and past P/F cuts from future moments and future P/F cuts.

Let us allow each vertical line in Diagram 4 to represent the same stretch of time. On each such line, bisection by the continuous diagonal can then be taken as the P/F cut that is present or as the present moment. Bisection by the shorter diagonals on that same line will then represent P/F cuts that are past and P/F cuts that are future, or past and future moments to which these cuts are relativized, according to whether they are below or above the major or present bisection.

But not merely do these bisections or moments on each vertical line form a set. As the diagram indicates, they also fall into a serial order, for the past and future sections have a comparative inclusiveness and exclusiveness relative to each other. Thus each member of the set is internally related to every other in unidimensional time somewhat as the members in a set of Chinese boxes, or the interlocking surface planes by which they are bounded, are internally related in three-dimensional space. Each member either encloses or is enclosed in one or other of the sections of each of the rest. Each member thus positions each of the others in relation both to itself and to the rest. Each member is self-ordering. That this, then, is the order imposed by the A-determinations distinctive of each member of the set gives it the status of the A-serial order of time.

For the very same reason it is, however, the B-serial order of time as well. In some sense of the present tense that I am about to use, one cut is(?) *temporally* before another, if it is(?) less inclusive in respect of its past section and (consequently) more inclusive in respect of its future section. It is(?) temporally after if the converse is true. More simply, one cut and the moment it identifies is(?) before another and the moment it identifies, if and only if it is(?) in the past relative to the latter moment. Again, it is(?) after, if and only if it is(?) in the future relative to that same moment. In spite of their provisionally indeterminate sense, in some sense these two statements seem to be true, and true furthermore by virtue of an inter-definability among the A-terms and B-terms they involve. That is what makes the before and after here belong to the temporal order rather than to an order of a non-temporal kind.[2]

Now in the diagram these claims are best represented by squeezing all the vertical lines horizontally into just one. Call this the vertical reading. There is, however, a more profound and more comprehensive significance in the converse procedure, i.e. in the status quo. Each moment in the series of moments $t^n - t^{n+4}$ is thus represented by a separate vertical line that has all the other lines squeezed into it, but yet in each case in a distinctive way. Call this the horizontal reading. The contrast represents a feature of the seriality of P/F cuts that is relatively hard to articulate. As vertically conceived, and with no reference to the horizontal dimension, each such moment or cut would be past or future merely in relation to some other moment or cut on the vertical and present in relation to itself. As horizontally conceived, however, the same series of cuts or moments acquires an absolutized aspect, though only consecutively member by member. Each moment on that axis is *tense-neutrally* the (present) P/F cut, other P/F cuts on one side or the other, or both, being relativized to times that belong to its past and future sections.

Thus in insisting that every moment or event is past, present, *and* future McTaggart was not being completely silly. The sophistry is not simply due to an abuse of relational terms. It is not comparable to the claim that a certain moment is both before and after, all at the same time, and hence in its nature conceptually incoherent. The appropriate response is not that a certain moment may be past relative to another, present relative to itself, and future relative to a third, but not all relative to the same *moment*, just as it may be before another and after a third, but not relative to the same moment. As well as having these A-determinations tense-neutrally relative to various moments, the moment also has them tense-neutrally *without further qualification*.

McTaggart's mistake was more complex in character – a combination of two misidentifications. First, he seems to have conceived absolutized A-determinations to be absolutized somewhat as the properties of largeness and smallness, despite a relational component, are absolutized. When we say that something is large or that it is small, there is commonly a tacit comparison of that thing with something that is accepted as standard in size for the same type of thing. In this way, through an absolutization of relational terms there is a genuine contradiction in saying of that thing that it is both large and small. Second, he interprets the ascription of A-determinations thus conceived as *tenseless*. Combining these two misidentifications he then claims that to ascribe all three A-determinations to a moment or event is to assert of either that it is in three incompatible relations to some one entity outside of time. But in this interpretation he is, of course, wrong. An absolutized ascription of three A-determinations to the same moment can be true only if it is tense-neutral. More lengthily, the conjunctive ascription is true – indeed truistic – if it asserts of any moment that it either was, is, or will be past absolutely, either was, is, or will be present absolutely, and either was, is, or will be future absolutely.

To this account of the serial nature of the A-series and McTaggart's contribution to the understanding thereof, one further qualification must however now be added. The convenience of regarding the A-series as a series of bisections – one in which the present is primarily the one that is dominant – is obvious. In practice it lends itself the most readily to a diagrammatic representation. However, time is commonly regarded as trisected rather than bisected by past, present, and future, even if as a duration the present is recognized as being much more confined than the past and the future between which it intervenes. Now so far as I can see without going more deeply into the matter, there is nothing to preclude the relativized and absolutized aspects of the A-series from being represented in terms of trisection rather than bisection. Thus as a beginning we could draw another continuous diagonal in our diagram, say from t^{n+2} on the left vertical to parallel the diagonal that intersects that same line at t^{n+1}.

But ontological considerations as well as those of convenience weigh against the view that time is to be cut in that manner. One might perhaps argue that events (as distinct from substances) cannot properly be said to exist as opposed to occur, at least if their existence is subject to tensing. But in any case, if they do have a tensed type of existence at all, it is primarily due to their tensed occurring. Thus those that existed are events that have already occurred by some past time, those that exist now are those whose occurrence has reached completion just at this instant, and those that will exist are those that are about to occur. In this way a dichotomy arises between what has occurred either before or by this instant and what has yet to occur. Time no doubt trichotomises in what has occurred, what is occurring now, and what will occur. But what is occurring now cannot be identified with events that now exist, for what is occurring now dichotomizes into one section that has just occurred and a remaining section that has yet to occur.

There may be some other rational way to tie the tensing of event-existence to that of event-occurrence. But what to avoid is the location in the present of the beginning as well as the end of an event that exists now. That would lead to the Null-Sandwich Paradox, unless we resort to desperate measures. Time degenerates into a temporally non-extended existent between two temporally non-existent extensions.

8.3 THE ONTOLOGICAL BASIS
OF THE A-SERIES — I

The vertical reading of the A-series as a series of P/F cuts has been relatively unaspiring. It interprets A-determinations in a purely relativized way. furthermore, the tense in which A-determinations as thus interpreted and B-determinations are interdefinable was left indeterminate. Ultimately, however, A-determinations are in some respect absolutized as well as relativized. This fact can no longer be left out of account. To what, then, does the A-series owe its horizontal aspect, i.e. the consecutive absolutization of its members?

In this section I shall consider a version of the B-theory answer to that question. It approximates closely enough to other versions of the same type to be given a representative status (see Russell, 1940, chap. 7; Reichenbach, 1948, §51; Smart, 1956, 224).[3] According to this version, the various past, present, and future tenses of tensed verbs, the A-adjectives such as "past," "present," and "future," and the A-adverbs such as "now" and "then" are all to be conceived as having an indexical function. More specifically they all point to the B-relations that the event or events, which they serve temporally to locate, have to linguistic or cognitive tokens that locate them. In other words, one locates the event or events about which one is talking or writing or thinking by virtue of the B-relations to the speech-act, or the writing or reading of the inscription, or merely the thought-act that refers to these events. In this way the various A-terms are supposed to function somewhat as do the personal pronouns, "I," "you," "we," and "they," and spatially locative adjectives or adverbs such as "here" and "there." More specifically and ambitiously, however, the analysis further insists that an event is past by virtue of being *tenselessly* before the linguistic or cognitive act that refers to it, present by virtue of being *tenselessly* simultaneous with or overlapping the act, and future by virtue of being *tenselessly* after. On this supposition, these tenseless sentences render the meaning of sentences that are tensed. Thus, to take one of our earlier examples, AB′ (i), "Jack's departure prior to Jill's arrival is future," would be rendered as logically equivalent to some such conjunction as "Jack's departure is (tenselessly) before Jill's arrival and the two events are (tenselessly) after this token."

Now there is a lot that is in principle right, as well as a lot that is in principle wrong, with this admittedly rather rough and ready presentation of the B-theory solution. Notice that it does provide an account of what it is to single out one P/F cut from the whole series of P/F cuts as present, of what makes the cut uniquely present, rather than present just in relation to itself. Notice too that it also accounts for what it is for the absolutization of that cut as present to be just one in a consecutive series of absolutizations in which each absolutized cut cancels or abnegates the absolutization of its predecessors. Thus the B-relationship of an event to the linguistic or cognitive token that describes and locates the event by a B-relational reference to itself can itself be something described and located by a subsequent linguistic or cognitive token through a B-relational reference to the latter. In short, the analysis does provide a rationale for the complex iterative character of A-terms that we reviewed in the previous section. Given that our thought-acts are self-referring, it even accounts in a manner for the trivial iterations *ad infinitum* of presentness, i.e. that which is present is at present present and so on.

Furthermore, there is no serious difficulty for the analysis in the fact that linguistic or cognitive tokens do not conveniently occur at all points in time at which we would like to suppose that a P/F cut does occur, i.e. at any point in time (Prior, 1967, 12 contra Smart,

1956).[4] There is no need to postulate an eternal supernatural being or an eternal series of less long-lived supernatural beings with cognitive equipment similar to ours. It is enough that there should be just a few such linguistic or cognitive acts sparsely scattered over a relatively brief finite period of time. That would permit distinctions between past and future sections of P/F cuts determined by moments that intervene between these acts, or fall outside that comparatively brief period of time. Thus, take an earlier and later moment both at a finite distance in the very remote past of an earlier and later activity-related P/F cut. Both moments may determine P/F cuts albeit indirectly, even though no linguistic or cognitive activity occurs anywhere near these two times. The later of the two cuts so determined abnegates the earlier at the later time just by being a shorter distance in the past of the later activity-related P/F cut than the earlier at the time that the later activity-related P/F cut abnegates the earlier activity-related P/F cut.

Nor again, and just to forestall misunderstanding, does the trouble lie in any attempt to render a temporally indefinite sentence as one that is temporally definite. Although the rendering is supposedly tenseless, that is not enough to make it temporally definite. In fact one can plausibly claim that the inclusion of the indexical "this" as qualifying an ephemeral type of event, i.e. a speech- or thought-token, imparts the necessary temporal indefiniteness that the rendering requires.

Where the main trouble lies is in something that the comparison between A-expressions and other indexicals is enough to suggest. There can be no logical equivalence between what an indexical sentence says and what it indicates or a conjunction of what it says and what it indicates. Thus, in the suggested rendering of AB' (1), to just what speech-, inscription-, or thought-token is the "this" supposed to refer? It cannot be to a token of AB' (1), for the logical equivalent of a sentence should be capable of replacing that sentence, thus preventing that sentence from being uttered. Furthermore, AB' (1) is ordinarily taken to be capable of stating the same fact as AB' (2), depending upon the times at which the respective sentences are uttered. But on the same interpretation the "this" in the conjunctive analysans of AB (2) would have to refer to a token of AB (2). Thus the two sentences would be stating slightly different facts rather than just the one. Nor in the light of these difficulties may one interpret a token to which the "this" refers as a token of the analysans rather than the analysandum. Given the logical equivalence of the one to the other, the analysandum would have to refer to that token as well. But how could it? An analysandum-token must be capable of referring to whatever it refers to in the absence of any analysans-token.

That, however, might conceivably be dismissed as a superficial objection. For certain purposes, one might suppose, it might be more perspicuous to replace a sentence like "It was raining" by another like "There is rain at a time before this token" or "There is rain at a time before K," where the "is" is tenseless and "this token" and "K" are respectively a definite description and a name not of the token replaced but of its replacement. Why one should suppose this is perhaps a problem. The phrase "this token" is just another indexical, and likewise for "K," if my account of proper names is approximately correct. One might reply that it can be illuminating, or at least mentally uncramping, to replace one set of indexicals by yet another once in a while. However, what this whole line of defence fails to appreciate is that, in relinquishing the claim that the proposed replacements are reductive analyses that are logically equivalent to what they replace, it removes from the hypothesis that a tenseless present is applicable in this context, whatever plausibility that hypothesis may previously seem to have had. If the replacement had been a reductive analysis of what it replaces, then indeed there would have had to be such a thing as a tenseless present for the verb in the replacement to be in. Otherwise, by virtue of circularity, the reductive analysis would have failed in what it attempts. As it is, the proposed replacements are just bad grammar.

We can shift, furthermore, to a quite different sort of complaint. The range of indexicals is somewhat wider than those that here have been taken as paradigmatic. Admittedly there is something highly subjective, indeed personal, about the way in which the use of such terms as "I," "you," "here," "there," "this," "that," and many others secure reference — so much so that when two or more people are conversing with each other about the same things, they cannot use exactly the same indexicals. What one person refers to as "I," "here," and "this," another may have to refer to respectively as "you," "there," and "that." Other indexicals are, however, far less personal in their mode of application — so much so that their indexical character may not be recognized. Here I refer to common and garden definite descriptions as in "The curtains are blue" and, once again, to proper names. In uttering "the curtains," two people may be referring to the same thing, even though the phrase does not describe one set of curtains absolutely uniquely, and so also with a name like "John," even though many males have that name.

Whereabouts, then, in this variety should we place the indexical "now" and its temporal congenors? There would seem to be no simple contrast. But in many contexts at least their appropriate use is less personal than that of the singular personal pronouns and spatial demonstratives. Where they occur in conversation or communication, it would seem that one identifies the time to which they refer by their relation to the communal act of communication. In this way, then, they are more like definite descriptions and names than personal pronouns, though of the latter two kinds of indexical perhaps the least like the singular pronouns.

These might seem to be relatively harmless afflictions. All they show is that the task of identifying a time need not fall exclusively upon speech- or thought-tokens that are peculiar to one person when that person is in communication with others. More to the point, I believe, is the fact that these referential identifiers are essentially thought tokens or cognitive acts rather than the linguistic tokens in which they find expression. That is because the distinction between past, present, and future is evident to us without the aid of language. Furthermore, these thought-tokens or cognitive acts must be *essentially* reflexive if they are to fulfil their function. That they are reflexive or self-referring cannot just be contingent. That is because of the essential if trivially iterative character of the present P/F cut. As we saw, if a P/F cut is present, then it is present at present, and present at present at present, and so on. Hence, if its presentness is identified by simultaneity with one's cognition of it, then one's cognition of it must implicitly at least involve one's cognition of the simultaneity of the cut with that cognition, and so on, *ad infinitum*.

Now I am far from saying that there is anything absurd about that. Its significance here is to be found in the fact that on the standard sort of theory of mind that underlies the B-theory, the property of essential reflexiveness is surely incomprehensible. If a cognitive activity were some kind of occurrence capable of causing or being caused by a physiological process, or if it were some kind of process that could at best only run parallel to a physiological process, or if it were just a physiological process itself, it would seem totally unintelligible that it could be essentially reflexive or self-conscious. Indeed, many would seem to concede as much at least by implication. Despite their other differences they agree with Ryle that our conscious activity is systematically self-elusive. The offered rationale is that a pointer in the act of pointing at something, or a scanner in the course of scanning, cannot simultaneously point at the pointing, or scan the scanning. What this then shows is that even

if the reflexivenes of conscious activity be taken as a datum, it is one
with which the more widely prevalent theories of mind are unable
to cope. If awareness, at least at the most basic perceptual level, is
to be conceived as some kind of reaction either in a spiritual substance or a physical organism with the object of awareness, then on
that sort of model even our apparently reflexive awareness must
involve some kind of time-lag that precludes the awareness of the
awareness's being identical with or included within the latter.[5]

8.4   THE ONTOLOGICAL BASIS
OF THE A-SERIES — II

What I propose is a form of A-theory both in a negative and a positive
sense. On the one hand, it denies that the ascription of A-determinations is to be defined, analysed, eliminatively reduced, or just
explicated in terms of ascriptions of B-relations, if the latter are
conceived as tenseless. On the other, it accepts that B-relations are
definable in terms of A-determinations, and likewise that A-determinations are definable in terms of B-relations, provided the latter
are conceived as tensed. As its basis it takes the Modal Identity Thesis
as already put forward. If we abstract the relativized from the absolutized nature of the members of the A-series, this same distinction
can be understood in terms of a similar abstraction of what is intimated from what intimates in the self-intimation both of OBO-
abilities and of the impendings of intentional action in which these
abilities are realized. Let me emphasize, however, that no attempt
will be made to regard the distinction as other than an abstraction,
i.e. as other than a distinction in aspect.

With this caveat, in its relativized or vertical aspect the A-series or
series of P/F cuts can be represented in terms of Diagram 5. Here
the branchings from each lettered node stand, whether hatched or
continuous, for actions. They indicate that each one such action is
possible relative to some node while impossible relative to others.
More specifically, the possibility is relative, not to the node from
which the action immediately branches, but to the node, if any, from
which that node branches. Thus relative to that less immediate node,
the actions that branch from the immediate node are all both equally
and exhaustively possible. Relative to the immediate node, however,
and to whatever nodes branch therefrom, none of the actions that
branch from it is *any longer* possible, save one. Furthermore, that
one action, here represented by a continuous line, is actual under
two aspects, rather than possible. Relative to the node from which
it immediately branches it is actually impending at the time that

Diagram 5

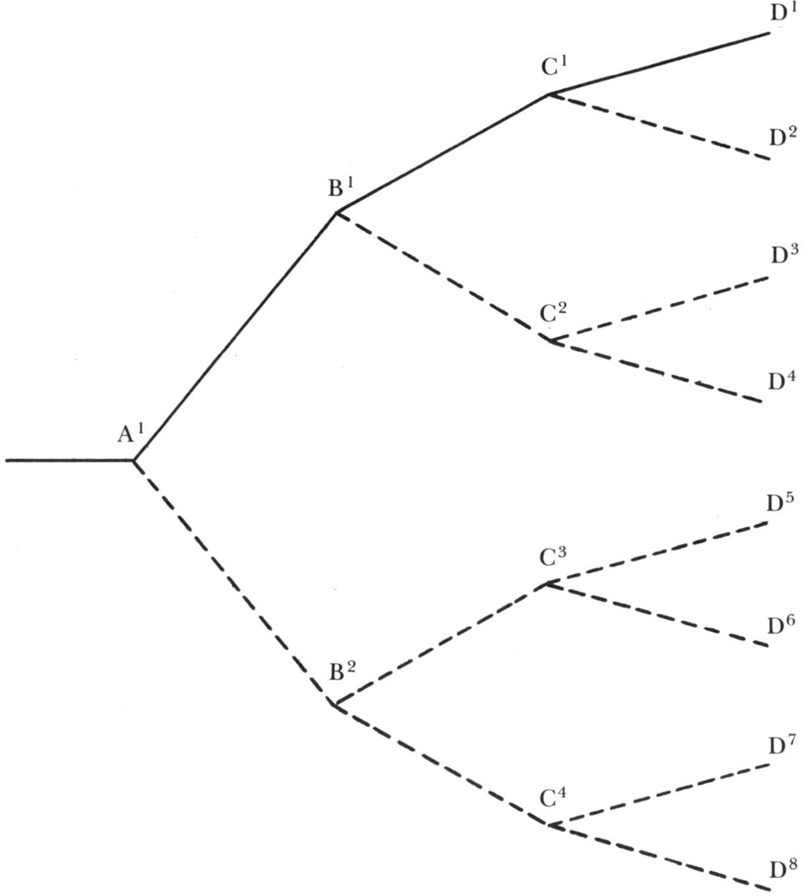

dates that node. Relative to the node towards which it branches and thereafter, it is in the past. (Notice that all these modalities are relativized and that all present-tense ascriptions are consistently tense-neutral). But, of course, the diagram at best is only an idealization of reality. To be more realistic it would have to be highly irregular in the distances between nodes, more hairy, and more extended in either direction.

Since the time of Bergson at least, philosophers have frequently warned against the dangers of spatializing time. This danger is particularly acute where one relies upon a diagram. Thus at its most superficial the diagram here might be taken to suggest that the distinction between past and future is to be reduced to some one-many relationship between *existents*. But what *could* happen in the future may never actually do so, and in that sense may never exist. Hence this suggestion must be resisted. The relationship is not one in which all the terms can be existent.

Then again, even on that understanding, an equally misleading suggestion may still linger. It may seem that the relationship in question is intended as more primitive than the A-serial order, in the sense that it is a relationship from which that order can be derived. That, however, is not what the diagram is designed to show. More specifically, its purpose is not to show that the temporal precedence of the past section of any P/F cut over the future section thereof is derivable from the asymmetrical transitivity of a one-many relation of determinate to indeterminate existents.

One may, perhaps, be tempted to say – as I once was – that the order of time is an ontological order, or an order of being. That sort of statement once commended itself to me for the purpose of explaining why one type of serial order rather than its converse is the serial order of time, if the serial order of time is to derive from some more fundamental relation. It allowed one to say that the temporal order of events, unlike any other event-order, was actually constitutive of the events that belong to the set that is temporally ordered. It encouraged one to liken events to the members of an exclusive club constituted solely for the purpose of electing aspiring members to its membership. Each member prior to his election owes, we may suppose, his eligibility for membership to nomination by a previously elected member. Accordingly, as a member each member falls into a certain constitutive order of priority. Similarly, then, the temporal order of two consecutive events would be conceived as constitutive of the events so ordered. The basis of the comparison would be that the *possibility* of one is causally dependent upon the actuality of the other and the actuality of the latter causally necessitated by the mere possibility of the former. There are, however, at least three reasons for not falling into any such kind of talk.

First, any attempt to derive temporal order from the asymmetry of any relation other than that of time itself is suspect. It presupposes the order it attempts to derive. Thus the derivation of an order, say, of mammals from the relation *smaller than* consists in taking the referent of the relation, say a mouse, first in time and the relatum, say a chipmunk, later in time.

Second, and more particularly, to represent intentions as non-causal dynamical residues, as I have done, is to require that the future section of each cut is initiated in something quite determinate. Thus as A^1, or sometime prior to B^1, the future beyond B^1 is certainly indeterminate. The agent can bring about at B^1 either B^1C^1 or B^1C^2 to the exclusion of anything else. But then at B^1 it loses its indeterminacy in a significant respect. According to what one then executively intends, whichever action one is *not* about to do is no longer something one *can* bring about, but merely something one *could have* brought about had one not been about to bring about the other. It is, then, only in further stages of the future section of a P/F cut that it can be said to be indeterminate.

Third, and in any case, the distinction between the actual and the merely possible cannot be drawn independently of the temporal distinctions in question. The A-terminology seems essential to set out the relationships between the various actual and possible cuts and events that the diagram represents. This is so even in the relational application suitable to our limited concern with the vertical aspect of the A-series. Thus, relative once again to the B^1 P/F cut being the present cut, we say that A^1B^1 *has happened*, that A^1B^2 could prior to A^1 *have happened* but no longer *can happen*, that B^2C^3 and B^2C^4 *could have been now about to happen* but no longer *can*, then passing to the future section, that say B^1C^1 *is about to happen* whereas B^1C^2 *could* likewise *have been about to happen* instead but no longer *can*, that C^1D^1 *can happen* and that C^1D^2 *can happen* though not conjointly, and so on.

Accordingly, the demand for some more primitive relation from which to derive the temporal order must be resisted. But the alternative is not to relapse into Bergson's irrationalism, nor to follow his prescription by ringing the changes among, or mixing, some stock of metaphors for the purpose of improving our insight. In place of a reductive analysis it is enough to supply one that is integrative – one that both illuminates and vindicates the application of A-distinctions by showing how applications of temporal and causal modal categories are interdependent.

What, then, is the point of the branching diagram and of the integrative analysis that the diagram serves? Well, simply to put the A-terminology to work, to show what is its purpose, i.e. what could not be done without it. It is needed to draw the necessary distinctions between the modalities of the respective cuts and occurrences that the diagram represents. Tense-inflections and their equivalents go hand in hand, in other words, with the distinctions within the subjunctive and indicative moods whereby we articulate what is implicit in the generalization that the past is *fixed* or *determinate* whereas the future is relatively *open* and *indeterminate*.

As an account of the A-series in its vertical aspect this, however, is not quite enough. No such account can stand if not at least con-

sistent with a satisfactory account of the horizontal aspect. If as well
it supplies the latter sort of account from within its own resources,
then so much the better. A further authority would thereby accrue,
for it seems natural to suppose that the vertical and horizontal aspects
of the A-series are conceptually connected. Now in interpreting the
A-series in terms of an interconnected series of OBO-abilities, we
secure this connection. With the self-intimation of such a series, two
aspects can likewise be distinguished, viz. what is intimated and what
intimates therein. Given, then, that the vertical aspect of the A-series
coincides with the intimated aspect of OBO-abilities as serially ordered, the intimating aspect of the latter must coincide with the
horizontal aspect of the former. Through this interpretation, furthermore, it becomes obvous as well why the A-series should present
both aspects. The intimating of that which is intimated must likewise
be intimated therein, since what is intimated is self-intimating.

Other accounts of the horizontal aspect do, of course, employ a
similar device. On one supposition, as we saw, when the cock is
cognized as crowing, the crowing is present absolutely and not just
present relative to itself or something simultaneous with it, because
it is tenselessly simultaneous not just with some activity of perception
but with the very activity whereby it is perceived. This activity is,
accordingly, accredited with the privileged and absolutizing role by
virtue of its self-reference.

On the Modal Identity Thesis, however, the order of analysis is
to some extent reversed. Thus instead of analysing the A-determinations that constitute a P/F cut in terms of a tenselessly B-relating
reflexive awareness, it analyses the reflexive awareness in terms of
these determinations. The series of P/F cuts consists of a series of
OBO-abilities in the sense that it is the function of all the A-determinations that constitute the former to articulate the serial order of
the latter. Given, then, that one's awareness of one's current OBO-
ability is both a component of that ability and in itself a conditional
form of the latter, it is likewise a component and conditional form
of the P/F cut that articulates that ability. Thus one's awareness of
the present situation, i.e. of what has occurred, of what is immediately about to occur, and of what less immediately may be about to
occur thereafter, is itself in part constitutive of the situation of which
it is an awareness. Accordingly, the absolutization of a given cut as
the present cut just consists in its being the cut of which one's present
consciousness is constitutive as well as conscious.

As in the B-theory, one's knowledge of the momentary absolute
present as that momentary absolute present is due to the reflexivity
of one's awareness. That of which one is reflexively aware, however,

does not consist of tenseless relations between independently existing and characterizable situations, on the one hand, and the awareness of which these situations are the objects, on the other. On that supposition – according to their respective tenseless relations to one's awareness – these situations would, presumably, have to be past, present, or future, even if, in addition to being aware of them, one were not aware of that awareness. On the contrary, the reflexivity of the awareness is simply due to that very awareness's being constitutive of the present situation, i.e. having a primary physical occasion-bound power, of which it is aware. Neither our awareness of the situation nor our awareness of that awareness is extra to that situation. Hence the reflexiveness is the essential sort required, as we saw in 8.3, by the essential iterativeness of presentness.

This integration of the vertical with the horizontal aspects of the A-series finds some further confirmation in what many have perceived as a particularly puzzling feature of time. Time is something within which we make our empirical discoveries. The function of experience is, among other things, to tell us *how* distinguisable phenomena are related in time, not *whether* they are related in time. That they are temporally related somehow or other is something the questions that experience can settle presuppose. In that sense, time is what Kant distinguished, with no doubt a misleading subjectivist emphasis, as a form of intuition. The explanation can now be seen to lie in the fact that what is responsible for time, viz. the newtork of actual and possible OBO-abilities, is likewise through its self-intimation responsible for the intimation of time. In intimating itself, what each such ability intimates includes the circumstances that distinguish it from the rest. But what they all must intimate, and cannot avoid intimating, is what they have in common, viz. the occasion-bound openness of possibilities upon which the temporality of the circumstances, whatever they are, depends.

Notice, too, that the same account does not ignore the relatively public or impersonal nature of A-distinctions. While in a community of interacting agents, each person's OBO-abilities are indeed personal to that person; nevertheless, one person's abilities are constitutive of another's. This fact introduces a kind of perspectival interpenetration that, in Whiteheadian language, might be characterized as that pertaining to a collection of windowed monads. (See Diagram 6.)

Consider a universe consisting of just two persons X and Y and whatever is required for them to interact. Suppose them to be so situated that at some time t^n they have to interact with each other in one way or another. Suppose further that at t^{n-1}, some short time

Diagram 6

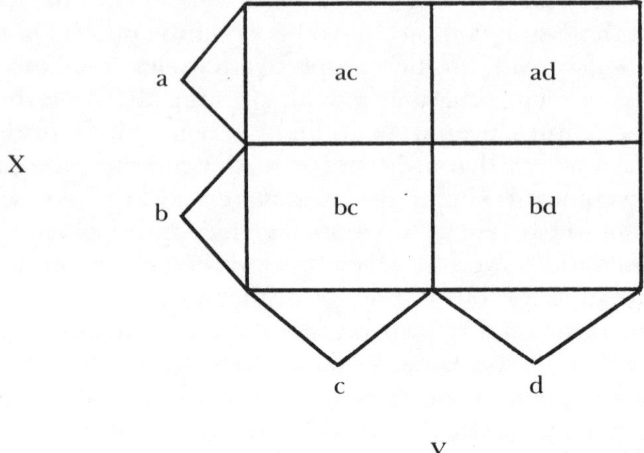

before, X has the mutually exclusive and exhaustive causal possibilities of doing *a* at t^n and of doing *b* at t^n. Likewise suppose that Y at t^{n-1} has the mutually exclusive and exhaustive possibilities of doing *c* at t^n and of doing *d* at t^n. Finally, suppose that the interactive activities at t^n, which causally at t^{n-1} are distributively possible, are exclusively and exhaustively *ac*, *ad*, *bc*, and *bd*, without any preferred order. In these circumstances there will be a perspectival structuring of possible interactions as follows. X at t^{n-1} has a choice of doing or bringing about either *ac* or *ad* rather than *bc* or *bd* or reversely at t^n. (Here the "rather than" serves as a bracketing device for each of its flanking disjunctions). In contrast Y has a choice at t^{n-1} of doing or bringing about either *ac* or *bc* rather than *ad* or *bc* or reversely at t^n. Theirs, then, is a cosmic game rather like "scissors, rock, and paper," though much simpler and with no necessary competitive incentive. Thus the possibilities at t^{n-1}, one or other of which it is up to each agent to realize at t^n, contain each within itself possibilities at t^{n-1}, one or other of which it is up to the other agent to realise at t^n.

At the same time, however, the same possibilities fall into an impersonal structure that is indifferent to the perspectival bracketing. Consequently, there is a corresponding impersonal or public structure of spacetime, in so far as the latter is determined by such causal disjunctiveness. This impersonal structure functions as a kind of common denominator within the diversity of personal spacetimes.

Then again, in addition to this kind of common denominator there has to be another of a more reduced or lowlier kind. The one that was higher was constituted by the primary powers of the agents concerned, within each case of which both the primary and secondary powers of other agents and things are involved. The lower kind, in contrast, consists just of the secondary powers both of things that have and of things that don't have primary powers. The secondary powers are in a qualified way dependent upon agents and primary powers. As a first approximation let us say that they are dependent in the way in which the general manual-toolishness of manual tools is dependent upon the skill of the hand. Consequently the world of those things that owe their mutable particularity to their possession of secondary powers is something of a public construct. Just as tools are regarded as tools irrespective of whether the hands of one of a community of two users have been temporarily deprived of their skill or not, so we think of such objects as mutable particulars irrespective of whether any of us happens to be asleep or in a coma or in some lesser state of ignorance.

8.5 REICHENBACH'S INDETERMINISM

Of course, if as an indeterministic theory the integration of the vertical and horizontal aspects of the A-series as above were open to the type of criticism to which other indeterministic forms of A-theory have been subjected, it would have at the very least to be revised. Accordingly, in this section I defend it against an objection of that type.

In distinguishing between the two sections of a P/F cut in terms respectively of what at the dividing moment is recordable (the past) and what is unpredictable (the future), Reichenbach (1953, 154–7; 1956, Appendix, 269–70) came under attack from Grünbaum (1967, 347–8), who writes

every event, be it Plato's birth or a birth taking place in A.D. 2000, *at all times* constitutes a divide in Reichenbach's sense between its own recordable past and its unpredictable future, *thereby satisfying Reichenbach's definition of the "present" or "now" at any and all times!* And if Reichenbach were to reply that the indeterminacies of the events of the year of Plato's birth have already been transformed into a determinacy, whereas those of A.D. 2000 have not, then the rejoinder would be: this tensed conjunction holds for any state between sometime in 428 B.C. and A.D. 2000 that qualifies as now during

that interval on grounds other than Reichenbach's assymetry of determined-
ness; but the second conjunct of this conjunction does not hold for any state
after A.D. 2000 which qualifies as now after that date. Accordingly, contrary
to Reichenbach, the now of conceptualized awareness must be invoked tacitly
at time t, if the instant t is to be non-trivially and non-arbitrarily singled out
as present or now by Reichenbach's criterion, i.e., if the instant t is to be
uniquely singled out at time t as being "now" in virtue of being the threshold
of the transition from indeterminacy to determinacy.

Now, on my reading of the passage Grünbaum partly quotes before making this comment, Reichenbach has in effect conceded the
point made in the last sentence above. Reichenbach's account of
becoming depends only in part upon his application of the indeterminacy relation of quantum mechanics. In its other part it depends
upon a token-reflexive analysis of tense of the kind outlined in my
account of the B-theory above. For our present purpose the difference between his account of tense and Grünbaum's is immaterial,
since both are in terms of supposedly tenseless ascription of temporal
relations. Accordingly, Grünbaum's criticism does not apply quite as
it expressly stands. It does, however, contain the further sufficiently
damaging implication that if the analysis of tense is independent of
any account in terms of the indeterminacy relations that Reichenbach
found necessary to invoke as well, then that analysis of tense alone
is sufficient for the purpose of explaining what constitutes the "now."
However, the implication does not reflect upon the indeterministic
theory I have offered above. We may note in passing that this theory
does not identify the indeterminacy of OBO-abilities with the quantum mechanical kind, nor do I subscribe to the token-reflexive analysis of tense or any reductive analysis of that genre. The main
difference lies, however, in the circumstance that for Reichenbach
the connection between indeterminacy and the reflexiveness of
speech or consciousness is external, whereas on my account indeterminacy and the reflexivity of consciousness are internally connected. Hence on my theory, contrary to what Grünbaum has
alleged, the analysis of tense and the absolutization of the A-series
therein invoked is not independent of the postulation of indeterministic relations.
Grünbaum's opening claim that every event that constitutes a divide between the determined and undetermined would do so *at all
times* may seem, indeed, to carry a certain independent polemical
force. However, Reichenbach's series of divides as it stands is comparable to the series of OBO-abilities in its purely vertical or relativized aspect. As we saw, the ordering of that series is tense-neutral

and not tenseless. In that ordering the question of which node constitutes the absolute present is not removed. It is merely not settled. Accordingly, in so far as Grünbaum's claim is true, what it merely says is that at all times every event that constitutes a divide either did, does now, or will do so.

8.6 ALETHIC BIVALENCE AND TIME-RELATIVITY

Does the Law of Alethic Bivalence (LAB) hold without exception? Some types of assertion raise a similar issue for the Law of the Excluded Middle (LEM), and hence for LAB as well. My present concern is not with them but only with those that raise an issue for LAB alone. More particularly, I want to consider whether a prediction, or future contingent proposition, that is confirmable as true or disconfirmable as false, when the time comes round to which it applies, must have had a truth-value antecedently, e.g. when it first was uttered. According to one reading of chapter 9 of *De Interpretatione*, his aversion to logical fatalism led Aristotle to deny that it must. On this reading he held that, given that certain admirals now have the choice whether to engage in battle tomorrow or not, then despite the fact that a sea-battle either is or is not about to occur as LEM requires, the future contingent proposition "There will be a sea-battle tomorrow," as uttered before the choice is actually made, cannot yet be either true or false. Whether this really was his claim is not my present concern,[6] nor even whether the claim is valid. Instead I will show that its implications are not genuinely anomalous in the way that some allege. Hence to that extent, should it be implicit in my indeterministic theory of time, it does that theory no disservice.

For some the contraint on bivalence has the smell of logical solecism. Here an assumption about canonical logical form has come into play. They demand that any proposition should be capable of formulation in sentences that are temporally definite, i.e. true (false) at all times if true (false) at any time. That assumption can, however, here be dismissed either as begging ontological questions about time or as allowing a jejune notational predilection to become their arbiter.

Some, however, sponsor a more arresting objection. It appeals to a general consensus that should a philosophical theory find itself at odds with scientific orthodoxy, it is the former that has to go to the wall. Is, then, the constraint on bivalence in this predicament? Debate on this issue usually appeals to the special theory of relativity as to a scientific touchstone. To that extent it is tacitly assumed that the

sort of considerations that require a general theory are not immediately to the point or would introduce an unnecessary degree of
complication. I conspire with this assumption for part of the way
only to reject it later on.

In either its special or general form the theory of relativity is
primarily a theory of invariance. Its major premiss is that the laws
of nature, including the physical constants, are invariant for all
frames of reference or co-ordinate systems (c-systems). From that it
infers that determinations of spatial distance, time-lapse, and temporal order that belong to the four-dimensional world-line through
space and time of any such system are ontologically no more privileged than those that belong to any other. What makes this inference
relevant here is that spatially distant events that in one c-system are
in one given temporal order may be simultaneous or even in reverse
order in some other c-system.

On this basis, then, the constraint on bivalence may seem to instigate an awkward dilemma. Let pt^o be a certain place-time in system
C^1 and let U be some uniquely specified event metrically simultaneous with but spatially distant from that place-time in that system.
Thus U may be a supernova, the explosion of a particular star,
perhaps the Star of Bethlehem, if that was a genuine historical phenomenon. Now since U is sufficiently distant from pt^o, residents of
C^1 are not yet in a position directly to observe its simultaneity. Suppose, however, that one of them by way of speculation were moved
to say at pt^o "U is occurring now." If that utterance is true, then
bivalence must apply. But is it true? I postpone an answer in order
first to ask another question.

Suppose that C^1 intersects at pt^o with another system C^2 at pt^o in
such a way that in C^2 U will only occur time later. If some resident
of C^2 were, again by way of speculation, to say at pt^o "U will occur,"
would that utterance then be true? Would bivalence apply to it as
well? The answer seems subject to the following constraint. If bivalence applies to the present-tense utterance, it must then apply to
the future-tense utterance as well; but if not to the latter, then equally
not to the former. In short, either bivalence applies to the present-
tense utterance or it does not apply to the future-tense utterance,
but not both.

Initially this sort of dilemma was conceived (Rietdjik, 1966;
Putnam, 1967; and Fitzgerald, 1969) merely as offering a Hobson's
choice. The assumption then was that statements that assert the
present or past occurrence of uniquely specified events such as U
must be subject without exception to bivalence. Hence the contention
was not just that the future is as real as any other part of time but

more specifically that it consists, without any indeterminate areas, of events that are real or actual. Should, then, this conclusion be accepted? Some (Stein, 1968; Lango, 1969; and Routley, 1980) have argued not. Here I shall join them by qualifying the major assumption.

First, let me stress the more obvious affinities that the special theory of relativity has to an interpretation of time in terms of OBO-abilities. For both types of theory there is a distinction of sorts, at any place-time in the world-line of any agent, between an absolute past and an absolute future. For both types of theory events in the absolute past and events in the absolute future belong respectively to the different components of the double cone of cause and effect contained in the double light-cone unique to that place-time on that world-line. For both, too, at that place-time there is a relativistic limbo, or whatever else you care to call it, falling outside that double cone. Accordingly, neither theory has room for a cosmic-wide simultaneous process of absolute becoming.[7]

Next let me point to a major difference. The special theory of relativity is exclusively concerned with inertial systems. The indeterministic theory of time is not. It represents certain double cones of cause and effect as each being the basis where it peaks of an OBO-ability. Now some at least of the potential manifestations of any such ability cannot be of an inertial nature. Hence in its application this theory of time is not subject to the constraints that are specific to the special form of relativity theory.

Note finally that the relativity-variance of temporal succession that has seemed problematic can only involve events that are spatially distant and not in any direct linear causal connection with each other (i.e. if causally connected at all only at the apex of some causal cone). The temporal order of events, as distinct from their temporal duration, on the world-line of any one agent is relativity-invariant — the same for all c-systems. Furthermore, the temporal order of events that are not on the one world-line but are in linear causal connection, e.g. arrivals and departures of light signals bouncing to and from each of two spaceships on different world-lines, is relativity-invariant as well. Hence, in terms of the specifics of our branching diagram, two actions — say, A^1B^1 and C^1D^1 — of the same agent could not have a different temporal order for someone on a different world-line from what they have for their agent.

Now it is the relativity-variance of the temporal ordering of events that are in no direct linear causal connection that is our present concern. On the hypothesis that bivalence does not completely apply to a certain specific sort of forecast, i.e. to forecasts of an agent's actions, e.g. to along which of several alternative world-lines the agent will continue, there is no anomaly in the implication that it does not apply completely to certain estimates of the temporal ordering of these non-linearly connected events. Notice in particular that the putative failure to comply with LAB that is common to those specific sorts of forecasts and estimates does not in any way detract from the contrast between the future, on the one hand, and the present or past on the other. As far as the forecasts are concerned the absence of fact that the lack of truth-value has to signify affects not the placing of one event in this rather than that temporal relation to another. Instead it affects whether the relativity-*invariant* series of events on some given world-line will after a certain place-time be continued in one way rather than in some other equally possible way, e.g. along which of several possible world-lines that world-line will continue. In contrast, as far as the estimates of temporal order are concerned, the absence of fact affects not the composition or continuation of any one world-line but rather the temporal order of one component on one world-line relative to one component on another. *Ex hypothesi*, of course, these two kinds of absence of fact are connected. The absence of fact about the continuation of the invariantly ordered world-line of an agent is responsible for the absence of fact about the variant order of components on one world-line relative to those on another. But this connection detracts neither from the difference between the two kinds of absence of fact nor from what distinguishes either the past or the present from the future. Hence I conclude that whether a constraint upon bivalence is or is not required by the indeterministic theory of time, it leads to no anomaly.

CHAPTER NINE

The Republic of Means

9.0

Why do moral claims about what is fitting, right, or obligatory have, if valid, the sort of authority they profess? I intend this question as primarily foundational rather than criteriological or epistemological. I am not primarily concerned with procedures for distinguishing valid from invalid moral claims. My primary concern is with why any valid moral claim upon our behaviour is considered to have the sort of binding power that it has, even where what it enjoins would seem to involve some self-sacrifice, i.e. even where we would seem to have very strong motives not to obey it.

As so expressed, what I am asking may appear rather vague. The notions of authority and binding power with which it conjures primarily belong to politics or law. In the context of morality they may seem to need some further explanation. Consequently, the question is susceptible to two kinds of approach. One may say that it tries to pass off something quite trivial as an enigma. More specifically, one may submit that all it asks is why one ought to do what one ought to do, and that to this there is no appropriate answer other than what the wording of the question itself directs, viz. that one ought to do what one ought to do because one ought to do it (Prichard, 1912). Alternatively, one may vindicate the question by identifying it with a more precisely formulated non-trivial question or series of questions. The mediating postulates and distinctions in 9.1 and 9.2 will have this clarificatory function. Those that come next in 9.3 and 9.4 will recapitulate conclusions of earlier chapters. Their function will be to prepare for the answer to the question or questions thus identified. The answer itself is due in 9.5 and 9.6.

It is not uncommon for a book on ethics to devote one chapter to ontology, and more specifically to the notion of free will. Almost as often some form of compatibilism is esteemed as convenient for this cursory task. The present work on ontology redresses that balance by devoting just one chapter to ethics, but in a spirit of reciprocity rather than retaliatory short shrift. On the one hand, the answer I give to my foundational question owes a debt to the antecedent ontology. On the other, an ability to yield the answer should make that ontology all the more credible.

By the end of this chapter I would also like the attentive reader to see, but with no further nudge or documentation from me, that the ethical problem has arisen, at least for us if not for Aristotle, from the distance he originally set between his ethical and his ontological conception of value, or between what he distinguishes as the good for us and the good by nature. My emendations to his Reificatory and Modal Identity principles are here advanced as removing the problem by curtailing that distance.

9.1 FROM DEONTOLOGY TO AXIOLOGY

My first postulate is ethical. It states that all deontological claims about what is right or obligatory are also of an axiological nature, i.e. that they are claims about what has a certain kind of worth, value, or goodness. This postulate is meant to be truistic. It is not to be confused with a narrower claim of a criteriological nature, viz. that all right and obligatory actions are contingently instrumental to the realization of something of worth. It leaves open as a possibility that an action that is right may have a worth that is intrinsic to itself rather than to some result from which it is distinguishable. I am in fact saying nothing more ambitious than that it is good to do whatever is right and bad not to do what is obligatory.

In itself, however, this postulate is still too vague for its clarificatory function. It refers to a *certain type* of worth, value, or goodness. To specify that type I introduce my first distinction. Goodness is either qualified or unqualified. The type of goodness here in question is unqualified, i.e. it is not of the qualified type that attaches to a good wine, athlete, accountant, harvest, jump, stroke, race, or audit, etc. These have their specific worth primarily as members of their respective sorts of thing. Since one and the same particular may instantiate a multiplicity of sorts, it may be qualifiedly good as a member of some of these sorts and bad as a member of others. A good athlete may be a bad student by virtue of the time and energy devoted to training and competition. In the same sort of situation, however, an attainment of qualified goodness specific to one sort can be at the cost of something more than the badness specific to another. Thus the sorts themselves may occupy some unqualified ranking in value irrespective of any ranking in terms of criteria specific to each. Athletic performance may be deemed superior to intellectual study or vice versa in an unqualified way. Alternatively, and irrespective of such ranking, if a student's future career, or ability to support dependents, is sacrificed to athletic proficiency, then the being a good athlete may under the circumstances be unqualifiedly bad.[1]

Nor is this subordination of the one type of good to another for the purpose of justification attribuable simply to the classificatory subordination of a more specific to a more general sort of thing, i.e. to the fact that human beings are a more inclusive class than athletes or students. After all, organisms constitute a wider class than human beings. Yet the goodness of being a good, i.e. a healthy, organism does not override that of being a good human being. We admire Sakharov and other dissidents for having resisted oppression for the general good of mankind to the detriment of their health. Moreover, there are alternative systems of classification that yield conflicting subordinations. One may classify wines, cheeses, steaks, and flitches of bacon either as foods or as gourmet items. Good members of any of these four types may also have to be good gourmet items. Whether they are also good foods (i.e. nutrients) is quite another matter again.

In drawing this first distinction there is some temptation to use our initial grasp of what it is to be qualifiedly good as an analytical tool for the understanding of unqualified good. Two main forms of prescriptivist theory have taken this course, viz. the linguistic and the existentialist. Thus Hare (1952, chap. 6) has proposed a quite general distinction between the meaning of the word "good' and the criteria for its correct application on the strength of the correct observation that different sorts of thing qualify for the application of that term on the basis of different criteria. Accordingly, the meaning of the term for Hare must primarily consist in its prescriptive or evaluative linguistic force. Sartre, in contrast, regards unqualified goodness as a sort of qualified goodness manqué (1946; 1949, 711–22). On his view, by virtue of our having free will and thus a certain ability to shape our own nature, we fall short of other sorts of thing in having no fixed essence, and hence nothing to fix absolute standards in terms of which our behaviour may be assessed. For him what standards we conform to are as much a matter of choice as is whether to conform to them or not.

My own procedure is the reverse. A more direct approach to unqualified goodness can bring its difference from qualified goodness into sharper focus. Like Sartre I maintain that ethics has a basis in the singularity of free will, and more particularly that key ethical concepts are analysable in terms of that singularity. Hence I reject Hare's distinction between meaning and criteria of application, for therein lies his further interpretation of the meaning of ethical expressions in terms of linguistic performance. This inhibits any attempt to analyse goodness, or to seek a foundation for ethics, either in psychological or in ontological terms. As well, however, I reject the specifics of Sartre's foundationalism. In taking qualified goodness as a kind of measuring stick for unqualified goodness, he misrepresents the singularity of free will and exaggerates the arbitrariness of ethical criteria.[2]

9.2 FROM AXIOLOGY TO PSYCHOLOGY

My first postulate connected the deontological to the axiological. The second connects the axiological to the psychological. It reaffirms the basic Socratic insight that the good, i.e. unqualified goodness, is in its nature attractive, i.e. it tends to attract. But not everything that is attractive is unqualifiedly good. What, then, distinguishes the unqualifiedly good from other attractive things, i.e. things that are unqualifiedly bad?

The answer lies in a second distinction, viz. between contingent and non-contingent desire. Contingent desires are desires that we could conceivably be without. Hence, the attractiveness they confer upon whatever satisfies them is a non-essential attractiveness. Our alimentary and erotic desires are of this type. Non-contingent desire, in contrast, is desire that we could not conceivably be without. What satisfies it has an essential attractiveness. In either case desire and the cognate attractiveness are primarily general in nature. The desire is for the future instantiation of certain properties, or things of a universal nature, without reference to any concrete situation in which the fulfilment of one desire may have to defer to fulfilment of another. Likewise, the attractiveness is of the related sort that pertains to future situations or states of affairs by virtue of their instantiating certain properties without reference to whatever other properties any such instances may, depending upon the concrete situation, instantiate as well. Thus any particular concrete situation or state of affairs may be essentially or non-essentially attractive in some respects and indifferent or unattractive in others.

In terms, then, of these distinctions I distinguish the attractiveness of unqualified goodness from other sorts as an essential attractiveness, unless it is just the sort of non-essential attractiveness that is in principle, as opposed to in every fully concrete instantiation, conjointly realizable with essential attractiveness. Accordingly, unqualified good is the object either of non-contingent desire or of any other sort of desire that is in principle conjointly satisfiable with non-contingent desire. That, in more specific terms than before, is my second postulate.

Notice here that I have followed Moore (1903, 97–9) among others in shunning the notion of a relative good, i.e. of a good that is supposedly good for one person but possibly bad for another. Provided that the realization of what attracts one person is not incompatible in principle with the realization of what is non-contingently or essentially attractive, then it is unqualifiedly good, and in a non-relative way. Of course, even in meeting the proviso it may also prevent the realization of what attracts another person, but that is merely a matter of one realization of unqualified goodness having to defer to another.

The mention of Moore will also remind that by this time I have fallen into his naturalistic fallacy. Here, however, is not the place to resuscitate the *ad hominem* polemic that Moore on this head has occasioned. Instead I shall merely insist that terms such as "desirable" and "attractive", when used as they are used on occasion to indicate that something is likely to cause desire or to attract, and the word "pleasing" used to indicate that something pleases or is likely to please, are all positively axiological in nature, at least in a defeasible way. The decisive factor in determining whether they are non-defeasibly axiological in any application is whether that to which they are applied satisfies, or at least does not in principle interfere with the satisfaction of, non-contingent desire.

But what could give the cognate notions of non-contingent desire and essential attractiveness an actual application? And if there is some way in which they could apply, what evidence is there that they actually apply in any such way as well? It is with these two more precise questions that my initial foundational question is now to be identified. The answer to the first will lead circuitously from psychology to ontology in 9.3 and back again to psychology in 9.4. The answer to the second will return to axiology in 9.5.

9.3   FROM PSYCHOLOGY TO ONTOLOGY — THE REIFICATORY PRINCIPLE

The next three distinctions recur to the Reificatory Principle mainly as emended in chapter 6. Thus the third in the total series is between an arbitrary and a non-arbitrary individual thinghood. The individual things with the thinghood of which I am here primarily concerned continue to be substances. As such they are capable of retaining their identity impartially from moment to moment through time in any one of a number of contrary states, i.e. each is capable of remaining the same thing throughout change. For its applicability, as we saw, this distinction rests upon what I now list as my third postulate. Whether a particular thing or substance has a non-arbitrary thinghood as such depends upon whether it inherently has causal powers of interaction with other such things. Things with inherent causal powers as individual causal agents have a non-arbitrary individual thinghood. Things that do not have such powers have a best only an arbitrary individual thinghood.

The fourth distinction is more narrow. It falls between an *intrinsic* and an *extrinsic* form of non-arbitrary individual thinghood. But this distinction depends in turn upon a fifth to which I immediately pass. The latter falls between two types of causal power, viz. primary and secondary, both of which confer a non-arbitrary thinghood. While all substances with non-arbitrary thinghood have *secondary* causal powers, substances with an intrinsic are marked out from those with an extrinsic non-arbitrary thinghood by their possession of *primary* causal powers as well.

I have identified the primary causal power with something that makes persons and other things that are sufficiently person-like unique, viz. the O-ability. Hence, since persons alone have this ability, at least to some degree (see chapter 7) persons alone have an intrinsic non-arbitrary thinghood. Many non-arbitrary things, however, do not have this sort of power. Instead they merely have the sort of power that enables them on an individual basis directly or indirectly to interact with each other and with things that have the primary power as thus identified. Such things, accordingly, have a mere extrinsic non-arbitrary thinghood.

The O-ability, as we further saw, is indeterministic. Where one has the O-ability as bound to a specific occasion, one's actions thereafter are causally underdetermined by the totality of what has gone on before, so that there is before one a range of mutually incompatible actions that (in this occasion-bound sense) are all causally possible. As so identified and interpreted, the primary power contrasts with secondary powers (at a macrophysical level with, e.g., brittleness, fragility, elasticity, inflammability, solubility, etc.) as a power that does not submit to analysis in terms of counterfactual *causal* conditionals with powers that do.

The O-ability's status as primary derives, furthermore, from its indeterministic nature. More specifically, the status of the secondary powers as *powers at all* derives from the incidence of that indeterministic power. Conversely, however, the precise form taken by the indeterministic, i.e. the primary, power on any occasion depends upon the secondary powers of things with which its bearer interacts. Here, the relationship between the respective powers of the hand and its tools is a serviceable analogy.

To conclude this section I cap my previous five distinctions with a sixth. It is between two kinds of responsibility, responsibility respectively for acts and for results. One's act-responsibility is one's responsibility for what one does. It amounts, in other words, to just the same thing as agency. Result-responsibility, in contrast, belongs both to what agents do (e.g. flipping the switch), or even more broadly to events (e.g. the flipping of the switch), and also to agents by virtue of what they do (e.g. the switch-flipper), for certain results (e.g. a light's going on). A confusion between these two types of responsibility lies behind the tacit assumption that agency is primarily some sort of causal or explanatory notion, which in turn is the source of much of the controversy over free will – but I will not dwell on that here. Instead I draw attention to the distinction for the purpose of identifying act-responsibility with non-arbitrary thinghood, and the sort of act-responsibility that is distinctive of bearers of O-ability with a non-arbitrary thinghood that is more specifically intrinsic.

9.4 BACK TO PSYCHOLOGY –
THE MODAL IDENTITY
PRINCIPLE

In this section I recur to the above-mentioned principle in its emended form, i.e. to the Modal Identity Thesis. The O-ability is not only the primary power, and as such the ultimate reifying or substantiating factor. It is also unique in being, while entirely physical, essentially intentionalistic. It is so in the more general sense, in that some sort of concurrent awareness of the courses of action that its possession makes possible, and of the situation out of which these possibilities arise, is logically essential to its possession. In this sense it is an intentionalistic power because in its occasion-bound form it is self-intimating. However, it is also intentionalistic in a more specific sense, for it is a desiderative power, and its subsequent realization in any of the actions it leaves open beforehand as possible must be intentional.

Yet, as also stressed, it is entirely physical. In other words, the mind or soul that is evinced in these intentionalistic activities is not some non-physical sort of entity. On the contrary, it is just the capacity to have the O-ability on certain occasions. In this sense the mind is an occasion-loose, as opposed to an occasion-bound, otherwising ability for physical behaviour (an OLO-ability as opposed to an OBO-ability). It is the constant component of the OBO-abilities that variable factors, such as our less constant capacities or skills and the diverse opportunities for their use that arise from time to time, tie down to specific junctures in our history. Likewise, the integrated mental process in which an OBO-ability intimates itself are nothing but a conditional form of that same ability, i.e. what would amount to the complete ability if both the requisite skills and the opportunity for performance are present as well.

Accordingly, although the possession and realization of any OBO-ability involve mental states and activity in the ways just mentioned, the realization of the power is primarily in physically overt behaviour. True, one does to a certain extent have the power to engage in or abstain from certain mental activities, e.g. imagining or thinking about some intellectual problem or deliberating how to act. That, however, would seem to be merely a matter of putting oneself in a favourable position for mental activity to occur. In the course that it specifically takes no such activity is antecedently programmed in an intention to engage in it in the manner in which, say, the raising of an arm may be antecedently programmed in an intention. When one sits down to deliberate, it is the sitting down and abstention from other more attention-demanding forms of physical behaviour, not the course taken by the deliberation itself, that may thus be programmed. In other words, the power one has to deliberate or otherwise, and more generally for engaging or not engaging in some form or other of mental activity, is a second-order sort of power. It is a power to put or not to put oneself in the sort of situation in which one may thereby acquire the sort of power for physical behaviour that is intimated in one's deliberation.

It is, however, in the intentionalistic and more specifically the desiderative aspect of the power that I am at the moment more interested. I have proposed as alone appropriate to the Modal Identity Thesis the Aristotelian conception of desire as a potency or power rather than as a psychic thrust, but more narrowly as a compotent of that power that is the O-ability. On this interpretation the primary function of our various special desires is just to propose, whereas that of intention, etc., is to dispose. It is by virtue of the attractiveness that certain general sorts of situation have for one that certain ranges of rival possibilities intimate themselves to us from occasion to occasion, thus constituting in part the OBO-abilities we may have that are specific to these occasions.

Conceived in this role desires have two salient features that Platonists, and even Aristotelians, have tended to suppress. The first is their plasticity. The process of deliberation in which to a greater or lesser extent our O-abilities intimate themselves is not a matter of our cognitively relating the circumstances in which we find ourselves to some more or less fixed battery of desires, i.e. to our finding to which of these desires they give an opportunity for satisfaction. It is rather a matter of our various special desires achieving their mutual differentiation through our progressive understanding of the sorts of non-compossibilities for action that arise from time to time within our physical, cultural, institutional, and technological environment. It is only in so far as our understanding of the situations in which we successively find ourselves has become stereotyped what we can declare an allegiance to some determinate set of desires, whether ranked or unranked.

The second salient feature is that of mutual defeasibility. The primary function of our special desires is to set our general goals. However, implicit in the sort of goal-allegiance thus secured by any one desire there is a deference to the general goals set by others. I have already said that desires propose where intentions, etc., dispose. Here, however, it is more useful to say that the special desires are conditional disposers, deference to each other[3] being written into their conditions, where intentions, etc., are categorical disposers. This implicit deference is a logical feature of these desires at least in so far as they function in the intimation of O-ability. It is an essential defeasibility.

In his description of the timocratic, oligarchic, democratic, and tyrannical souls, Plato has effectively plotted a process of progressive degeneration in this defeasibility-feature of desire and the successive stages of soul-disintegration that go therewith. I differ from him only in my emphasis that their mutual defeasibility is essential to the contribution that the special desires have to make to the soul-unity that the O-ability confers upon things with an intrinsic individual thinghood.

I shall have more to say about soul-pathology in 9.6, when finally I return to deontology. My more immediate objective is, however, to complete the limited psychological mission of this section. The way in which the distinction between contingent and non-contingent desires *could* have an application lies at last before us. The special desires that we have been discussing are all contingent. That we have special desires of some sort is no doubt essential to our possession of O-ability and our intrinsic thingood, but not that they should be of just the specific sort that they are. Any one of these desires is a desire that the person who desires could conceivably be without. However, in addition to being desiderative through the differentiation between special desires, the O-ability is *self*-desiderative in the sense that to have it requires that one desires the continuation of its instantiation. As such it is non-contingent, i.e. *a desire that one cannot conceivably be without.* To have it is a necessary condition of having the intrinsic thingood by virtue of which one is intrinsically the subject of attributes, the agent of action, and the possessor of any kind of desire whatever. In relation to the special desires, furthermore, this self-desiderative desire wields a distinctive authority. Like them it is defeasible, but unlike them – as it is a necessary condition of intrinsic thinghood – it is not *essentially* defeasible.

9.5   BACK TO AXIOLOGY

Provided, then, that the O-ability is essentially self-desiderative, there is such a thing as non-contingent desire. So far, however, that the ability is indeed self-desiderative has fallen rather short of support.

By way of remedy one might, perhaps, cite our desire for self-preservation. It is very evident that we do have the latter. Indeed, if the reifying factor upon which the intrinsic individual thinghood of any individual depends were an individual essence unique to that individual, then the self-desideration would have to be so identified. However, my argument in chapter 2 still stands. I take it to have established that there are no such things as unique individual essences whereby actual and possible particulars are all individuated from each other. It may well be thas as a matter of contingent fact no two particulars are exactly alike in the properties intrinsic to each, but it is upon their extrinsic properties of spatial separation from each other that their numerical difference is in the last resort dependent. Consequently, in our numerical differences one from the other there can be no essential basis for a preference of one over another. That upon which our intrinsic thinghood as individuals depends neither affords in itself, nor can conspire with anything in us, to provide any such basis. But in any case, given that the reifying factor here in question is the O-ability, it must be a universal. It is what things that fulfil the minimum individuating condition of being spatially separate from each other have in common, if the individual thinghood that thus they have is also intrinsic. Consequently, the reifying factor cannot be some uniquely individuating essence. What would otherwise have been a reason for identifying the self-desideration of that factor with the desire for self-preservation can therefore be dismissed.

Furthermore, to show of any desire whatever that it is a form – even the only form – that a self-desideration of the O-ability could take is not to show that the ability is indeed self-desiderative. It is not to show of any desire that it has non-contingent status. One might perhaps aver that one searching one's inmost heart one finds a feeling there that as a project there would be some conceptual incoherence about willing or not resisting one's own death. But the force of this phenomenological datum is somewhat impaired by the undeniable fact that considerations of either a prudential or an eth-ical kind sometimes persuade people under certain circumstances that their own death is preferable to any available alternative. Con-sequently, if there is any such incoherence about the project in ques-tion, it must be subject to some further qualification.

I turn, then, instead to the ethical, and more specifically axio-logical, sort of consideration by which the desire for self-preservation is sometimes defeated. We do regard the survival of persons other than ourselves as just as unqualifiedly good as our own, except to the extent that the survival of one person interferes with that of others. We may, of course, be more strongly attached to the survival of ourselves or of those dearest to us than to that of others. But in itself the strength of the attachment is beside the point. That one's own survival is more worthwhile than that of someone else has to have some basis other than merely that one is more strongly attached to it. To this one should further add that the satisfaction of other more special desires is also unqualifiedly good, no matter to whom these desires belong, at least to the extent that such desires are conjointly satisfiable. To take a quite visceral example, how more enjoyable it is to eat when one has cooked for oneself and others than when one has cooked for oneself alone.

Now, just because they concern unqualified goodness, it is for the explanation of axiological intuitions such as these that, through the mediation of certain analytical hypotheses, the notion of non-con-tingent desire is particularly suited. My proposal, accordingly, is to take these same intuitions as evidence for the existence of that sort of desire. The mediating hypotheses consist in my earlier axiological claims (1) that the unqualified good consists in whatever is essentially attractive together with whatever is non-essentially attractive without being essentially unattractive, and (2) that what distinguishes the essentially from the non-essentially attractive is that the former is, whereas the latter is not, the object of non-contingent desire. What better evidence that we have a certain desire than that we deem a certain sort of thing attractive? What better evidence that we have a non-contingent type of desire than that we deem a certain type of thing essentially attractive? Given, then, our analysis of the unqual-ifiedly good in terms of the essentially attractive, that we deem certain types of thing unqualifiedly good is evidence of our having a non-contingent type of desire.

Since, furthermore, the same intuitions about what is unqualifiedly good are altruistic in character, they demonstrate not only the ex-istence of non-contingent desire but the latter's impartial character as well. Given, then, that the non-contingency of the desire consists in the self-desideration of the O-ability as reifying factor, what these intuitions further show is that our proper allegiance is not to a kingdom of ends, as Kant would have it, but rather to a republic of means. Each one of us should regard him/herself as but one possible means among many towards the continued instantiation of the rei-fying factor as a universal, no one such means having priority over and other. It is that impartial continued instantiation that is essen-tially attractive. Moreover, given that it is through striving towards some of the goals proposed for each one of us by our special desires that each one of us instantiates the O-ability as a universal, we should act with deference towards the desires of others as well as our own so long as the satisfaction of these desires does not interfere with anybody's function as a member of the republic of means.

The relation of each one of us to the OLO-ability is somewhat like that of a musical performance to the composition performed. For each performer, if moved purely by aesthetic considerations, there is (in principle at least) at least as much value in any other perfor-mance as in the performance that the performer is actually per-forming. To that extent, then, the performance of each performer is for that performer but a means to the realization of the universal, which is the composition that all these performances perform.

No doubt certain performers may be motivated by a certain degree of personal ambition, which, potential superiority as to performance aside, may lead them to place a preferred value upon their own performance. Similarly, presumably because of its evolutionary sur-vival value, in all of us there is a genetically in-built selfish component whereby we tend to give preferential value to our own survival and future well-being. However, this component should not be identified too closely or completely with the legitimate concern each one of us has for his or her own survival or well-being, any more than the personal ambition of some virtuoso should be identified too closely or completely with an ability to put himself or herself heart and soul into the performance of the composition.

There is, indeed, something very basic about one's concern for one's own survival that distinguishes it from one's concern for the future being of others. It may seem, superficially at least, that one's desires need not be desires that involve any action on one's part. One may desire very sincerely that famines and wars should cease forever, without necessarily believing that there is anything that one could do about it. Yet for a desire to be one's desire there must be some sort of commitment (defeasible no doubt) on one's part to do something towards its realization, if only under certain hypothetical conditions, the fulfilment of which one may reckon to be unlikely. One may desire, no doubt, that famines and wars should cease forever, and also desire as strongly that the task of bringing that about should not fall in any part upon oneself. Even here, however, one would own to one's having a commitment towards the implementation of the former of these two desires under certain conditions, the latter desire being a desire that these conditions should never be fulfilled.

Neglect of this fact might, then, suggest that the impartially I have claimed on behalf of the desire for a continued embodiment of the OLO-ability could leave no room for, or give no sanction to, one's special regard for the continuation of one's own embodiment of that ability. In so far as one does place a particular importance upon one's own survival and well-being, that would have to be attributed, it might seem, to an unregenerate selfishness that the foundational thesis does not condone. To the contrary, however, a special concern for oneself has a legitimate basis. First, it is towards the survival of one's own person that one usually can be of the most direct and greatest service. Second, one's being of service to the survival of anyone entails one's survival at least for the limited period of time that the service requires – at least in so far as this service is an implementation of one's desire.

I have identified unqualified good in 9.2 with whatever is consistent with the satisfaction of non-contingent desire, desire that we could not conceivably be without. I have explained in 9.3 and 9.4 what kind of desire that could possibly be in terms of the self-desideration of a reifying factor, i.e. a desire essential to the possession of the O-ability for the continuation of that possession. In this section I have shown that the notion of a non-contingent desire as thus elucidated has an application. The specific nature of our axiological intuitions supplies the evidence. In all this, of course, my aim has been primarily foundational, as I have already insisted. Here, however, before I take the next and final step, there is room for an epistemological aside. These same axiological intuitions share the same self-grounding quality as belongs to the intuitions that apprise us of our free will, for they are integral to these intuitions. In other words, once the reifying factor to which they testify is properly understood as what it is, they account for themselves as essential components of that to which they testify.

9.6 BACK TO DEONTOLOGY – MORAL RESPONSIBILITY

That the free will and the good will are necessarily the same is a doctrine of some antiquity. My claim that the instantiation of O-ability is unqualifiedly good is very similar. Similar enough, indeed, to seem as beset by a standard sort of objection to that doctrine as the latter itself may seem. If the free and the good will are the same, and if – as I have already postulated – it is bad to do what is morally wrong, then so long as one acts freely one can never do moral wrong. Hence it may seem to follow further – given that freedom and responsibility are as closely tied as they are commonly supposed to be – that, contrary to what ordinary practice presupposes, no one is ever responsible for doing what is morally wrong.

However, the error that leads to this result is not in the identification of the free with the good will. It lies in the rather vaguely worded further assumption, viz. that freedom and responsibility are as closely tied as they are commonly supposed to be. In one sense, of course, this assumption is quite harmless. That the notions of freedom and responsibility are closely tied not only is commonly supposed. It is correctly supposed as well – or so I shall assume. Nevertheless, whether there is a common consensus as to what the nature of the tie happens to be is dubious, and in any case the notions of freedom and responsibility here involved are too polymorphic to allow the assumption as it stands to function as a reliable premiss.

I have already distinguished act-responsibility from result-responsibility. Act-responsibility is simply the equivalent of the agency that belongs to substances, and primarily to those substances that have an intrinsic non-arbitrary thinghood. Indeed, in this primary manifestation it just is intrinsic non-arbitrary thinghood. Result-responsibility, in contrast, is more widely spread. It belongs both to the events that cause certain results and to substances, if any, the actions of which are the events that cause such results. Thus the specific function of the former ascription is that of descriptive narration, and that of the latter is explanation. It is the specific function of neither to praise or blame. That is the function of the ascription of a further and quite distinct type of responsibility, which thereby presupposes an ascription of at least the first of the preceding two, while at the same time being something more. What persons do may be deplored as morally wrong or commended as morally right. In short, they are held to have a *moral* responsibility for what they do.

How, then, is responsibility of this specifically moral kind tied to an agent's freedom? Act-responsibility and the O-ability amount to the same, provided that the former is of the primary kind and that the latter confers freedom in an indeterministic sense – or so I have claimed. But need the tie of moral responsibility to freedom be similar? For an answer to this question first consider an ascription of responsibility that is only quasi-moral.

When spectators at a ball game vilify a player for fumbling a pass, in so doing they are holding him responsible for the loss of an opportunity. Do they, however, thereby presuppose that in the circumstances he could have done otherwise than fumble? Well, whether they do or not, the fact remains that if they did they would in one sense probably be wrong. The loss of the opportunity may have been due to some momentary physical exhaustion or inattention that in the heat of the fame was inevitable: and even if those factors in turn could be attributed to some act of his prior to the game, e.g. not resting enough the night before, the latter in turn might have been as inevitable, e.g. due to a squalling baby.

Furthermore, if the player were to cite the inevitability by way of excuse, that would hardly appease his critics. It might even incense them further. For them, irrespective of his fatigue on the field or lack of sleep the night before, there are certain standards to which he should, and in fumbling failed to, conform. Nor is their censure offered merely in the spirit of keeping him up to the mark or as inducement to exceed previous limits to his capacities. Censure from the coach may have this purely deterrent or reformatory purpose. From the resentful crowd its purpose is in the main downright retributive.

I do not contend that this sort of ascription is rational or even morally unreprehensible. In fact I think it is neither, unless it is informed by conscious camp. That, however, does not impair its value as a parallel for the moral sort of ascription. Already it has indicated that inevitability may not serve as an excuse. It will also suggest an explanation of why that should be so. The opprobrium of which he has become the target is just the sort of thing the player, in aspiring to be and remain on his team, has let himself in for. In his commitment as a player he subscribes to the standards by which he is judged – he prescribes them for himself. Furthermore, in so far as the crowd's behaviour does have a deterrent or reformatory influence, he must accept it as something even more than that, i.e. as in keeping with his own purpose as a member of the team. In short, his responsibility for what he does on the field, in so far as the responsibility is a liability to blame as well as to praise, is something he has contracted into.

Consider now the ascription of responsibility that is genuinely moral. My claim is that behaviour for which an agent is being held morally responsible is, if bad, just as inevitable as the ball-game gaffe may have been. For the will to be a will at all the special desires, within the domain of which it disposes, must to some extent defer to each other. To be a will at all it must to this extent be free. However, only where the will is good do the special desires, which inspire the specific promptings to which it is susceptible, defer to each other and to the master desire without exception. Only thus can it be completely free. Where, on the contrary, the will is bad to any degree, the special desires fail to that degree so to defer, and then the will is correspondingly unfree. In a will of that sort subsets of special desire cluster into relatively restricted or hierarchically structured coteries of mutual deference. Only within any such coterie or hierarchical stratum is the inferior will free. Outside these confines it is pathological and unfree, for there the mutual deference ceases. More specifically, one's will may be free in a situation that provides the opportunity for nothing beyond the more or less immediate satisfaction of any, but no more than, one member of some such coterie or stratum. But if beyond that the opportunity is for the more or less immediate satisfaction of other special desires besides the former, one's will may not be free. Thus desires for food, drink, sexual partners, children, entertainment, reputation, and a few others may defer to each other in proposing options just as options, but not be deferred to, say, by a desire for power on occasions when opportunities for the satisfaction of any one (or small subset) but no more than one (or that same small subset) of these desires arise.

In some ways, then, the ascription of moral responsibility is comparable to the ascription of responsibility in the case of the ball game in the sort of freedom it presupposes. Where the anger as well as the adulation of the crowd has the useful function of keeping their recipients up to or beyond the mark, so does moral praise and blame. To this extent my account is very similar to quite standard compatibilist accounts of how moral responsibility ties in with free will. On this standard sort of account of free will and responsibility the former merely consists of some such fact as that one will act otherwise if one chooses, and the latter in the further fact that how one chooses can be influenced by one's knowledge that one will be made to answer for what one chooses. However, the moral differs from the quasi-moral ascription in three main ways.

First, the standards of behaviour that the spectators prescribe for players, and players for themselves, are of a relatively arbitrary or artificial nature. Except in so far as they are limited by moral injunctions, they can be changed at any time for no other reason than that they may improve the competitiveness of the game and its interest for spectators. In contrast, the moral standards of behaviour that we prescribe for ourselves and others as members of a republic of means are neither arbitrary nor artificial. They are the standards we meet in so far as we have an intrinsic non-arbitrary thinghood.

Second, the standards that the spectators prescribe for the players and the players for themselves are not standards prescribed for the spectators as well, unless certain additional rules for spectator-participation are somehow specifically prescribed. Moral standards, contrariwise, are prescribed for all who prescribe them, for all who prescribe them are members of the republic of means for whom they are prescribed. Indeed, the very act of holding others, and in some cases even oneself, to be morally responsible must itself come under a moral review. It may have a manipulative purpose that requires some degree of moral justification.

Third, as already emphasized, the player's liability to the quasi-moral ascription of responsibility is something that he has let himself in for, i.e. contracted into. It is a let-in or *in*contractual commitment. That was why inevitability could not be allowed as an appropriate plea. Contrariwise, one's liability to the ascription of moral responsibility is something one cannot let oneself, or contract, out of. It is a no-let-out or *non-ex*contractual commitment. One cannot consistently contract out of the republic of means and the obligations one has as a member thereof, or complain against measures that are designed to keep that republic as inviolate as possible. One has the intrinsic non-arbitrary thinghood that qualifies one as something that does anything at all, including the repudiation of moral responsibility, only in so far as one defers to the non-contingent desire for a continued impartial instantiation of what confers that thinghood. One cannot even consistently commiserate with oneself in the privacy of one's heart on becoming the target of deserved reproach, for such private goings-on are but a part of the self-intimation of the reifying factor the self-desiderativness of which prescribes the standards to which we have failed to conform.

CHAPTER TEN

Towards a Psychocentric Physicalism

10.0

A concluding chapter is a bit of a bore if it simply restates what came before. Luckily, then, my revision of the Axiological Principle in chapter 9 is much too recent to call just yet for repetition. Luckily, too, the gist of my earlier emendments to the Reificatory and Modal Identity principles can be found in 9.3 and 9.4, where as a basis for the Axiological Principle they had further work to do. Hence, as a target for recapitulation my emendment to the Psychocentric Principle is all that is left to try the reader's patience. But our meed of luck has not yet run out. That emendment merely amalgamates the others. It puts, indeed, the finishing touch to my rendering of the Integrative Program. In brief it merely states that the mind or soul is the reifying factor. Accordingly, we now are free to reflect quite generally on the course that the program has taken, and to mull over some further problems.

10.1 THE TWO STYLES OF ANALYSIS

The Integrative Program is more clearly defined in the climate of today, indeed more clearly integrative, than it was in Aristotle's. Not only have integrative and disintegrative styles of analysis become more sharply differentiated and increasingly irreconcilable since then. As well the latter have long been in the ascendent. Nowhere is this more evident than in our current understanding or misunderstanding of the concepts of subjectivity, causal modality, and time. More or less overtly a dualistic interpretation of subjectivity is prevalent (least overtly in mind-brain identity theories and eliminative forms of materialism, but there all the same). This places the mental and the physical either in existential tandem or as rivals either for the same or for the dominant (i.e. subsumptive) existential status. Then, on the basis of this interpretation correlative features of these respective concepts have come unstuck. Thus causal necessitation and causal uniformity have been respectively and opposingly subjectivized and objectivized in the manner of Hume. The same applies to the interdependent A-determinations and B-relations of time. More specifically causal necessity, on the one hand, and A-determinations on the other have been reduced in one way or another to extraneous sorts of relationships that mind-independent uniformities and B-related sequences have to a mind. With yet other concepts, furthermore, those, e.g. of personal identity and the good, correlative features, once unstuck, then become antithetical. Thus as criteria of personal identity, continuity of memory and continuity of body have come into conflict. Likewise the attractiveness and the non-relative character of the unqualified good appear as difficult to reconcile.

My psychocentric form of physicalism can counter this trend. Its function has been to integrate subjectivity, causality, and time by showing how the first constitutes the logically implicit self-intimation of the second in the form of OBO-ability and how the language of the third as A-determined is inseparable from the language in which the various modalities that constitute OBO-ability are to be rendered articulate.

For the present, however, my main concern is with a further contrast between the two styles — one that is spiritual. Remember the eighteenth-century gentleman who – as Boswell reports – felt forced to abandon his philosophical studies because cheerfulness kept breaking through. Practitioners of the disintegrative style of whatever persuasion have been largely responsible for giving philosophy its reputation as a dispiriting activity. They contrast the vastness of the universe, the boundless magnitudes of space and time, with the tininess of the human body and the brevity of its history, and then interpret the quantitative disparity as a sign of man's insignificance. They make out the lot of any living person to be like that of some mariner adrift for the span of his existence in some boundless ocean, his only haven from the elements makeshift constructions from flotsam and jetsam around. Then, to counteract the dispiriting effect they have thus on themselves, they tend to divide into three main parties. One of these contends that by meeting, however ineffectually, the challenge posed by nature at large we achieve in our paltry portions of space and time a distinctive dignity to which that by which we are challenged can never attain, for which indeed it does not even qualify. In other words, where you are going to lose in any case, change the rules of the game so that you win. Another faction finds consolation in the thought that after all we are a part, however humble and diminutive, of the totality of natural processes by which we are eventually devoured. If you cannot beat them, join them — or better still declare yourself onside all along. The third party, dissatisfied with these two tactics, postulates existence of some supernatural immaterial realm, better adapted to the requirements of the spirit, to which we may be translated when in the natural realm we receive the final *coup de grâce*.

Now it may not be the function of philosophy to give solace to the spirit. However, at least to forestall confusion, it is prudent to show that the spiritual hallmarks of the *isms* that fall somewhere within the spectrum of disintegrative analyses are not essential to physicalism as such. As conceived through the integrative analysis of the psychocentric physicalist, space and time in their respective magnitudes are not to be regarded as alienating us from the rest of the universe. That is not to underestimate the hazards that lie in wait at every turn. But it is within the dispersions of space and the longeurs of time that the possibilities, to the mutual discrepancies of which we owe our intrinsic thinghood, divide and proliferate. Conversely, it is through the diminutive portions of matter to which intrinsic thinghood pertains that the spatio-temporal order presupposed by this division and the proliferation of possibilities — the boundless spreadoutness and endless succession by which the respective magnitudes are defined — acquire a non-arbitrary status as the basic physical order. Finally it is this being, of which the magnitudes of space and time are constitutive, and to which they owe their fundamental and non-arbitrary physical status, that is in itself an absolute fulfilment, i.e. the good.

These remarks on spirit also bear on a question that so far I have suppressed. If cognitive activities belong to the self-intimation of OBO-abilities, in what way do our present integrative activities, our progress on the Path to Enlightenment, fit in with this claim? In part the answer lies in what I have described as the plasticity of our desires as manifest in the interdependence of our cognitive and desiderative faculties for which I have already argued. The contrasting effects of the disintegrative and integrative styles on our spirits, i.e. our attitudes, give further evidence of the same sort of phenomenon. Ignorance of one's relation to the rest of the cosmos as a primary source and centre of intrinsic thinghood can, like ignorance of anything else, actually diminish the degree to which one can realize that thinghood. It may do so by lowering our expectations of what through our being we can achieve. Shout it out, then, from the rooftops. Publish it in the purlieus of academe. First philosophy, yea metaphysics, is of use after all! It can articulate, and hence protect, our tacit knowledge not only of ourselves as the primary source of being but of that being as the unqualified good that is the fulfilment of non-contingent desire. The object of this knowledge is what is knowable by nature. Hence the knowledge, whether articulated or just tacit, is itself indispensible to the realization in some measure both of that being and of that good.

10.2 EMERGENT COMPOSITION

In this section and the next I confront another question to which so far I have neglected to attend except in a tangential way. If so much really depends upon us, what would reality be like without us? Suppose that this planet happened to be the only habitat in the universe for any localized form of life, sentience, affective awareness, intelligence, or intentional activity. Suppose that tomorrow or in the days to follow all these localized phenomena were wiped out by means that seem already within our technological compass. What would the leavings be like?

It is arguable that the answer to this question should come primarily from physics, i.e. physics conceived as a special science. Some precedent for this can be found in Aristotle's psychocentrism, and more specifically in the elementalism that is its physical basis. Of course, the intellectual activity that is the ultimate form of which all other forms are a lower manifestation is conceived by him as eternal, and hence as coeval with the basic stuffs. Therefore the latter never would exist on their own without the existence of the former to which to conform. Nevertheless in themselves they are, as we have noted, spatially and quantitatively indeterminate. Their only intrinsic distinguishing features are of a purely qualitative nature.

Having long been obsolete, Aristotle's elementalism in itself is ineligible as an answer to my question. It has, however, a contemporary counterpart. I refer to the Copenhagen interpretation of quantum mechanics and more particularly to the psychocentric version of that interpretation offered by Wigner (1967, essays 13 and 14)[1].

For Wigner matter as a composite of subatomic particles is, while unobserved, in that sort of probabilistic state that is mathematically represented by a wave function, and this state is further conceived as spatially indeterminate – as a distribution (among other parameters) of alternative locations. Indeed, even a system that includes such particles and an observer who observes them is, in Wigner's estimation, similarly indeterminate while unobserved by further observers, i.e. in relation to these further observers. However, in any system taken as a whole, the wavelike quantum superposition of its subatomic particles, which the wave function represents, is collapsed or reduced to a determinate reality through interaction with the mental activities of that system's observer.

This interaction has, furthermore, to be quite other than that between the particles and, say, a photographic plate in a laboratory during the absence of any onlooker. The difference, as Wigner conceives it, between the plate and the onlooker is other than the mere difference of complexity between the former and a neurophysiological recording mechanism. It must be a difference of kind. Otherwise the ontological indeterminacy of the system prior to observation would, when the system is observed, merely extend to include the observer instead of collapsing. Likewise any higher-order addition of observers would merely lead regressively to further indeterminacy.[2]

Wigner's psychocentrism, like Aristotle's, is dualistic. For him, however, the reifying psychological factor is not coeval with what it reifies. How more exactly the mind is to perform its reifying function is left, furthermore, uncomfortably vague. He seems to have a pre-theoretical conception of the mind as some physically transcendent *deus ex machina* (his own phrase, by the way). In this the status of the mind's own thinghood does not appear as problematic. For him, it would seem, an accomplishment of contemporary physics has been to update Descartes just by offering a more radical conception of what the effect of the mind's intervention must be. On this view, in addition to affecting the motion and rest of the physical world, the mind imbues that realm with the phenomenological definiteness that it observes therein.

Psychocentrism of this sort is, however, transposable into one that is physicalistic. The order of explanation can just be reversed. Thanks to the Modal Identity Thesis, instead of attributing the introduction of determinate physical characteristics to the intervention of the mind, we can identify mind or its activities with the introduction of a certain degree of determinacy. The hypothesis must be that in certain parts of the cosmos the quantum-mechanically determined particles aggregate through the course of time into physical ensembles of a distinctive kind. These ensembles constitute a form of emergent composition whereby the wave functions of their components collapse progressively and conjointly into determinacy. This conjoint collapse just consists in the continuous possession of the series of OBO abilities that constitutes a person as a person throughout the series of P/F cuts thereby defined. We must suppose, in other words, that the probability distributions are channelled into divergent branches of equally possible determinate alternatives any one of which may serve as a node for the divergent branching of further channels. This, no doubt, still makes a mystery of what the cosmos is like when none of the required types of ensemble happen to exist. But that is a mystery to which contemporary physicists are for the most part resigned.

10.3 EMERGENT DECOMPOSITION

Compared with Wigner's psychocentrism as thus transposed the more direct implications of the psychocentric physicalism I have been expounding may seem rather tame. The transposition has set out to explain how a reality that instantiates determinate characteristics in an indeterminate way can come to instantiate these characteristics determinately. What my form of psychocentrism has set out to determine is which of all the determinate instantiations of determinate characteristics are instantiations by non-arbitrarily individuated things. Accordingly, what it more directly suggests is that without us or beings like us reality would be more like what it currently is than psychocentric ontologies are commonly supposed to permit. The one crucial difference would be that in their thinghood no localized or spatio-temporally limited particulars could any longer be non-arbitrary. Not unlike the classroom furnishings that Nozick (1981, pt 1) recalls – items classifiable indifferently as vertical fixtures with seat in front and desk-top behind or desk-consoles with seat behind and desk-top in front – their individual thinghood would be indeterminate in status, only more so.

It is prudent at this late stage to leave the status of secondary qualities such as colour, sound, taste, smell, and certain tactual qualities somewhat in a limbo. Not to be completely craven I suggest that they are to be included among the perspectival or body-centred phenomena through which our OBO-abilities intimate themselves as ours. But if we set that issue aside, then in the psychically bereft universe now being imagined or conceived it would not be as if some Kantian veil of appearances were suddenly to disperse leaving things in themselves by themselves in some state of austere incomprehensibility. All that would happen is that by themselves they would no longer be individuated as things in themselves, at least if we forget what they would owe to their past history, if any. They would merely be arbitrarily distinguishable parts of the whole.

Nevertheless it is only in opposition to other and more traditional forms of psychocentrism (e.g. Berkeley's) that the extent of the deprivation can be thus downplayed. Again, if we forget any debt to past history – the damage would be cosmically pervasive. It would destroy the basis for a number of ontologically salient features. These include (a) the bifurcation of time into past and future, (b) the related bifurcation of space from time, as a multidimensional extension at an instant in a further single dimension from the further single dimension, (c) the ontological priority of mutable particulars over spacetime worms or EVENTS, and (d) the secondary potencies to which certain mutable particulars owe a non-arbitrary extrinsic status as mutably particular. In short, the universe in these respects at least would become very like what many contemporary philosophers believe it actually is.

Furthermore, and even more devastatingly, with the elimination of the primary powers upon which the psychocentric structure of the universe is ultimately dependent there could no longer be any of the real in-the-actual-world causal possibilities that give the counterfactual implications essential to any actual causal relationships their ontological point. In stating what would happen given causal antecedents other than the actual causal antecedents in any situation, one would merely be stating what would be happen in another logically possible world *if it were sufficiently like the actual world*. One would not be stating what would be happening in this world. In short, causal laws would be very like what on Humean accounts they basically are, viz. extrapolatory generalizations about actual past, present, and future conjunctions – with their counterfactual nature attributable mainly to their extrapolatory purpose and the limitations to human knowledge to which such extrapolations pander.

It has sometimes been alleged that no form of psychocentrism can be comfortable with the relatively late emergence within the cosmos of the sort of life and intelligence by which any such form supposes the cosmos to be structured. To this line of criticism my physicalistic psychocentrism may seem as vulnerable as any idealistic kind in view of the devastating consequences adduced above. One may then be tempted to toy with some fairly strong anthropic principle, e.g. of the sort proposed by Wheeler (1977), which assigns to observership a retroactive participatory role in the genesis of the antecedent conditions that were indispensible to its emergence, or turn alternatively to some axiarchical principle to the effect that the value of what ought to be, e.g. the existence of creatures such as ourselves, has a creative power whereby what ought to be is eventually actualized (Leslie, 1979, 1982, 1983).[3]

These principles, of course, have had a somewhat different problematic provenance. Their protagonists have begun with the problem of cosmogony whereas that is where I am ending. For them it is the creation of the universe as presently structured that is psychocentric, rather than anything further in the structuring itself. Thus the former of the two principles has the function of explaining why the evolution of the universe has been so delicately attuned as to bring about just that very specific kind of cosmic environment that, among countless and physically equally probable cosmic environments, is alone conducive and hospitable to life. Likewise, according to the disjunction proposed by Leslie, to explain the exceeding improbability of our universe's being actual either there must be countless other universes besides ours, (i.e. the equally probable other universes are likewise actual) or, if ours is the only actuality, some anthropic or axiarchical principle must have steered its evolution.

But though the claims made for these principles have had a rather different provenance from a psychocentrism such as mine, do they not perhaps address a problem that is specific to the latter as well? The answer I believe is negative. While by cosmic standards the existence of persons may be exceedingly belated and brief, it is timely and long enough to act as a kind of ontological leaven throughout the reaches of spacetime.

Consider, first, the spatio-temporal immensity between the Big Bang and the synthesizing in sufficient abundance of carbon and other chemicals that constitute the raw materials essential to the formation of life as we know it. From within this immensity a set of three-dimensional volumes could be arbitrarily selected as slicing that spatio-temporal totality, somewhat as a set of parallel planes slice a three-dimensional cone. This set could then be ordered equally arbitrarily in terms of the asymmetrical relation *smaller than*, rather than the latter's converse. Thus the singularity of the Big Bang would come first and the universe of stars and galaxies towards the end, though in terms of the converse relation *larger than* the order would be reversed. But now, by virtue of the continuity of that chunk with that part of spacetime occupied by persons, the arbitrarily selected slices may parallel the non-arbitrary bifurcation of the spatial from the temporal dimensions within the latter. If so, they will acquire a non-arbitrary status of an extrinsic kind. Furthermore, that their temporal ordering should coincide with a certain size-ordering, so that the smaller is also the temporally antecedent volume, will likewise acquire a non-arbitrary extrinsic status. And finally, what applies in this way in the backwards direction applies reversely in the forward direction from now on in spacetime as well.

Accordingly, the devastating consequences of our absence at any time from the universe would only prevail in a universe in which we had at no time been and at no time will be – though, given the dependence of time upon us, that is a rather Irish way of making the point. More importantly, however, radical though these consequences are, they bear out my earlier claim. They merely relate to the structure of reality as a whole, i.e. to the non-arbitrary individuation and ordering of its parts. There is nothing in my version of the psychocentric hypothesis to indicate that the determinateness of reality would be impaired by the absence of things such as ourselves. Quite to the contrary indeed. On my hypothesis presumably that absence would abolish the openness of the future, and to that extent make reality more homogeneously determinate.

Where, then, does physics enter the picture? Has it any further contribution to make to our grasp of what the absence would be like? More particularly, has the Copenhagen interpretation of quantum mechanics, supposing it to be on the right track,[4] any further contribution to make? To this question there are, I believe, at least two answers.

For one of the two my transposition of Wigner's idealistic into a physicalistic form of psychocentrism is to be taken as merely a specification of the more general type of theory I have been developing. In other words, the outcome is to be regarded as merely adding more detail to the picture of absence that the more general type of theory paints. I have some difficulty, however, with this mode of conciliation. It seems to concede to reality in our absence some measure of the sort of structure that on the supposedly more general theory is due to our presence. The non-emergence of the emergent composition that would constitute that presence would seem to be a non-emergence in a non-arbitrarily constructed time. Likewise the non-composition would seem to be a non-composition of non-arbitrarily individuated particles with certain secondary causal powers, even if the nature of these particles and of their powers are of a somewhat indeterminate kind. These structural features would seem to be more than merely retrospective, i.e. introduced retroactively by the "emergence" of intelligent beings. On the contrary, the intelligibility of the transposition seems to depend upon their being intrinsic.

Accordingly, I prefer the other answer. On this alternative the advent of mind in the universe consists in an emergent *decomposition* whereby the physical reality is differentiated non-arbitrarily into spatio-temporally separate or separable parts. The phenomena of quantum mechanics are then to be interpreted as due to a certain recalcitrance on the part of reality as a whole to decomposition beyond a certain level. In other words, beneath a certain quantitative threshold the parts of the total structure do not submit to determinate non-arbitrary individuation as bearers of secondary causal powers. On this hypothesis, furthermore, no temporal or particulate structural features are attributed as intrinsic to reality in our absence.

10.4 DISORDER IN TIME

My final problem has a more heterodox basis. Quite a few people claim to have precognized, usually in dreams, situations in which they find themselves at a later date. One may doubt whether these experiences really took place as distinct from being retrospectively imagined as having done so, or else dismiss their verisimilitude as coincidental. Unless, like J.W. Dunne (1929), one has made a practice of recording one's dreams in a bedside book upon waking, one certainly has no better check on one's apparent memory of dreams than one normally has of memories that one accepts without question as veridical. But if one happens to belong to the number who are occasionally visited by such experiences, then — somewhat like Ayer on recovery from his clinical death and a more apocalyptic vision of space and time — one cannot remain completely at ease with attempts of this sort to shield the world of everyday normality.

That being the case, my A-theory of time as an explanation of temporal becoming may likewise come under suspicion. If precognitive experience is taken at its face value as veridical, it may seem incompatible with anything but some form of B-theory. In other words, it may seem that the future must be as determinate or fixed as the past, even though for some reason it is normally hidden. Given, then, that this is so, events must have a temporal ordering that is independent of the division of time into series of P/F cuts. These doubts, furthermore, should extend to the theory of reification and the Modal Identity Thesis upon which my A-theory is based.

I used to think that the latter could account quite readily for the possibility of precognition in the following way. Some of the possibilities of action before us that diverge from a single node of time might in some exceptional cases converge eventually by a causal necessity into other nodes. As a consequence the overall direction of time would be preserved because of the main divergent trend, but in isolated areas a temporal disorder would impinge. Thus times and experienced events that would be in sequence relative to the overall order would also be simultaneous in their relative isolation. However, I now believe that this attempt at assimilation won't do, or at least that it cannot account for precognition of the sort in question. If some of the possibilities that diverge from a single node did eventually converge, then it would seem that in the area where divergence and convergence meet events in time would appear to go in the reverse of their normal development. But so far as I know no such experience has been reported.

There is, however, a simpler alternative. It would seem that sometimes *by choice* at some earlier time we are predisposed to put ourselves in the way both of having the opportunity to perform and of performing certain actions at a later time. Between these two times, however, we are called upon to make choices between alternatives the respective outcomes of which will not interfere with the arrival of the opportunity and the subsequent performance which the latter makes possible. At least in some of its segments one's lifeline may be like a Mandarin's sleeve. The latter, being much more voluminous than the arm it covers, is free to flap and billow along its length in more directions than the arm itself can turn, but not beyond limits set by the latter. In these circumstances my version of the A-theory allows the prediction that one may have an immediate experience of unforeseen circumstances attending the performance of the action at the later date, at a time when one is still in the midst of the occasions for the intermediate choices. It also allows the prediction that one's experience of these later circumstances should occur during sleep where temporarily one's ability to carry on with these intermediate choices is suspended.

The Non-causal Self-fulfilment of Intention[1]

I. WHY ARE INTENTIONS, IF NOT CAUSES, SO LIKE THEM?

Apart from the fact that what we do often depends on what we intend, intentions are conspicuously quasi-causal in at least one other way.

An explicit intention antedates the action intended. This, of course, is clearest where the intention has been formed early enough to be revoked, or forgotten, before the time for fulfilment comes round. But even where it persists right up to, or occurs just at, the executive moment of action, it precedes in the sense that it is there at the moment when the action takes off. Some actions, no doubt, are intentional without being intended. Though in no way premeditated, their performance is under the control of the agent's intelligence. A casual contribution to a conversation is, for instance, usually of this kind. More often than not we do not think what to say before saying it. Consequently, it is sometimes inferred that intentionality without premeditation – and even what is essential to intentionality as such – consists of nothing that antedates the intentional action. But, though I believe the inference to be hasty, I shall set it temporarily to one side by confining myself initially to intentional actions that are intentional because intended.

Now, in the present context, a cause is taken as in some sense a crucial component of a set of states or events that, relative to natural laws, are together a sufficient condition of whatever is caused. Like intentions, such causes quite often precede, though sometimes they may coincide in time with, what depends upon them. Should intentions, then, be classified as causes? And if not, why are they so cause-like? Both of these questions are the concern of what follows.

II. TWELVE CLUES

Clue 1. Typically a categorical or unqualified intention is expressed by an anticipatory form of utterance such as "I am going to X," or "I shall (will) X," or "I am about to X."[2] It can also be expressed in a non-anticipatory way by some verb of volition as in "I intend to X," or "I have decided to X." But the latter are indirect. They leave inexplicit the important difference between the agent's attitude at the time towards his intended action and the attitude of someone else who reports the agent's intention in some such formula as "He intends to X."

An epistemic analogy may show more clearly why.
The three kinds of sentence in question,

    S_1. "I intend to X,"
    S_2. "He intends to X,"
    S_3. "I am about to X,"

compare respectively in function to

    S_1'. "I believe Richard Hughes was born in 1900,"
    S_2'. "He believes Richard Hughes was born in 1900,"
    S_3'. "Richard Hughes was born in 1900."

On some occasions the verb "believe" as in S_1' has a so-called parenthetical use we shall set to one side. On other occasions it simply ascribes a specific belief-attitude to the speaker. S_1' then ascribes what S_2' would ascribe, if used by someone else to refer on the same occasion to the speaker of S_1'.

But S_2' conveys accurately what its speaker means only where his assumption is that the subject of the ascription has a conviction that could be accurately expressed by S_3'. Should the subject have any reservation about what S_3' states, then S_2' would convey its speaker's meaning inaccurately. A sentence of the form "H is inclined to believe ..." would have been better chosen. Consequently, since *ex hypothesi* S_1' and S_2' ascribe the same belief-attitude to the same person, S_3' expresses the belief-attitude that S_1' ascribes.

Now this illustration of the distinction between what a sentence ascribes, or reports, and what it expresses helps us to differentiate the respective roles of S_1, S_2, and S_3. S_1 and S_2 may both ascribe the same intention to the same person. In that case S_3 expresses the intention both ascribe, provided it is uttered by the speaker of S_1. His linguistic behaviour would be inconsistent if, upon uttering S_1, he were to add "But due to circumstances outside my control I am not about to X." It would be as incongruous as that of a speaker of S_1' who denies what S_3' conveys.

As already noted, however, when S_1 and S_2 convey the same thing, S_1 gives an *indirect* expression to its speaker's intention. Its inclusion of "I" indicates that the person to whom it ascribes the intention is the utterer, and hence that the utterer also subscribes to the expression of that intention in S_3. Similarly when S_1' and S_2' convey the same thing, S_1' gives indirect expression to its speaker's belief. Its inclusion of "I" likewise indicates that the person to whom it ascribes the belief is the utterer, and hence that the utterer also subscribes to the expression of the belief in S_3'. But in neither case can what the "I" indicates be identified with any part of what the sentence including it states. Otherwise we would have to abandon our hypothesis that what each sentence and its third-person partner states or conveys is identical (Rankin, 1964). Consequently, the expression of the intention, in the one case, and of the belief, in the other, is only indirect.

Clue 2. When X-ing is possible, and someone's intention to X is formed in all cognizance of the circumstances that make it possible for him, his intention is fully appropriate. But all the same it would seem odd to give his utterance of S_3 the accolade of "true" or "correct," or to congratulate him for perspicacity in uttering it, even though his intention will be fulfilled. What is true or correct is his assessment of the circumstances – not his commitment to S_3. For S_3 it is a matter of the facts matching up to the words, rather than the words matching up to the facts. We can sum this up by saying that expressions of intention lack *paradigmatic truth-value.*

Sometimes, of course, we may express an intention by saying "It is true that I am going to do what he says I am" or "It is false that I am going to resign." Here, however, the words "true" and "false" belong to the actual formulation of the intention rather than evaluate it. Hence their inclusion does not give the expression that includes them paradigmatic truth-value.

Sometimes, too, we may refer in a proprietary way to someone's *true* intention. But his true intention is simply what he *really* intends, just as his true belief is what he really believes. The proprietary is quite distinct from the non-proprietary, viz. the paradigmatic "true." Thus *his* true belief need not be true, i.e., *a* true belief, a belief expressible by a true sentence. It may be false. And it seems unnatural to describe *his* true intention as either true or false.

You might object that my expression of intention in S_3 must be paradigmatically true or false because of its undoubted consistency with your report of my success by "He did it." But does the comparable consistency of my performative "I bet" with your informative "He bets" similarly entitle the former to truth-value? Not if we are to believe Austin. When I say "I bet," I succeed or fail in betting rather than say something true or false, correct or incorrect. And even if we are saying something true or false, etc., by virtue of succeeding or failing, the truth or falsity can hardly be described as paradigmatic.

Clue 3. Unlike some other types of utterance that lack paradigmatic truth-value, expressions of intention are, first and foremost, expressions of something mental. No doubt commands like "You shall report here at 2.30 p.m.," promises like "I will return it tomorrow," and performatives like "I bet" or "I promise" have to express such mental attitudes as wishes or judgments to have any point. But unlike expressions that are nothing but expressions of attitude, such expressions are used in the type of illocutionary act that is definable in terms of its perlocutionary effect (see Searle, 1969, 71). Thus a command is, roughly, the sort of expression of a wish that conveys by linguistic convention that, should the person addressed fail to take reasonable steps towards satisfying the wish, he will become liable to some penalty.

Clue 4. In spite of its lack of paradigmatic truth-value an intention is an anticipation, and judgmental in character. In forming an intention you subject you attitude to the criteria of consistency. Unless schizoid, you cannot knowingly intend to perform incompatible actions, nor can you form a categorical and unqualified intention to do something while subscribing to an inductively formed, and firm, belief that the action will not occur (see clue 1). Likewise your intention will be held by others to be inappropriate, if they believe that what you intend will not come about. By contrast, wish-attitudes – though like intentions in some respects – are non-judgmental. You may know that the realization of one wish precludes satisfaction of another and yet wholeheartedly have both. Likewise your wish is not reckoned inappropriate by others just because they think it will not be realized.

Clue 5. As a verb, "anticipate" like "believe" can be used to ascribe a disposition. Someone may anticipate a rise in salary next year, in the sense that if you take up the matter with him he may say, and will believe, that his salary will then be raised, even though the thought does not often cross his mind. But "anticipate" can also be used to refer to the sort of occurrence in which an anticipatory disposition is *realized*, i.e. to the fact that it *occurs* to someone that something, e.g. a rise, is on the way.[3]

Such occurrents, however, are admittedly somewhat singular. Sometimes they are the result of some process of deliberation, or resolution of uncertainty. As such *results*, they come about quickly or slowly, easily or with difficulty, etc. Sometimes, however, they come without any process. Hence they do not seem to fall within the Rylean category of achievement as a correlative of process. Sometimes, too, however they come, they may persevere continuously, or intermittently over a period of time, if on first occurring they refer to an occasion sufficiently far ahead. On such occasions they seem as complete in any small segment of their duration as in the whole. To this extent they are like states. But surely it may occur to one quite instantaneously, without consciousness of time-span, that something will occur just before the happening does occur. To that extent they are more like changes from one state to another.

I may intend now, for instance, to do something rather exacting at a later date. Since what I intend will require all my resolution, my intention may remain in the forefront of my mind continuously, or intermittently as when I waver or spend time in sleep, right up to the occasion for action. And for as long as it continues, it will be as complete, as an intention, at any one time, or for any one time-span, as at, or for, any other. However, perseverance through a stretch of time does not seem essential to the occurrence. The formation of intention may occur just at the moment of action.

Clue 6. Anticipating, intending, and certain other kinds of mental occurrent are rather singular in yet another way. They have temporal duality. Thus anticipating refers to something that is due to take place later, and remembering what has happened refers to what has taken place earlier.

Clue 7. Likewise they have an act-content structure. Each distinct occurrent is characterizable by a judgmental content, though one may have the same content as another. Consequently, where the content has paradigmatic truth-value, the occurrent, quite straightforwardly, belongs to the sort of thing that we do rightly or wrongly, correctly or incorrectly, etc. Where a perceptual judgment is false, the perceiver has misperceived, etc. Even where the content lacks paradigmatic truth-value in the way that the content of intending does, his intending is something the agent does appropriately or inappropriately, depending upon whether or not it is based upon correct assessment of the situation. Now it is by virtue of being either right or wrong, etc., that mental occurrents of these kinds have the status of being acts, though, of course, in contrast to intentional action they are more like ordinary happenings.

Clue 8. Anticipations of intention are *indexically committed* to the first grammatical person or some equivalent. The judgmental acts of different people can have a common content in cases other than intention. This holds even where the content of one person's judgment refers solely to himself. Thus "I am over eighty" and "He is over eighty," as uttered by different persons, potentially express judgments with the same content. Such contents, accordingly, are uncommitted to the first, rather than the third, person. But one person's intention cannot have quite the same content as any sort of judgmental act of another. As an expression of intention, S_3 is not translatable into S_4 "He is about to X" uttered by another in reference to the same action of the same agent. There are at least four indications of this:

a Normally S_4 expresses simple anticipation, not intention.
b This anticipation is formed on a twofold basis, viz., that the agent intends to X *and* that he has the opportunity, including the capacity, to X. In contrast, the anticipation of intention is formed solely on the basis that the opportunity, including the capacity, obtains.
c The anticipation of intention lacks the paradigmatic truth-value that the other anticipation possesses.
d Less normally, S_4 might be short-hand for "I am going to induce him to X." But then it expresses the intention of another agent to perform a different action that will result in the first agent X-ing.

To appreciate the full significance of these considerations, we can turn once again to our previous analogy in which all four are reflected.

a' Normally, to say "He is betting" or "He will return tomorrow" is respectively neither to bet nor to promise.
b' These things are said appropriately on a twofold basis, viz., that their subject has uttered performatives like "I bet" or "I will return tomorrow" *and* that the circumstances are appropriate for betting or promising. But the performatives themselves are appropriately uttered solely on the basis that the circumstances are appropriate.
c' The performatives lack the paradigmatic truth-value that their third-person counterparts possess.
d' Less normally, these counterparts might be shortland respectively for something like "I guarantee he will bet" and "I will see to it that he will return tomorrow." But then their utterances become quite different performative acts of another speaker.

Now all four of these considerations point to a parallel indexical commitment in performative utterances, whereby they are untranslatable into third-person counterparts. Despite the analogy, however, there are important differences between expressions of intention and other kinds of speech-act such as performatives. We have indicated these in clues 3 and 4. The true basis for the analogy will become clearer in the clues which follow.

Clue 9. Anticipations of intention are to some extent self-fulfilling. When the agent has an opportunity to act in opposing ways, it is essential to, and, if he has the capacity, sufficient for, his acting in any one that he intends to do so then – except in three types of case.

(a)   He may be instantaneously competent to act appropriately. Thus he may be instanteneously competent to punch his tormentor on the nose, or to give his name when asked. Here his actions tend to be intentional, but not intended. He comprehends the situation in terms of the appropriate reaction to it – *as to be handled in such-and-such a way*, e.g., as a nose to be punched, or a question to be answered by giving his name (cf. Bradley, 1935, 39, 504–5; Polanyi, 1960, chap. 1). One might say that he does not distinguish expressly between the challenge and his impending response. Notice that this act-oriented type of comprehension is antecedent to the act. That is why I questioned the inference in my introduction that intentionality without intention consists of nothing that antedates the intentional act.

(b)   When an agent has an opportunity, including a capacity, to act in any of several opposing ways, one of the actions would have been necessary, through a teleological sort of inertia, and the rest impossible had it not occurred to him that he might do something other than the former (also see 6.2). To begin with more universal types of case, in most situations it is necessary that I continue breathing or blinking unless it occurs to me to desist for a time, perhaps to attend more carefully to a faint sound, or indistinct object, or to test my endurance. Similarly, in the case of well-established patterns of habitual behaviour, such as driving home at the end of the day, once set off, we necessarily carry them through unless it occurs to us to modify them in some respect. But even where neither the operation of our autonomic nervous system nor of habit is at issue, the same principle holds. When I am seated, normally the situation is such, e.g., the chair is sturdy enough, that I continue seated *necessarily*, unless it occurs to me to stand up, or slither down, etc. Accordingly, intention cannot be essential to the performance of any action that we would perform through the kind of inertia illustrated in these three ways, where it does not occur to us that we might act otherwise.

(c)   Where in performing one action we necessarily perform, or will perform another, the intention to perform the second is not essential to its performance. It is enough that we intend to perform the first. Thus, if I were to discern a star in the sky, if and only if I were to stop blinking for a while, I might in fact discern the star without intending to, if I had intended simply to stop blinking and did stop in fact. This example, however, suggests a complication to the present exception. What I do in stopping blinking is more likely to occur to me as trying to discern a star than simply as stopping blinking. In fact, it may not occur to me as stopping blinking at all. Hence, for reasons given in b above, the intention to discern a star would be essential to my discerning it by stopping blinking. The same complication, however, might not arise in other cases of doing one thing in, or by, doing, or having done, another.

Clue 10. No agent can be blind to the distinction between his intention and non-self-fulfilling types of anticipation. If an anticipation of mine expressible by "I shall not inhale while under water" does not present itself to me as distinct from a non-self-fulfilling anticipation, I am probably in for a nasty shock after I submerge.

Clue 11. The self-fulfilment of intention must be distinguished from that of other kinds of self-fulfilling anticipation. The performance of an intentional action is quite unlike, for instance, a patient's recovery from what would otherwise have been a fatal illness only through confidence in his doctor's assurance that he will recover. "I am going to recover" is in these circumstances the expression of a mere anticipation – not of an anticipation of intention. The patient has been taken in to some extent, and possibly his anticipation could not have withstood the insight that his belief in recovery is an essential condition of his recovery. In contrast, an anticipation of intention does not seem to be in any way diminished where the agent has explicit insight into its self-fulfilling role.

Clue 12. Anticipations of intention are also unlike those of the self-faith-healer who has acquired insight into the self-fulfilment of his anticipation of recovery. There are five indications of the difference.

(a)   The self-faith-healer's insight is epiphenominal to the self-fulfilment of his anticipation. The therapeutic power of his anticipation, in other words, is not dependent upon his insight, provided he really does anticipate. Whether the anticipation is induced by himself, his doctor, or by something else is quite immaterial. According to clue 10, however, the agent's insight into the self-fulfilment of intention is essential to the self-fulfilment.

(b)   Success in administering faith-therapy to oneself seems dependent upon the degree of confidence, or certitude, with which one can sustain the anticipation. In contrast, the self-fulfilment of intention is not tied to certitude to the same extent. Sometimes the strongest anticipation of intention that an agent can commit himself to is expressible by nothing stronger than a formula like "I shall try to X." The uncertainty about the possibility of X-ing that this manifests need not interfere with successful performance. True, a person who doubts his ability to pronounce unslurred a tongue-twister, e.g. "The Leith police dismisseth us," may have less success than someone more confident, even though both suffer from the same degree of inebriation. However, his uncertainty may have the contrary effect, by making him exercise greater care.

(c)   The ability of the self-faith-healer is an ability that, upon gaining insight into the therapeutic value of the anticipation of recovery, he has to acquire. Or at least he has to possess the pre-existing ability not to be put off by his insight. He has the ability despite the insight. But there is surely no question of agents being put off intending upon acquiring insight into the self-fulfilment of intention.

(d)   The ability of the self-faith-healer is something he may acquire and apply for a purpose. He anticipates his recovery *in order to* recover. This anticipating may in fact be sufficiently deliberate to be intended as well as intentional. It may be intended as a means to an end, i.e., the end of recovery. But in that case the anticipating must be distinct from the intending to recover. It becomes part of the action intended, in the same way as reading aloud in order to amuse a child is part of the intended action of amusing the child. And if we ignore this conclusion by supposing the anticipating not to be distinct from the intending, we would be obliged to suppose that the intending was also an intentional action.

(e)   Intending can be accompanied by insight into its self-fulfilling character without the anticipation incurring *on that count* the charge of irrationality. The self-faith-healer's anticipation of recovery does, however, contain an element of irrationality. A doctor who has insight into the therapeutic effect that his assurance of recovery has upon his patient can anticipate the patient's recovery in a rational way on the basis, among other things, that the patient has accepted his assurance. But the self-faith-healer is not assured until he commits himself to the anticipation of his recovery. His anticipation consequently cannot have a complete rational basis. It may, of course, be rational in a pragmatic way, viz. as an effective means towards the recovery anticipated. But as shown in (d), intentions cannot be regarded as means towards their own fulfilment. Are we then to suppose that intending is irrational? Surely the agent who does what he does through the teleological sort of inertia is less rational than the agent to whom it occurs that he can act otherwise and who consequently does whatever he does intending to do it.

III. WHY INTENTIONS ARE NOT CAUSES

In their respective ways these clues suggest a very simple interpretation. They indicate that intention is the sort of anticipation in which his anticipating is a *logically* necessary condition of the agent's being about to act in the way he anticipates.

Clues 1, 3, and 4, on the one hand, and 9 on the other bring the quasi-causal features of intention into sharper focus. Intentions anticipate what is intended not simply by way of coming before but also in the way that cognitive acts or attitudes of anticipation anticipate. Likewise, with the exceptions noted, what is intended depends upon intention specifically as a necessary, not a sufficient condition.

If, however, the future occurrence of the anticipated action were *logically* independent of this necessary condition, then the agent's anticipating would presumably have paradigmatic truth-value. It would be "objective" in one of the senses commonly given to "objective," i.e. true or false logically irrespective of whether someone believes it to be true or false.[4] Hence clue 2, the lack of paradigmatic truth-value, indicates that this sort of anticipation is not logically independent of cognitive attitude.

If, on a contrary hypothesis, the anticipator's action were *causally* dependent upon his cognitive attitude, the logical status of his anticipation as paradigmatically true or false would not be diminished. If anticipations of intention are analogous to performatives, causally operative anticipations would be analogous to certain perlocutionary acts. Thus, if you frighten yourself by saying "I frighten myself," what you say, unlike a performative, is paradigmatically true.

The indexical commitment of intention, to which clue 8 testifies, provides further evidence that the necessary condition is logical. Where an indexically *uncommitted* proposition about someone refers to him in the first person, the expression does not *state*, but only *indicates*, that the person expressing the proposition as his belief is the person to whom the proposition refers. At least a distinction between *stating* and *indicating* is needed, if we ever want to say that an utterance whereby one of us refers to himself or herself by means of "I" expresses the same proposition as an utterance whereby another of us refers to the same person by means of "you," "he," or "she." Where, however, an anticipation is indexically committed to the first person, what its expression *indicates* is also implicit, at least, in what it states. What the speaker states as his anticipation logically implies that he anticipates as stated. And what he so implies is exactly what his first-person expression indicates. Consequently, his anticipating must be a logically necessary condition of his being about to act as stated.

This conclusion is reinforced by clues 10 and 11. Since the agent's anticipation of intention is essential to his being about to do what he anticipates, it is to that extent self-fulfilling. And since it is logically essential, the agent must have at least implicit knowledge of the difference between his anticipation of intention and any non-self-fulfilling anticipation.

Clue 12, in conjunction with 10 and 11, precludes the possibility that the agent's anticipating is *causally* a necessary condition of the anticipated action instead of, or in addition to, its being logically essential. If the anticipating were causally a necessary condition, no insight, explicit or implicit, would be essential to its self-fulfilling operation. And, indeed, it is conceivable that any such insight might interfere with the self-fulfilling operation, as the case of faith-healing would seem to illustrate. Anticipations of intention, contrariwise, require implicit insight at least into their self-fulfilling operation and are certainly not rendered inoperative by such insight.

If despite these arguments, however, they were causally self-fulfilling, they would have to resemble the anticipating of the self-faith-healer.[5] But they are quite unlike the latter in important respects, for reasons already given by clue 12. But if the anticipating is logically a necessary condition of its substance, none of these reasons apply any longer.

1 The agent's insight cannot be epiphenomenal upon self-fulfilment of his anticipating, since to understand his anticipation he must understand, implicitly at least, that his anticipating is a logically necessary condition of his being about to act as he anticipates. Here, of course, I am arguing from the principle that to understand a proposition one must understand, implicitly at least, not only what is implicit in it but also that it is implicit.

2 The degree of certitude with which we hold a belief does not prevent what is implicit in it from being implicit in it. Hence, if that we hold the belief is logically implicit in it, the absence of certitude does not prevent the belief from being logically self-fulfilling.

3 Likewise we need acquire or possess no special ability to be able to withstand insight in the belief's self-fulfilling nature. The ability to withstand the insight is in fact inseparable from the ability to have the belief.

4 And finally, the anticipating cannot be regarded as irrational. In a logically true proposition like "If this is a rose, then it is a flower,"

the truth of the consequent is a logically necessary condition of the truth of the antecedent. But the truth of the consequent is not one of the truths on the basis of which we should infer the truth of the antecedent. Similarly, as a logically necessary condition of what we anticipate in intention, our anticipating does not place itself in the impossible position of having to function in part as its own epistemic basis.

It will be observed that the arguments in this section are of two main kinds. The first kind represents the connection between an anticipation of intention, and its substance as logical, more directly than the second. And the second represents the connection more directly as non-causal than the first. This double attack protects my interpretation from the type of criticism to which the first type of argument has been prone in the past. Because causes are often described functionally in terms of their tendency to produce certain effects, the connection between them, when so described, and these effects is logical as well as causal. Hence, certain standard arguments that establish a logical connection between intention and intended action fail to show the connection to be likewise non-causal. For the latter purpose it is not enough to point out that, typically at least, intentions are specified in terms of the description of the action as intended, or that, "other things being equal," it is logically necessary that given the intention, the action will occur. Now possibly my first kind of argument might turn out to be subject to this kind of criticism. But the second kind does not seem vulnerable in the same way.

Notes

CHAPTER ONE

1 In his aporetic agenda in *Meta.* B he distinguishes one difficulty (chap. 4) as "the hardest of all and the most necessary to examine." The difficulty so described seems identifiable from what comes next as the one-over-the-many with certain Aristotelian offshoots superimposed.

2 That Plato at all times recognized the problems of the one-over-the-many and Heraclitean flux as distinct from each other or from further problems is perhaps not entirely clear. See T.H. Irwin (1977).

3 We can neglect the complication that some Forms fall under other Forms, and that all Forms are treated in a way as perfect particulars.

4 I am not denying the undeniable, viz. that Aristotle uses Aristotelian distinctions quite explicitly to attack the Theory of Forms. But at his most explicit he seems to have used them for the purpose of creating problems for the theory rather than for removing the apparent need for it.

5 For a more conservative reconstruction, which cleaves more closely to technical distinctions that Aristotle actually observes, see Montgomery Furth (1988, 10ff). On Furth's interpretation, the general relationship of predication that the formula "X is Y" expresses takes, on deeper analysis, two specific forms: (1) the relation of *inhering in* a subject (e.g. as bravery inheres in Socrates) and (2) the relation of being *said of* a subject (e.g. as man or animal or their differentiae are said of Socrates, or virtue is said of bravery). Relation 1, and that relation to a subject alone, is cross-categorial. Relation 2, and that relation to a subject alone, is in contrast intra-categorial. It is distinguished from 1 as the *said-of* relation, he ingeniously suggests, by virtue of the respective involvements of its referents in the *logos* or definition of a thing

or its kind. Unfortunately Furth's study of Aristotle's metaphysics appeared too late for me to react to any of his reconstructions except in afterthought sorts of footnote. For the moment, however, it is enough to observe that his reconstructions have, as in this case, the purpose of offsetting what he interprets as comparatively minor lapses in how Aristotle articulates his doctrine. In contrast, my reconstruction at this point is designed to remove major and stultifying error. See also 13 below.

6 The need to keep predicatives and substantives distinct has been shown very thoroughly by Wilfred Sellars (1960). However, his further exploitation of the distinction in support of nominalism is arbitrary. H.P. Grice (1979) has argued specifically for a dual conception of Aristotle's category-distinctions that is sensitive to the same need.

7 More accurately, it might seem to be *the* courageous that he describes as a paronym of the substantive courage, thus apparently defining the relation as between two kinds of substantive. Greek, however, does not distinguish as sharply as English between noun and adjectival uses of adjectives. Hence my use of the term "paronym" may not be as contrary to Aristotle's as initially it might seem. This comment arises, indirectly perhaps, from an objection made by Mohan Matthen.

8 The need to take these measures only became clear to me under pressure from an objection by Ali Ahktar.

9 The syntactical nature of the category confusion in many category-confused predications and identifications can be made evident in terms of articles 4, 5, and 6. Thus when we substitute "one thing that one or more than one thing is (or is not)," viz. "wise" for "wisdom" in "Socrates is wisdom," it becomes clear in that context that the name-frame is redundant, and hence that the substitute can only have a predicative, not a substantive function.

10 This comment responds, perhaps indirectly, to an objection raised by Mohan Matthen. Notice further that, though by our quasi-Quinean criteria differentiae of natural kinds, e.g. two-footedness, rationality, belong to the secondary categories, even in his *Categories* (see chap. 4) Aristotle consistently exempts them from that status. Perhaps that can be explained as in part a misrepresentation of a distinction that has to be drawn within the secondary categories between contingently and necessarily existing things.

11 Notice that the so-called "is" of composition is as much a piece of mythology as are the "is" of predication and the "is" of identity. Thus when Parfit argues (1984, 211) that in "This statue is a piece of bronze" the "is" is of composition, not of identity, it is strictly correct to say that it is neither. There is, however, a more crucial issue, i.e. whether the sentence identifies one thing with another or not. On

Parfit's interpretation it states that the statue is composed of, *not* that it is identical with, a piece of bronze. His reason for this conclusion is that to melt the statue destroys the statue without destroying the piece of bronze. But the survival of a piece of bronze as such after the statue has been destroyed indicates no more than that the piece of bronze was identical with the statue for a period of time and not thereafter. Consider the sentence "This piece of bronze is a statue," used perhaps to demonstrate what a statue is. Here it is crystal clear there is no implication that the piece of bronze is composed of the statue. On the contrary, it is being identified with the statue. But if it is identical with the statue, then conversely that statue, contrary to Parfit, must be identical with the piece of bronze.

12 But notice in "A man is an animal" the indefinite article is equivalent to the quantifier "any" in its first occurrence but not in its second. Thus the proposition as a whole is equivalent to "If anything is a man, then it is an animal." Here the indefinite article in neither occurrence is the quantifier "any" and the antecedent and consequent alike are indefinite identification.

13 It is a limitation of Furth's conservative sort of reconstruction that at this point (1988, 25) he neither attempts to overcome this difficulty for Aristotle's notion of substantial primacy nor even acknowledges its existence.

14 D.W. Hamlyn (1977–78) has argued that Aristotle did not subscribe to a Fregean distinction between sense and reference. Hence, on that assumption, the distinction between a semantical and an ontological basis for the dependency would not (need not?) arise – at least for Aristotle.

15 As illustrations of more contemporary interest Hamlyn (1977–78) suggests "wants," as applied respectively to introspected and unconscious wants, and "knowledge," as applied in accordance with the various conflicting criteria to which ordinary discourse seems to subscribe.

16 To describe a nexus of terms bound together by focal meaning as naming things that are homonyms may extend the application of the notion of homonymy beyond what Aristotle seems strictly to allow in the *Metaphysics*. It is, however, a useful extension and already in vogue. See Joseph Owens on Equivocals (1963, 110–18) and G.E.L. Owen (1960).

CHAPTER TWO

1 On Julius Moravcsik's interpretation (1971; see Vlastos, 1971), "it is reasonable to assume that both the paradox and its proposed solution

are interpreted by Plato to apply to a priori contexts only." But this does not go far enough. It is in keeping with Plato's a priorism, that he should be suggesting that the paradox can be solved only in a priori contexts, and that therefore a priori inquiry is the only genuine form of inquiry.

2 This problem has been identified and debated in more modern times as the paradox of analysis. See C.H. Langford (1942) and Moore's inconclusive response (1942). For further discussion, see Paul Feyerabend (1957–58), R.M. Hare (1960), Wilfred Sellars (1967), and M.S. Gram (1969) in Klemke (1969).

3 In this context we may permit ourselves to take the Scotist notion of *haecceitas* to be equivalent to the notion of bare particularity, for both are invoked as the basis of the difference between particulars that have exactly the same properties. In that capacity the notion of bare particularity is not specifically invoked for its further purpose of misrepresenting the notion of substratum as that in a thing that underlies all the thing's properties.

4 For arguments against solution A that are similar to, and sometimes more ample than, some of those provided here, see Quinton (1973, chap. 1).

5 As candidates for the status of a unique individual nature Alvin Plantinga (1974) has offered properties of the two types: (1) a thing's property of being identical with itself, e.g. Socrates' being Socrates, or Socrateity, and (2) those properties of a thing, which it alone has in some possible world ("world" = "maximal state of affairs"), taken as indexed to that world, e.g. Socrates' property of being married to Xantippe in the actual world. These two types of property are uniquely essential because they belong uniquely to whatever owns them in all possible worlds in which the owners exist. But in the case of type 1, if we allow the being Socrates, or Socrateity, to be a property, as such it could only lend itself to the task of uniquely securing reference to Socrates, if it could be cashed in for some account or intuition – falling either under solutions A or B – of what it is to be Socrates uniquely, other than the triviality that to be Socrates is to be Socrates. As for type 2, those world-indexed properties could only be cast in the role of a unique individual nature by a caricature of the latter notion. In effect properties that as a matter of contingent fact only one thing happens to have, but other things could have, would be presented in that role. But by definition a unique individual nature is a nature that no more than one particular *can* instantiate, and only as so defined could such a nature play any part in *assuring* uniqueness of reference. At best, world-indexed properties, if there are such things at all, determine the essence of the world specified in the indexing. It is part of the essence of the actual world that P uniquely

instantiates F in the actual world, since that P does so is true in all possible worlds. Strictly, however, it is not the property but the unique instantiating by P of the property that constitutes the essence of the actual world. Indeed if, as I believe, pure properties (i.e. those unadulterated by particulars as constituents) exist necessarily, i.e. in all possible worlds, the indexing of properties to particular possible worlds lacks the contrastiveness that could give it significance. For a more general criticism of Plantinga (1974), see Fabrizio Mondadori (1976, 354–63).

6 Michael Loux (1978, 122) has correctly observed that bundle theorists in general exempt themselves from criticism that would take a bundle to be just a set; for they explain their bundle metaphor variously in terms of "some relation between properties which those properties only contingently enter into." If, however, as Loux himself believes, all (pure) properties exist in all possible worlds, even in those in which they are not instantiated, it is difficult to see how any group of properties so understood could enter into any given relation between themselves in one possible world without so doing in all possible worlds, save indirectly through a relation to some non-property, i.e. a common instance, that exists in that possible world but not in all.

7 This stipulation, of course, makes no commitment to a bundle theory as such, i.e. a theory that identifies an individual particular with a bundle of properties. Yet it would seem that any explication by a bundle theorist of the bundle metaphor in terms of "some relation between properties which these properties only contingently enter into" would have to be a specific interpretation of this stipulation – at least where the quasi-Quinean affirmation is understood as contingently true.

8 For the particularist conception of properties, see G.F. Stout (1921, 1923, 1940). For a compromise between exclusively particularist and exclusively universalistic conceptions, see Norman Kemp Smith (1927). I have formulated the reformed notion of bundling in terms of the compromise position purely for convenience.

9 E.g. as in D.M. Armstrong (1979, 1:91–7 and 1:97–101).

10 A somewhat more recent and more elaborate version of the Bundle Theory than those I have been considering can be found in the Guise Theory of Hector-Neri Castañeda (e.g. in 1974, 1975a, 1975b, 1978, 1982). Castañeda takes the operator that bundles together a set of properties into a guise as a primitive that derives its ontological credentials from the ability of Guise Theory to illuminate a whole swatch of puzzles and paradoxes (1982, 334–7). Hence he need not, and presumably would not want to, accept any of my suggestions, or anybody else's, about how to give the notion of a bundle an intelligibility that is independent of its problem-solving utility. Hence again, his version

remains impervious to any criticism one might educe from these suggestions. However, in treating properties as ontologically basic it does come into conflict with my Special Theory of Being. While the latter arose likewise from the need to solve certain problems, the notion of substance, of properties, and of the categorial relation between them it proposes has a prior intelligibility. One can understand what the notion is without the paradoxes that arise from misunderstanding it ever having occurred to one. In general it would seem legitimate to postulate unobservable theoretical entities for the nomological systematization of what is observable in a piecemeal way. But the parallel procedure of postulating unintelligible theoretical entities for the purpose of logically systematizing what is intelligible in a piecemeal way is, I submit, not legitimate. That is because the unintelligibility of the postulate defeats the purpose of the logical systematization, which is to make all that is intelligible piecemeal conjointly intelligible. Here, then, lies a disanalogy. There is no good reason for supposing that the unobservability of a postulated entity defeats the purpose of a nomological systematization of all that is observable piecemeal. Even were it the purpose of the latter in some sense to bring about a conjoint observability of what is observable piecemeal, the postulation of an unobservable would not defeat that.

11 The concept of a particular stripped bare of all its properties may have been inspired by Aristotle (*Meta.* z3.1029a10–25). Aristotle, however, may have been referring exclusively to the stripping away of those properties (he mentions length, breadth, and depth) required by something being at *this*, e.g. a casket, rather than *thaten*, e.g. wooden. See further 4.1 and also 3.3.

12 My insistence that if bare particularity distinguishes at all, it must distinguish actual from merely possible, and merely possible from merely possible, as well as actual from actual particulars may seem unduly to prejudice the issue. Why should the distinguishing role of bare particularity not be limited to actual qualitatively identical particulars? Well, if the distinguishability of one particular from another really were to depend upon both having actual existence, it surely would have to depend upon the extrinsic spatial relationship that the two have to each other. It could not be intrinsic to the particular.

13 I use the term "characterization" with the maximum flexibility that its syntax allows. Sometimes a characterization can be taken to be a character or characteristic, at other times the attribution of a character or characteristic. In the latter case the attribution may either be by an adjectival or by a noun expression. Thus identification as well as predication are characterizations in this sense.

14 Less straightforward uses of the first-person pronoun as in the subordinate clauses of statements about beliefs have been distinguished by

Castañeda under the headings of purely quantificational, partly indexical, and quasi-indexical uses. See the interchange between him and John Perry in Tomberlin (1982) and the bibliographies attached thereto. A fuller treatment of referring expressions than I can allow myself here would have to take these into account.

15 An explicit identification of proper names as indexicals has been proposed by Tyler Burge (1973, 1974, 1982). However, his account of their indexicality, unlike the one I give here, rests on the supposition that there is a covert use of some such indexical expression as "that" in their application.

16 A degree of vagueness in their respective accounts suggests that Kripke and Donnellan themselves do not consider that proper names function in the indexical fashion I have described.

CHAPTER THREE

1 To insist upon synchronic coinstantiability as a criterion for the status of being a universal may seem too stringent. Note, however, that pure universals – those that imply the existence of no particular – do satisfy this criterion. Whether the being located somewhere is interpreted in terms of absolute or relative space, it is not a pure universal. Interpreted absolutely the somewhere just is an absolute kind of particular, part of absolute space. Interpreted relativistically it is just a spatial relationship to concrete particulars.

2 Quinton (1973, 4) has claimed that "Aristotle's view that every concrete individual is a compound of shareable form and individual matter is the first clear formulation of the positive theory of individuating substance." Given that in neither the diachronic nor, as I later claim, the synchronic case do the matter-form and instance-universal distinctions exactly coincide, clarity is not a salient feature of Aristotle's formulation. But see also 4.4.

3 Someone might claim that the two distinctions must fit after all because there must be an ultimate kind of matter, i.e. diachronic prime matter that satisfies three conditions: (1) it can lose all the characteristics it has at any one instant and acquire others instead; (2) in no case would such loss and acquisition amount to a case of DR4 and DR5; (3) all cases of DR4 and DR5 would be reducible to the losing or acquiring of characteristics by matter that meets conditions (1) and (2).

As an objection, however, the claim is not relevant. At best, all it could show is that the diachronic matter-form distinction might conceivably be applied in such a way that *de facto* it coincides perfectly with the instance-universal distinction. But a *de facto* coincidence as such is not a conceptual coincidence.

Notice further that even if there were *de facto* coincidence its *de facto*

nature would have to have a causal basis. There would have to be
some reason for deciding that what we commonly deem to be cases of
generation or dissolution are, more fundamentally, only cases of one
or more than one of the other three types of change. Without that
basis, to assert that there is prime matter would seem to have no more
content than to observe that instances of generation and dissolution
do occur, that even the most durable properties pass. But if this is to
be conceded, further difficulties abound.

Aristotle, whose own allegiance to a notion of diachronic prime
matter appears at best to have been patchy (Charlton, 1970, in his appendix argues that Aristotle had no such allegiance), was sensitive to
one of these (*De Cael.* 4.5.312b2off). If there were a diachronic prime
matter, then things in the world would exercise only one kind of
diachronic power. Now that they do is obviously false – or so he
thought. But even if he were wrong about this, a more fundamental
objection remains. The fundamental diachronic causal power possessed by the prime matter has to be possessed, either by the prime
matter instantiating some mediating property by virtue of which it
possesses the power, or directly just by the matter instantiating the
causal property of having the power. In either case some property is
constitutive of the matter, and in relation to that property, at least,
the diachronic matter does not function as diachronic matter.

4 This claim should not be confused with one made by Sellars (1959,
  1967), viz. that an Aristotelian form is in a primary sense a *this* and in
  a secondary sense a universal. The *this*-ness of an Aristotelian form
  should not be identified with the form's role as an instance. It pertains primarily to a form taken as sublimated from matter (see
  chap. 4) – at which point the distinction between instance and universal no longer applies. Further, within the latter distinction the universal component is primary. The distinction between material and
  formal particular aspects of the same concrete particular is surely mediated by the distinction between material and formal universals that
  these two particular aspects respectively instantiate.

5 That the synchronic matter-form distinction occurs at both the particular and the universal level may explain, at least in part, why in some
  places (*Meta.*, z4.1029b13–15; z11.1037a5–9) Aristotle appears to
  treat a specific case of S-form, viz. the soul, as individual, e.g. as what
  it is to be you or to be Socrates. That he does so need not, in other
  words, be taken as suggesting that he postulates a unique individual
  nature for every individual natural substance. To offset this explanation, however, one must bear in mind that he treats individual souls at
  least in their highest contemplative form as approximating in their
  nature to the Prime Mover, which in its own nature must be unique.

6 Some translators use the terms "potentiality," "potency," and "power"

to represent distinctions Aristotle draws. I use these terms inter-changeably.

7 Aristotle distinguishes between a primary or strict and a more ex-tended or useful sense of "potentiality" (*Meta.* Θ 1. 1045b30–6a35 and 6). It is in the primary sense that potentiality is an active or passive interactive power. If active, it is an originative source of change in an-other thing or in the thing itself qua other. If passive, it is an origina-tive source of, or susceptibility for, something's being changed by another thing or by itself qua other. However, of these two kinds of interactive power he seems to place the greater emphasis on the pas-sive – and naturally so, for the reasons I have given. The more ex-tended sense, in contrast, covers a non-interactive as well as the interactive type of power. But Aristotle fails to delimit the full scope of the non-interactive type in a clear and unambivalent way.

8 One might say that S-potentiality is for *remaining* in a certain state as distinct from *attaining* any state. As such, then, it could be more accu-rately described as a special type of D-potentiality. However, as it re-lates S-matter to S-form, it is convenient not to.

9 This distinction between D- and S-types of potentiality has an oblique relation to Aristotle's complex distinction between two kinds of actual-ity in terms of a distinction between movement (in the sense of change) and activity (e.g. *Meta.* Θ6.1046a30–8b38). For an aporetic discussion of this distinction see Ackrill (1965). For more constructive treatment see Penner (1970). Movement, according to Aristotle, is in its nature incomplete. It is from a whence to a whither, and when complete is not movement but rest. It is, furthermore, more or less swift or slow. Activity, by contrast, is neither from a whence to a whither nor more or less swift or slow. Like movement, it may per-haps have to endure for some finite time, if it is to exist at all. But unlike movement, it is complete at every instant within its duration. Aristotle's most remarked-upon examples of activity, e.g. sensing, un-derstanding, and contemplation, all happen to be of a psychological kind. As such, however, they are archetypal rather than typical within the full range of activities as such. They occupy the most eminent po-sitions in a hierarchy within which superior members set some sort of standard for the relatively inferior. Nevertheless, any S-form, what-ever its hierarchical status, is an activity.

Since, then, movement and activity apparently are distinct and mu-tually exclusive, the potentiality for movement and the potentiality for activity must be likewise. Indeed, it thus may seem to be the very same as the distinction between the D- and S-potentiality, as I have just drawn the latter. But that cannot be *quite* right. Ultimately Aristo-tle wanted to identify actuality with activity, despite his distinction of the latter from movement. Furthermore, he appears to facilitate this identification by representing movement as an actuality only *of a sort*, without qualifying the actuality of activity in any comparable way. More specifically, movement for him is only the actuality of the potential qua potential (*Phys.* 3.1.201a10–18; 3.1.201b9–15). Thus the process of building is the actuality of the buildable qua buildable. Presumably, then, he conceived movement as being in a manner a limiting case of actuality, activity, and S-form, though more strictly as not a case of these three at all. Accordingly, the potentiality for movement must be a limiting case of S-potentiality, and not identical with D-potentiality after all.

There is, however, an oblique relation between the two respective potentiality-pairs. Presumably his intention, at least in part, was to compare the *actualization* (see Penner, 1970, 430) of the D-actuality of a D-potentiality with the relation of S-form to S-matter. The actualization of the house, as distinct from its non-actualization, and the constructability of the construction materials into a house are appropriate to each other in much the same way as the distinctive character of wine, as opposed to that of vinegar, is appropriate, in Aristotle's estimation, to the distinctive character of water. In other words, in this comparison D-potentiality is made to serve a dual role. It functions first as genuinely itself, a potentiality of D-matter for D-form, and second as quasi S-matter that is or constitutes the potentiality for a quasi S-form. Strictly speaking, of course, neither the D-potentiality nor the movement in which it is actualized are respectively S-matter and S-form, but the relation between them and the two latter is sufficiently alike, in Aristotle's estimation, to allow them to be treated as if they were.

10 See n 8.

11 The hierarchy of hylomorphic levels can be conceived as falling either within the same substance, as in my illustration, or as relegating a set of separate substances to different ranks.

CHAPTER FOUR

1 A number of commentators – e.g. Charlton (1970, 99) and Sorabji (1980, 40 passim) – have elucidated Aristotle's notion of cause in terms of that of explanation. Their main purpose has been to reject an equivalence between his notion and that of necessitation. Taken out of context this places undue emphasis on the epistemological at the expense of the ontological aspect of the notion, though that seems not to be the intention.

2 It is generally admitted that causal powers are at the very least conceptually and epistemologically distinct from their categorical bases, i.e. that to determine what powers an object may have is not *ipso facto*

to determine what are the properties, if any, by virtue of which it has these powers. However, to assume as I do here that a causal power is not identical with its categorical basis is more controversial (see Alston, 1971, 125–54; Armstrong, 1973, 11–15). I rest this assumption on two considerations. First, if any state of affairs a', categorical or conditional, is a sufficient causal condition of some categorical or conditional state-of-affairs a'', then a' and a'' are not identical. Suppose that if, when p (i.e. a certain rubber band R is pulled) then s (i.e. R stretches), then one can say R is such that if p then s. In other words, in these circumstances R has the causal power of elasticity. Suppose further that R's elasticity is due to b, i.e. that it has a certain molecular structure. Then b is the sufficient causal condition of R's being such that if p then s. In other words, b is the categorical basis of the elasticity by virtue of its detachment from the causal conditional "if b and p, then s." Hence, given my initial premiss, b cannot be identified with R being such that if p then s. Second, that each of two separately characterizable properties constitutes, other things being equal, the categorical basis of exactly the same set of causal powers would seem uncontroversially to be a criterion for taking the two properties to be identical. Yet the same criterion could have no uncontroversial application for the purpose of identifying the two properties with the set of causal powers of which they constitute the categorical basis. It would be like employing the principle of the identity of indiscernibles for the purpose of identifying two particulars that have all their properties in common with that set of common properties. See further Prior, Pargetter, and Jackson (1982). Without underwriting my sort of application of the categorical/modal distinction in this context, they argue persuasively that any causal disposition has to have a causal basis, that the causal basis must be distinct from the disposition itself, and that the disposition itself is causally impotent. It is the last two of these theses that I support.

3 Versions of this option are not without contemporary support. Thus Father Joseph Owens (1963, 1967) concludes

The Aristotelian matter has not been superseded nor even touched by the stupendous advance of modern physics. Nothing that is measurable can perform its function in explaining the nature of sensible things, and by the same token it cannot be brought forward to account for anything that requires explanation in measurable terms ... but is rather a very different means of explanation for sensible things on another scientific level, the level of natural phisolophy.

More recently Montgomery Furth (1988, 168–9), adopts, only a shade less supportively, a position of historicist tolerance. In dealing with the "coalescence" of the individuative and the essence or constitutive properties of substantial kinds that proceeds from the same option, he writes

Our ability to make a distinction does not imply that an ancient thinker who apparently lacks the means to do so is therefore succeeding only in "lisping" what we can pronounce; and there is no reason to assume that Aristotle would be interested in helping himself to our distinctions, had he access to them ... It is natural that in the newly forged concept of substance, the properties of (b) "forming" and (a) "individuating" should have been seen as deeply connected, merging in an overall notion of "unifying" that covers them both. If closer to our own time they have decoupled, as indeed seems to be the case, that fact should be taken account of; but I find no basis in that fact for criticism of the form in which they originated.

My own reaction to Furth's attitude is that what one might require from Aristotle is more a matter of his eliminating confusions in his own distinctions than of his helping himself to ours, for ours still are in need of emancipation from confusions in his.

4 This translation follows the emendation of Schwegler. If the traditional reading were followed, "separately" would be replaced by "inseparably." See Joseph Owens (1957, 296, n 44) for an account of how various scholars have divided on this issue. In his edition of the Greek text and in his later translation Ross follows Schwegler. Nevertheless, in his note to the relevant part of the text, he opines that "regarded as a concession, the sentence is satisfactory enough with the traditional reading." Jaeger supports the emendation with greater enthusiasm. See his *Aristotle* (1962, 217). He has a twofold rationale, (1) that "separately" may in some contexts be appropriately interpreted as meaning "transcendentally" (separately from matter) and in others as meaning "independently," and (2) that in this context the latter interpretation alone would be appropriate. His speculation is that someone altered the text on the assumption that "separately," or rather its Greek equivalent, could only have the former of the two interpretations, and that so interpreted the passage could not convey Aristotle's meaning. My position on 1 is that the distinction to be drawn is between a fuller and a lesser actualization of separateness rather than between two meanings, and on 2 that while most mutable things in Aristotle's estimation have the lower form of separateness, some (i.e. our intellectual activities) have the higher.

5 The discrepancy-reconciliation thesis is, of course, Jaeger's (1962, chap. 7).

CHAPTER FIVE

1 It would seem to be this spatial opposition that Aristotle has in mind in his definition of time as number of motion in respect to before and after (*Phys.* 4.11.220a24–5). At 4.11.219a13–14 he says "The distinction of 'before' and 'after' holds primarily between places."

2 In *The Modularity of Mind* (1983) Jerry A. Fodor has taken the following quotation from Spearman (1927) as his opening motto:

One curious feature about these formal faculties has yet to be mentioned. The doctrine loses every battle – so to speak – but always wins the war. It will bend to the slightest breath of criticism; but not the most violent storm can break it. The attacks made long ago ... appeared to be irresistible; no serious defence was ever attempted. Yet the sole permanent effect of these attacks was only to banish the word "faculty" leaving the doctrine represented by this word to escape scot free.

Fodor himself gives an even stronger support to faculty-psychology than Spearman in this passage, for he writes (1983, 26)

In retrospect, then, the supposedly decisive methodological arguments against faculty theory were, on the face of them, so silly that it is hard to believe (much) in their historical significance. And, indeed, isolated arguments – like isolated experiments – generally don't alter the course of history. What usually does the job is the emergence of an alternative theoretical enterprise. As I indicated above, it seems pretty clear that what did for faculty psychology was the promise of an associationistic theory of mind. For just as Empiricist epistemology offered an account of the origin of mental *contents* which dispensed with the Cartesian postulation of innate ideas, so associationism offered an account of the ontogeny of mental *processes* which dispensed with the postulation of innate cognitive architecture – which, in short, dispensed with the need for faculties.

3 If neophrenologists such as Fodor (1983) were to limit themselves to the claim that different parts of the brain are the seat of different brain faculties, I would have no objection. But since they seem to claim that these faculties are faculties of the mind, my objection is that the sort of organic unity that obtains between such putative brain-faculties is not the sort that obtains between the soul-faculties or faculties of the mind that are more traditionally identified as such.

4 In going on to claim that sensing is an activity of judgment or under-

standing in its most basic form I do not claim that sensing is necessarily a form of believing, but merely that it is as essentially propositional in its nature as believing. In work as yet unpublished I argue that sensing is analysable in terms of perceiving where the content of the latter is conceived as involving a belief-commitment to some propositional content. More specifically, to sense that such-and-such is for it to be with one as if one were perceiving that such-and-such in such-and-such a perspective.

5 See also Rankin (1961, 113–22).

6 Kemp Smith's distinction (1929) between pre-critical, semi-critical, and critical elements in Kant's first *Critique* is too often seen as if it stood or fell with his explanation of how these disparities occurred. The validity of his distinction does not depend upon whether the first *Critique* is, as he supposed, a collation of writings that date from different periods in Kant's life. Works of philosophical originality are likely to show complicity with deeply engrained assumptions they are in process of sloughing off, whatever the manner of their composition. My suggestion that the Kantian method is a half-way house between two methods mirrors Kemp Smith's remark (from the podium) that in its maturest aspect Kant's philosophy is a half-way house to realism.

7 Notice as well that Aristotle's form of dualism is exempt from certain objections to Descartes'. As critics have pointed out, Descartes' Cogito gives no guarantee that one exists as an enduring substance other than when thinking, or as the same substance at any one such time as at any other. Nor on an assumption it seems willing to allow, viz. that the mental activity impinging on two different bodies could be qualitatively identical, can it find any basis for distinguishing the mind conjoined to the one body from the mind conjoined to the other. For Aristotle's transcendent Cogito, i.e. the Prime Mover, there are no such embarrassments. What it reifies is intended both as eternal and as absolutely unique. Presumably, too, when first philosophers reach the point of contemplating the essences of things, they transcend themselves. Hence that their identities should be distinct when they contemplate the same essences, and that they should retain their identity through successive acts of contemplation, need not be essential.

8 Descartes' Cogito has quite commonly been taken as an inference to the existence of the subject of thought from the self-intimation of the thinking. But as Hintikka (1962) has shown, with perhaps an over-pre-emptive emphasis, it also functions as a self-reifying performance whereby one hoists oneself into existence by one's subjective bootstraps. Self-intimation and self-reification, indeed, are complementary

aspects of the reflexive Cartesian cogitation, as much as they are within the self-enchantment of Aristotle's Prime Mover.

CHAPTER SIX

1 It may be prudent to observe at this juncture that certain standard regimentations of such terms as "necessary," "possible," and "impossible" may not be flexible enough to sanction certain perfectly legitimate colloquial applications of these terms which have given rise to philosophical problems of long standing. Thus M.R. Ayers (1968) has "refuted" determinism (with a view to giving it undercover support) on the basis that it is modally fallacious to say, e.g., of any future event that it is causally necessary (possible, possible but not necessary, impossible) that it will occur. It is only such things as a sequence consisting of certain causal antecedents followed by the event that on this view can properly be said to be causally necessary (possible, possible but not necessary, impossible). For a brief refutation of this refutation see Rankin (1971). For a fuller treatment in terms of more flexible regimentations see Thorp (1980, 16–64).

2 Hence, it may need emphasizing, the Modal Identity Thesis does not expose itself to Kripke's objections (1980) against contingent-identity forms of physicalism.

3 Sensory modalities are not faculties in relation to each other. They overlap and supplement each other in the information that they yield, rather than complement each other.

4 Following Moore, Austin describes this kind of relation as implication *as distinct from* either entailment or presupposition.

5 For these two reasons, of course, further exceptions to the H-to-M entailment have to be admitted.

6 A promotion of persons or agents to the status of prime movers receives some encouragement from Aristotle. After all, he does represent the human agent and, more generally, animals as first causes. However, there are at least two ways, and possibly three, in which he conceives his Prime Mover's causing as very different from ours. First, in their action as first causes of movement in other things, animals including ourselves move other things by themselves being in motion, i.e. by changing in some way. As first causes their own movement is self-movement. In contrast, his Prime Mover does not itself move, i.e. change in any way. Second, as first causes animals are primarily efficient causes, whereas the Prime Mover is a teleological first cause. Hence the manner in which the former are first causes is compatible with their being caused directly or indirectly by the Prime Mover.

Third, even as efficient causes, the title of any animal to the status of first cause may have to be qualified. Thus some commentators, e.g. Thorp (1980, 96–9) on the basis of *Phys.* 8 and EE 2.8, have argued that Aristotle's notion of self-movement is compatible with universal causal determination. This interpretation has, however, been challenged by others. Thus, in the second of her interpretative essays on *MA* Nussbaum has argued that the relevant passages in *Phys.* 8 fail to support a conclusion of that sort. I myself find *Phys.* 8, at least on the compatibilist interpretation, hard to reconcile with *De An.* 1.4.408b, which states of movement "that sometimes it terminates in the soul and sometimes starts from it." Perhaps we should not impose consistency upon passages presumably penned at different times.

7 For a critical, if generous, discussion of the notion of agent causality, see Irving Thalberg (1976).

8 Note that, in distinguishing the sort of responsibility specific to causes as explanatory, I am not reneging on my previous rejection of any analysis of the notion of causation in terms of the notion of explanation. In rejecting any such analysis I do not deny that to specify a cause is to provide the material for an explanation where an explanation is sought. However, as well as making the point that to identify you as the agent of your action is not to provide a sort of explanation of the fact that you did that action rather than another, I might also have made the even more obvious point that it does not specify anything *by virtue of which* you did the one rather than the other.

9 Further, that each possible world has a structure that is truly causal, that is something that each owes to its membership of the set as a whole – and hence extrinsic to it – given that the existence of a causal relation between two events is one with counterfactual implications, i.e. about what is the case in other possible worlds.

CHAPTER SEVEN

1 It is obliquely relevant to notice that Strawson's objections to the no-ownership theory fail to anticipate Kripke's distinction (1980) between the necessary and the a priori. While the theory certainly does take the dependence of my mental states upon my body to be contingent (because causal), simultaneously (pace Strawson) it does not render that dependence necessary, i.e. non-contingent, by identifying mental states as mine by means of this dependence. It merely renders that dependence as holding a priori. Though I can give no reference, I suspect that this has been noticed by others before – probably, indeed, by Kripke himself.

2 Armstrong's use of his notion of a closed causal circuit is not quite the same as its application here. He sets out to explain why the locus of an intentional object of vision is out there rather than, say, on the retina. His answer is in two steps, (1) that the locus of the intentional object of perception is tied to the locus where the *objective* of the will is to be carried out, and (2) that the latter locus is at the farthest outreach of the closed causal circuit formed by the perceiver's actions and their reactions upon his sensing. Thus what the child sees is a blue block because his objective is to place the blue block in a blue box. That – rather than the modification of a retinal image that will thereby take place – is his objective because it is the modification that occurs the farthest out.

  Neither part of Armstrong's answer seems to allow for the cases where the child is manipulating the blue block indirectly with the help of a mirror and an assortment of rods. In such cases the mirror may be farther away from or nearer to the child than the block. Likewise, the rods may be the more directly active on something that is farther away or nearer. In short, the locus of what is the more directly seen, i.e. the mirror and reflections therein, need not coincide with that within which the objective is to take place.

  My position is that what distinguishes the objects of our direct experience at a given time from others is that it is their potentialities that are the most directly constitutive of our OBO-ability at that time. As constitutive of that ability, those potentialities and the objects' situation relative to the agent's body are intimated in the self-intimation of the possibilities for interaction of which the ability consists.

3 This argument does not directly meet the extremer version of the two-minds hypothesis advanced by Puccetti (1973, 1976), who argues that even for normal uncommissurotomized subjects – or for commissurotomized subjects in normal situations in which stimulation from the environment is independently duplicated in each hemisphere – there are two qualitatively identical total fields of experience, and hence two persons. For an argument that this inference from the data is unjustified, see Marks (1981). For an argument that the conclusion is wrong, see my further application of the Modal Identity Thesis. That in a normal person each hemisphere substantially duplicates information that is fed into the other only shows that one and the same OBO-ability, and the intimating component thereof, may have an overdetermined neural basis, just as the one house may have a doubly sufficient foundation.

4 Marks (1981, 13–16) discusses the relative merits of two candidates for the status of necessary condition for the simultaneous conscious

experiences e_1 and e_2 belonging to the same unified consciousness, viz.

1. that they do so only if they are known, by introspection, to be simultaneous, and
2. that they do so, only if they would, given certain conditions, be known by memory or introspection to be simultaneous (attributed to Grice, 1941).

Condition 2 may seem an improvement on 1, for the occasion might be such that one is unable to attend simultaneously to e_1 and e_2 by introspection, while yet later one remembers that they occurred simultaneously. Even if later one is unable to remember this, it might be that had one been exerting less concentration on the occasion one would later have been able to remember their simultaneous occurrence. Marks rejects 2, however, on the ground that the split-brain patient after the experiment that demonstrates disunity of consciousness may, by exchange of information between the disconnected hemispheres, e.g. by cross-cuing, be able to remember that e_1 and e_2 occurred simultaneously.

5 One might argue on behalf of Nagel that the Modal Identity Thesis fails to fit our ordinary perception of mind in at least one respect. Ordinarily one thinks of experiences like perceiving, remembering, and thinking as things that are done by us. On the Modal Identity Thesis, however, our relation to them is not that of agent to action but rather that of bearer to what is borne or subject to attribute. A suitable reply is that the ordinary concept of action is highly accommodating. Sleeping and dying are spoken of as things that we do. Yet at the same time they consist of our being respectively in a comatose and a moribund state.

6 Since this kind of fuzziness, or incomplete immanence of intrinsic thinghood, specifically pertains to abnormal cases, the amount of attention that here it has been apportioned may seem excessive. If more normal psychological limitations, such as our apparent inability to give introspective attention to all the contents of our consciousness simultaneously, were to lend support to the fuzziness thesis, that would surely be more impressive. However, the abnormal cases examined here have the particular value of raising more directly the issue of how consciousness is related to the nervous system and of giving some degree of empirical confirmation to the Modal Identity Thesis, as opposed to other theories of mind, as an account of that relation.

7 This proviso is needed to distinguish the post-fission bodies from the bodies A, B, and C of the three-bodied person S imagined by Straw-

son (1959, 90–2). Each of the latter three bodies were conceived as contributing a distinctive feature to the same individual perceptual state of S – A's eyelids being open to S's seeing anything at all, the orientation of B's eyeballs to what falls within S's field of vision, and the position of C to where S sees from. For an examination of this fiction's coherence, see Rankin (1976).

CHAPTER EIGHT

1 This is rather rough. If proper names have indexical features as I have earlier argued (2.4), then the truth-value of sentences containing them is affected by variability as well. More accurately, the truth-value of a tensed sentence containing a proper name may be variable in different ways. Thus a sentence in one tense containing the name "Jack" may be affirmed truly on one occasion and falsely on another, because "Jack" is not being used to refer to the same person. However, where "Jack" is used to refer to the same person, the sentence may be used truly on one occasion and falsely on another according to whether the utterance is before, simultaneous with, or after an action that fits the action-description being used.

2 This derivation of B-relations is quite different in type from various other attempts at derivation. These have been derivations from the asymmetrical transitivity of certain nomological or *de facto* invariable relations between temporally sequential physical states. They represent a relation that links the separate stages of some physically universal kind of physical process as logically more primitive. Candidates for this primitive status, separately or in mutual collusion, have been the causal relations between events (Reichenbach, 1957, §21), the microstatistical entropy relation between total ensembles of physical branch-systems within the universe (Reichenbach, 1956, §14–16), the macro-statistical entropy relation between an event recorded and the event that records it (Reichenbach, 1956, §18), the indeterminacy relation of quantum physics (Reichenbach, 1956, §27), and the relation between wider and narrower rings in the propagation of wave-motion (Popper, 1956a, 1956b, 1958).

In the derivation of the B-series of moments from their A-determinations the moments are recognized as self-ordering. In other words, their temporal relation to each other is recognized as intrinsic to the terms of the relation. Furthermore, the derivation is analytic a priori, for it depends on interdefinability. In these other derivations, in contrast, the temporal relation is derived from some more primitive asymmetry between events that occupy such moments. Furthermore, the converse of the temporal order could have been derived from the converse of the more primitive asymmetry. Hence that the temporal order is derivable from the primitive asymmetry rather than its converse is something that could only be established a posteriori, if it could be established at all, i.e. by observing whether it is the primitive asymmetry rather than its converse that relates earlier to later events. Granted, however, that the notions of necessary truth and of a priori truth are distinct, the a posteriori nature of the derivation does not rule out the possibility that it might be *necessarily* true that, say, the B-serial order of time is derivable from, say, the relation *more disordered than* rather than from the converse of that latter order, even if that derivability only became known to us a posteriori. Nor, for that matter, does it rule that in.

3 For a variant version of B-theory see D.H. Mellor (1981). Mellor denies that tensed sentences are translatable by tenseless ones and also that tensed judgments are dispensable. He merely insists that tensed sentences have tenseless ones as their truth-conditions. However, there would seem to be only two ways in which one could try to show that these same tenseless sentences are tenseless in the required sense rather than merely tense-neutral. On the assumption that a tensed sentence is perfectly syntactical and that some putatively tenseless sentence is its equivalent in meaning, one might argue that the latter sentence must be syntactical as well. Alternatively, one could rely on a parody-prone proof such as McTaggart's to show that contradiction is latent in the application of A-determinations and tense. Mellor rightly avoids the former course. However, in his attempt to show that McTaggart's proof works he presupposes what neither he nor McTaggart has a right to presuppose, viz. that certain sentences that ascribe the A-qualifiers "past," "present," and "future" are tenseless.

4 Prior himself goes on to outline a reply to his objection to Smart on the basis of Reichenbach's analysis of the more complex tenses, such as the past, present, and future perfects. As Reichenbach has shown (1948, §51) these tenses require one to distinguish between the "point of speech" (which features in his analysis of the simpler tenses) and a "point of reference." This, of course, indicates the possibility in principle of an unlimited number of points of reference all different both from each other and from the point of speech. Just because the point of speech is thus in principle outnumbered, Prior, rather cavalierly, goes on to infer that it doesn't deserve the special status it occupies in Reichenbach's analysis. This move amounts to an attempt to represent the series of P/F cuts purely in terms of its vertical dimension, and A-determinations as purely relational.

5 As Robinson (1982, chap. 4, § 6) has shown, there is a further deficiency in mechanistic models for self-scanning. With specific reference

to Armstrong's brain-scanning model for consciousness, he argues that, because of the physiological continuity between the "scanning" and "scanned" brain-states, they do not have the clear separateness that would qualify them for the respective roles with which they have been thus charged.

6 Several commentators (e.g. Anscombe, 1956; Fine, 1984; Hintikka, 1973; and Rescher, 1968) have argued that the claim is one that Aristotle himself rejected.

7 Some writers on time, e.g. D.H. Mellor (1985), quite recently have argued that an A-theory of time must be inconsistent with the theory of relativity. In so doing, however, they have failed to reckon with an A-theory of the psychocentric kind that I offer here.

CHAPTER NINE

1 But notice that the qualified type of good is subordinate to an even more absolute ethical limitation. In this it is like the hypothetical type of imperative. There are some things one ought not to do even if they are instrumental to one's purpose. Thus it is inappropriate to say "You ought to put poison in your parents' coffee, if you want to get rid of them." Similarly, we are reluctant to describe certain sorts of thing as good in a qualified way where we regard any member of that sort as bad in an unqualified way. Thus we would not normally refer to any epidemic as a good epidemic or to a burglar as a good burglar, though we might be quite happy to refer to either as a good specimen of its sort.

2 Like Sartre I associate self-consciousness very closely with freedom and being. However, I have derived self-consciousness and (intrinsic) being from freedom. He, on the other hand, derives freedom conversely from a supposed self-elusiveness of the conscious self, the incessant flight of being *en soi* from being *pour soi*.

3 My account of desire is, in a way, a securalized version of Kierkegaard's. His distinction between an aesthetic and an ethical life-stage is simply a distinction between two opposing ways in which one's occasional freedom to choose between non-compossible ways of being satisfied appears obversely as a freedom to choose between non-compossible ways of being *dissatisfied*. In the aesthetic stage one's response to this obverse aspect takes the more overt forms of anguish. In the ethical stage one responds with more covert despair by finding fulfilment in a moral self-discipline. In contrast, in the third stage, both on Kierkegaard's view and on mine, one's freedom sheds the observe aspect that afflicts it in the other two. Kierkegaard attributes this emancipation to faith in God as having the miraculous power of

somehow rendering the non-compossible ways of satisfaction compossible. I attribute it to a state of soul-integration (ideal if not miraculous) in which the variety of desires whereby various non-compossible forms of satisfaction commend themselves mutually defer to each other, so that in achieving satisfaction in one way rather than another we satisfy the whole self instead of simultaneously frustrating ourselves in one way rather than another.

CHAPTER TEN

1 For a particularly trenchant account of the various quandaries out of which the Copenhagen and other interpretations of quantum mechanics arose, see Hilary Putnam (1975–79, vol. 1).

2 For an argument to the effect that Wigner's hypothesis can only be saved from incoherence by postulating backwards causation, see Paul Davies (1980, 133–4).

3 It is noteworthy that Leslie has favoured a deterministic B-theory type of universe for the operation of his axiarchical principle. Hence to that extent his form of psychocentrism, if that is what it is, radically opposes mine.

4 For provocative objections to Copenhagen interpretations, see Sir Karl Popper (1982). Perhaps he has shown that so far the arguments for these interpretations have been unconvincing. Yet the case made out by Galileo in support of the Copernican hypothesis fell short of being conclusive too. Maybe the Copenhagen school offers more ammunition for the themes of such works as Koestler's *The Sleep Walkers* and Feyerabend's *Against Method* (1975).

APPENDIX

1 As a supplement to the analysis of intention offered in 6.1 this appendix consists of the first three sections of Rankin 1972 with certain minor modifications that bring the references and notes in line with the format of the previous chapters.

2 Perhaps we should distinguish present-tense anticipatory forms, like "I am going to X," from past-tense anticipatory forms, like "I was going to X." A peculiarity of the latter is that it in no way commits its utterer to a belief in the subsequent occurrence of the action specified, whereas the former does. Throughout this appendix, with the present exception, I identify anticipatory forms of utterance exclusively with present-tense anticipatory forms.

3 The Rylean dichotomy "Either dispositions or occurrent, but not both" would require that the sort of occurrent anticipation that real-

izes an anticipatory disposition cannot itself be a disposition. A requirement on that basis would be unacceptable to those who go along (correctly, I believe) with William P. Alston (1971) and D.M. Armstrong (1968) in rejecting the dichotomy. There are, however, other grounds for regarding the realizing and realized anticipations as not dispositions in the same sense. Some of these are derivable more or less directly from later clues.

4 In this sense the truth of a belief may fall short of objectivity in at least two ways. Either sincerity of belief is logically necessary or logically sufficient for the truth of the belief. Anticipations of intention exhibit only the former shortcoming. The belief that one is in pain is commonly regarded as exemplifying the latter.

5 My method of refutation here does not assume that any mental act whatsoever, whether the anticipation of a self-faith-healer or anything else, ever is genuinely a cause. The assumption, however, would be hard to avoid were it not for the case that anticipations of intention do not function as causes, and that other more cause-like mental acts play a constitutive role in intentions.

Works Cited

All quotations from the works of Aristotle in the text are from Oxford translations. With the exception of his works and Plato's, items listed below have been cited mainly by name of author and date. The date is not necessarily that of first publication, particularly where some more accessible source is available.

ABBREVIATIONS

Aristotle

Cat.	Categories
De An.	de Anima
De Cael.	de Caelo
De Sen.	de Sensu
EE	Eudemian Ethics
GC	de Generatione et Corruptione
MA	de Motu Animalium
Meta.	Metaphysics
NE	Nicomachean Ethics
Phys.	Physics

Plato

Cra.	Cratylus
Meno	Meno
Prm	Parmenides
Philb	Philebus
R	Republic
Soph.	Sophist

Ackrill, J.L. 1965. "Aristotle's Distinction between Energeia and Kinesis." Bambrough 1965.

Allaire, E.B. 1963. "Bare Particulars." *Philosophical Studies* 14. Repr. in Loux 1976b.

Allaire, E.B. 1965. "Another Look at Bare Particulars." *Philosophical Studies* 16. Repr. in Loux 1976b.

Alston, W.P. 1971. "Dispositions and Occurrences." *Canadian Journal of Philosophy* 1, no. 2 (December).

Anscombe, G.E.M. 1956. "Aristotle and the Sea Battle." *Mind* 65. Repr. as revised in Smart 1964.

Armstrong, D.M. 1968. *A Materialist Theory of Mind*. London: Routledge and Kegan Paul.

— 1973. *Belief, Truth and Knowledge*. Cambridge University Press.

— 1979. *Universals and Scientific Realism*. 2 vols. Cambridge University Press.

Austin, J.L. 1961. "Ifs and Cans." *Philosophical Papers*. Ed. J.O. Urmson and G.J. Warnock. Oxford: Clarendon Press.

— 1962a. *How To Do Things with Words*. Ed. J.O. Urmson. Oxford: Clarendon Press.

— 1962b. *Sense and Sensibilia*. Reconstructed by G.J. Warnock. Oxford: Clarendon Press.

Ayer, A.J., ed. 1959. *Logical Positivism*. Glencoe, Ill.: Free Press.

Ayers, M.R. 1968. *A Refutation of Determinism*. London: Methuen.

Bambrough, R., ed. 1965. *New Essays in Plato and Aristotle*. New York: Humanities Press.

Bergman, G. 1964. *Logic and Reality*. University of Wisconsin Press.

Bergman, G. 1967. *Realism*. University of Wisconsin Press.

Bettenson, H., ed. 1950. *Documents of the Christian Church*. Oxford University Press World Classics.

Black, M. 1952a. See Geach and Black, eds., 1952.

— 1952b. "The Identity of Indiscernibles." *Mind* 61.

Borst, C.V., ed. 1970. *The Mind/Brain Identity Theory*. London: Macmillan.

Bradley, F.H. 1927. "The Vulgar Notion of Responsibility." *Ethical Studies*. Oxford University Press.

Braithwaite, R.B. 1956. *Scientific Explanation*. Cambridge: Cambridge University Press.

Brand, M., and D. Walton 1976. *Action Theory*. Dordrecht: Reidel, Synthèse Library 97.

Burge, T. 1973. "Reference and Proper Names." *Journal of Philosophy* 70.

— 1974. "Demonstrative Constructions, Reference and Truth." *Journal of Philosophy* 71.

— 1982. "Russell's Problem and Intentional Identity." In Tomberlin 1982.

Butts, R.F., and J. Hintikka, eds. 1977. *Foundational Problems in the Special Sciences*. Dordrecht: Reidel.

Castañeda, H.-N. 1974. "Thinking and the Structure of the World." *Philosophia* 4, no. 1.

— 1975a. "Individuation and Non-Identity: A New Look." *American Philosophical Quarterly* 12, no. 2.

— 1975b. "Identity and Sameness." *Philosphia* 5, no. 1–2.

— 1982a. "Reply to John Perry: Meaning, Belief, and Reference." In Tomberlin 1982.

— 1982b. "Reply to Alvin Plantinga: Method, Individuals, and Guise Theory." In Tomberlin 1982.

Charlton, W. 1970. Translation, with introduction and notes, of *Aristotle's Physics I, II*. Oxford: Clarendon Press.

Chastain, C. 1975. "Reference and Context." In Gunderson 1975.

Chisholm, R. 1964. "J.L. Austin's Philosophical Papers." *Mind* 73, no. 289 (January).

Chisholm, R. 1966. "Freedom and Action." In Lehrer 1966.

— 1976. *Person and Object*. London: Allen and Unwin.

Cranston, M. 1953. *Freedom*. London: Longmans, Green & Co.

Davies, P. 1980. *Other Worlds*. New York: Simon and Schuster.

Donellan, K. 1966. "Reference and Definite Descriptions." *Philosophical Review* 75. Repr. in Schwartz 1977.

— 1968. "Putting Humpty Dumpty Together Again." *Philosophical Review* 77.

— 1974. "Speaking of Nothing." *Philosophical Review* 83. Repr. in Swartz 1977.

— 1979. "The Contingent A Priori and Rigid Designators." In French, Uehling, and Wettstein, eds., 1979.

Dunne, J.W. 1934. *An Experiment with Time*. London: Faber & Faber.

Eccles, J.C., ed. 1966. *Brain and Conscious Experience*. Berlin: Springer-Verlag.

Feyerabend, P. 1957–58. "Die Analytische Philosophie und das Paradox der Analyse." *Kant-Studien*.

— 1963a. "Mental events and the brain." *Journal of Philosophy* 59. Repr. in Borst 1970.

— 1963b. "Materialism and the Mind-Body Problem." *Review of Metaphysics* 17. Repr. in Borst 1970.

— 1975. *Against Method*. London: Verso.

Fine, G. 1984. "Time and Necessity in De Interpretatione." *History of Philosophy Quarterly* 1, no. 1 (January).

Fitzgerald, P.K. 1969. "The Truth About Tomorrow's Sea Fight." *Journal of Philosophy* 66, no. 11 (June).

Flew, A.G.N., ed. 1951. *Logic and Language*. Oxford: Blackwell.

— ed. 1956. *Essays in Conceptual Analysis*. London: Macmillan & Co.

Fodor, J.A. 1968. *Psychological Explanation*. Random House.

— 1983. *The Modality of Mind: An Essay on Faculty Psychology.* Cambridge, Mass.: Bradford Books, MIT Press.

Foot, P. 1962. "Free Will as Involving Determinism." In Morgenbesser and Walsh, eds., 1962.

Frege, G. 1952a. "Function and Object." In Geach and Black, eds., 1952.

— 1952b. "On Concept and Object." In Geach and Black, eds., 1952.

— 1952c. "On Sense and Reference." In Geach and Black, eds., 1952.

French, P.A., T.E. Uehling, and H.K. Wettstein, eds. 1979. *Contemporary Perspectives in the Philosophy of Language.* University of Minnesota Press.

Furth, M. 1988. *Substance, Form and Psyche: An Aristotelean Metaphysics.* Cambridge University Press.

Gale, R.M. 1966. "McTaggart's Analysis of Time." *American Philosophical Quarterly* 3, no. 2 (April).

— 1968a. *The Language of Time.* London: Routledge & Kegan Paul.

— ed. 1986b. *The Philosophy of Time.* London: Macmillan.

Geach, P.T., and M. Black, eds. 1952. *Translations from the Philosophical Writings of Gottlob Frege.* Oxford: Blackwell.

Gram, M.S. 1969. "The Paradox of Analysis." In Klemke 1969.

Grice, H.P. 1941. "Personal Identity." *Mind* 50. Repr. in Perry 1975.

— 1979. "Aristotle on Being and Good." Presented at the Victoria Conference on the Philosophy of Aristotle, January 1979.

Grünbaum, A. 1963. *Philosophical Problems of Space and Time.* New York: Alfred A. Knopf.

— 1968. "The Status of Temporal Becoming." In Gale 1968.

Gunderson, K., ed. 1975. *Language, Mind and Knowledge: Minnesota Studies in the Philosophy of Science* 7. Minneapolis: University of Minnesota Press.

Hacker, P.M.S. 1982. "Events and Objects in Space and Time." *Mind* 91, no. 361 (January).

Hall, E.W. 1961. *Our Knowledge of Fact and Value.* Chapel Hill: University of North Carolina Press.

Hamilton, W., ed. 1895. *The Philosophical Works of Thomas Reid.* Edinburgh: James Thin.

Hamlyn, D.W. 1977–78. "Focal Meaning." *The Aristotelian Society* 78.

Hare, R.M. 1952. *The Language of Morals.* Oxford University Press.

— 1960. "Philosophical Discoveries." *Mind* 69, no. 274 (April).

Hintikka, J. 1962. "Cogito, Ergo Sum: Inference or Performance." *Philosophical Review* 71, no. 1.

— 1973. *Time and Necessity.* Oxford University Press.

Hintikka, J., in collaboration with Unto Remes and Simo Knortilla. c1977. *Acta Philosophica Fennica* 29, no. 1.

Hobart, R.E. 1924. "Free will as involving determinism and inconceivable without it." *Mind* (January).

Honderich, T., ed. 1973. *Essays on Freedom and Responsability.* London: Routledge and Kegan Paul.

Hume, D. 1739. *A Treatise of Human Nature.*

Huxley, A. 1952. *The Devils of Loudun.* New York: Harper & Row.

Irwin, T.H. 1977. "Plato's Heracliteanism." *Philosophical Quarterly* 27, no. 106 (January).

Jaeger, W. 1962. *Aristotle.* Oxford: Oxford Paperbacks.

Jackson, F. 1977. "Statements about Universals." *Mind* 86, no. 343 (July).

– 1982. See Prior, Pargetter, and Jackson 1982.

Kemp Smith, N. 1927. "The Nature of Universals III." *Mind* 36.

Kim, J. 1966. "On the Psycho-Physical Identity Theory." *American Philosophical Quarterly* 3, no. 3 (July).

Klemke, P., ed. 1969. *Studies in the Philosophy of G.E. Moore.* Chicago: Quadrangle Books.

Koestler, A. 1959. *The Sleep Walkers.* London: Hutchinson.

Kripke, S.A. 1972. "Naming and Necessity." In *Semantics of Natural Language,* ed. D. Davidson and G. Harman. Dordrecht: Reidel.

– 1980. *Naming and Necessity.* Cambridge: Harvard University Press.

Langford, C.H. 1942. "The Nature of Analysis in Moore's Philosophy." In Schilpp, ed., 1942.

Lango, J.W. 1969. "The Logic of Simultaneity." *Journal of Philosophy* 66, no. 11 (June).

Lehrer, K., ed. 1966a. *Freedom and Determinism.* New York: Random House.

– 1966b. "An Empirical Disproof of Determinism." In Lehrer 1966a.

Leslie, J. 1979. *Value and Existence.* Oxford: Blackwell.

– 1982. "Anthropic Principle, World Ensemble, Design." *American Philosophical Quarterly* 19, no. 2 (April).

– 1983. "Observership in Cosmology." *Mind* 92, no. 368 (October).

Lewis, D.K. 1966. "An Argument for the Identity Theory." *Journal of Philosophy* 63, no. 1 (January).

– 1976. "Survival and Identity." In A. Rorty 1976.

Locke, J. 1690. *An Essay Concerning Human Understanding.*

Lockwood, M. 1975. "On Predicating Proper Names." *Philosophical Review* 84.

Loux, M. 1976a. "The Existence of Universals." In Loux 1976b.

– ed. 1976b. *Universals and Particulars: Readings in Ontology.* Rev. ed. University of Notre Dame Press.

– 1978. *Substance and Attribute.* Dordrecht: Reidel.

MacMurray, J. 1953. *The Self as Agent.* Gifford Lecture Series, *The Form of the Personal,* vol. 1.

McTaggart, J.McT.E. 1908. "The Unreality of Time." *Mind,* 68 (October).

– 1921. *The Nature of Existence.* Vol. 1. Cambridge University Press.

– 1927. *The Nature of Existence.* Vol. 2. Cambridge University Press.

Madell, G. 1981. *The Identity of the Self.* Edinburgh University Press.

Marks, C.E. 1981. *Commissurotomy, Consciousness and Unity of Mind.* Cambridge, Mass.: MIT Press.

Mates, B. 1979. "Identity and Predication in Plato." *Phronesis* 24, no. 3.

McMullin, E, ed. 1963. *The Concept of Matter in Greek and Medieval Philosophy.* Notre Dame: University of Notre Dame Press, Indiana.

Mellor, D.H. 1981. *Real Time.* Cambridge University Press.

Mondadori, F. 1976. Review of Alvin Plantinga 1974 in *Journal of Philosophy* 73.

Moore, G.E. 1903. *Principia Ethica.* Cambridge University Press.

– 1942. "A Reply to My Critics." In Schilpp 1942.

Moravcsik, J., ed. 1967. *Aristotle.* New York: Anchor Books, Doubleday.

Moravcsik, J. 1971. "Learning as Recollection." In Vlastos 1971.

Morgenbesser, S., and J. Walsh, eds. 1962. *Free Will.* Englewood Cliffs: Prentice-Hall.

Nagel, T. 1975. "Brain Bisection and the Unity of Consciousness." In Perry 1975.

Nozick, R. 1981. *Philosophical Explanations.* Cambridge, Mass.: Harvard University Press.

Nussbaum, M.C. 1978. *Aristotle's De Motu Animalium.* Princeton University Press.

Odegard, D., ed. 1988. *Ethics and Justification.* Edmonton: Academic Printing & Publishing.

Owen, G.E.L. 1960. "Logic and Metaphysics in Some Earlier Works of Aristotle." In *Aristotle and Plato in Mid-Fourth Century*, ed. I. Düring and G.E.L. Owen. Göteberg.

Owens, J. 1963. *The Doctrine of Being in the Aristotelian Metaphysics.* Toronto: PIMS.

– 1963. "Matter and Predication in Aristotle." In McMullin 1963. Repr. in Moravcsik 1967.

Parfit, D. 1975. "Personal Identity." In Perry 1975.

– 1984. *Reasons and Persons.* Oxford University Press.

Pargetter, R. 1982. See Prior, Pargetter, and Jackson 1982.

Penner, T. 1970. "Verbs and the Identity of Actions – A Philosophical Exercise in the Interpretation of Aristotle." In Wood and Pitcher 1970.

Perry, J, ed. 1975. *Personal Identity.* Berkeley: University of California Press.

– 1982. "Castañeda on He and I." In Tomberlin 1982.

Pitcher, G. 1970. See Wood and Pitcher 1970.

Plantinga, A. 1974. *The Nature of Necessity.* Oxford University Press.

Polanyi, M. 1960. *The Tacit Dimension.* Garden City, NJ: Doubleday.

Popper, K. 1956a. "The Arrow of Time." *Nature* 177.

– 1956b. "Irreversibility and Mechanics." *Nature* 178.

– 1957. "Irreversible Processes in Physical Theory." *Nature* 179.

– 1982. *Quantum Theory and the Schism in Physics.* Hutchinson.

Prichard, H.A. 1912. "Does Moral Philosophy Rest on a Mistake?" *Mind* 21.

Prior, A.N. 1967. *Past, Present, and Future.* Oxford University Press.

Prior, E.W., R. Pargetter and F. Jackson. 1982. "Three Theses about Dispositions." *American Philosophical Quarterly* 19, no. 3 (July).

Puccetti, R. 1973. "Brain Bisection and Personal Identity." *British Journal for the Philosophy of Science* 24.

– 1976. "The Mute Self: A Reaction to Dewitt's Alternative Account of the Split-Brain Data." *British Journal for the Philosophy of Science* 27.

Putnam, H. 1967. "The Nature of Mental States." In *Art, Mind, and Religion*, ed. W.H. Capitas and D.D. Merrill. Pittsburgh: University of Pittsburgh Press. Repr. in Rosenthal 1971.

– 1975. "The Meaning of 'Meaning.'" *Mind, Language and Reality. Philosophical Papers*, vol. 2. London: Cambridge University Press.

– 1975, 1979. "A Philosopher Looks at Quantum Mechanics." *Philosophical Papers*. Vol. 1. Cambridge University Press.

– 1981. *Reason, Truth and History.* Cambridge University Press.

Quine, W.V. 1953. "On What There Is." *From a Logical Point of View*. Cambridge, Mass.: Harvard University Press. Repr. in Loux 1976b.

Quinton, A. 1973. *The Nature of Things.* London: Routledge and Kegan Paul.

Rankin, K.W. 1961. *Choice and Chance: A Libertarian Analysis.* Oxford: Blackwell.

– 1964. "Referential Identifiers." *American Philosophical Quarterly* 1, 3 (July).

– 1971. Review of Ayers 1968. *Philosophical Review* 81, 1 (January).

– 1972. "The Non-Causal Self-Fulfilment of Intention." *American Philosophical Quarterly* (October).

– 1976. "The Trinitarian Vision of P.F. Strawson." *Philosophical Archives.*

– 1980. "Ifs as Labels on Cans." *Canadian Journal of Philosophy* 10, 2 (June).

– 1981. "McTaggart's Paradox: Two Parodies." *Philosophy* 56, 217 (July).

– 1982. "The Complete Reality of Substance." *Mind* 91, 363 (July).

– 1988. "Responsibility as an Ontological Basis for Ethics." In *Ethics and Justification*, ed. Douglas Odegard. Edmonton: Academic Printing & Publishing.

Reichenbach, H. 1948. *Elements of Symbolic Logic.* New York: Macmillan Co.

– 1953. "Les Fondements logiques de la méchanique des quanta." *Annales de l'Institut Henri Poincaré* tome XIII, facs. II, Paris.

– 1956. *The Direction of Time.* Berkeley and Los Angeles: University of California Press.

– 1957. *The Philosophy of Space and Time.* New York: Dover.

Reid, T. 1785. *Essays on the Intellectual Powers of Man.* Repr. in Hamilton 1895, vol. 1.

Rescher, N. 1968. "Truth and Necessity in Temporal Perspective." Gale 1968.

– ed. 1969. *Essays in Honor of Carl G. Hempel.* Dordrecht: Reidel.

Robinson, H. 1982. *Matter and Sense: A Critique of Contemporary Materialism.* Cambridge University Press.

Rorty, A.O., ed. 1976. *The Identity of Persons.* Berkeley: University of California Press.

Rorty, R. 1965. "Mind-Body Identity, Privacy and Categories." *Review of Metaphysics* 19, 1 (September). Repr. in Borst 1970.

— 1970. "In Defense of Eliminative Materialism." *Review of Mataphysics* 24, 1 (September). Repr. in Rosenthal 1971.

Rosenthal, D.M., ed. 1971. *Materialism and the Mind-Body Problem.* Englewood Cliffs: Prentice-Hall.

Ross, W.D., ed. 1924. *Aristotle's Metaphysics.* Rev. ed. Oxford University Press.

— 1930. *The Right and the Good.* Oxford University Press.

— 1939. *Foundations of Ethics.* Oxford University Press.

Routley, R. 1980. *Exploring Meinong's Jungle and Beyond.* Departmental Monograph #3, Philosophy Department, Research School of Social Sciences, Australian National University.

Russell B. 1903. *The Principles of Mathematics.*

— 1940. *An Inquiry into Meaning and Truth.* London: Allen and Unwin.

— 1949. *Human Knowledge: Its Scole and Limits.* London: Allen and Unwin.

— 1956. "The Philosophy of Logical Atomism." *Logic and Knowledge: Essays 1901–1950,* ed. R.C. Marsh. London: Allen and Unwin.

— and A.N. Whitehead. 1913. *Principia Mathematica.* Cambridge University Press.

Ryle, G. 1949. *The Concept of Mind.* London: Hutchinson University Library.

Sartre, J.P. 1946. *L'Existentialisme est un humanisme.* Paris: Nagel.

Schilpp, P.A., ed. 1942. *The Philosophy of G.E. Moore.* Library of Living Philosophers. New York: Tudor.

Schwartz, S.P., ed. 1977. *Naming, Necessity and Natural Kinds.* Ithaca and London: Cornell University Press.

Searle, J.R. 1958. "Proper Names." *Mind* 67.

— 1969. *Speech Acts.* Oxford University Press.

— 1983. *Intentionality.* Cambridge University Press.

Sellars, W. 1960. "Grammar and Existence: A Preface to Ontology." *Mind* 69, no. 276 (October).

— 1967a. "The Paradox of Analysis: A Neo-Fregean Approach." *Philosophical Perspectives.* Springfield, Ill.: Charles C. Thomas.

— 1967b. "Aristotle's Metaphysics: An Interpretation." *Philosophical Perspectives.* Springfield, Ill.: Charles C. Thomas.

Shaffer, J.A. 1968. *Philosophy of Mind.* Englewood Cliffs: Prentice Hall.

Smart, J.J.C. 1956. "The River of Time." Flew 1956.

— 1959. "Sensations and Brain Processes." *Philosophical Review* 68. Repr. in Chappel 1962 and slightly revised in Borst 1970.

— ed. 1964. *Problems of Space and Time.* New York: Macmillan Co.

Smith, W. 1980. "Dummett, and Rigid Designators." *Philosophical Studies* (January).

Spearman, C. 1927. *The Abilities of Man.* New York: Macmillan.

Sorabji, R. 1980. *Necessity, Cause and Blame: Perspectives on Aristotle's Theory*. London: Duckworth.

Sperry, R.W. 1964. "The Great Cerebral Commissure." *Scientific American* 210, no. 42.

— 1966. "Brain Bisection and Mechanisms of Consciousness." In Eccles 1966.

Stein, H. 1968. "On Einstein-Minkowski Space-Time." *Journal of Philosophy* 65, no. 1 (January).

Stich, S.P. 1983. *From Folk Psychology to Cognitive Science: A Case against Belief*. Cambridge, Mass.: Bradford Books, MIT Press.

Stout, G.F. 1921. "The Nature of Universals and Propositions." British Academy Lecture. London: Oxford University Press.

— 1923. "Are the Characteristics of Particular Things Universal or Particular?" *Proceedings of the Aristotelian Society*, supp. vol.

— 1940. "Things, Predicates and Relations." *Australasian Journal of Philosophy and Psychology* 18.

Strawson, P.F. 1953–54, 1976. "Particular and General." *Proceedings of the Aristotelian Society* 54. Reprinted in Loux 1976b.

— 1959. *Individuals*. London: Methuen.

Taylor, R. 1963–65. *Metaphysics*. Englewood Cliffs: Prentice-Hall.

— 1966. *Action and Purpose*. Englewood Cliffs: Prentice-Hall.

Thalberg, I. 1976. "How Does Agent Causality Work?" In Brand and Walton, eds., 1976.

Thorp, J. 1980. *Free Will: A Defence against Neurophysiological Determinism*. London: Routledge and Kegan Paul.

Tomberlin, J.E. 1982. *Agent, Language, and the Structure of the World*. Indianapolis: Hackett.

Vlastos, G., ed. 1971. *Plato: A Collection of Critical Essays*. Vols. 1 and 2. Garden City, NY: Doubleday.

Walsh, J. 1962. See Morgenbesser and Walsh, eds., 1962.

Walton, D. 1976. See Brand and Walton 1976.

Wheeler, J.A. 1977. "Genesis and Observership." *Problems in the Special Sciences*. In Butts and Hintikka, eds., 1977.

Whitehead, A.N., and B. Russell. 1913. See Russell and Whitehead 1913.

Wigner, E.P. 1967. *Symmetries and Reflections*. Indiana University Press.

Williams, B. 1973. "The Self and the Future." *Problems of the Self*. Cambridge University Press. Also in Perry 1975.

Williams, D. 1958. "Form and Matter." *Philosophical Review* 67.

Wilson, G. 1978. "On Definite and Indefinite Descriptions." *Philosophical Review* 87, 1.

Wittgenstein, L. 1922. *Tractatus Logico-Philosophicus*. London: Kegan Paul.

— 1953. *Philosophical Investigations*. Oxford: Basil Blackwell.

Wood, O.P., and G. Pitcher, eds. 1970. *Ryle: A Collection of Critical Essays*. New York: Doubleday.

Woodfield, A. 1976. *Teleology*. Cambridge University Press.

Index

Because of their frequent occurrence in the text, terms such as "hylo-morphic," "matter," "diachronic," and "synchronic" do not appear as main entries below. Please refer to the Table of Contents for their particularly topical use.